THE PHILOSOPHY OF MYSTICISM

THE PHILOSOPHY OF MYSTICISM

BY

EDWARD INGRAM WATKIN

AUTHOR OF
"SOME THOUGHTS ON CATHOLIC APOLOGETICS"

NEW YORK
HARCOURT, BRACE AND HOWE
1920

PRINTED IN GREAT BRITAIN BY THE RIVERSIDE PRESS LIMITED
EDINBURGH

TO
MY MOTHER

O Lord Almighty, my spirit has fainted within me because it has forgotten to feed upon Thee. I knew Thee not, O my Lord, when I went after vanity. Who can free himself from base and mean ways, if Thou, O my God, wilt not lift him up to Thee in pure love? Thou wilt not take away from me, O my God, what Thou hast once given me in Thine only begotten Son Jesus Christ, in Whom Thou hast given me all I desire. I will therefore rejoice, Thou wilt not tarry if I wait for Thee. The heavens are mine, the earth is mine, and the nations are mine: mine are the just, and the sinners are mine: mine are the angels and the Mother of God; all things are mine, God Himself is mine and for me because Christ is mine and all for me. What dost thou then ask for, what dost thou seek for, O my soul? All is thine, all is for thee; do not take less, nor rest with the crumbs that fall from the table of Thy Father. Go forth and exult in thy glory, hide thyself in it, and rejoice, and thou shalt obtain all the desires of thy heart. O my love, all for Thee, nothing for me: nothing for Thee, everything for me.

St John of the Cross.

(Trs. David Lewis.)

*From the " Prayer of an Enamoured Soul
and Aspiration to God."*

PREFACE

At a time when so many volumes issue from the Press on the subject of mysticism, Western or Oriental, Christian or non-Christian, Universal or the mysticism of an individual or School, it will be well to indicate the aspect under which mysticism is viewed in this Work. Many modern writers confine their treatment of mysticism to its psychological aspect, for they regard mystical experience as a wholly subjective state, devoid of objective validity or intellectual significance. For example, Professor Höffding views this experience as pure feeling whose epistemological interpretation is derived *ab extra*, and Miss Evelyn Underhill, without adopting so extreme a position, emphasises the volitional and sentient aspects of mystical experience at the expense of the cognitive. To me, however, it is as impossible to divorce cognition from experience as it would be impossible with Mr Bertrand Russell to banish value from ontology. It is true that the categories of discursive reason are inadequate to render the knowledge content of mystical experience, as indeed they are inadequate to render the knowledge content of any experience not given immediately by themselves. Nevertheless they can render something of the truth apprehended by the mystic. Otherwise we should possess no mystical literature. After all, the mystics have not been dumb, though knowing well that anything they can tell us falls infinitely short of their experience. All other forms of experience are employed as data for the construction of philosophies necessarily stated in terms of discursive reason. The highest form of human experience, that of the mystic, must therefore provide most valuable data to metaphysics. Historically the most satisfactory metaphysic has employed mystical data. I have therefore endeavoured in this book to state the metaphysic implicit in mystical experience, a philosophy of mysticism. This philosophy is the body of truth about the nature of ultimate reality and of our relationship to it to be derived from the content of mystical experience.

This metaphysic of mysticism I find to consist in a doctrine of ultimate reality, of God, as the Unlimited, and of the consequent relationship between man's limited soul and the Unlimited. Thus the philosophy or theology, call it which you will, of mysticism is a philosophy of the Unlimited. In my first chapter I vindicate the epistemological and transubjective validity of mystical experience. I then discuss the nature of its Object as given immediately or by implication in this experience. I proceed to treat of the general character of the mystic way, to determine the principles which constitute and condition the via mystica. After this I describe its stages and discuss their character, causes and value. Throughout I have followed as my guide St John of the Cross. By general consent he is among the very greatest mystics for actual attainment, and in the intellectual exposition of his experience he is, I believe, unrivalled for penetration, clarity and harmony. Many mystics have been too apt to describe their experience in a confused and disordered manner. Magnificent passages abound, but there is a lack of coherence and methodical exposition. With the Spanish School of mysticism this defect of method was, for the first time, largely overcome. In the German School, and especially in Eckhart, there is indeed a metaphysic. But the Spaniards are the first to provide a methodical description and arrangement of the forms and stages of mystical experience based on accurate psychological observation and distinction. Naturally this scientific treatment is imperfect. Human language can never be free from ambiguity and obscurity, when it describes an experience so transcendent of the images and concepts of our natural life and knowledge. But it is here attempted for the first time, and with no small degree of success. After this period there is indeed an exaggeration in the opposite direction to the old disorder, an over-systematisation of mystical states and stages of union beyond the possibility of real distinction by concepts and conceptual terminology. The Spaniards, whose supreme representative is St John of the Cross, keep the golden mean between these two extreme methods of mystical exposition, lack of system and unreal schematisation. Where St John is silent, his silence is supplied by Saint Teresa and by another Spanish writer, as yet hardly known, a Carmelite nun, Mother Cecilia. In my opinion her work is of an extraordinary value, both for her attainment and for her exposition. Lest it be objected that the doctrine of these mystics is not derived from their experience, but from the dogmatic teaching of their Church, I have shown in a final chapter that Richard Jefferies, despite his intellectual atheism, bears witness as a mystic in the same sense. Nevertheless, though I am convinced, and hope in this Book to have proved, that there is a philosophy or theology derivable from the data of mystical experience, this theology is too exceptional in its attainment, too obscure in its mode and too incomplete in its nature to suffice by itself for the religious need of mankind. It requires to be supplemented by a metaphysic of natural experience and of discursive reasoning. Both these require the further supplement of a Divine revelation. As a Catholic I believe that this revelation is given to us in the *de fide* teaching of the Catholic Church, and that this revealed doctrine, though it has neither caused nor conditioned the essential deliverance of mystical experience, has confirmed and supplemented its utterance. Catholic theology has also interpreted mystical experience by guarding against false interpretations derived from other external sources, and by providing the mystic with an accurate vehicle of expression, which he recognises as faithful to his experience, and to which, therefore, he in turn lends the sanction of his vision.

For lack of this traditional medium of expression non-Catholic mystics have often been driven to speak in idioms peculiar to themselves and difficult to interpret. Böhme was compelled to adopt the terminology of alchemy, which has involved his doctrine in a very considerable and quite unnecessary obscurity. Blake, by employing a language altogether his own, has rendered his message well-nigh unintelligible. Moreover, Catholic doctrine has shown the application of the data of mystical experience in wider spheres than that experience could of itself attain. Thus both theologies are confirmed by their mutual harmony.

My quotations from St John of the Cross are taken from Lewis's translation corrected from the Edicion Critica, in which, for the first time, we possess the accurate text of the Saint. Those from Mother Cecilia are of my own translation from the Spanish. My obligations to mystical writers, to theologians, philosophers and men of letters are, I think, acknowledged in the course of the Book. I will only mention here the name of Baron Von Hügel, to whom, though I do not accept all his positions, my debt is of peculiar magnitude. But I cannot leave unmentioned the name of a friend, to whom I owe most valuable and most fruitful suggestions. One, indeed, of these has worked itself out in my mind among the *idées directrices* of this Book. I refer to Mr H. C. Dawson. In a previous work I had occasion to acknowledge my great intellectual debt to Mr Dawson. I am very glad of this opportunity to repeat my acknowledgement.

A final word of personal explanation. I am not a mystic, only a mystical philosopher. By temperament I am a book-and-garden Epicurean. But the stern truth of the Carmelite mystic has, almost against my will, convinced my understanding. For truth is determined neither by temperament nor by desire, but by facts. Nevertheless, this work is a theoretical exposition. It is possible to be a mystical philosopher in an arm-chair, to be a mystic only on a cross. Certainly every Christian not wholly self-alienated from supernatural union with God is a potential mystic. For mysticism is the blossoming of Christianity,[1] the epiphany of supernatural life. But this potency cannot be actualised, this epiphany cannot come to pass save through the passion and death of the lower, earthy, MERELY natural life. Thus the way of Divine union, of which the mystical way is but an advanced stage, is necessarily a way of the cross. A soul can leave that way or halt at its beginning. By study of the mystics I have learned of the beauty of this divine way to God, but I have learned also of its pain. The mystic, wearied with toil and scorched with heat, is climbing Mount Nebo with Moses, to die with him on the summit of vision. I linger in a comfortable hotel at Sittim, with a magnificent view of the Hills of Moab and a shady corner of garden under the palms. There I sit in sight of the Holy mountain, its steep ascent of crags, its summit red in the rays of the sun. From the Mountain of God I cannot turn away my eyes. But I dare not leave the garden. Yonder peak every soul must climb to see God. For this mountain is also the mount of purgatory. The mystic makes the ascent in this life. Blessed is he. He and he alone sees the vision. If I did not know that this Book would never have been written. But the price of the vision is mortal pain. As each is called, each must choose his response.

SHERINGHAM, *October*, 1919.

---

[1] The non-Christian mystic is thereby shown to be a member of Christ—an implicit unconscious Christian.

CONTENTS

15

NOTE.—*Where an asterisk appears in the text it indicates that a note will be found at the end of the book.*

CHAPTER I

INTRODUCTORY

DISILLUSIONED of the past and the present, men are everywhere seeking in the future ways to a better life, a life of higher and richer values for mankind. But no future can provide these values unless they exist somewhere as a present reality. The mystic claims that he has found a reality of inexhaustible value. To no golden past nor golden future need we chase a mirage of satisfaction. It is an eternal reality which the mystics have seen and attained and which they present to us. It is, therefore, of the first importance to discover, if we can, whether this claim of the mystic is justified, and if this prove to be the case, to learn from him the nature of that reality and worth which he has found. To set before my readers the mystic's report of the object apprehended in his experience and of the manner and way of his progressive apprehension of that object is the aim of this book I have attempted a study of the truth given in mystical experience, a philosophy of that experience. This study I have based on the principles laid down and explained with unrivalled clearness and penetration by St John of the Cross, and applied by him with a remorseless severity of logical reasoning, a clearness and severity aptly symbolised by the hard contours and sharp outlines of the barren, sun-scorched sierras of his own Castile.

We possess four indubitably genuine works of St John, in addition to poems, sayings and a few letters. These four works—two of which are fragments—are treatises of mystical theology. Two of these, *The Ascent of Mount Carmel* and *The Obscure Night of the Soul*, are concerned with the purgation necessary in order to attain the supreme mystical union ; the remaining two, *The Spiritual Canticle of the Soul* and *The Living Flame of Love*, are concerned with that supreme union itself. The teaching of these four great books will be the foundation of all I have to say in this exposition of the philosophy of mysticism. I shall, however, make large use also of three other treatises. One of these, *The Obscure Knowledge of God*, may perhaps be the work of St John himself, the remaining two, *The Treatise on the Transformation of the Soul in God* and *The Treatise on the Union of the*

Soul with God, are by a Carmelite nun, Mother Cecilia of the Nativity. These treatises belong to the Johannine [1] school of Mysticism, and serve to throw light on certain points left obscure in the four authentic treatises of the Saint.

I have entitled this work "The Philosophy of Mysticism." I disclaim by the very title any practical scope. Mysticism as an art, as a state of prayer, as the practical way to Union with God, can only be taught by one himself experienced in this way. My concern as an outsider is with the theoretical aspect of the matter, with mysticism as a theory, or science, with "mystology," if I may coin the expression. Every art presupposes a body of theoretical truth on which it is based. The higher the art, the greater in depth and scope must the underlying truth be. If there be an art or practical way by which the human soul is united to God, that art or way must be based on, and must reveal to us, truth about God. The philosopher, the student of religion, above all the Christian apologist, cannot afford to neglect the body of truths about God, the Supreme Reality, which underlies the practice of mysticism. Indeed, metaphysics have always tended to pass over into mysticism, or at least into the theory of mysticism. For the subject-matter of metaphysics is ultimate reality. Hence that art or practice whose end is union with ultimate reality must, if it be a true art, a fruitful practice, yield the most valuable data for metaphysical knowledge of that reality. A practice based on a false view of reality would prove barren in exact proportion to the falsehood in its underlying theory. The practice of mysticism has, however, been supremely fruitful. Its adepts have, as they declare with a unanimity of consent that transcends all divergence of philosophy or creed, attained the union with the Absolute of which they were in search. Therefore at their hands we must expect the fullest and deepest, and therefore the truest, knowledge of the ultimate reality that is attainable, apart from positive revelation. [2] As we shall see, the practice of mysticism is largely passive—the reception of an experience given from without. Mysticism, or mystical theology in the strict sense, is this experience, the philosophy of mysticism, or "mystology," is its intellectual interpretation.

---

[1] The term Johannine is throughout this book, save where the contrary is expressly stated, the adjective of St John of the Cross, not of the Evangelist.

[2] Even that revelation was itself largely given through the medium of mystical experience.

What then is this mystical experience that is to yield the highest knowledge of ultimate reality ?   The full answer to this question is, of course, the entire teaching of mystical philosophy.   Nevertheless, that we may attain at the outset some clear notion of the true meaning of a term often most loosely applied, I will define mysticism or mystical experience as a union-intuition of God. In chap. xvi. of Book II. of *The Ascent of Mount Carmel,* St John of the Cross says : " In the high state of the union of love God . . . communicates Himself to the pure and naked essence of the soul, through the will." This union, however, normally involves a certain direct consciousness of its object.[1] Mystical union is thus a union of the entire soul through the will, involving a consciousness of the object of union.   This consciousness is an intuition—by which is meant an immediate apprehension of reality, as opposed to an axiom or a conclusion of discursive reasoning, whose object is reality apprehended *mediately* through concepts abstracted from sensible experience.   Intuition, on the other hand, being thus an immediate apprehension, is essentially not a concept or idea.   The intuition that is the conscious concomitant of mystical union is, of course, superrational above the conceptual understanding of discursive reasoning, not an infrarational sensation.   There is, however, an intuition or instinctive apprehension which is found in animals and indeed in man in the inferior regions of his soul life.   This lower intuition or instinct has been wrongly confused, by M. Bergson, with the superrational intuition.[2]   It is, on the contrary, essentially infrarational.   Though it apprehends reality more directly than discursive reasoning, it does not penetrate to so deep a level.

[1] As will be seen later, in the certain phases of mystical union this positive consciousness is temporarily replaced by a strange negative consciousness, whose character will hereafter be discussed.

[2] On page 339 of *L'Évolution Creatricice*, 8th ed., M. Bergson seems indeed to conjoin infrarational intuition in its form of sense-perception with discursive reason in opposition to superrational intuition there distinctly recognised.   Nevertheless even in this passage the former intuition is supposed to pass into the latter as violet into red through the colour scale.   Moreover reason is unduly opposed here also to the superrational intuition.   If we consider the general tenor of M. Bergson's philosophy, we shall find that it amply bears out the criticism of my text.   The superrational intuition of the philosophy of the future is to be obtained by a return to the instinct intuition element of the evolutionary nisus which has hitherto been most highly developed in certain insects.   That the higher intuition is rather a development and eminent inclusion of the discursive reasoning which it transcends is a truth ignored—or almost ignored—by the Bergsonian philosophy.

Mystical intuition is the highest form of superrational intuition, for it is the consciousness of union with the Infinite Being of God, Who, as we shall see, is beyond the definition of the essentially limited concepts of the discursive reason.[1] I also name the Object of the mystical union-intuition God, not, with Miss Evelyn Underhill, Reality with a big R. My reason for so doing is not merely that as a theist and as a Catholic I know the ultimate reality to be a personal God, but because no other term expresses so well the Object of mystical experience, as revealed in that experience itself. To use the term Reality is to say too little. Everything that is—is Real—if it were not real it would be nothing. Every being, in so far as it is or has being, is or has reality. If anything is more real than another, it is because it has more being. If we say *Supreme* or *Ultimate* Reality our definition will indeed be correct, but unnecessarily vague in its formulation. The most real is that which has most being. Spirit, however, has more being than matter, the personal than the impersonal. There is more being and therefore greater reality in a living soul than in a lifeless stone ; more in a human personality than in an impersonal force ; more in love than in hunger ; more in my friend than in my walking-stick. Therefore ultimate or absolute reality must have more being than less ultimate realities, must be above, and more than the highest beings that are but derivative and contingent, not lower and less than they. If, however, the ultimate reality, the Absolute Being

[1] Corresponding with these two forms of intuition—below and above the level of discursive reason are the two passions (Erotes) or non-rational loves. The lower is natural desire in its varied forms, the force of life reaching out blindly and instinctively. The higher is the love of the will reaching out towards an un-limited Good beyond the conception of reason. The history of religion often shows us mystical or quasi-mystical cults and doctrines taking over or spiritual-ising—as expressions and vehicles of the higher Eros, cults and myths originally deifications of the lower Eros. Thus did Orphism adopt the cult of the Wine God Dionysus, spiritualising the infrarational impulse set free by intoxication into superrational ecstasy. (*Cf.* also the mythology of the Sirens as explained by Miss Jane Harrison, *Prolegomena to the Study of Greek Religion*, pp. 197-207.) Since, however, such mysticism lacks the guidance of revelation and the elevat-ing dispensation of sanctifying grace the lower Eros, become in fallen man a per-verse concupiscence, pollutes and distorts the higher nisus towards spiritual good, ever dragging it back to its own level. Hence that unhappy confusion or mingling of lower and higher impulses and loves which marks so many forms of non-Christian mysticism, a confusion rendered easy, as is the analogous Bergsonian confusion of the intuitional aspects, by the common element of divergence from discursive reason present alike in the lower Eros of life-instinct and in the reason-transcending force of spiritual love.

were material or impersonal, an unconscious force for example, it would have less being or reality than the human soul. Therefore, ultimate reality, the Absolute, must be above, not below, finite and dependent spirits. It must be supra- not infra-personal.

We must therefore maintain that the nature of Ultimate Reality, though the ground of all being, is such that it is more adequately represented by the spiritual and the personal than by the material and the impersonal. Moreover, the union between the mystic and Ultimate Reality is essentially personal in character—a union through love, a union moreover more satisfactory of our need for personal communion than is any union with a fellow-man. If, however, this union-intuition were without a supra-personal Object it would be less personal and less satisfactory than union through love with a fellow-man. Moreover, as we shall see in the course of this book, mystical experience in its higher stages does reveal certain characters of its Object,[1] and these the characters of a personal Spirit. We have therefore good ground, simply as students of mysticism, to affirm that the Object of mystical experience is a Being Who is more truly represented by and is more akin to the Spiritual and the Personal than to the Material and the Impersonal.

Nor can we with the Monist suppose that Ultimate Reality is simply the totality of matter and consciousness, of the personal and the impersonal. Such an absolute Monism would involve the ascription of equal reality and ultimacy to all its constituent elements. We should therefore touch ultimate reality in equal measure in each and every portion of our experience. We should touch this ultimate reality as truly, and participate in it as fully, in eating as in scientific discussion or æsthetic intuition, and as truly in all these as in prayer and in mystical intuition. It is, however, of the very essence of mystical experience that it is a penetration to a deeper level, the attainment of a greater, fuller and more ultimate reality than is afforded by any other form of human experience. Hence the object of this experience is not simply the sum total of all being and experience, but the underlying ground of all the lesser realities and more superficial levels touched by the other forms of experience. The pantheist will, however, urge that this ultimate reality is the true being of the less ultimate and is manifested of necessity in and through these. But we should then be compelled to admit that it is conditioned

[1] Not, however, as they are in Him. See Chapter IV.

and so limited by the limits of these lower forms of being in which It is of necessity manifested. But the most complete "personality" is the human soul that is least dependent on creatures lower than itself. Therefore the suprapersonal Reality must be wholly independent of beings lower than Himself. Moreover, as we shall see later, the object of the mystical intuition is essentially experienced as transcendent and free from all limits, as the wholly Unlimited. Hence the limited cannot be its necessary self-manifestation. In vain does Pantheistic mysticism seek to evade this difficulty by teaching the complete illusoriness or non-reality of the limited, of the relative as opposed to the Absolute.[1] Even if this were the case, ultimate Reality, the Absolute, would be conditioned and limited by its necessary causation of this illusion, that is of the limited appearance, whose phenomenal existence at least is undeniable. Moreover this denial of reality to the limited or relative contradicts our lower experience, whose validity within its own limited sphere is as immediately given as is the validity of the mystical experience itself. For this lower experience is a real experience of a real object. Otherwise it would be non-existent. It follows, therefore, that if we would accept, as we must accept, the entire content of experience in all its forms, both mystical and non-mystical alike, as given immediately in those experiences and mediately through their abstraction, comparison and combination, we must grant that the finite objects of our ordinary experience are possessed of some degree of reality, and also that the ultimate Reality which is the object of mystical experience is wholly free from their limitations. But the acceptance of these truths demands the acceptance of a theistic as opposed to a pantheistic interpretation of the nature of ultimate reality. Neither can we identify the Object of mystical experience with the *durée* which, according to the system of M. Bergson, underlies and is opposed to the more unreal, indeed artificial, time series. If the mystic were *en rapport* with a mere *durée* or even with an impersonal life therein existent, there would be no ground for his exultant certitude of communion with a Personal Being infinitely superior to his own personality. Moreover, one essential feature of mystical experience—or at least of certain forms of that experience—is that it is a consciousness or apprehension not of any kind of succession or duration but of Eternity—the *totum simul* equally present

---

[1] So teach certain schools of philosophic idealism.

to all time, the Everlasting Now in which all time exists and is comprehended, both clocktime and soultime alike. This is well brought out by Baron von Hügel, both in *Eternal Life* and in *Mystical Religion*. In the *Autobiography* of Bl. Henry Suso, a rapture granted to that great mystic is described as " a breaking forth of the sweetness of eternal life, felt as present in the stillness of unvarying contemplation" (Suso's *Autobiography*, trs. Fr. Knox, ed. 1913, p. 10. Burns and Oates). "I have observed," writes Lucie Christine, "that during the prayer of passivity and especially in the state of union the soul loses all sense of the duration of time. . . . There is one single moment only . . . the soul being raised to that state lives according to the mode of life in Eternity, where time is no more, neither past nor present, but one eternal Now" (*Spiritual Journal*, Eng. trs., p. 52). The well-known lines of Henry Vaughan, perhaps based on an actual experience, are a most beautiful and at the same time a most clear and concise expression of the mystical experience of eternity.

> I saw Eternity the other night,
> Like a great ring of pure and endless light,
> All calm, as it was bright ;
> And round beneath it, Time in hours, days, years,
> Driven by the spheres
> Like a vast shadow moved.
>
> VAUGHAN, *The World*.

It is, however, impossible to identify the experience of eternity with an experience of a successive *durée*. Nor yet is the Ultimate Reality apprehended in mystical experience a stream of Becoming, an *élan vital* pushing its way onwards and outwards whether aimlessly or aimfully through an opposing matter. For just as the object of mystical intuition is given as eternal, so is it given as absolutely perfect and in complete rest. All the mystics are agreed that their experience is of this kind. Moreover, the object of mysticism is the infinite, the unlimited, and Becoming is essentially limited. The object of mysticism is fulness that is perfection of being, whereas Becoming is incomplete and imperfect, being constituted by being and not being. Indeed, the goal of mysticism has ever been escape from strife to rest, from flux to permanence, from becoming to pure Being. Certainly the object apprehended by the mystic is an activity—but an activity that is rest, because it has no obstacle to overcome nor deficiency to satisfy a life that is so full, as to need no complement for its preservation or increase. Thus does the object of mystical experience as given in that experience itself exclude the limitations alike of an external and hostile matter and of any kind of becoming. Mysticism, therefore, has *not* found its philosopher in M. Bergson. Enough surely has been said to show that we need have no hesitation in terming the object of mystical experience, not reality nor even ultimate reality, but God. If, however, any reader prefer it, let him by all means keep for the present to the less definite terminology. The following chapters on the nature of the object of mystical experience as revealed in that experience will prove it to possess precisely those characters which constitute the theistic and Christian understanding of the term God, and will, therefore, be a fuller argument for the identity of the former with the latter. Till then let him, if he will, define the object of mystical experience as the ultimate Reality. I prefer to term it from the outset what it will prove in truth to be, God —the God not of pantheism or semi-pantheism but of Christian theism.

Now, however, I have to face a more fundamental objection to my definition, the objection that this mystical intuition or experience is false, a delusion from beginning to end. If the objector means by this that no man has ever had any such experience, and that all those who claim it are liars, he is like a blind man who should affirm that all those who claim vision are liars. As well should the inartistic man deny that the artist perceives the beauty and significance that to him are wholly imperceptible. Doubtless, however, he will mean that this mystical experience is purely subjective—due to the physical or psychical condition of the recipient. It is urged by many psychologists that the psycho-physical condition of the mystic fully explains his experience, which has thus no objective validity. This explanation would make the experiences of a St Paul and of a St Teresa the fruits of a nervous derangement. This materialistic explanation is, however, opposed to the axiom that the effect cannot be greater than its cause. A psychical phenomenon may be conditioned, but cannot be wholly caused, by a physical fact. The more common, and assuredly the more powerful attack upon the trans-subjective validity of mystical experience proceeds from the psychology that would explain mystical experience as simply a manifestation of the subconscious, subliminal or subjective mind or self. The existence of this subconsciousness has indeed been amply proved by modern psychological research. The evidence will be found in such a book as Myers' *Human Personality*, and substantially the same teaching is expounded in a more popular form by Hudson in his *Psychic Phenomena*. No candid student of these works can doubt the existence of the subconscious or subliminal mind, that is to say of a sphere, aspect or function of the soul normally hidden from self-conscious observation. Moreover there is every reason to believe that this subliminal sphere is the seat of mystical experience. For the central depths of the soul are not normally above the threshold of consciousness: are, therefore, normally subliminal. But, as we shall see later, these depths are the special seat of the Divine Presence and Action in the soul, since they are the most remote and the most free from the conditions of sense, and are thus the least limited by the limitations due to the senses and their material data. Therefore, when the Divine Presence and Action enter the field of consciousness, as they do in the mystical union-intuition, the normally subliminal depth—the subjective mind—that is the seat of that Presence and Action is also revealed through the Divine Presence and Action therein. Thus the subliminal is the special vessel and organ of mystical experience. This fact, however, is by no means the admission that mystical experience proceeds simply and entirely from the subconscious soul, is nothing but a subliminal uprush into the field of normal consciousness due to autosuggestion. If that were the case it could not present, as it does, the constant characteristic of a self-evidént experience of a Reality other and immeasurably greater than the self revealed in normal consciousness. Since mystical experience thus produces, nay, consists in, a self-evident conviction of contact with an objective being or reality other than the mystic himself, if the mystic be not really in touch with a Being outside himself, his entire spiritual life is based upon an experience which is essentially illusion and self-deception. Can we in reason believe that the lives and work of the mystics are thus the fruit of illusion and hallucination ? It were surely as reasonable a belief that the achievements of art and science are the products of illusion. Moreover, the result of illusion must surely be the detriment, indeed the destruction, of the soul's higher life, in proportion to the closeness of relationship between the illusion and that life. Illusion and unreality must ever produce emptiness and death, never fulness and life. The result of mystical experience, however, has been the growth and elevation of life. Hence that experience cannot be illusory. Moreover, no function of the soul can produce wholly out of itself anything external to the self. The understanding, for instance, cannot know any external object which has not first been presented to it from without. Therefore the subconscious function or level of the soul cannot produce out of itself what it has not received either from the conscious level or from stimuli—suggestions, if the term be preferred—received subconsciously from a source external to the self. The subliminal mathematician, for example, the "mathematical prodigy," is in subliminal contact with an objective truth, a reality external to his own being whether supra-liminal or subliminal (see Myers' *Human Personality*, p. 60 *sqq.*). The subconscious self is no conjurer's hat which can produce out of itself a rabbit or a palm-tree. Indeed Myers himself states distinctly of the man of genius that "from his subliminal self he can only draw what it already possesses." "We must not," he continues, "assume as a matter of course that the subliminal region of any one of us possesses that particular sensitivity—that specific transparency—which can receive and register *definite facts from the unseen. That* may be a gift which stands as much alone . . . in the subliminal region, as, say, a perfect musical ear in the supraliminal" (*Human Personality*, p. 84). The mystic, however, receives in and from his experience a satisfaction of consciousness and will, a fulness of spiritual life and energy, a certainty of communion with an ultimate and Divine Reality external to himself, that is in obvious excess of all that he has obtained by the exertion of his conscious faculties, a reality and life indefinitely superior to and quite other than the knowledge of religious truth and the force of spiritual life obtained by conscious instruction and religious exercises. This reality and life must, therefore, have been received into the subconscious depths of the soul from a source external to the soul.

Again, if we accept, as we must, the testimony of the mystic to the fact of his experience we ought to admit his testimony to its nature as being essentially a self-evident experience of a transubjective Reality. Just as the fact of sense perception carries with it an immediate certainty of the existence of an external object of that perception, so also does mystical experience involve an immediate certainty of the existence of an external object of that experience. There have been, indeed, and at present there are, philosophers who deny the transubjective validity of sense perception. Such a scepticism, however, can never be accepted by the unsophisticated common-sense of mankind at large. It is surely equally irrational to refuse similar validity to the experience of the mystics, which, despite its comparative rarity, is as undeniable as the fact of ordinary sense perception.[1] The objective validity of this experience is indeed being realised by modern thinkers, and this realisation is making mysticism more popular to-day than it has been for a long while past. Thus the late Professor William James, despite the great stress he lays on the subliminal, distinctly says that " the reference of a phenomenon to a subliminal self need not exclude the notion of the direct Presence of the Deity. The notion of a subconscious self ought not . . . to be held to exclude all notion of a higher penetration. If there be higher powers able to impress us, they may get access to us only through the subliminal doors " (*Varieties of Religious Experience*, pp. 242, 243). Again, in his summary at the end of his book, Professor James maintains in principle the truth of this objective reference.

It is true that the term of this reference is in the opinion of James a finite being, one of the many gods, or rather demi-gods, of pluralism. This interpretation, however, is in contradiction to the experience which it professes to interpret. Mystical experience is, as will be shown later, essentially an experience of communion with the unlimited, the Absolute, the All.[2] So much is this the case that, as the history of mysticism abundantly proves, it is extremely liable to misinterpretation in a Pantheistic sense. Pantheism, however, is the antipodes of pluralism. Hence the pluralistic explanation of James is arbitrary in the extreme ; was, in fact, not a conclusion reached by his psychological research but

---

[1] We must, however, beware of Miss Evelyn Underhill's attempt (*Mysticism*, chap. i.) to *contrast* the objective validity of mystical experience with the mainly subjective and illusory character of sense perception. If we must accept St Teresa's testimony to the existence of the Divine Being immediately given in her mystical intuition, we must equally accept the plain man's testimony to the objective existence of the brick wall immediately given in his sensible vision. The world of common-sense in which the plain man is at home is real within its own narrow limits, and with its own limited degree of reality, although the world of the mystic above and beyond the sphere of common-sense is a real world without limit and real with an unlimited reality. Nothing could be more pernicious to mysticism than attempts to found it on a basis of philosophic idealism or scepticism.

[2] For the theistic and Catholic understanding of this term see the following chapters.

a metaphysical "overbelief" violently forced upon his psychological conclusion. That conclusion in itself—namely, that mystical experience is transubjective—is surely neither invalidated nor even weakened by the addition of this alien element introduced from a false metaphysic.* Moreover, Hudson also affirms the transubjective validity of "subconscious" experience. It is already evident from the quotation made above that the great pioneer of subliminal investigation admitted this transubjective validity. A page or two further he explicitly recognises this validity in the case of the mystical experience of "a Francis" and "a Teresa" (*Human Personality*, p. 89). Doubtless Myers' interpretation of the Objective Reality given in their experience was inadequate. Nevertheless he does recognise that Reality, as other than the subliminal self of the mystic, as "a spiritual Universe" from which "the soul can draw strength and grace," "a spirit accessible and responsive to the soul of man" (p. 91). Surely enough, indeed more than enough, has been said. Both argument and the explicit admission of investigators of the subliminal abundantly prove that mystical experience cannot be the merely subjective experience of the subconscious self, as certain anti-mystical psychologists have affirmed, but is, on the contrary, the apprehension of an objective spiritual reality.

Moreover, this reality must be the most fundamental attainable by the human soul. For the nobler the instrument of perception the higher is the reality perceived. Sight, for instance, gives more knowledge of reality than taste. Discursive reason working on the data of sense furnishes a still deeper knowledge of reality. Surely then the intuition of the soul through its highest and most spiritual faculty must constitute a far higher and truer apprehension of reality. If the sense-conditioned intuitions of the artist or poet penetrate depths of reality hidden from the discursive reason, far greater and more ultimate must be the reality attained by the intuition of the mystic. We have, however, already seen that this Reality must be a Being not devoid of the highest characters of our own spiritual life, that is a personal, or, more strictly, a suprapersonal God. I therefore repeat and emphasise with all confidence as the starting-point of these studies my definition of Mysticism or mystical experience as the union-intuition of God, the personal God believed and adored by theists of all ages and creeds.*

We must, however, beware of the prevalent error of supposing that all mystics, whatever their creed, whether Christian, Mohammedan or Buddhist, teach one truth *wholly* identical and differ only in a terminology externally adopted. It is true that the essential mystical experience is one and the same in all. But the Catholic will maintain that (1) since the Christian revelation is true, its doctrines interpret the experience of the mystics better than any other, and (2) that Christian mysticism is higher and more complete than any other. It is higher in that Christian mysticism has led its followers to a higher degree of union with God than that attained by non-Christian mystics. Such, at least, is the general rule, though admitting perhaps of exceptions. Moreover the Christian mystic has possessed a personal love of God which is often lacking in non-Christian mysticism, a love arising out of devotion to the Incarnate Jesus. It is more complete because Christian mystics have often been granted the direct intuition of certain distinctively Christian doctrines—*e.g.* the intellectual vision of the Blessed Trinity. Nevertheless the experience even of non-Christian mystics is, as such, a true experience of God—a union-intuition of Him.

There are certain principles which should be borne constantly in mind while reading the writings of the mystics. The concepts of discursive reason, based as they are on the data of sense, are inadequate to express the purely spiritual reality apprehended in mystical experience. The categories of the reason are too narrow to grasp it and break down under the attempt. Any formulation of this reality in terms of the discursive reason must therefore be taken simply as a signpost to a region beyond clear rational apprehension. It is, moreover, of the essence of conceptual thought to abstract. The discursive reason cannot make its abstractions living realities. But the object of mystical experience is not an abstract concept or a system of abstract concepts, but a living reality. Hence mystical experience as it is in itself is transcendent of all the images and concepts of the understanding, and is, therefore, ineffable. Moreover, the Unlimited Godhead cannot be expressed by the essentially limited operations of the created intelligence. Hence the mystics unanimously tell us that their experience can only be understood by those who themselves possess it. " It would be foolishness," writes St John, " to think that the language of love and the mystical intelligence . . . can be at all explained in words of any kind for the spirit of Our Lord who helps our weakness . . . dwelling in us makes petitions for us with groanings unutterable for that which we cannot well understand or grasp so as to be able to make it known. . . . For who can describe that which He shows to loving souls in whom He dwells ? Who can set forth in words that which He makes them feel ? And, lastly, who can explain that for which they long ? Assuredly no one can do it ; not even they themselves who experience it. That is the reason why they use figures of special comparisons and similitudes ; they hide somewhat of that which they feel and in the abundance of the Spirit utter secret mysteries rather than express themselves in clear words " (Prologue to *Spiritual Canticle*). After a truly sublime description of the supreme mystical union Suso adds : " Now, daughter, remember that all these figures and images, *with their interpretations*, are as remote from and unlike the formless Truth as a black Moor is unlike the beautiful sun " (*Autobiography*, trs. Knox, p. 283). Discursive reason divides truth into partial aspects, and those partial and severed aspects cannot by that thought be unified into a complete self-consistent whole. The intuition of the mystic, however, which is a concomitant of the unifying love of the will, apprehends truth in its totality and unity. This intuition cannot, therefore, be consistently formulated in terms of discursive thought. Hence the concepts and images which the mystics are compelled to employ, being essentially partial and incomplete, can never be taken exclusively. In so far as they are positive they are true —for God is eminently all the positive being of creatures (see Chapter II). In so far as they are negative, excluding by their finitude other aspects of positive being or reality, they are false. Hence we must always so understand and use the images and concepts of the mystics as not thereby to deny images and concepts apparently opposed, but really complementary. Rather we shall find that the only possible utterance of the ultimate truth given in mystical intuition is a series of paradoxes. There is much paradox in the teaching of Our Lord, and the teaching of the mystics can only be expressed in that form. The reader will not be able to peruse the earlier chapters of this book without finding himself in face of such a paradox as that God is all and God is also nothing. The discussion of this and the other great paradoxes of mysticism I leave to their proper place. My present object is simply to urge the student of mysticism to bear in mind that, as was pointed out above, its Divine Object cannot be represented by a logically coherent concept or conceptual system.

Rather is it the fundamental characteristic of mystical truth—to be so transcendent of our concepts that it can only be indicated—expressed it never can be—in their terms, by means of statements apparently contradictory—that is, by paradoxes—whose opposition is soluble by experience alone, not by discursive reasoning. If we remember this we shall not label a mystic pantheist for statements which, taken exclusively, would be pantheistic, as, for instance, certain statements of St John or St Catherine of Genoa concerning the Divine Immanence, agnostic for statements of the essential unintelligibility of God, anti-sacramental or anti-incarnational for statements of the necessity of transcending forms and images. On the contrary, we shall see in all such statements diverse aspects of one infinite truth, as positive, true, as exclusive of complementary aspects, false.

Moreover, the same spiritual fact or process will be described by a series of different sense-derived images which regard that one fact or process from different points of view. The mystical way may, for instance, be regarded as a motion upwards, an ascent from creatures to God—as a motion downwards into ever-increasing depths of increased reality, until God the one absolute Reality is reached—as a motion outwards away from the finite with its narrow limits to the infinite—as a motion inwards to the depth of the central ego away from the superficial operations of the exterior matter—handling and sense-conditioned powers. It may be conceived positively, as the ever-increasing attainment of reality, or negatively, as the ever-increasing denial and rejection of the unreal or negative or limiting element in the creature. It may be described by means of impersonal images as—*e.g.*—the consumption of wood by fire ; the impregnation of air by light ; a plunge deeper, ever deeper into the sea ; or by means of personal imagery such as the passionate human love of bride and bridegroom ; the simple confidence and self-abandonment of an infant to its mother. All these images are complementary, not mutually exclusive, and are true only in their positive being, false in their essential limitations, exclusions and negations. In such sense is the teaching of the mystics to be understood.

Indeed the whole of mystical philosophy is an attempt to express one inexpressible thing in a variety of wholly inadequate ways. Other and lower branches of knowledge have a multitude of distinct things to tell us clearly and adequately * ; a multiplicity united only at a deeper level than that which these sciences

attain. "Mystology" has for subject matter *one* thing—
the *unum* necessarium—the union of the unified soul with the
absolute unity of God. Its multiplicity is a manifold, apprehended as the diverse aspects of an underlying unity, the manifold
aspects of the One Divine Being, and of a soul life or psychosis
that is substantially unified in the soul, when fully united to God,
and made by that union godlike. Do not, therefore, ask of
mystical theology a series of clear definitions and of distinct
facts—her work is not to express, far less to explain, but simply
to indicate the One that contains an inexhaustible manifold which
is mutually inclusive, not mutually exclusive, and in virtue of
that exclusion discrete and *distinct*. Never, reader, press her
images or her similes to the exclusion of contrary images or
similes, for they are, as we saw above, true only as positive, not as
negative. Pardon much repetition, for it is no variety of distinct
ideas or concepts, but one supreme reality of infinite content that
is to be set within the vision of your soul. Above all remember
that, when all has been said, nothing has been said. A finger has
pointed the way to a reality which reason, and much less its verbal
expression, can never attain. On that dark Reality, the Infinite
God, fix the will in adoration ; if God so call you, in desire also,
and veil the eyes of reason before the light unapproachable, the
hidden Presence, that is the Alpha and Omega of all the truth and
being made known by philosophy and science, by art and practical
experience. So shall mysticism indicate to you the first principle
on which these depend, and falling down you shall adore the God
Whom on earth you can never know as He is, and shall pray for
that open revelation in the world to come.

The preliminary chapters of this book will consist of an attempt
to expound more fully the matter already touched upon in these
prolegomena, the teaching of Christian mysticism as represented
by St John of the Cross and Mother Cecilia as to the nature of
God as the Object of mystical experience. I shall then discuss
the essential character of this union-intuition between the soul
and God, the chief degrees of that union, the principles of its
action and the way by which the soul is prepared to receive it.
This preparation will be discussed not with a view to practice,
but as a part of the theoretical study of the nature of mystical
experience. I will begin by considering the teaching of mysticism
in regard to the Divine Immanence as apprehended in the mystical
union-intuition.

CHAPTER II

THE DIVINE IMMANENCE

*The Lord appeared in a flame of fire out of the midst of a bush,
and the bush was on fire and was not burnt.* EXODUS iii.

Ex quo, per quem, in quo sunt omnia.

*Lift the stone and then thou shalt find Me: cleave the wood and
there am I.* OXYRHYNCUS, *Logion.*

> *Mi Amado las montañas.*
> *Los valles solitarios nemorosos.*
> *Las insulas extrañas.*
> *Los rios sonorosos.*
> *El silbo de los aires amorosos.*
>   ST JOHN OF THE CROSS,
>   *Spiritual Canticle of the Soul.*

THE doctrine of God as the Object of mystical experience is a
doctrine of the relation to Him of creatures in general and in particular of the human soul. Of Himself, as He is in Himself, we
have, as we shall see, no knowledge—that is, no clear, conceptual
knowledge. Even the doctrine of the Trinity is revealed, so to
speak, inferentially from the working of the Three Persons in our
Redemption and Sanctification. Moreover, we know by faith
that the Godhead is possessed in Three Persons, but not what is
the nature of the Godhead thus possessed or the nature of that
triple possession.

God is the first cause and the immanent ground of all creatures.
The existence of creatures is essentially dependent. They are
kept in being by the conserving will of God. "In Him we live
and move and are." The creature may be regarded under two
aspects—a positive and a negative. By the very fact of its
creatureliness the creature is finite, exclusive of other beings—is
not—as well as is. The positive being of the creature is a copy
of some aspect of the Infinite Being of God, of some idea of the
Divine Mind. Whatever positively is in the creature is therefore

C   33

in God. God is eminently all created being. Creatures, because they are creatures, are essentially distinct from God. But the ground of that distinction is the finitude of their being and its consequent relativity and dependence, that is their lack of being, what they are not. That which differentiates the creature from God is thus no positive being—non-existent in the Divine Being, but the negation-limitation of the creature, whereby its participation of the Being of God is essentially constituted as a being distinct from Him. St John of the Cross insists on this truth when he says of certain created beauties : " All that is here set forth is in God eminently in an infinite way, or rather, every one of these grandeurs is God and all of them together are God. . . ." The soul " feels all things to be God " (*Spiritual Canticle*, st. 14). It follows that symbolism is not merely an external and arbitrary representation of spiritual realities by material figures. It is rather that the ultimate reality of the symbol is its participation and reflection of the spiritual reality or idea symbolised : and thus ultimately of God, of Whom all ideas are aspects. The essence, for example, of some beautiful scene in nature is precisely this, that it is an external, sensible reflection and presentation of spirit. All that is positive in it, as opposed to the negation of its materiality, is the participation of a spiritual reality, ultimately of a type-idea existent in God, a participation therefore of the Divine Being. Thus, for instance, the ascent of a mountain is no merely arbitrary emblem of the Godward ascent of the soul. A mountain ascent is essentially an elevation and consequently the attainment of a wider horizon, no longer bounded by the narrow limits of the valley below. This material elevation and emancipation of vision themselves embody and thus represent and participate in a spiritual elevation and emancipation of vision. These spiritual realities constitute the positive being of a mountain ascent. Their material embodiment is but a limitation or negation of being. This spiritual elevation, this spiritual emancipation from limits, is an activity of the creature Godward, a relation therefore of the finite creature to the infinite God : so finally God Himself as essentially constitutive of such an activity and relationship in His creation. Thus in very truth " My beloved *is* the mountains," as St John says in this same stanza.

It is also clear that the higher the created being, the more fully does it reproduce the Divine Being of the Creator. A living soul possesses more of God than a mass of lifeless matter. For it is less limited, less exclusive. A material substance, indeed, differs from a spirit by the lesser degree of its being, by its greater exclusion of other beings. There is less being in an electric current than in thought, and electricity therefore reproduces less of the Divine Being than thought. God is therefore more immanent in, more present to, creatures possessed of higher and fuller degrees of being,[1] than He is immanent in and present to creatures possessed only of lower and scantier degrees of being. For the increased limitation—that is, lack of being of the latter—excludes Him to a greater degree by its greater defect of being—that is, its greater exclusion of his boundless plenitude of Being—than the lesser limitation of the former, constituting as it does a fuller degree of being, and therefore a lesser exclusion of His Unlimited Being. Hence God is more immanent in spirit than in matter, more in reason than in mere sentience, more in life than in the inorganic, more immanent also in the more purely spiritual, and therefore less limited functions of the human soul than in its more sensible and therefore more limited functions. Hence every creature is a revelation of God, and the higher in the scale of being that creature is, the more fully does it reveal Him. Consider some beautiful flower, for example, a peony glowing amidst the tender green of May. All its grace of form, all its glory of colour is a representation, a participation, though infinitely inadequate and scant, of the Beauty of God. But the beauty of a loving heart is a far more adequate representation, a far ampler participation, albeit still infinitely inadequate and scant of that Divine Beauty. Created being is thus on its positive side the reproduction of the Divine Being, under diverse aspects and in divers degrees, so that there is no positive being in them, that is not in God ; that is not their participation of God, God in them. The Vulgate used by St John of the Cross read, in the first chapter of St John's Gospel : " Whatsoever was made, in Him was life." Whether this be the true reading or not,[2] it was certainly the classical expression of the truth for St John of the Cross, for he recurs several times to this text. By it is meant that the true being, the living reality of the creature is the Divine Idea, the Aspect of the Godhead which it represents, this Idea being no dead concept but one with the Divine Life, an Idea moreover whose willed externalisation

---

[1] Strictly speaking, they are rather present to Him than He to them. See *Transcendence*, chap. iv.

[2] It is the reading accepted by Westcott and Hort.

constituted the creature in being, and conserves it in being.
Thus the being of the creature is rooted in the Godhead, its
Creator; its continuance in being is grounded in the Godhead,
its Conserver.   Without the Divine Conservation and Co-operation
the being and action of the creature would cease.   Thus is the
life of the creature wholly in God.   In the fourth stanza of *The
Living Flame of Love*, we read : " As St John tells us, all things
in Him [God] are life, and in Him they live and move and are, as
saith also the Apostle.   Hence it is, that when this mighty Emperor
moves in the soul . . . all things seem to move together, even as
in the earth's motion all the natural things thereon, move, as if
they had been nothing. . . . Nor do they only move.   They also
disclose the beauties of their being, their virtue, beauty and
graces, *and the root of their duration and life*.   The soul now sees
how all creatures both on high and here below have their life,
force and duration in Him. . . . Although it is true that the soul
sees that these things are distinct from God, in that their being
is created, and sees them in Him with their force, root and strength,
she also knows that God is in His being in an infinitely pre-
eminent way, all these things."   Mother Cecilia repeats this same
doctrine with particular emphasis.   " The Soul," she says,
" beholds how creatures, although they are dead in themselves,
in God are life " (*Trans.*, st. 4).   In such wise is this " vision of
God " imprinted on the sight of the soul that in it she beholds all
things in and through God, and sees Him in them all.   She beholds
them, as it were, bathed and penetrated by their Divine Lord, and
*when she contemplates them as they are in themselves she sees that
they are like accidents without substance* (*Transformation of the
Soul in God*, st. 1).   She does not indeed say that apart from the
Divine Being creatures *are* mere accidents whose substance is
God.   That were sheer pantheism.   What she does mean by her
bold language is that since the substance of creatures is but an
externalised Aspect of the Godhead, a participation of the Divine
Being, differentiated from Him by their creaturely limitation, and
wholly dependent upon, and grounded in His being, it is by
comparison unreal and accidental.   Ruysbroeck expresses this
same doctrine in another terminology when he speaks of the Divine
Being as the uncreated superessence of our created essence
(*Sept Degrés d'Amour*, chap. xiv).   Not only is God the positive
being of all creatures in the sense explained above.   He is also
the agent of all their activity.   As Dame Julian tells us : " God

doth all things, be it never so little. . . . There is no Doer but He "
(*Revelations*, chap. xi).   Every created activity *qua* positive activity is an act of God, for that activity is sustained, moved, kept
in motion by His co-operative will, and is a finite reproduction of
His activity.   Even the ruthless determinism of natural energies
veils the beneficent action of Personal love operative therein.
This activity of God in all Action, as the concomitant of His
presence in all being, is taught by Bl. Angela of Foligno in the
following energetic language.   "I understand," she says, "that
He [God] is present . . . in everything that hath being, *in the
demon*, in the good Angel, in hell, in Paradise, *in adultery*, *in
murder*, in every good work " (*Visions and Instructions*, chap. xxvii.
Trs. A Secular Priest).   Hence it follows, as Dame Julian points
out, that *every act*, even an act that is morally evil, is, as a positive
act, good.   The evil is simply an undue defect of being limiting
that positive goodness.   Moreover, even this undue defect is overruled and supplied by God for the general good of the universe
—indeed the good of every part of the universe—in so far as each
part is capable of good—a capacity largely dependent in the case
of rational spirits on their free choice.   The doctrine of immanence—as apprehended by mystical intuition—whereby God
is perceived as the positive being and activity of all creatures is
the firm foundation of this further optimism of faith.   Because
God " is the only Doer," " He can and will make all things well."
The life of every creature is thus rooted in the Divine Life of God
—so that, although the created life is by its creatureliness and
consequent finitude infinitely distinct from the Divine Being and
Life of God, the Divine Being is intimately present as the ground
and ultimate cause of that created life.   Moreover, it is by this
Divine immanence that we can explain satisfactorily the evolutionary phenomena now being discovered by the natural scientist.
Natural selection can no longer be regarded as an adequate explanation of the evolution of species.   The sudden mutations
discernible, for example, in certain plants, when brought into a
new environment, mutations whose end is the formation of new
species, better adapted to that environment than the parent
species, point to a purposive nisus in organic life—as is admitted
by many modern biologists.   But it is surely impossible to regard
that purpose, which has in view the future welfare and improve-
ment of the species, as something inherent in a life that is
irrational and, in the case of plants, not even conscious.   We

must see in it therefore the working of a Reason other than the organism in question—yet intimately present in that organism—which directs the nisus of the organism in view of a good which it is incapable of foreseeing. This immanent Reason or Spirit (unless indeed it be an angel, which would justify anew the scholastic belief in angelic beings at work behind the phenomena of nature) must be God Himself immanent in His creation. The intimate immanence of purpose—so intimate as to give rise to the error that it is inherent in the organism itself—points to the latter as the true explanation. The view of evolution adopted by the Jesuit scientist, Fr. Wassmann, is polyphiletic. He believes that our present species have been evolved from a far more limited number of species, each the ancestor of a group of species. The origin of these type-species he refers to special creation. The general consensus, however, of modern scientists is in favour of a monophyletic evolution, whereby all species have been evolved from one rudimentary form of organic being. I can see nothing in the defined teaching of the Church to prevent our acceptance of this hypothesis, if the evidence seems to demand it, provided, however, we admit the special creation of the immortal soul of man, and that in the case of every individual. I am too ignorant of natural science to put forward with decision any view of evolution. It does, however, appear to me that modern scientific research has (1) rendered monophyletic evolution extremely probable ; (2) laid increasing stress on sudden mutations. The great mutations which have brought into being new type forms seem to me due not to special creation but to the operation on the subject of the mutation of an external stimulus, the stimulus of the Divine Spirit immanent in creation. This special operation of the immanent Godhead would effect a mutation greater in kind and degree than could be effected by the operation of natural causes. It would, moreover, be but the intensification at special points of the evolutionary process of the continuous co-operation of God with the course of evolution, wherein He is immanent for its motion and its direction. Thus do the discoveries of modern science, which at first occasioned such needless alarm to the religious soul, tend to make us realise as never before the immanence of God—even in His lowest creatures—not only to sustain them in being and action but to direct that action to the common good of the material creation. This good is an ever more adequate representation of the Divine Being, and this more adequate representation is (as we shall see) a closer union with Himself. It is then no exaggeration of devotion but a fundamental truth that the creature, alike its being and its energy, apart from God, is nothing. All created being and activity is a partial reproduction of God, and is eminently contained and existent in Him. The creature has and is nothing of its own, save its creaturely limitation, which is sheer negation of being. Nevertheless, that limitation is essentially constitutive of *created* being. Therefore created being is not a limited mode or aspect of Uncreated Being. This pantheistic error, as was pointed out in the previous chapter, would make the Unlimited necessarily manifested by the limited, and would therefore subject the Unlimited to limitations, a patent self-contradiction. On the contrary, created being, in virtue of its essential limitation, is, as created being, infinitely apart from the Uncreated Being, of Which, as being, it is a participation. A paradox assuredly of discursive reason, but the truth of mystic intuition.

CHAPTER III

UNITY OF GOD

Hear, O Israel, the Lord Thy God is **One** *God.*

To be, is no other than to be one, in so far, therefore, as anything attains unity, in so far it " is." For unity worketh congruity and harmony, whereby things composite are, in so far as they are: for things uncompounded are in themselves, because they are one ; but things compounded, imitate unity by the harmony of their parts, and, so far as they attain to unity, they are. Wherefore order and rule secure being, disorder tends to not being.

ST AUGUSTINE,
De Morib. Manich, chap. vi.   Quoted and trs.
Pusey, in note to *Confessions,* chap. i.

BEFORE discussing the complement of the Divine Immanence, the Divine Transcendence with its consequence, the unknowableness [1] of God, as He is in Himself, I must speak of the Divine Unity. We will approach this from the scale of reality and truth. The lower the rank of creatures in the scale of being—that is, the less they possess of positive being or reality—the greater is their mutual exclusiveness : that is to say, the more do they exclude other creatures, other aspects and kinds of being. One material atom or electron is wholly external to another. Matter is indeed a principle of exclusion and separation. The higher the being the greater is its unity, a unity, however, which is imposed upon an ever-increasing multiplicity. Life, and still more, thought, is inclusive and unifying. How much greater is the unity of the spiritual than the unity of the material is evident from a simple example. A stone consists of separable molecules, a perception, however many its objects, is one indivisible act. Life unifies in one nisus directed to one end a complex manifold of forces, otherwise divergent, and subordinates to itself a variety of material elements. Thus is constituted the unity of the organism whose members are united by their essential relation to the whole, and are

---

[1] By creaturely knowledge—that is, the knowledge proceeding from a created intelligence as its first principle.

so mutually interdependent that in proportion to the perfection of the organism the nature or activity of each increasingly demands and implies those of the others. When life departs the principle of unity is removed. The subordinate elements or forces then work independently of each other and corruption sets in. Above sentient life is thought, and thought is more unifying than sentience. It unifies an indefinitely greater number and diversity of elements, and their union is far more intimate. The higher, more powerful and more deeply penetrating the thought, the wider is the scope and the more intimate the nature of its unification.

It is said to be the essential characteristic of genius to find resemblances between things apparently most unlike—in other words, to unify diverse phenomena by their reduction under general laws. A great scientific hypothesis is such a principle of unification. Intuition, however, unifies more completely than discursive thought. By intuition I mean the intuition of the mystic (and in a secondary sense of the artist), not the lower intuition, which is blind instinct.

In like manner a dominant aim in the will unifies by subordination the minor aims which would otherwise distract and divide and so " corrupt " the higher spiritual life. Thus throughout creation an increased unification of an increased multiplicity denotes an increase of reality and a greater perfection. Lowest of all is elemental matter, with its external and mutually exclusive multiplicity united solely by external interrelation.* In chemical combination there is the same externality of parts, but a higher unification has been achieved, by the fusion of diverse elements to form a compound, which is qualitatively distinct from its components, not merely their external sum total. Above this is organic life unifying diverse material elements by subordination to one nisus. Above that is consciousness, in which a greater multiplicity of forces, desires and subject materials is quasi-consciously unified by a direction to one end, through an immediate instinctive apperception of their relation to that end. Sentience also unites subject and object in the act of sense perception. We then rise in succession to discursive reason uniting sensation to sensation, idea to idea, fact to fact, and framing unifying hypotheses, to rational will unifying minor ends by one supreme aim, to artistic intuition, vaguely conscious of an ultimate unity which it cannot grasp, and, above all these, to mystical intuition—which is at once volitional and intuitive, apprehending though without clear comprehension the Unity of God, and of all things in Him as their ground and cause. Thus as the scale of being and its concomitant activity rises upward by its increase of content, and of qualitative level, there is discovered an ever-increasing unification of an ever-increasing multiplicity. The approach to God, both objectively in the scale of being itself and subjectively in the apperception of reality by creatures capable of psychical action, is thus the way of an ever greater unification of an ever fuller manifold. Hence God must be the " Absolute " Unity of an infinite manifold, and the Vision of God —of which mystical intuition is but the obscure beginning —the perfectly unified apperception of His All-inclusive Unity. This notion of a scale of being ascending upwards to the One God in proportion to its increasing unification of an increasing manifold is corroborated by the teaching of Mr Bradley's philosophy of the Absolute. Mr Bradley finds in this increased unification of an increased multiplicity a criterion of greater reality. He regards the soul as a more adequate presentation of reality than matter, because " the relation of unity and multiplicity is not so external in the soul-life as in physical nature." But this unification is obviously incomplete in human psychology. " Perfect experience would consist in an all-comprehensive content, unified with full consequence and harmony into a whole." [1] This ideal multiplicity-in-unity of Mr Bradley is realised in that perfect unification in One Simple Unity of an infinite multiplicity, which is the Divine Being of Catholic theology. Mr Bradley concludes that since we cannot attain to this ideal unification of multiplicity, we cannot attain to reality, and hence that our knowledge is confined to appearance. This is a truth falsely expressed. Our natural knowledge is not indeed of appearance in the sense of the merely phenomenal, but it is of a reality which is but unreality and appearance *by comparison* with God the absolute Reality. It is also true that our natural knowledge, confined as it is within the limits of the finite, of the external multiplicity of sense images and distinctive concepts derived therefrom, can never attain to knowledge of the nature of the ultimate or absolute Reality—that is, of the nature of God. It is only by the supernatural elevation of the soul, by the light of glory and in a veiled and imperfect manner here, by sanctifying grace—that we can receive this knowledge of God as He is in Himself.

Mr Bradley's insistence upon the logical need of unification, and

[1] Professor Höffding on Mr Bradley. *Modern Philosophers*, pp. 63-64.

his application of the principle that unity in multiplicity is the criterion of reality, has thus led him to a view of the Absolute which is largely coincident with the doctrine of God taught by the Catholic mystic. Unhappily, that view is weakened by a conclusion which makes the external imperfectly unified multiplicity of " Appearance " a necessary and inherent expression of the absolute. If, however, the absolute of necessity expresses itself by this external multiplicity, that perfect unification which Mr Bradley rightly demands is, after all, lacking in his absolute. Nevertheless he has done good service in thus emphasising the necessity of this unity, since it is a principle of the first importance for mystical theology.

Since the scale of increasing reality is an increasing unification of an increasing manifold, so also must it be with our knowledge and practical handling of reality. As that knowledge and handling penetrate to greater depths of reality and approach closer to the ultimate reality, they are increasingly unified alike in object, mode and act. Of this I will now give some examples.

In internal politics the goal of the true statesman is the unification, for the common good of society, by co-ordination in view of that good, of the multiple activities of individuals, each freely developed. In international politics his goal should be the unification under one world-wide authority of a multiplicity of subordinate societies, each of which makes in complete internal freedom its peculiar contribution, a contribution which is the fruit of its particular history and character, to the commonwealth of the world-state and thus to the common good of the human race. We may hope with the authors of a stimulating little book, *The War and Democracy*, that such a unification of a multitude of internally autonomous states will be at least the ultimate solution of the present European problem. The late war was radically due to a false patriotism, which aims at the self-realisation of one nationality as independent and exclusive of, and therefore as opposed to, the full self-realisation of other nationalities. For no single nation or race can possibly be the full expression and realisation of a civilisation which can only be adequately expressed and realised by all its component nationalities and races together. Hence to maintain and to work for the realisation of one national or racial ideal or culture or character as exclusive of and in opposition to the ideals, cultures and characters of other nations or races, is to maintain, not only what is positive in that national ideal, character or culture, but also its limitation : that is, its negation of other ideals, characters and cultures. Even if one national culture is better than another, it is not identical with that other, and therefore the two cultures are richer and contain more positive good than the one alone. The unity of man's common good demands, therefore, an inclusive patriotism which expresses itself in the desire that the patriot's country shall make the largest contribution to the common treasury of mankind, not the exclusive patriotism which seeks the lower material welfare of that country at the expense of the well-being of other countries : the love of one's country as *against* other countries. This latter patriotism is a mischievous illusion, whose fruits are division, ignorance, prejudice, suspicion, hatred and suicidal wars. It is a limitation and the parent of limitations. The inclusive unity of the unlimited demands the former patriotism and wholly rejects the latter.   Let us hope that the false patriotism which attaches to a system of sovereign states and which is a principle either of division, exclusion and mutual destruction, or, if one such state acquires world-wide supremacy, of a wasteful and barren unification, shall in future give place to a world commonwealth of subordinate states that will include in its unity the greatest possible multiplicity.

Even a very superficial acquaintance with the fluctuations of philosophical systems should suffice to bring home the fact that the only final and satisfactory philosophy—and by philosophy I mean the intellectual presentation of human experience as an interconnected whole—must be a synthesis of all that is positive in every interpretation of experience made by the human soul, whether of the totality of experience, or of any partial aspect, or portion of experience.   That synthesis must, for instance, possess the unification of Monism without its limitation of God by the limitations proper only to finite beings. It must possess that sense of the Divine Transcendence which belongs to Agnosticism without the refusal of Agnosticism to satisfy the soul's demand for immediate experience of ultimate Reality—that is, for personal communion with God, which is the essence of religion. For this refusal really implies that ultimate Reality is infra- not supra-personal, and therefore *unable* to place the soul in such a relationship with itself as that in which one person stands to another. Such a philosophy must also admit the self-evident dualism of matter and spirit, and that more fundamental dualism of the

unlimited Creator and the essentially limited and hence comparatively unreal creature. It must, on the other hand, reject a dualism which denies one principle causal, and therefore explanatory,
of the totality of experience and (by extension) of being. It must
insist on the discontinuity of the scale and process of evolution, by
the introduction of new principles and new beginnings. But it
must ascribe all these new principles and beginnings to one first
cause and supreme principle, Who manifests aspects of his one
infinite being in all these, and Who is immanent in the course of
evolution to produce these new beginnings and introduce these
new principles while ever remaining infinitely transcendent of
His creation. Our philosophy must also lay due stress on the
uniqueness of the individual and on the free will of the rational
soul, without losing sight of the dependence of the individual on
his environment, both present and past, and of the solidarity of
human society, and guarding always a wider consciousness of the
universe as a whole. It must accept, not only the data of science
and the logical deductions of the discursive intellect, but the
intuitive perceptions of art, and the facts of conscience and of
religious experience. It must utilise all these manifold data of
human experience, accepting all that is positive in them and rejecting the negations arising out of the inadequacy of each partial
datum or series of data. It will thus harmonise and unify, as far
as it is possible to do so. It will, however, accept the obvious
impossibility of any complete unification by our finite understanding, whose accessible subject matter is, moreover, so incomplete and so narrowly limited. Therefore it will not attempt a
false harmony by the rejection of any indubitable datum of
experience. Moreover, when all these data have been accepted,
such a philosophy will recognise the inadequacy of human experience and its philosophic interpretation, even at their richest and
deepest, to satisfy the need of the human soul, which craves a
fuller knowledge of God and a closer union with Him than her
unaided and purely natural understanding and activity can
supply. It will therefore seek a revealed religion and a dispensation of supernatural grace which will fully satisfy this need,
while at the same time accepting and unifying all the positive
truth which this most " positive " and synthetic philosophy—the
philosophy of the unlimited—must, as we have seen, accept and
subsume ; in short, a revelation which is a world religion. Such
a world religion must clearly possess this inclusive unification of

the greatest possible multiplicity, which is a reflection of the divine unity of God. It cannot, however, be a syncretism of all existing and future cults, beliefs and purported revelations. Such a syncretism would result in the substitution for a number of living beliefs, of a philosophical abstraction which would fail to provide those concrete objects and aids, faith and worship and grace required by the religious sense of man. Moreover, such a syncretism would involve the rejection of that very element which transcends the natural theology in which our philosophy concluded, but which it found so inadequate. Therefore our synthetic philosophy must look for its religion to some one definite religious system of divine revelation, which contains in itself all that is positive in every other creed and worship and rejects only their limitations and exclusions. If no such revealed religion were forthcoming, we should be obliged to fall back on the inadequacy of natural theology. Such a religion does, however, exist. It is the Catholic religion, which can be shown to be a synthesis of all that is positive in all other creeds and worships, and which also necessitates and implies a synthetic philosophy of the type which I have outlined above. We find, for example, in Catholicism a synthesis of monotheism and polytheism, of the pantheism of the Upanishads and the transcendence of Mohammedanism, of sacerdotalism and personal religion, of sacramentalism and mysticism, of communism and individualism. The Catholic synthesis reconciles and unifies all these divergent elements by rejecting their mutual negations and accepting what is positive in all. Catholic theology is the unification of the manifold of religious beliefs and creeds, as any philosophy wholly acceptable in her eyes must be the unification of the manifold of philosophic systems, and of the data from which they have been built up. It is true that Catholic theology does not propose, any more than sound philosophy can propose, to provide a perfect rational unification of this manifold of positive truths. It is faith, not beatific vision. It does, however, accept all positive truths, even when it cannot completely harmonise them, and unifies them at least potentially by referring all to the Triune God, Who is the Absolute Unity of an infinite multiplicity. In any case an incomplete unification, with a potency and promise of completion hereafter, of the entire manifold, that constitutes the totality of experience, is preferable to a complete unification of a lesser manifold that is but a portion of that totality : a unification artificially attained by the acceptance of certain data only of experience, to the exclusion of other data. Moreover, as our union with God increases, we enjoy an increasing perception of the ultimate unity of dogma and of experience in their first principle, the unity of God, the revealer of dogma, the cause and ground of experience. This synthetic character of the Catholic Faith is surely the most cogent proof of its Divine origin and of its faithful representation of the absolute unity of infinite variety which is the Being of God. This universality of Catholicism has indeed never been perfectly actualised, nor can it be until and unless the Church comes into vital contact with all the civilisations, philosophies and religions of mankind. For the Catholic synthesis, the unification by Catholicism and the philosophy which it presupposes, of the entire manifold of all religious and metaphysical truths, indeed, of experience as a whole, is not a static reality already completed once for all.[1] It is, on the contrary, a living, organic growth—a growth due, not to further revelations, but to an increase of the human experience and its scientific explanation which interpret and develop the body of truth once for all revealed to the Apostles, and which that revelation in turn interprets and unifies. We cannot therefore finally acquiesce in the present divorce between the Catholic religion and secular thought and culture. It is surely undeniable that Catholicism attained in the mediæval synthesis the fullest, widest and richest of presentation hitherto achieved. In that synthesis every branch of human knowledge and art was made subservient to the understanding and explication of the Catholic revelation. From the Renaissance onwards secular culture—speculation and art alike—has been increasingly dominated by a naturalistic humanist immanental and therefore this-worldly, anti-supernatural and anti-religious tendency. This tendency is now so far triumphant that transcendental, other-worldly religion, and especially its most complete representative, the Catholic Faith, has been driven from the main current of our European civilisation into its backwaters. Every province of secular life, speculation and art has been wrested in turn from the empire of religion. All branches of human activity and speculation now find their end no longer in eternity, but in time, no longer

---

[1] Nevertheless there is a very important static element in Catholicism unlike in this the trend of modern thought which is one-sidedly dynamic. A revealed dogma can never be set aside as false, nor can its *fully ratified* development be rejected. (See my *Apologetics*, sec. 15.)

in God, but in man, no longer in the supernatural, but in mere nature. On the other hand, the living presentation of Catholicism has lost enormously in scope and wealth through lack of the stimulation and material of secular culture. A narrowness of outlook, a lack of sympathy for all that is good outside the Church, an excessive suspicion of all novelty, even at times a dislike of art and speculation as such, have inevitably marked the spirit of counter-Reformation as opposed to pre-Reformation Catholicism.[1] Now it may perhaps be—as the late Mgr. Benson imagined it in his gloomy novel, *The Lord of the World*—that the anti-supernaturalist tendency will attain an almost complete triumph and culminate in the full revelation of Antichrist—that is, of pure naturalism *as opposed* to the supernatural—in the great apostasy and thus in the Second Coming of Our Lord. If, however, this is not the case, and many records of past disappointment warn us against too confident an expectation of an imminent parousia, then the naturalist tide must inevitably turn. The human soul can never be finally satisfied with the creature, because the creature is essentially limited and the soul needs the unlimited—the infinite. At the epoch of Our Saviour's birth naturalism was also dominant—a dominance expressed in the entire structure and life of the Roman Empire. Then, as to-day, the achievements and possibilities of man, the reality and sufficiency of the material, or, at least, of the purely natural, overshadowed and dimmed, for the imagination at least, the spiritual and the Divine. Some three to four hundred years passed by, and lo ! the emperors and the great ones of the earth listen in reverence to the teachings of desert hermits and pillar ascetics—the extremest representatives of the supernatural and the transcendent. But the movement did not end with this conquest of the immanental and the natural by the transcendental and the supernatural. A higher synthesis had yet to be accomplished, wherein the positive truth and value of the former should be incorporated into and utilised by the latter. Natural philosophy and culture had scarcely been vanquished by the supernatural revelation than they were accepted by it as its faithful servants, by whose aid alone its own wealth and depth of truth could be fully manifested. The Alexandrine fathers first, and later the pseudo-Dionysius and St Augustine, who largely incorporated Plato and Neoplatonism, began this synthesis,

---

[1] The fuller mediæval Catholicism continued in Spain until after the sixteenth century, as is evident in St Teresa and St John of the Cross and in Mother Cecilia.

which was completed by the scholastic Christianisation of Aristotle
—itself but a part of that wider synthesis of Catholicism and
Graeco-Roman civilisation which constituted mediævalism. Since
the Renaissance another cycle of history has begun. We have
again the thesis of pure naturalism. Unless the end come we
shall assuredly have the antithesis of a reaction to supernaturalism and the final synthesis of both tendencies.[1] Indeed, as before,
the commencement of the synthesis must be in part concomitant
with the antithesis. The Alexandrine fathers began their work
before the second century of Christianity had passed, and a
century earlier St John had utilised the Platonic-Philonian conception of the Logos. So must it be now at this return of the
cycle. The stream of secular philosophy and literature must be
reunited with the stream of Catholic Faith and its development.
We cannot believe, for example, that Spinoza and Locke, Berkeley
and Kant, Hegel and Schopenhauer, Eucken and Bergson, or
again that Goethe and Schiller, Beethoven and Wagner, Wordsworth and Shelley, Ibsen and Maeterlinck, or yet again that
Newton and Laplace, Darwin and Kelvin, Haeckel and Huxley,
Charcot and Freud have nothing to contribute to the development and the enrichment of that increasingly fuller and wider
presentation of reality, which is utilised and unified by the Catholic
revelation. It is no doubt true that we cannot substitute Kantism
or Hegelianism or indeed any other of the post-Renaissance philosophies, for scholasticism, as the most adequate metaphysical
expression and instrument of Catholicism. Indeed the attempt
at a " Catholic Kantism " has been officially condemned. The
reason, however, is that these systems are essentially limited and
one-sided—interpretations of experience harmonised artificially by
the rejection of indubitable data of that experience. Scholasticism, on the contrary, accepts frankly the totality of experience.
Hence in principle scholasticism will be permanent, as against
these later, more limited systems.* The religion of the unlimited
cannot accept as adequate a philosophy of the limited. But the
scholastic synthesis will be indefinitely expanded and modified by
the incorporation of the positive truth contributed by these partial
philosophies.

Among the ancient philosophies the monistic system of the
Stoics could not be accepted by the Church to the degree in which

---

[1] My use of Hegelian terminology does *not* imply a Hegelian conception of
reality as a whole.

D

Aristotelianism, Platonism and Neoplatonism were accepted. Nevertheless the presence in scholasticism of an element of Stoic provenance is indubitable. May we not expect to find in the neo-scholasticism of the future elements similarly derived from the philosophies of—*e.g.*—Kant and Hegel, although such philosophies must ever remain, as a whole, unacceptable, on account of their intrinsic limitations. Such elements might conceivably be, in the case of Kant, his insistence on the supreme value of the argument from conscience to the existence of God, beyond that of the Onto-logical, Cosmological and Teleological arguments, though we cannot follow him in his denial of all value to these latter. From Hegelianism might be accepted the conception I have myself utilised above of the cycle of thesis, antithesis and synthesis as a law of historical progress. Thus should Neoscholasticism be scholastic in its fundamental principles, which are the permanent elements, the fundamental constituents of human experience ; in its detailed teaching largely affected by modern anti-scholastic philosophies. All that there is of positive truth in the phil-osophies and in the various branches of science developed by the naturalist trend of the past few centuries will be built into the Catholic philosophy of the future. The new synthesis will doubt-less owe a far greater debt to the discoveries of modern physical science than to the speculations of modern philosophy, since the modern age has been the golden age, not of metaphysics, but of the natural sciences. So shall we attain a presentation of Catholicism that will be indefinitely fuller and richer than was even the presentation of the thirteenth century, a synthesis more adequate than any yet reached by human thought. Catholicism will achieve the unification of a manifold enormously more various, more complex and more extensive than that which was unified by the schoolmen.[1] In this progressive unification of an ever-increasing manifold Catholicism will, both in itself and through its subordinate philosophy and culture, ever more and more fully

[1] This can, of course, only be accomplished by the careful maintenance and frank teaching of the entire deposit of revealed dogmas. No portion of this deposit — *e.g.* eternal punishment and diabolic possession, and in ethics the absolute indissolubility of marriage—can be denied, explained away, or practically ignored in order to suit the passing exclusions and imitations of contemporary thought and feeling, in the name of a false charity. The divinely unlimited cannot admit of these human limits. I would add that by eternal punishment I understand a final self-exclusion from supernatural union with God, together with the consequences that follow of necessity from that exclusion. (For diabolic possession see Appendix to Chapter VIII.)

manifest the unity of infinite multiplicity which is the nature of its Divine Author—the unlimited and therefore all-inclusive God.

Nevertheless the *present* existence in Catholicism of this potential unification—indeed, its partial actualisation—is a conviction which the study of other religious and philosophic systems brings home ever more strongly.

Thus in the development of society, both civil and religious, and of philosophy and theology, the law of progress is the increasing unification of an increasing multiplicity. But the law of progress is the law of Godward ascent. The most perfect social organisation, the most complete philosophic system, and the true revelation in its fullest development,, are in their several kinds the closest possible approximations to the Divine life and Nature, because they contain the maximum of positive being, and that is the maximal participation of His Being. Thus the most perfect unification possible of the greatest multiplicity is the fullest participation and reflection of God. Therefore God the Ultimate Reality must be Himself the perfect Unity of an Infinite Multiplicity. We have reached this conclusion by the consideration both of the scale of created being and of the nature of human activity and speculation. In both the same law was found to be operative. We shall now attempt to reach the same conclusion from a more narrowly ontological standpoint.

We have already seen that the positive being of the creature is in God eminently, being a reproduction of His Being under one aspect. As such the positive being of one creature cannot exclude the positive being of another, since both are ultimately aspects of One Absolutely Simple Being, the Being of God. In proportion, therefore, as we perceive the positive being of creatures in its ground, apart from the limitations of its finite creaturely embodiment, we see this positive being as one throughout, a representation and manifestation of the One Divine Being. For the external multiplicity of creatures is due to their negative distinction, whereby one being is not another ; is constituted, not by their positive being, but by their creaturely negation or limitation of being. When, therefore, that negation is transcended, their positive being is seen as one in God, their mutually exclusive distinction disappearing with the limitation which gave it birth in that Divine all-positive Ground of their being. Hence in mystical intuition the many are seen as one—aspects of one, positively, not negatively, distinct, the positive being of one not excluding but including the positive being of the others. The one is a harmony and the many the notes that compose it. Moreover God, since He is the Fulness of Being, without negation or limitation of any kind, must be without the external multiplicity, the negative distinction inherent in the creature as such. He is thus altogether One, the Absolute Unity, the Perfect unification of an infinite manifold that is without negative distinction or mutual externality. He is The One in Whom is All, and in Whom All is One. This Absolute Unity of the Godhead, embracing in its all-inclusive unity the positive being of the external manifold of creatures, a manifold thus unified in its Divine Ground and Source, has been well expressed by Dante in the *Paradiso*, when he says of the beatific vision :

> Nel suo profondo vidi che s'interna
> Legato con amore in un volume
> ciò che per l'universo se squaderna
> Sustenzia ed accidenti e lor costume
> quasi conflati insieme per tal modo
> che ciò ch'io dico è un semplice lume.
>
> *Par.*, xxxiii. 85.

"Within its depths" (*i.e.* of the Deity) "I saw ingathered, bound by love in one volume, the scattered leaves of all the universe ; substance and accidents and their relations, as though together fused, after such fashion that what I tell of is one simple flame " (Trs. *Temple Classics*). Theologians express this Unity of God by saying that He is each of His attributes. St John of the Cross dwells on this doctrine in the third stanza of *The Living Flame of Love*. He there says : " We must remember that God, in His one simple Being, is all the virtues and grandeurs of His attributes. . . . Since He is all these things in His simple Being, when He is united with the soul . . . it sees distinctly in Him all these virtues and grandeurs, such, for example, as omnipotence, wisdom, goodness and mercy. As each one of these is the very Being of God in one Person, either Father, Son or Holy Ghost, each attribute is God Himself." Mother Cecilia also speaks, in her treatise on the Union of the Soul with God, of the " measureless abyss— which is Our God, wherein there is no variety or diversity of things but a most simple unity in His Divine Being, for the entire Being of God is a most pure and *infinite* substance, in whose unity all differences are embraced and in Him are made life and pure substance." The Unity of God is thus the Perfect Identity of

His attributes. But the Divine attributes themselves include their subordinate ideas and forms which, when externalised by the Creative Will, are the positive being of creatures. Hence the Unity of God unifies, as we have seen, the manifold of created being. Moreover, since the Divine Being is infinite, it also embraces and unifies a literally infinite multiplicity of possible being. The Divine Unity is therefore the very opposite of that bare and abstract oneness which the mystics from Plotinus downwards have often been accused of substituting for the manifold of human experience. (See the following chapter.) The Supreme Unity is the unity of infinite multiplicity—not the negation of multiplicity. The Absolute Being of God is not One because It abstracts from differences and is bare, abstract existence, for this would be the minimal reality, but because Its Infinite Fulness unifies all differences. " The entire Being of God is a most pure and infinite substance, in Whose unity all differences are embraced and in Him are made life and pure substance." [1] For, as we saw above, the limitations inherent in the created being of diverse creatures are absent, so that they are no longer mutually exclusive. St John of the Cross expresses this truth by saying that in God there are no modes. By mode he means a limited aspect or quality of being distinct and ultimately distinguishable from other aspects and qualities. For in God all aspects of His infinite Being, though distinguished by our inadequate and limited concepts, are not really distinct, but are identical with His One Simple Essence. Therefore does St John say that in God there are no modes—that is, separate aspects—for such modes belong essentially to the external, mutually exclusive multiplicity of finite creatures. God the Object of mysticism is thus the One Who contains and makes one in His perfect Unity an infinite multiplicity, that is only to an infinitesimal degree represented in His creation.

How God is Absolute Unity and Simplicity and nevertheless contains in Himself an infinite variety, is beyond our comprehension. Why it must be so I have attempted to indicate in this chapter. The mystic, however, perceives in his intuition the fact of this Unity, though not its manner.*

The Immanence of God may be regarded as the starting-point of mysticism, and His Unity as the way. The goal is His Transcendence, to which the following chapter will be devoted.

[1] Mother Cecilia, *Union of the Soul with God.*

APPENDIX TO CHAPTER III

THE EPISTEMOLOGICAL SIGNIFICANCE OF THE DIVINE UNITY AS THE GROUND OF THE UNITY OF CREATION

SINCE God is the sole unification of created multiplicity, it is clear that no created principle will provide that complete unification which would be the unitary explanation of experience as a whole. We find in experience various planes of being which interact and are interrelated, planes constituted by different principles of being. There is, for example, the plane of mass and energy—that is, of mechanism—the plane of vegetable life, the plane of sentience and the plane of intelligence, with its correlative free will. Science and metaphysics have attempted in vain to secure a unification of experience by the reduction of these diverse planes or principles to one plane or principle—*e.g.* to explain the entire cycle of phenomena by mechanical energy, by life or by thought. This has proved a failure. One plane cannot be explained in terms of another. The existence of more than one principle or plane must be admitted. If, however, these planes are regarded as ultimate, we are unable to account for their inter-actions and combinations. To maintain this is to deny the possible existence of any ultimate unity and therefore of any ultimate intelligibility of experience. We must therefore posit an ultimate principle of unity lying beyond and above these created principles—the common ground and unification of them all. This must be either a common being, self-manifested in these diverse planes, which are aspects of this being, or a transcendent Being containing these principles eminently in Himself. The former alternative is taught by Pantheism, the latter by Theism. My intention here is not to discuss the arguments for and against these rival unifications—but, taking theism for the true alterna-tive—to point out that in God alone can we obtain the unification necessary to a complete explanation of experience.[1] From this

---

[1] Science having failed to explain phenomena by one principle alone has no ground for denying the possibility that the ultimate principle that transcends and causes the others—the Divine Creator—can intervene in the series of phenomena

we conclude (1) that, since the Divine Being as He is in Himself is unknowable by our earthly knowledge (see the following chapter), we cannot hope to attain a complete rational explanation of experience ; (2) that since we can apprehend God by faith or mystical intuition, we can obtain a certain knowledge that such a unification does exist ; hence that experience is wholly intelligible in itself, though only partially intelligible by human reason. We can and, as we shall see later, do attain a sense of the ultimate unity of experience, although we cannot comprehend that unity. Moreover, since God is thus the sole principle of complete unification, religion must always possess an epistemological value. God is the epistemological unification, because He is the ontological Unity.

among the created principles which there interact, Miracles are therefore possible. If in other ages the autonomy of natural science required vindication, to-day the most urgent necessity is the vindication of the autonomy of theology, metaphysics, ethics, and of certain aspects of psychology menaced with servitude to the principles and methods of physical science.

CHAPTER IV

THE TRANSCENDENCE OF GOD

I see a mighty darkness
Filling the seat of power, and rays of gloom
Dart round, as light from the meridian sun,
Ungazed upon and shapeless ; neither limit,
Nor form, nor outline ; yet we feel it is
A living spirit.

SHELLEY,
Prometheus Unbound, Act II., sc. 4.

Yen el monte nada.

FINITE being is, as we saw, constituted by two elements, a positive element, which is the external reproduction of some aspect of the Divine Being, and a negative element, whereby it is finite and dependent being. This essential finitude, this negative element, renders finite and relative being *infinitely* distant from the Infinite and Absolute Being of God. God infinitely transcends creatures. They are related to Him as their cause, ground and conserver. He is not related to them, else He would be conditioned by them, and to some degree dependent on them. This would involve some being possessed in common by Himself and them, the ground of this mutual relationship. This common being would be a *summum genus* of which He and they are species—a common category to which He and they are reducible. Such reduction under a common category would mean that God was not Absolute and Infinite Being—but relative to the creation, as belonging to a common category with it, and finite because there would be some other being outside Himself that possessed existence as He possesses it, and by its existence added to the sum of being. God would thus be a part of a larger whole, which whole would be greater than He, its part. It would moreover result from such relationship of God to creatures that the ground of such relationship—the common being or category, uniting both terms, was itself the Absolute—God but a subordinate deity. We should

56

further have to inquire whether this absolute were Itself related to God and the created universe, and should thus be brought to an infinite regress. Therefore God cannot be related to creation.[1] Nor do creatures share with God the common category of being. On the contrary, created being, as compared with the Absolute Being of God, is sheer not-being, or, if we consider created being as being, then in that sense of being God is not, is, as certain mystics have said, nothing. From the pseudo-Dionysius onwards mystical theology has dwelt much on this Divine Transcendence and on its consequence that our knowledge of God is negative, rather than positive, a knowledge rather of what He is not than of what He is. Indeed, it is a dictum of theology that we can know that God is but not what He is.[2] In his *Mystical Theology* Dionysius takes all the grades of being in order, from matter to spirit, and points out that God is none of these. "We say, then," he writes, "that the Cause of all, which is above all," has not "shape, nor form, nor quality, nor quantity, nor bulk—nor is in a place—nor is seen—nor has sensible contact—nor perceives, nor is perceived, by the senses, nor has disorder and confusion as being vexed by earthly passions . . . neither is It, nor has It, change or decay, or division, or deprivation, or flux—or any other of the objects of sense. . . . It is neither soul, nor mind, nor has imagination, nor opinion, nor reason, nor conception, neither is expressed, *nor conceived* ; neither is number, nor order, nor greatness, nor littleness ; nor equality, nor inequality ; nor similarity, nor dissimilarity ; neither is standing, nor moving ; nor at rest ; neither has power, nor is power, nor light ; neither lives, nor is life ; neither is *essence,* nor eternity, nor time ; *neither is Its touch intelligible,* neither is It science, nor truth ; nor kingdom, nor wisdom ; neither one nor oneness ; *neither Deity nor Goodness ; nor is It Spirit according to our understanding*; nor Sonship nor Paternity, nor any other thing of those known to us or to any other existing being; neither is It any of non-existing nor of existing things, nor do things existing know It as It is ; . . . neither is there expression of it, nor name nor knowledge " (*Mystical Theology,* chap. iv. 5. Trs. Parker). This doctrine is not agnosticism

---

[1] See Höffding, *Philosophy of Religion,* p. 42. Professor Höffding seems to regard such relationship as involved in the theistic doctrine of creation and attacks the doctrine on the basis of that misconception.

[2] This remains true despite qualifications attempted by St Thomas in certain passages.

—because it is based on the knowledge that God is the cause of all creatures. The agnostic does not know, if there be a first cause distinct from creation. Even if there be such a cause, the agnostic is ignorant, whether it may not be more akin to the lower forms of created being than to the higher. The mystic knows that the first cause must be above, not below " His highest effects." We have seen already that by the doctrine of Immanence God is affirmed to possess eminently all the positive being of creatures, and therefore that the more of positive being they possess the closer they resemble God. The doctrine of Transcendence supplements this teaching by pointing out that while the positive being of creatures is in God (in the sense explained above), their limitation, which is the ground of their exclusive distinction, of their particularity, is not in Him. No created being, therefore, whether material or spiritual, can adequately represent God or possess being in the sense in which He is. For created being is essentially limited and therefore exclusively distinct or particular. The higher it is the less limited it is—but it is always, and must essentially be, limited ; and by its limitation exclusive of other beings. God, therefore, being unlimited and inclusive of all being, is infinitely more unlike any creature than He is like it. He is therefore unintelligible because all concepts or images are essentially finite and He essentially infinite. Another reason why no concept is applicable to God is this. As Professor Höffding truly points out : " It is a fundamental law of all our concepts that they express relations . . . and therefore that no concept can be formed of a something which stands in no relation to any other something " (*Philosophy of Religion*, p. 69). Therefore the Absolute, which is unrelated to anything outside Itself, is beyond all concepts. This reason is reducible to the former. What is related is limited by its relationship. A relation is a limit. Therefore our concepts, which always express or imply relationship, are inapplicable to the Unlimited. Therefore Ultimate Reality, the Unlimited, cannot be represented conceptually by a logically coherent concept, or conceptual system, but only by series of paradoxes. (See pp. 30-31.) Hence agnostics infer that we can have no knowledge whatever of Ultimate Reality. For modern agnosticism and positivism are based on the assumption that it is unreasonable to believe that which we cannot show to be logically coherent. This assumption is, however, false. We have not, we cannot possibly have, sufficient knowledge of Ultimate Reality, nor, indeed, even of ultimate created reality, to give a logically coherent account of its nature. We cannot attain a logically coherent conception of the nature of matter or force or life or knowledge or the human soul—indeed, of any pure or elemental substance, but only of their effects, compositions[1] and relationships. That is to say, we cannot comprehend pure or elemental substances, but only their operations, compounds and relations. Thus even our own soul is incomprehensible. How then can we expect to attain a logically coherent conception of the Divine Being that is the Ultimate Reality ? How can we hope to comprehend God ? " By what understanding," asks St Augustine, " shall man comprehend God when He comprehendeth not his very intellect, whereby he would fain comprehend Him ? (*Aug. de Trin.*, v., sec. 2. Quoted by Pusey in note 1, *Confessions*, vii. 2). Nevertheless we have knowledge of created elemental substances and of our own soul. For their being is evident, the most evident of realities, despite our impotence to comprehend them. In like manner we can know that God is, albeit we cannot comprehend at all His Nature. Nay, we know of Him that He must necessarily be incomprehensible, a Being of whom it is beyond the power of our understanding to give a logically coherent account. Moreover, as we have seen, we do know that Ultimate Reality cannot be without certain characters, must be above, not below, the highest dependent and created being, more, not less, than our highest object of knowledge. We know also that it must be free from the limits of beings lower and less real than Itself, and that since the highest, most spiritual of these is the least limited by the others, the Supreme Being must be altogether unlimited, unconditioned by and independent of aught outside Itself. Therefore they can be neither a portion nor a necessary manifestation of Ultimate Reality. This knowledge is, however, as was pointed out in the introductory chapter, the affirmation of theism in opposition to atheism, agnosticism and pantheism. To reject this knowledge and its consequent theism because we cannot form a logically coherent concept of the Deity thus affirmed is unreasonable, and would be unreasonable even if revelation and mystical intuition were entirely wanting. The " agnosia " of the Christian mystic is far removed from this irrationally *negative* agnosticism—or more truly negative gnosticism. The

---

[1] I refer to our ability to reduce compounds to their constitutent elements. Such analysis is a conception of their character *qua* composition.

Unknowable of Dionysius—known only in "ignorance" (agnosia)
—is thus by no means identical with the unknowable of modern
agnostics.* The mystic, unlike the agnostic, knows that every
created perfection—that is, all the positive being of creatures—is in
God—that He is infinitely more than they. He knows therefore
that in Him we shall find not only all the positive content of our
highest ideals but also an infinite excess. Since our highest ideals
are essentially limited, their fulfilment would be the limited, the
exhaustible. But, as we shall see, there is in human nature—
and this is the basis of all true religion—a need of the infinite, of
the inexhaustible.[1] The doctrine of the Divine Transcendence
guarantees the fulfilment of this desire to all whom God raises to
that fruition of Himself which is above conceptual knowledge. It
also involves the practical consequence that the way of approach
to God is progressive detachment from the limitations of creatures,
of the particular—of images and concepts—in naked adherence to
the unlimited and unintelligible Being of God. This doctrine of
the Divine Transcendence is taught by St John of the Cross in
numerous passages. "The whole creation, compared with the
infinite Being of God, is nothing. . . . All the beauty of the
creation, in comparison with the infinite beauty of God, is supreme
deformity. All the goodness of the whole world together, in
comparison with the infinite goodness of God, is wickedness rather
than goodness. All the wisdom of the world, and all human
cunning, compared with the infinite wisdom of God, is simple and
supreme ignorance" (*Ascent of Mount Carmel*, Bk I., chap. iv).
"Among all creatures, the highest and the lowest, there is not one
that unites us proximately with God, or that bears any likeness
to His substance. For though it be true that all creatures bear
a certain relation to God and are tokens of His being, some more,
some less, according as their being is more or less essential" (*i.e.* as
it is less negative and limited), "yet there is no proportion between
them and Him; yea, rather the distance between His Divine
Nature and their nature is infinite. Hence it is impossible for the
understanding to attain perfectly unto God, by means of created
things, whether of heaven or of earth, because there is no proportion of similitude between them. . . . All that the understanding
may comprehend, all that the will may be satisfied with, and all

---

[1] I mean, of course, subjectively. The Christian religion is not, as the modernist would have it, the creation of this need. It is its satisfaction by a special
Divine interposition from without.

that the imagination may conceive, is most unlike unto God, and most disproportionate to Him " (*Ascent of Mount Carmel*, Book II., chap. viii). "He that will draw near and unite himself unto God must believe that He is. That is saying in effect, he that will attain to the union of God must not rely on his own understanding nor lean upon his own imagination, sense or feeling" (for these are of necessity limited and therefore negative of being, as well as positive of it), "but must believe in the Divine Essence (which is absolutely positive and therefore) not cognisable by the understanding, desire or imagination nor any sense of man " (because all these essentially involve limitation or negation). "Yea, in this life " (when as yet we lack the peculiar communication of God's infinite self-knowledge which is the beatific vision, and are dependent on finite modes of knowledge) "our highest knowledge and deepest sense, perception and understanding of God is infinitely distant from that which He is " (*Ascent of Mount Carmel*, Book II., chap. iv). "All these forms are never represented so as to be laid hold of but under certain modes and limitations ; and the Divine Wisdom . . . admits of no such particular modes or forms, neither can it be comprehended under any limitation or distinct particular conception, because it is all pureness and simplicity. . . . God is not comprehended under any form or image or particular conception " (*Ascent of Mount Carmel*, Book II., chap. xvi).

This doctrine is stated more clearly still in the second chapter of the *Treatise of the Obscure Knowledge of God*, a treatise, be it remembered, *possibly* the work of St John of the Cross himself. This passage is of the utmost importance and value and, indeed, summarises the entire doctrine of mystical negation. "According to the teaching of St Dionysius and other saints, there are two different manners of contemplation, for there are two ways of attaining knowledge of God. One of these is by affirmation. We attribute to God those things which are perfections in the creature." That is, we know that all that is positive being in the creature is in Him—but in another way—without the limitations of the creature and therefore with an infinite transcendence. "For instance we contemplate God as infinitely good, wise, powerful, merciful and the like. In the same way we ascribe to Him all the other things that are perfections in the creature. In this contemplation we ascend, as it were, by degrees from the perfection of the effects to the perfection of the cause." In this way is excluded modern agnosticism, which admits the possibility that the cause of personal spirit is an impersonal, unconscious force—far less positive and less real than the effect. " The other way is negative. We set aside the contemplation of the perfections of creatures and consider how inferior they are to the Creator. We thus ascend to contemplate in God a Being so incomprehensible, so superior to and so far excelling all that can be imagined, that we can find no created name that will suffice to describe Him." Observe that this negative way is the complement of the other—God *is* all the positivity of creatures, *is not* their essential negativity. *Thus this negative way is really ultra-positive—it denies nothing of God—except limitation which is non-entity. This point cannot be urged too strongly, since the failure to understand it is the root of all the attacks on mysticism, alike its theory and its practice.* " In this way we attain indeed to a knowledge of God, but we do not know Him as a substance, or as goodness, or as wisdom, or as mercy " and so on. " For this way consists in denying of God any attribute or perfection whatsoever, *to whose knowledge we can attain.*" * The emphasis lies on the qualification. We deny the attribute *as knowable* by our essentially limited knowledge. " This knowledge is therefore called knowledge by negation or privation, because we proceed by denying of God everything that we attributed to Him in the affirmative way." *NOT* of course in the sense in which we affirmed it—which would be a contradiction—but by denying the limitations. The terms employed by mystical writers—as in this text before us and in the precedent text from Dionysius—seem indeed to imply absolute negation. This language, however, is employed to bring home the fact that the distance between our limited concepts—even the highest and most spiritual—and the unlimited Being of God, is *infinite.* " We say that God is not being, because He is more than being, not wisdom, because He is more than wisdom, not goodness, because He is more than goodness, and more than any other perfection. In fine, we come to understand Him as something that exceeds all the sensible, all the imaginable and all the intelligible, that is indeed above everything, that has being. The latter way of knowing God is higher and more perfect than the former, as St Dionysius tells us, and Pope St Gregory also, who says : " Then may we say with truth that we have knowledge of God, when we understand that we can know nothing of God, and when we realise most clearly His incomprehensibility, which, because of its infinite splendour, is invisible and impenetrable in this life " (chap. ii).

We must remember, however, that while the majority of our concepts are essentially limited or closed—that is to say, all concepts of material being and concepts essentially expressive of created spiritual being—there are certain which are not thus closed. The primary ideas, such as being, unity, goodness, truth and beauty, are not concepts limited and therefore strictly definable. They express something absolutely positive, which admits of infinite degrees of fulness. They are like clues whose end we hold in our hand, but which extend altogether beyond our grasp or even vision. When they are understood, or rather used in this unlimited manner, as unclosed or incomplete concepts, they are predicable of God formally—that is, not as merely contained eminently in God, but as being true of Him, as they are in themselves. But of course, when used thus as unclosed concepts, they are themselves transcendent of all limits and created understanding. We have, for example, a considerable knowledge of the nature of created goodness. Infinite or absolute goodness is transcendent and incomprehensible. These fundamental ideas, however, when taken as limited or closed concepts, may be understood in two ways. They may be understood of the maximal degree of their presence conceivable by our understanding, or they may be understood of their minimal presence as the lowest common denominator, so to speak, of all the things that participate at all in them, a bare minimum attainable by abstraction from all these concrete participators. Thus, for instance, goodness may be understood of the greatest goodness conceivable by us, or of the minimal degree of goodness that is common to all things that are in any way good—the bare goodness which we obtain by abstraction from all good things. In either case they are no more predicable of God formally than are the concepts and images of material objects, or other essentially closed concepts. Unhappily, there has often been a confusion between the unclosed use of these ideas, their unlimited fulness, which is predicable formally of God, and the abstract minimal that is almost nonentity and is therefore all but the opposite pole to the Divine Being. Neoplatonic speculation, whether pagan or Christian, never freed itself from this confusion, from Plotinus downwards to Marsilio Ficino. It has resulted in endless obscurity, self-contradiction and barren logomachy. Hence a prejudice has arisen against mysticism as substituting an empty abstraction for the fulness of the Divine Being and Life. This substitution was never really made by these mystics or mystical philosophers. It is clear that their philosophy is based upon and leads up to an intuition of the supreme Reality, as the unlimited fulness of the positive being contained in ultimate ideas, such as Unity, Goodness and Being. They often, however, seek to justify this intuition by arguments which are guilty of illicit transition, from the unclosed fulness to the abstract minimal, from goodness absolute to abstract goodness, from the supreme Unification to barren oneness, from fulness of Being to being in the abstract without content, from Being unqualifiable, because containing eminently all qualities, to being unqualifiable because every quality has been abstracted from it. A very good example of this intellectual confusion is exhibited by Marsilio Ficino's commentary on Dionysius. Language encourages it and the baneful prejudices thence arising. I trust, however, that it is now well out of our way and will no longer hinder our appreciation of the true doctrine of transcendence first plainly formulated by this Neoplatonic school of "mystology"—the doctrine which this chapter attempts to explain. Though the ideas which can be used thus unclosed are our nearest conceptual approaches to God, and their realisation our nearest actual approaches to Him, nevertheless, even when they are conceived or realised even in the higher closed manner as the maximum conceivable by our thought or practicable by our efforts, they are infinitely inadequate to the intuition-union of Him in Whom alone the human understanding and will find their last end and complete satisfaction.

It follows from the doctrine of the Divine transcendence that theological statements are true rather positively than negatively. Every theological term or statement is of necessity finite and therefore inadequate to express the Infinite God. " Low, defective and improper," says St John of the Cross, " are all the words and phrases by which in this life we discuss Divine things, and utterly impossible (it is) by any natural means . . . to know and consider of them as they are (*Dark Night*, ii. 17). Nevertheless, in so far as a statement or term is positive—that is, in so far as it affirms being and denies limitation, which is absence of being— it is true. We cannot, however, get rid of the finite and therefore limiting and negative element in the statement or term. We therefore use it, without thereby binding ourselves to this negative element, and we posit complementary terms and statements which deny the negation of the first term or statement. All heresy is the attempt to insist on the truth of some theological statement in an exclusive sense—maintaining the truth, not only of its positive assertion but of that seeming denial of other aspects of the truth which its finite character compels. All statements of theological truth in human language are like comets whose orbit is not closed. As the path of these comets is distinct and clear when it approaches the sun, so are these dogmatic statements definite and intelligible while they are within the sphere of human reason, that is, in so far as they are concerned with facts falling within the sphere of human experience,[1] or employ analogies drawn from that experience. When, however, the astronomer tracks the comet's departing orbit farther and farther, it is lost in the depths of space. In like manner, when we strive to penetrate the meaning of these dogmas, it vanishes into the Infinity of God. Thus the study of theology should end in the reverential awe of adoring ignorance—not the ignorance of the agnostic, who knows not whether the ultimate reality possesses the highest goodness of creatures, but the ignorance that realises how infinitely below the Divine Being is the highest created being, how infinitely inadequate to the Divine Truth is the highest created truth. The study of theology is for the Catholic directed to a fuller realisation of his faith. But the author of *The Obscure Knowledge* is at pains to insist on the apparent paradox that the end of the faith is to know what God is not; not the apprehension of positive truths about God, but the full and vivid realisation that He is unintelligible by concepts and statements intelligible to our finite understanding—the realisation of the Divine transcendence and infinite excess of any limited being or concept. Later on we shall consider the teaching of St John that faith unites the understanding to God by detaching it from all particular images, concepts and ideas which as such are essentially limited, in the loving apprehension of the infinite and therefore incomprehensible Godhead. This is indeed the work of the infused gift of faith. The study of theology, however, should lead us indirectly and externally to the state to which infused faith leads directly and internally. " In this state," says St John, " they feel so highly of God as to see clearly that they know Him not at all, and that perception, that His Deity is so immense that it cannot be perfectly understood, is

---

[1] I mean within the totality of that experience, possible and actual. A virgin conception, for example, is outside the sphere of our actual experience, but as a physical act is within the sphere of human sense-conditioned knowledge.

E

a very lofty understanding." " One of the greatest favours of God . . . is to enable the soul to see so distinctly and feel so profoundly that it clearly understands it cannot comprehend or feel Him at all.   Those souls are herein, in some degree, like the saints in heaven, where they who know Him most perfectly, perceive most clearly that He is infinitely incomprehensible " (*Spiritual Canticle*, st. 7).

This truly is the goal of the mystic way to God, the rest of the human soul—to lose itself in the Divine infinity, the Divine incomprehensibility.   This negative knowledge is neither abstract nor empty, but a limitless fulness that the soul can never exhaust —no, not in infinite eternities.   We shall realise better how this is so if we consider a few indubitable facts of human experience. Those who see no depths in life beyond the superficial aspects open to their understanding are necessarily dissatisfied, dull and *blasé*.   Art or thought confined to the most limited and superficial regions of experience is frivolous, and shallow, and soon wearies. The perception and suggestion of unfathomed depths of spiritual significance is the function of art.   There is no beauty where the entire meaning is obvious.   To understand the entire meaning of a work of art is to have spiritually consumed it—to have eaten the cake and thus to have finished it.   Certain colours and forms are beautiful, because they are in some inexplicable fashion suggestive of spiritual realities beyond the comprehension of sense or reason. Others are ugly, because they do not possess this transcendental suggestion.   In proportion to the presence of this suggestion is the degree of beauty; in proportion to its absence the degree of ugliness.   Transcendence is thus the criterion of æsthetic worth. It is the same with scientific hypotheses and with metaphysical conceptions.   They are of small value, unless they open out inexhaustible vistas of truth.   Indeed, this is a universal law of truth-values.   Those truths that are most particular and most limited in their applicability are the superficial truths, which are merest rudiments of knowledge.   The great depths of truth are those general truths not limited to a narrow sphere, but indefinitely applicable to the most varied spheres and inexhaustible in their suggestiveness.   Here then is our measure of beauty and truth. The more limited, *particular* and superficial is the uglier, and the more untrue (in the ontological sense, of course) ; the more unlimited, general and inexhaustible of significance—that is to say, the more incomprehensible and mysterious—is the truer and the more beautiful. All created beauty and truth are, however, essentially ugly and false, if regarded as ultimate values, because their content is sooner or later exhausted. At best they are messengers of Infinity; they cannot *qua* created notions or images impart that infinity. The most perfect created beauty, the deepest, widest truth of creatures are, as *finite* being, essentially limited and negative. They stimulate a spiritual thirst which they cannot quench. Sooner or later the soul touches the negative element of their essential limitation. Thus with all that is finite the soul comes at length to the end. Its thirst remains unappeased; its blessed gift of wonder is replaced by weariness and dissatisfaction. Alexander weeps that there are no more worlds to conquer.

Far other is it with the supernatural grace-mediated fruition of God begun here, consummated in eternity.

In the infinite abyss of the Divine fulness of positive being without limit, never to be exhausted, the " good containing in itself all good together at once," [1] there is the perfect rest of entire and everlasting satisfaction, a rest, however, which is also untiring, eternal energy. This all-satisfying fruition, as we have seen, is indescribable. Only the limited can be formulated by limited concepts and images. The soul has, however, now transcended all the barriers of created limits by full participation in the Unlimited Being of God that is transcendent of all limits, and therefore of all created being in its essential limitation. The only report the mystic can bring us of the Unlimited Object of his intuition is that of an ultrapositive nothingness eminently containing all created being and worth, and nevertheless infinitely unlike any creature. *God is all*, therefore He is nothing, for all things are essentially finite. God is nothing, nothing finite and particular, therefore He is All and the positive being of all. God All, therefore Nothing, Nothing therefore All, absolute Being uncreated, therefore absolute non-being created, absolute unity, therefore the unification of an infinite manifold, unmoved yet perfect energy, one perfect and absolute energy, yet unchanging and unmoved, possessed of and containing all the virtues and qualities of creatures, yet possessed of none as we know them in the limitation of the creature, such are the seeming paradoxes that bring home to the soul the Infinity and the Transcendent Majesty of God, until contemplation is merged in sheer adoration—and

---

[1] St Teresa, *Autobiography*, chap. xviii.

our sole prayer is the cry of the Apostle : "O the depths of the riches of the wisdom and the knowledge of God. How incomprehensible are His judgments, and how unsearchable His ways."

Truly O God is "Thy way in the sea, and Thy paths in many waters, and Thy footsteps shall not be known."

This doctrine of the Divine transcendence can alone save belief in God's finite self-revelations and manifestations from leading to a limited and indeed to an anthropomorphic conception of the Deity. If the background were removed from a landscape, that landscape, now consisting solely of the foreground, would not lead the vision out to the far horizon, but would imprison it within the narrow compass of the objects nearest at hand and most immediately visible. In like manner, if the background of this Dionysian transcendence were removed from our presentation of the Catholic creed and practice—which are deeply incarnational and sacramental—the Catholic religion would become *for us* limiting, inadequate and anthropomorphic, probably superstitious, and in any case opposed to our highest thoughts and intuitions of the Divine. The presence of that infinite background, on the contrary, invests the more immediately present incarnational and sacramental dispensation—the foreground of our faith—with its own infinity, rendering these incarnational and sacramental doctrines and practices avenues to the Unlimited. It is therefore of the first importance to the Catholic desirous of a fuller understanding of his faith to grasp firmly this background teaching,[1] and to follow up the line of thought that is based upon and leads to the Absolute Transcendence of God.

This line of thought has, I know, often issued in grave error. In the hands of the Modernists it has led to the doctrine that all theological truth is merely symbolic, that every creature, even the Sacred Humanity, is simply a symbol of the infinite, incomprehensible Reality. The fundamental error of the Modernist is to regard Christ crucified as being as wholly and as purely a symbol as a crucifix actually is. For the thorough-going Modernist Christ crucified is but a living crucifix, and nothing more than that, a representation of the Divine love in human life and act, even as the crucifix is a representation of that Love in a lifeless work of art. It may be urged that the fundamental error of Modernism

---

[1] As the mystical way is followed this background becomes more and more the foreground of religion, though never excluding the other elements of our faith and practice.

is rather the denial of a supernatural order divinely superimposed on the natural—as, indeed, in another work, I have myself maintained. Both errors, however, are but different aspects of one and the same error. The rejection of a distinct supernatural order, which enters into and superimposes itself upon the order of nature at special times and places, and in special ways, the rejection of a special revelation and *a fortiori* of a Divine Incarnation, is essentially the rejection of the doctrine that particular concrete persons, things and events have been taken into a peculiar relationship to God, a relationship of a different and higher order than the relationship of creatures to God in the natural order. This rejection, in turn, necessitates the treatment of the Incarnation and its consequences as mere symbols of a spiritual reality, with which they possess no special or supernatural relationship or union whatsoever. This position leads inevitably to a denial that the Infinite God *can* place a finite being in a peculiar relation and union with Himself.[1] Such an assertion is an unwarrantable dogmatism—and is in absolute opposition not only to the teaching of the Catholic faith but to the fact of mystical experience. For mystical experience, thus far supporting the revealed dogma of the hypostatic Union, proves that God can raise and has raised finite beings to a most intimate union with His infinite being. To deny the possibility of such a special relationship and union logically involves the assertion that all created being is equally distant from God—the Unlimited, and therefore equally limited. This is, however, patently false. Spirit, for example, is less limited and therefore nearer to God than matter, and a good than a bad man. Moreover, unless certain creatures were in closer relationship to God than others, we should be united to God as well by eating and drinking as by prayer and meditation, as well by vocal petition as by the sublimest contemplation. Moreover, self-denial and mortification would be useless. This is, however, in flagrant contradiction to the universal experience, the practice and the teaching of all mystics, whatever their creed. For they have all alike found, and taught others to find, God more fully

---

[1] This Modernism is not all so modern as its name would imply. Already in the fifth century B.C. a treatise ascribed to Hippocrates affirms its fundamental principle and its logical consequence, sheer pantheism. " Nothing," he says, " is more divine or more human than anything else, but all things are alike and all divine " (Treatise on Airs, Waters and Sites. Burnet, *Greek Philosophy*, Pt. I., Thales to Plato, pp. 32-33). Moreover, Mr Burnet points out the essentially *irreligious* character of this Ionic pantheism.

in the more spiritual—that is, in the more unlimited—than in the less spiritual—that is, in the more limited—have therefore renounced the latter for the former, and have taught their disciples the same renunciation.[1]   Hence we must conceive of one person or thing as related more closely to God than another on account of its lesser limitation, and of God as operative and manifest more fully in one person or thing than in another.   This leaves open the possibility of a special revelation in and through particular persons and things, and even of a hypostatic union between a created being and God.   Indeed, the fact that in the natural order God is revealed more fully in one person or thing than in another renders it probable that this graduated revelation should be crowned and completed by a special supernatural revelation through particular objects taken from the diverse degrees of natural being, and through personages and events of human history.   Moreover, we should expect that the things, persons and acts thus raised to the supernatural order as instruments or recipients of faith and grace should be as diverse in their manner and degree of freedom from limitation and consequent participation of the Unlimited Deity as are the beings of the natural order.   This expectation is, of course, amply fulfilled in the diverse measure of revealed truth and sanctifying grace and consequent union with God, possessed and communicated by the instruments and recipients of the Judæo-Christian revelation and economy of grace ranging, as it does, from the first gleams of revealed truth vouchsafed to the patriarchs to the fulness of the Apostolic deposit ; from the grace communicated by a devout use of the least of the sacramentals to the grace conferred by a fruitful communion ; and from the union with God possessed by the most imperfect Christian in the state of grace to the hypostatic union of Jesus Christ.   I pointed out above that the Modernist places crucifixion and crucifix on the same level of pure symbolism.   Still he would no doubt admit that the crucified Jesus, as a living and reason-endowed man, nay, more, as a man of supreme holiness, was in closer relation to God and more adequately representative of God than the lifeless image. In making this concession, however, he would be making an illogical return on his own path.   For he would have admitted,

---

[1] A certain qualification seems required in the case of Blake.   But (1) what was the degree of mystical union attained by Blake ?   (2) Certainly it was far from the highest.   (3) His life was in practice ascetic and involved a severe renunciation of lower goods.

as all theists must admit, that one creature is nearer to God and therefore more closely united to God and more fully representative of His Godhead than another. Short of adopting pure pantheism, our Modernist must concede this and in the concession he has, as we have just shown, conceded the underlying principle of revelation and the Incarnation. The fact of diverse degrees of union with God, even in the natural order, pleads in favour of that supernatural elevation of particular creatures to a higher supernatural union with the Godhead, whose affirmation is the fundamental distinction between Christianity, with its doctrine of special revelation and the Incarnation, and " natural religion," which denies this special supernatural union. Mr C. Webb, in his interesting Wilde Lectures on Natural Religion, points out that a religion which teaches a special manifestation of God in the peculiar relationship to God of a special concrete fact is of a higher type than one which rejects any particular concrete historical embodiment or manifestation of the Divine. " So far," he says, " as by ' historical element in religion ' we mean the element of sacred history, a belief in which forms an important element in some religions, it is a mark of higher development in a religion to emphasise this element. For in the recognition of such a sacred history religion comes to recognise itself as the most concrete and individual form of human experience, concerned, not with mere abstract universals, but with concrete individuals, those and no others, in which, and not elsewhere, the universals with which we have to do are, as a matter of fact, particularised, apart from which they possess no actual reality. A religion which involves as part of its essence a sacred history is, in this way, at a higher level than one which, while setting forth certain universal principles, moral or metaphysical, is ready to symbolise them by anything that comes to hand, as it were, and is comparatively indifferent to the particular symbol chosen " (*Nat. Theol.*, pp. 292-300). But this rejection of the particular and concrete is the very essence, not only of Modernism but of a certain theory of mysticism very popular to-day—a theory of mysticism such as is exemplified by utterances of Miss Evelyn Underhill,[1] which treats the dogmas of the historical religions as so many more or less indifferent symbols of one purely spiritual reality.

---

[1] She is not, however, a consistent upholder of this position. The book in which this " indifferentism " is most thoroughly maintained is unfortunately her latest—namely, *Practical Mysticism*.

This is truly, as Mr Webb says, to reduce religion to a lower level.

That the existence of a special revelation, and the recognition that God is revealed and possessed more fully by higher grades—that is, by more unlimited degrees, of being—are thus closely connected as manifestations of one and the same principle, is shown by the history of modern thought. The rejection of revelation has tended with religious temperaments to result in a pantheism which deifies all beings alike. It may, indeed, be objected that pantheism is the result of a perverted doctrine of immanence and cannot therefore be the result of a perverted doctrine of transcendence, and further, that Modernists are hyper-immanentists rather than hyper-transcendentalists. Extremes, however, meet, and an exclusive doctrine of transcendence will be found to issue in the pantheism to which an equally exclusive doctrine of immanence is another passage. Some Modernists, and these the mystical-minded, have tended towards pantheism by the former route; others, more naturalist in temper, by the latter. Ultra-immanentism, as we have already seen, issues in pantheism by exaggerating the participation of finite beings in the Godhead as the source and ground of their positive being, into the assertion that they are elements and modes of the Godhead. Ultra-transcendentalism, on the other hand, reaches the same goal from a different starting-point. The truth that the finite does not possess Reality and Being in the sense that these are possessed by the Infinite Deity is perverted into a denial of all reality and being to the former. It is regarded as mere appearance and illusion—Maya, as the Indians term it. The sole reality underlying this appearance is the One Absolute Godhead. This form of pantheism, termed specifically acosmism, has been incurred by the mystics who have abandoned theism in the interpretation of their experience. It is the pantheism of the Upanishads, of the Sufis and of Eckhart.[1] Thus do the denial of the reality of creatures and their identification with the Deity blend into a common pantheism. Indeed ultra-transcendental pantheism, when it regards the finite as but a manifestation of an underlying Godhead, *ipso facto* regards the finite as a mode of that Godhead, and becomes thus identical with ultra-immanentist pantheism. Catholic mysticism bars both passages to this common error. It bars the immanentist approach by insisting on the absolute distinction of

[1] Who, however, did not intend to abandon either theism or Catholicism.

finite beings from God, in virtue of their essential finitude. It bars the transcendentalist approach, and therefore the mystical modernism that is taking that way, by its doctrine of special relationships, including, as it does, its doctrine of personal identity between a created being and God, in the Incarnate Word. If we hold fast to this complementary doctrine of special relationship, the doctrine of the Divine transcendence will not lead us with the Modernists and mystical undenominationalists to reject historic revelation and the Incarnation.

The best way to secure our firm grasp of special relationship is by tenacious adherence to and emphasis of its supreme exemplification, the Divine Humanity of Jesus. For God has united Himself with and has manifested Himself in the Sacred Humanity of Jesus Christ after a fashion immeasurably fuller and more intimate than in all His other unions and manifestations with and through created beings. In that Humanity dwells bodily the fulness of the Infinite Godhead.[1] Hence a truly Christian mysticism, while duly insisting on the Divine transcendence, will never lose sight of the Sacred Humanity of Christ as personally one with the all-transcendent Deity.

It is true that the passages in *The Ascent of Mount Carmel* where St John repeats explicitly St Teresa's teaching, that the mystic can never transcend the contemplation of the Sacred Humanity, are interpolations. Nevertheless we cannot doubt that they truly represent his opinion on this point. Mother Cecilia devotes a special stanza of her work on *The Transformation of the Soul in God* to the statement that :

> In order to travel in safety
> After a Divine fashion
> The mysteries of Christ have been her [the soul's] path.

As the entire passage is of the utmost importance I will quote it here : " It is impossible that the soul should be safe without this foundation of faith, comprising, as it does, the mysteries of Jesus Christ Our Lord. It was the Father's will that He should be our guide and the means whereby we unite ourselves to Him and remain in union with Him. Truly then did our glorious Mother Teresa of Jesus say that the soul cannot ascend far save by this path, and that we cannot attain any good unless our souls are stamped and saturated with these Divine truths, that is, unless

---

[1] St Paul, Colossians.

we seek the Redeemer, apart from Whom there is no redemption, and unless we love the Beloved, for Whose sake God loves us." [1] " We should not regard it as a hindrance to beginners to contemplate this Divine Beloved, provided they realise the truth of His Godhead and contemplate this Divinity in union with His Humanity.   Those who travel by the right path know very well what assistance they have received towards the attainment of their spiritual treasures from this Divine and human Lord.   Not only is such contemplation no hindrance ; it is a spark whereby the soul is kindled, like tinder, with the fire of Divine love, so that even if she does not intend it, she loses all thought of self, being wholly lost to herself.   She has now entered deeper into Christ, because she is in Him and in His Father and in the Holy Ghost, and abides far more deeply penetrated with His love.   Even so was it with St Paul the Apostle after he had been in the third heaven and had seen Jesus.   He was thenceforward penetrated so deeply by Jesus Christ that he could say : ' I live no longer, but Christ liveth in me.'   This exclamation reveals how intimately St Paul possessed Christ within himself, since not only his thoughts, but his very life, was Christ's and he was another Christ, since he possessed Him in himself.   No one will feel any great surprise at this who knows the capacity of the human soul, capable of containing God, and therefore of containing Christ, Who as man is less than God, and also all mysteries and scriptures, in a word an infinity of things, for all things are less than God."   " Now there is nothing so dear to God as the only begotten Son, in Whom He loves us, and our human nature thus raised to Himself in the very person of the Eternal Word.   We cannot, therefore, possess truth unless we are united with this Truth, nor can any path be the right one which does not lead to Him.   The soul that ascends highest does so with the aid of this greatness of Divine Truth." . . . " The soul that possesses this Truth is united to the Essential

[1] This doctrine, in so far as it demands explicit knowledge of the Sacred Humanity in order to every degree of mystical union, is indeed untenable in face of the indubitable existence of true mystics outside the pale of Christianity (e.g. Plotinus, Richard Jefferies, certain Sufis and possibly Buddha).   This can be denied only by a refusal to attach credence to the self-reports of men whose sincerity is unquestionable.   Such treatment of their evidence would invalidate all appeal to the testimony of Catholic mystics.   In the case of Plotinus, Fr. Sharpe admits at least the possibility of the genuineness of his experience.   It is, however, certain that any mystical graces granted to non-Christians are granted entirely through the merits and for the sake of Jesus our Lord—the sole name whereby we must be saved.

Truth Who is God, Who has taught us the particular truth of His mysteries in order to our salvation, and that they may be the means and foundation of this supreme transformation. Since it is impossible truly to reach this transformation without this foundation, nor can the soul travel in safety without it, it is said that

> In order to travel in safety
> After a Divine fashion
> The mysteries of Christ have been her path."

In this important passage it is clearly laid down that God has raised certain creatures into a peculiarly close relationship with His own Divine Being—and in particular has placed Our Lord's Sacred Humanity, created though it was out of nothing, in the relationship of hypostatic or personal union. We can never dispense with this Incarnational and Sacramental economy, nor transcend Jesus or His mysteries. Since Jesus is in this unique relationship with the Infinite God, through Him we are united to God, and His Sacred Humanity, far from limiting the soul by Its limits and particularity, introduces the soul into the Unlimited Godhead, with Whom It is personally One. Nevertheless the mystic must make this use of the Incarnation. He must find God in Jesus, and not rest in the Humanity as such, in a knowledge of Christ as man, after the flesh, as St Paul terms it. This is clearly explained by Mother Cecilia in the passage immediately following. " We must, however, take particular notice of the words, ' after a Divine fashion,' because there are many different fashions in which we may profit by the mysteries of Christ. From all there is great profit to be derived. But there is a certain divine fashion or method which enormously exceeds all others in its power to bring us speedily to the goal of our journey. . . . This Divine method is an immense force and light, whereby the soul knows the Divinity of God in the person of the Incarnate Word. The Eternal Word has exalted His Most Sacred Humanity in Himself with an infinite excellency. The soul contemplates this Humanity exalted in God, after a Divine fashion, and apprehends the Humanity as existing in the eternal Divinity, in a most sublime and most Divine experience, which cannot be explained to anyone who has never known it. In this experience the God-Man communicates to the soul a Divine virtue of His Divinity and Humanity, whereby she knows Him with a knowledge so subtle

that it cannot be described by any other name, but must be
termed His Divinity Itself.   It is with this mode of knowledge
that the soul contemplates and knows Him in all His mysteries ;
when the soul is penetrated by the contemplation of His wounding
and blood-shedding, or of any of the other incidents of His life,
death and resurrection, when she contemplates Him as He is now
in heaven, and as He will come to judgment—in a word, whenever
she contemplates anything wherein her Beloved has part, she is
penetrated in conjunction with His Humanity, by His eternal
Divinity, and that after a fashion unspeakably sublime, which
is termed Divine because it proceeds from God Himself. . . .
But these communications differ greatly among themselves, and
great also is the difference between the communications enjoyed
by the same soul at different times.   For although these truths
are always the foundation of her prayer, they are understood in
a manner that is ever more and more spiritualised. . . . The
fashion of the soul's ' apprehension ' of Christ ' and life ' in Him
is now far more spiritual and Divine, for the Divine communication has now been completely transferred to the most spiritual
and secret part of the soul. . . . The substance of the soul is penetrated by God and His eternal truths after the most sublime and
spiritual fashion possible.   To this great blessing the soul has
attained by this Divine method, above described, of contemplating Christ and His mysteries.   It is now evident to what a
height of glory and bliss the way of this Divine Lord has led the
soul from the beginning onwards.   He went on increasing continually His love in the soul until she was thus Divinely penetrated by Him and was made Divine in His Divinity.   As
the soul has been from the outset grounded in the truth, she
now possesses the Father, the Son and the Holy Ghost, and
in this immense and Divine Being of the one true God she abides
consumed and transformed in Him as in her true and last
end, having begun to enter into that immensity which has no
end " (*Transformation*, st. 7).   The way of the soul's progress is
thus not the rejection of the Incarnational and the Sacramental,
of the particular creaturely fact, but an ever-increasing spiritualisation of its understanding and reception of the particular, of the
creature.   This spiritualisation is a progressive apprehension of
the Unlimited Deity, present in and through the creature, due to
the soul's progressive union with God, to Whom that created
being has been in a special fashion united.   Why, then, does St

John bid us reject the particular ? Because by the particular he means just that negative element, limited, limiting and exclusive, from which the soul must escape. The closer, however, a particular creature is united to God the unlimited, the less does its particularity limit and exclude. When, therefore, the relationship of a created being to God is that of personal or hypostatic union, the positive manifestation and representation and possession of God so infinitely transcend the creaturely limitation and exclusion [1] that the latter becomes practically non-existent for the soul that contemplates and loves the positive interior reality. That is why the Humanity of Christ and his Human mysteries need not and should not be rejected or transcended, even with that temporary rejection and transcendence requisite for the mystic in the case of other creatures in order to escape their limitations. There must be, however, that increasing spiritualisation of his contemplation of Christ and His mysteries which is indicated in the above quoted passage by Mother Cecilia. This spiritualisation involves, indeed, a certain transcendence, in that the soul no longer rests in the external and human facts of Our Lord's life but penetrates through these to the Infinite Being of God contained therein—but it is *through* them that she always penetrates, not beside and apart from them. " We shall," so Ruysbroeck summarises the Cecilian teaching, "*through the personality of Christ* transcend . . . the created being of Christ and rest . . . in the Divine Being in eternity " (*Adornment of the Spiritual Marriage*, Bk. II., chap. xlvii. Trs. Wynschenk Dom.). Thus the Incarnation and mystical negation are not opposed, but complementary. We must also remember that this mystical spiritualisation is but the continuance of a process visible in every Catholic, whose religious education is proportionate to his general mental development. (This, unhappily, is by no means always the case.) A child conceives, for example, of heaven and hell, of the Trinity, of the Resurrection and Ascension by imaging them after the fashion of the sensible phenomena of this life. Heaven is a palace among the clouds, hell a furnace in the centre of the earth. The Trinity is represented by an aged man on a throne, a younger man on another throne and a dove above their heads. The Resurrection is the revivification of Our Lord's Body, exactly

---

[1] Though the Sacred Humanity was created and is therefore finite, It must not be termed a creature, having received the dignity of the Godhead with Whom It is personally one.

as It was in His earthly life, and the Ascension His going up through the white clouds and blue sky to a gem-built palace, where His Father awaits Him on a throne of gold.   The religious progress of that child consists not in the denial of the positive truth of these things but in an increasingly spiritual under-standing of them.   The prayer progress of the mystic is but the indefinite continuance of this process, with its progressive destruction of limiting concepts and images, and its progressive apprehension of the unlimited, and therefore unimaginable and unintelligible Being of God present in and through the mysteries of faith.   Such a progressive spiritualisation by the individual soul of the created elements of revealed truth has had its counterpart in the development of revelation itself.   One very important mode of the Judæo-Christian revelation has been the spiritualisa-tion of already existent religious ideas.   Thus, for instance, Our Lord took the notion of a largely material and earthly Messianic kingdom and spiritualised it into the teaching of a spiritual kingdom of God, beginning in the Church on earth and fulfilled in the society of the blessed in heaven.   We must, however, observe, and it is important to do so, if we would escape the Modernism easily incurred by this line of thought, that, alike in the giving of the revelation and in its understanding by the individual, and in the continuance of that process in mystical prayer, the process of spiritualisation works in two distinct ways. Sometimes the conception to be spiritualised limited a spiritual reality by a material embodiment which was inconsistent with it. For example, the child's imagination of the Trinity ascribed anthropomorphic limitations to the Divine Being itself.   Spiritual-isation here involves the entire rejection of the material expression. Partially, but only partially, within this first category is the case of a spiritual reality, which has indeed a certain external and material embodiment, which cannot therefore be transcended or rejected, but which was originally conceived so externally and materially as to be unduly limited and materialised by that con-ception.   For instance, the kingdom of God has its external and material aspects in the earthly Church and the future resurrection. Nevertheless the original conception of that kingdom so limited and materialised the spiritual reality as to destroy its unlimited significance and to render it altogether finite.   Hence spiritualisa-tion meant in this case the *partial* rejection of the concrete material embodiment, which belonged to the original conception.   To this first category of spiritualisation must be referred the spiritual understanding of prophecies false, if taken in their external and material form—true in their interior and spiritual meaning or substance, a spiritualisation which St John discusses in the second book of *The Ascent of Mount Carmel*. " In the Holy Scriptures," he says, " we read that many prophecies and divine locutions disappointed in their fulfilment the expectations of many of the ancient people, because they understood them too much according to the letter and in their own way." " The chief purpose of God in sending visions is to express and communicate the spirit which is hidden within them. . . . This is much more abundant than the letter, more extraordinary and surpasses the limits thereof. . . . We must, therefore, reject the letter, which is of sense, and abide in the obscurity of faith, which is the spirit, incomprehensible to sense " (ii. 19). This gradual discovery of the true sense of prophecies, the sense intended by the Holy Spirit, is part of that mystical interpretation of Scripture which the Church and her doctors have ever used to interpret all scripture whose surface meaning bears no direct reference to the infinite and spiritual Reality of the Divine Being or to the self-manifestation, donation and union of that Infinite God to man.[1] It is otherwise with the central substance of the Christian revelation, the Incarnation and its extensions, which lie outside the sphere of this first mode of spiritualisation. For the very essence of the Incarnation and its extensions is personal identification or intimate union between the limited nature of man, alike in its physical and spiritual constituents, and the Infinite Creator, a union of the transcendent Being of God with an individual created being. The fundamental ground of the dogmas of Our Lord's human life, Church and sacraments is the dogma of the Incarnation itself, and the inmost significance of the Incarnation is a unique manifestation of the Infinite through and in the finite, a complete self-donation of the Infinite to the finite, a union of personal identity between the Infinite and the finite, the Infinite remaining all the while in its own illimitable infinity. The Nativity, the Crucifixion and the Resurrection are thus no mere symbols of a spiritual Reality that is not bound up in any special manner with the external facts. They are rooted in the concrete fact that the Man Who was born, crucified and raised from the dead was one person with the infinite and incomprehensible God. Moreover, in the

[1] See, for a fuller treatment, Chap. XIII.

presentation and conception of these incarnational dogmas by Catholic theology, the external and material element has never been so conceived as to limit or materialise the inward and spiritual significance. In the case of the Incarnational dogmas the material element is therefore neither wholly nor mainly symbolic,[1] and thus is not such a presentation of spiritual truth as taken literally limits the apprehension of that truth, and therefore an element to be spiritualised entirely or partially away. Therefore in the case of these and similar dogmas, spiritualisation cannot mean (as it does in the case of dogmas wholly or partially of the former class) the rejection of the particular external and material fact, as a limitation of the inward spiritual reality, and that, for the very reason that the external and material fact, instead of limiting the inward spiritual reality, is itself given an infinite significance by its peculiar union with that reality. Spiritualisation can here only mean—as we have seen—the ever-increasing apperception of that infinite Divine reality thus so intimately and so indissolubly united with the external finite fact.

The Divine Being is indeed so infinitely transcendent of created being that not only is God incomprehensible by any creature, indeed unknowable by any created mode of knowledge, but, while remaining immutably in that infinite transcendence of all creatures, unrelated to any creature, He is able, by the fiat of His omnipotent will, to bring a created being into a relationship of personal identity with Himself, so that in virtue of that personal identity that created being is no longer a pure creature. God in His infinite transcendence is unrelated even to the Sacred Humanity of Christ, and nevertheless that humanity is so intimately related to God as to be one person with Him. How this can be is beyond human conception. It is another insoluble paradox. But it is equally a paradox that one finite being can be nearer to and participate more fully in the Infinite than another finite being. Must not all finites be equally removed from the infinite ? Yet, as we have already seen, the latter paradox at least must be accepted by all who would not place the material on the same level with the spiritual, in defiance of the obvious absurdity of such equal valuation. Why, then, need any boggle at the former paradox of our faith ? Indeed, both these paradoxes are ultimately reducible to the paradox of the co-existence of the finite and the infinite. If we grant this co-existence it follows that some

---

[1] No doubt there is also present a quite secondary element of symbolism.

finites are nearer to the infinite than others. It is undeniable
that thought is less limited than material mass, life than lifeless
energy. The less limited must surely be nearer to the unlimited
than the more limited, and nevertheless both are infinitely distant.
Moreover, it is equally clear that if the finite and infinite co-exist,
the former must be related to the latter, but not the latter to the
former, for the infinite cannot be limited by relationship.* The
ultimate and basal paradox is therefore the co-existence of finite
and infinite. Yet this co-existence, however inexplicable, is a
fact. It cannot be escaped by denying the existence of an infinite.
Whatever view be adopted of the nature of ultimate reality, there
must be an infinite. The all, or the totum of reality, cannot be
in all respects limited. If the universe were not created out of
nothing by God, it must be everlasting—*i.e.* unlimited or infinite
in duration. Moreover, we should also have then to admit that
a thousand years is more akin to and participates more largely in
that everlasting duration [1] than one second, because the less
limited duration must be more akin to and partake more fully of
the unlimited duration than the more limited duration.[2] The co-
existence of finite and infinite is therefore one of those antinomies
inevitable whatever metaphysical system be adopted. The
mystic's philosophy of the Unlimited and All Transcendent is no
more burdened with such antinomies than any other, and cannot
fairly, on that account, be rejected. The existence of these final
antinomies or paradoxes makes us realise that reason cannot
wholly explain or harmonise experience, cannot solve all its
problems. If it attempts to do so, it destroys itself and the thinker.
Reason must recognise its limitations. A culture or a philosophy
that attempts to obtain a complete rational explanation of experience is attempting an impossible task, only too likely to end in
intellectual despair. The existence of paradoxes, such as that
of the co-existence of the finite and infinite, should not be the
occasion of an unwarranted scepticism. It should serve rather to
bring home to us the utter incomprehensibility, the unfathomable
mystery of the Divine Being Who is the Ultimate Reality. This
incomprehensible mystery is the meeting-place of two parallel

---

[1] Not eternity. That is disparate from becoming, which would, however, be
ultimate in this pantheist universe.

[2] Yet from another point of view both periods are seen to be equally distant
from the infinite duration. Herein consists the internal self-contradiction of an
everlasting duration, as opposed to the *totum simul* of eternity.

F

truths, incapable of union by our finite intelligence. One of these is God's complete transcendence of creatures, the other His immanence in them, an immanence which culminates in the Incarnation. These parallel truths thus meet, as parallel lines are said in geometry to meet, in infinity.

We must, however, always remember that the perversions of Modernism and agnosticism are perversions of a great truth, a truth of supreme religious value, the truth that the Divine Absolute Being is so absolutely transcendent of the essentially limited finite being that even when that finite being is in personal union with God it is by comparison sheer non-existence. If we therefore keep a firm hold on two truths (1) in the sense in which God *is*, every creature is not; (2) through Christ, His Church and His sacraments, human nature has been brought into a most intimate relationship with God, we shall avoid the false agnosticism of the agnostic and the Modernist, which is the destruction of faith, and we shall at the same time maintain the true agnosticism of the mystic which is the perfection of faith. We shall realise that all that is revealed to us of God in Christ and His mysteries is absolutely and eternally true—but that it is also infinitely inadequate to exhaust or express the Divine Being as It is in Itself. We shall then perceive that of sheer necessity the dogmas of theology cannot be grasped or harmonised by human reason, that any religious system which is completely harmonious and intelligible is *ipso facto* proved to be false, and that rationalism in religion is supremely irrational, because it limits God by the concepts and images of our finite intelligence, just as agnosticism is irrational, because it does not see that God the first cause must infinitely transcend the highest categories of dependent being, and therefore cannot be infraspiritual or infrapersonal. Like the transcendence the unity and the immanence of God are ultimately reducible to the fact that Infinite Being, as unlimited, excludes all negation and exclusive distinction. " I Am that I Am " was the Divine title revealed to the Jews by God Himself. In this I Am are constituted the Divine Immanence, as the ground of all created being—which is essentially relative and dependent on the Divine Being of which it is but a reflection and participation, the Divine Unity, for absolute positivity admits of no mutually exclusive differences, and the Divine Transcendence, for the Unlimited Being must be infinitely distinct from being which is essentially limited and as limited negative. As Moses of old beheld Jahwe in the bush burnt yet unconsumed by His Presence, so to the Christian mystic is revealed this Absolute and Divine "I Am," burning through the universe of finite being which nevertheless is not, as pantheism falsely teaches, consumed by His Indwelling. Let us therefore who draw nigh to behold with him this Divine Vision put off the shoes of human reason [1] and adore the Mystery of Infinite Godhead Immanent in all things, yet of all transcendent, that makes this world of creatures wherein we live in very truth a holy ground.

Note 1. *The Divine Purity*

The Divine Purity is a subordinate aspect of the Divine Transcendence of all limits. In chap. ix. of the first section of vol. ii. of *Modern Painters*, Ruskin maintains that purity is essentially energy unimpeded. Theology teaches that God is perfect energy—essential and absolute energy, the *actus purus*. By this *actus purus* is meant that the Divine Being is always one fulness of act without any potentiality as yet unactualised. Unactualised potentiality in creatures arises from their limitations, which give rise to division and opposition. Pure energy is absolute positivity, without that defect of being which constitutes the unrealised potentialities of creatures. Created substances are pure in so far as they possess their fulness, their completion of being and energy, unalloyed and unimpeded by alien substances. Pure wine, for instance, has not its vinous properties and effects impeded by the presence of non-vinous liquids. Pure love is not impeded in its operation towards its object by the presence of hostile or even neutral will aims.

God therefore is essential purity because a Being unaffected by the presence and action of any alien nature, a fulness of energy unimpeded by any limitations. St John of the Cross has stated this in a passage already quoted from *The Ascent of Mount Carmel*, ii. 16. "The Divine Wisdom . . . admits of no such particular ways [modes], neither can it be comprehended under any limitation or distinct particular knowledge, because it is all *pureness* and simplicity." God's purity is thus His perfect energy ; that is, His absolute positivity without the negative element involved in the finite and relative being of creatures. God's purity is therefore His Absolute Being, the I Am under another aspect.

---

[1] Like shoes, necessary in its own lower sphere.

Mother Cecilia says : "The Divine Being is termed pure on account of the simplicity of His most pure substance." God is here termed pure, " not only because He is most clean and free from all stain, but from the nature of His essence which transcends all that can be attributed to it, and because He is a pure act working in Himself, through Himself, and for Himself " (*Transformation*, st. 1).

Note 2. *Personal and Impersonal Representations of the Godhead*

Personal finite spirits, human spirits at least, lack certain positive characters of material and impersonal forces. A human soul does not, for instance, possess the power and scope of an elemental force of nature, though higher far in the scale of being. Now, as has been already pointed out, the Infinite Being of God is eminently all that is positively existent in creatures. Therefore the vastness of an impersonal force represents an aspect of His being, not represented by the human soul. For this reason mystics are obliged to use images taken from impersonal forces and elements, to indicate the Divine Being, side by side with intimately personal images. The philosopher of mysticism will perhaps incline more to the impersonal images—the practical mystic will be attracted to the more personal.[1] Both are true positively, both false negatively, true in their affirmations, false in their limitations. As the personal images or categories have more positive being than the impersonal, they are more adequate representations of God than the latter, though ever infinitely inadequate.

[1] Nevertheless it is largely a matter of individual temperament. St John of the Cross prefers personal, Mother Cecilia impersonal, imagery.

INTRODUCTION TO CHAPTER V

1. *Relation of the Infrarational Creation to God.*—Before we consider the relation between the human soul and God, it would be well to say a little as to the relation of the infrarational creature to the Creator. One great purpose of the infrarational creation is certainly the service of man, and that in two ways—by ministering to his material being and well-being, and by ministering to his spiritual well-being. This latter ministry itself falls under two heads. The infrarational creation ministers to man's spiritual good, by giving him occasion to glorify God in thanksgiving for the use he has of creatures—but far more by man's knowledge and praise of Him as the first cause and eminent possessor of all their perfections—that is, of their positive being. Material creatures are sacraments of spiritual realities, the Divine attributes which they represent. To use nature as a sacrament is to be brought into contact with its underlying ground, the Divine Being in His various aspects. This is the noblest use of the visible creation. Since the fall the infrarational creation subserves also man's spiritual well-being as an obstacle to be overcome—that is, as a more or less recalcitrant matter, to be moulded with great toil to human and spiritual ends, a task which brings into play the moral virtues. It subserves man in this office by way of temptations to sensual pleasure, the resistance to which purges and perfects his spiritual life. It subserves him also as a scourge for his discipline and chastisement. But this ministry to rational creatures cannot exhaust the significance of the infrarational creation—no, not if every planet and star in space were populated with rational beings. The investigations of modern science bring home to us with ever-increasing force the incalculably immense amount of inorganic elements and forces and the incalculably vast multitude of living beings, vegetable and animal, that have only the most accidental reference—often none at all—to man and his needs. But we have seen already that all created being is a representation of the Divine Being under various aspects. As such it is not only sacramental to man of that Being but is in itself an external manifestation of

God, which is His accidental glory. A difficulty arises in the case of certain creatures—for example, the octopus—which seem to possess ugliness in the sense of a privation of due form—not its mere absence, which would be a foil to the beauty of other creatures. Such ugliness seems sacramental rather of spiritual evil than of spiritual good. This privative, and therefore repellent, ugliness is emphasised by Richard Jefferies, not, I think, without exaggeration, in *The Story of my Heart*. We should remember that the liturgy and tradition of the Church seem to presuppose a certain power of the evil spirits over the lower creation. For the reality of this power there is ample warrant. It is presupposed by the forms of benediction employed by the Church, also by certain scriptural expressions—for example, "the powers of the air," "the rulers of this darkness," "the prince of this world cometh." We may also compare many well-attested incidents in the lives of saints. Its exact nature and extent are altogether indefinite and unknown. Might it not extend to an interference with the course of evolution, introducing into it an element of privative ugliness? If we admit this explanation we are surely compelled by the discoveries of geology to postulate with Mr Webb the existence and activity of this evil power in the world before man fell or, indeed, had any existence. Whether or no the evil spirits have thus interfered with evolution, the strife and waste so obvious, alike in the present condition of the earth, as in the course of its past history, are, to a very great degree at least, due to the very nature of the limited, to the limit inherent in every creature not emancipated by supernatural union with God. Though it is doubtful whether the actual suffering and ugliness existent in the extrahuman creation be explicable without the operation of the privative limit of moral evil, it is surely undeniable that the limit as such involves defect, and therefore a certain degree of inevitable physical evil. Moreover, the limit involves exclusion and consequent division, and therefore strife.[1] Nevertheless, despite all this waste, strife, suffering and ugliness, creatures are essentially representations and sacraments of the Godhead, and that to the degree of their positive being.

Moreover God is the end of creation. Every created being tends to become as like to God as it can. This is true, alike of the

---

[1] In the new heaven and earth of the Resurrection this defect arising from the limit will, in so far as it involves ugliness, pain or strife, be remedied by a special dispensation of supernatural power.

individual, of the species, of the class and of the entire Universe. The course of evolution is no blind and aimless striving, but is a purposive progress. This progress is a gradual perfecting of the subject of evolution. The effect and aim of this evolutionary progress is the actualisation of the latent possibilities of its subject being. But we have seen already that the more of positive being there is in any creature, and therefore the more its potentiality is actualised, the better does it represent the Divine Being, for the more being a creature possesses the closer does it approach (though always infinitely distant from) the fulness of Absolute Being. Moreover the greater the multiplicity of forms of being and life harmonised in the unity of the specific character, and of the individual life, the fuller is the revelation of God, Whose attributes and their unity are manifested thereby. No one has more strongly insisted on the onward striving energy of life than M. Bergson. He has, however, treated this striving as blind and aimless. Certainly it is so in the individuals who partake of it in various grades. To treat it as in itself aimless is, however, the abandonment of explanation—the acknowledged bankruptcy of philosophy. How infinitely rich, on the contrary, is the Christian conception outlined above. All the marvellous contrivances and adaptations, far exceeding any possible conscious intention of their subjects, which are revealed to us by science, and whose immediate end is the conservation and reproduction of the species and whose more indirect end is its evolution, are seen to be a progressive manifestation of God, an increasing approach to His Divine Being. On a polyphyletic view of evolution this manifestation of God and approach to His Being will be bounded by the essential limitation of certain fundamental types. When this limitation is reached the capacity of each type is exhausted and God's being has been shown forth and represented to the utmost extent possible to that type. If, however, we accept a monophyletic view of evolution, not only will the potentialities of each type form be thus actualised but new potentialities will be added in the course of evolution. For we surely cannot believe that all the high and complex forms of life and sentience to be found in the vegetable and animal kingdoms were present potentially in the most rudimentary organism. They must therefore have been added by the stimulus and operation of the Divine Spirit immanent in the evolutionary process. These new elements, however, like the actualisation of potencies contained already in the type forms, only to a far greater degree than the latter, are additions of being, the removal of limits and accordingly an increasing representation of God and a closer approach to His Infinite Being. This manifestation of the Godhead through the ordered hierarchy and pushful life of creatures has never been expressed more clearly than by Dante in the first canto of the *Paradiso*.

> Le cose tutte e quante
> Hann'ordine tra loro ; e questo è forma
> Che l'universo a Dio fa simigliante.

> [All things whatsoever observe a mutual order ;
> And this is the form that maketh the universe
> Like unto God.]

We know far more of this order, its incalculably vast extent and variety, than did Dante and his contemporaries, and the result of this new knowledge should be a fuller realisation of the Divine glory shown forth therein.

> Qui veggi-on l'alte creature l'orma
> Dell'eterno valore, il quale è fine
> Al quale è fatta la toccata norma.

> [Herein the exalted creatures trace the impress
> of the Eternal Worth, which is the goal whereto
> was made the norm now spoken of.]

Not for the consideration of man alone, with his narrow knowledge, has the order of the universe been decreed, but for the adoring contemplation of the angelic intelligences.

> Nell'ordine ch'io dico sono accline
> Tutte nature, per diverse sorti
> più al principio loro e men vicine ;
> onde si movono a diversi porti
> per lo gran mar dell' essere, e ciascuna
> con istinto a lei dato che la porti.[1]

> [In the order of which I speak all things incline by
> diverse lots, more near or less unto their principle ;
> wherefore they move to diverse ports o'er the great
> sea of being, and each one with instinct given it
> to bear it on.]

---

[1] That the means of this progress should be so largely a remorseless competition—a struggle for existence—is part of the mystery of evil unfathomable to the understanding, even when illuminated by faith and further by mystical intuition. See, however, above.

Upward ever upward to God, such is the law of created being and life.   In the light of modern knowledge we are able to realise this law more fully than was possible to the men of the fourteenth century.   It is ours to behold with clearer vision than theirs the order of created energy and life, its striving and evolution, as a moving stairway ascending from story to story of diversely graded being till it reaches at length the steps of its Creator's throne.

2. *A Few Words on Psychology.*—The discussion of the relationship between the human soul and God must be prefaced by a few words as to human psychology.   The psychology adopted by St John cannot be regarded as an adequate scientific system—for the time for such a complete and wholly scientific psychology had not yet arrived.   Indeed, such a psychology is still in its infancy. The scholastic psychology employed by St John seems to me to be rather a description of the general features of human life and consciousness, expressed in clear and definite formulæ.   As such it can no more be overthrown by the fuller and more scientific psychology of the future than the obvious facts of our physical constitution, as known by simple observation and common-sense, can be discredited by the more radical explanations of medical science.   All the psychologies other than the scholastic, hitherto adopted, have been defective in every sense—even as descriptive, because they have tried to explain man's psychical life by the denial of some essential factor or element.   Since the scholastic psychology is thus fundamentally sound in its acceptance of all the known facts or aspects of our psychical experience, I will adhere to its principles in this work.   Such adherence, however, will not commit me to the adoption either of its details or of its exact terminology.   Wherever I feel that I can bring home my meaning more forcibly to the modern reader by the use of terms unknown to or otherwise employed by the schoolmen, I shall not hesitate to do so.   Moreover, I accept in substance the modern psychology of the subconscious.

The human soul has a twofold function—in two diverse planes. It is in the first place the form of the body—by which we mean this, at least, that the soul is the principle of organic life and growth and of bodily sentience.   So far as this function is concerned it is identical with the soul of brute beasts.   But the rational soul has another function on a higher plane—namely, the spiritual or rational life.   As such the soul transcends the limitations of physical existence, and attains to a knowledge of abstract or spiritual ideas—general ideas—as also to self-knowledge, and in the rational will it transcends the necessary motions of sensible desire.   This higher life is divided by the schoolmen and by St John into three chief functions, called faculties or powers—understanding, memory and will.   Modern psychology, it is true, dislikes the term faculties as implying distinct entities, whereas these so-called " faculties " are but different functions of one activity, different aspects of one entity.   Nevertheless a certain distinction must be admitted.   Thought is not the same as volition, though it is the one indivisible soul that wills and thinks.   Therefore that one soul has in it a power of willing and a power of thinking.   To these we may surely apply the term faculty, without implying entities substantially distinct from each other and from the soul. In this book I will retain the old faculty terminology employed by St John, understanding by a faculty a distinct function of the soul. I will therefore speak indifferently of " faculty " and " function." St John's three faculties of understanding, memory and will may, I think, be reduced with profit to two supreme faculties, the cognitive and the conative faculties or functions.   By the cognitive function we are conscious of general ideas and notions, as also of spiritual beings, whether apprehended by discursive reasoning or by intuition.

Throughout these chapters this cognitive faculty or spiritual consciousness will often be termed understanding—since that is the name given to it by St John and the schools.   Nevertheless the term, if understood strictly, is somewhat misleading.   It suggests discursive reasoning and the apprehension of distinct concepts.   The spiritual consciousness, however, while inclusive of these activities, transcends them, both naturally, in a superrational intuition of truths not distinctly grasped by discursive reason, and supernaturally in the intuition of God through faith and the crown of faith, the veiled intuition of the Divine presence, which is a constitutive element of mystical experience.   Some may object to the use of the term intuition as indicative of the unveiled intuition of the beatific vision, and prefer to regard the faith-intuition of mysticism as an idea supernaturally impressed.[1] This objection is, however, ill-founded and misleading.   It is surely undeniable that the mystical consciousness of God—independent,

---

[1] As in an interesting study of mysticism in *The Journal of Ecclesiastical Studies*.

as it is, of sense data and transcendent of the clear concepts of reason—is what is generally understood by the term intuition. Attached to the spiritual consciousness is the memory of the ideas and beings of which it is conscious, and a certain element of spiritual as opposed to sensible feeling ; for example, spiritual joy and sorrow. The conative faculty or function is the will, stretching out to good, as apprehended by the cognitive function, together with the spiritual emotion, which is attendant in greater or lesser degree on the act of will. Spiritual feeling, in so far as it is *affection*, is subsumed under the conative or volitional element, as heat under energy. Both functions, however, the cognitive and the conative, are concomitant. We cannot will without some consciousness of the object willed, nor know without attention of the will to the object known. These two functions are aspects of one indivisible soul, as also are the lower or sensible functions. All the functions of the soul, sensible and spiritual alike, are united by proceeding from one centre—the central, fundamental ego or self. In strict terminology the ego or self is the entire man, the complex of soul and body. The body, however, and the psychic functions conditioned by and dependent upon the body are parts of the ego only in virtue of their union with the central selfhood. Therefore I think it justifiable and tending to greater clarity to use the term ego of this central selfhood which is the source of the individual unity of the entire person.[1] This centre, from which all the separate functions of the soul proceed as rays from the sun, is termed by the mystics the centre of the soul, or the ground of the soul, or synderesis.[2] Since this centre is the least conditioned by the limitations of sense, it is nearest to the Unlimited Being of God. Hence it is the special seat of the Divine Being and Action, in which He is most immanent. It is in the centre that He dwells in an especial fashion, because there are fewer limits of non-being to bar Him out. It is in and from the centre that He acts in the soul. Of this centre or synderesis our knowledge is mainly indirect.

---

[1] Here I must part company with the schoolmen who regarded the body as the principle of individuation. This doctrine makes it very difficult to believe in the individual survival of the disembodied spirit.

[2] It is, however, but fair to point out that I depart from the scholastic understanding of the synderesis in two points : (1) I regard it as normally subliminal ; the scholastic philosophers and theologians did not. (2) They regarded it as identical with the intellectual faculty or function by which axioms are apprehended. I cannot admit this identity. (*Cf.* Scheeben, *Dogmatik*, Fr. trs., vol. ii., p. 13.)

The inmost ego is normally known only in and through its functions. All our psychical functions are largely subconscious, as modern psychology has clearly demonstrated. Mainly subconscious are the deeper, more fundamental and more purely spiritual energies of the cognitive and conative faculties—namely, intuition and radical will. As intuition underlies the conscious cognition of discursive reason, so the radical will is the fundamental disposition of the will, the orientation of the entire self, which underlies particular volitions which are not thus completely expressive of the soul. At comparatively rare intervals this fundamental will emerges in a conscious decision, as also the subconscious intuition becomes on occasion a conscious perception. Most fully subconscious, however, is the centre or ground from which these cognitive and conative functions proceed. Hence the conscious manifestation of the Divine Being and Activity in the soul involves as its concomitant—its " epiphenomenon," the entrance into consciousness of depths and functions normally subconscious—an uprush from the subliminal, as modern psychologists term it. Therefore the subject of mystical experience is that portion of the soul which is normally subliminal, though by no means always entirely subconscious, even in man's normal and purely natural life. We must, however, remember that the opposite pole of the psychical life, the most extremely superficial functions—those, namely, that pertain to the vegetive life of the body—are also normally subconscious or subliminal. There is, as Miss Evelyn Underhill aptly remarks (*Mysticism*, chap. iii), no special faculty or function of subconsciousness, no distinct entity, such as the " subjective mind " of Hudson. It follows that when we term a state of consciousness an uprush from the subliminal we really mean only that it is the consciousness of functions, faculties or energies, whether superficial, medial or central, of which we are normally unconscious, whether or not there is also the consciousness of a transubjective reality apprehended by or active in the " emergent " functions. Moreover, the assertion does not tell us what functions they are of which the soul has thus become conscious. Hence " subliminal uprush " is an exceedingly inadequate explanation of any psychological phenomenon. Certainly there is a subliminal uprush in mystical experience—since this involves a consciousness of the central depths through which the Divine Being and Action are manifested. But there is also a subliminal uprush from the opposite pole in an attack of indigestion. We have already discussed the modern error which identifies the Divine Being and Action manifested in and through the central depths that are normally subliminal—with a simple consciousness of those normally subliminal depths and their natural content—the error which regards mystical experience as simply subjective. I need not, therefore, say more here on this point. There is, then, in the soul a normally subconscious central ego, and proceeding from this central ego a fundamental, spiritual consciousness or cognitive faculty, which, as it comes to the surface of consciousness, produces the increasingly limited and increasingly sense-conditioned forms of consciousness and a fundamental, spiritual will or conative faculty, which, as it comes to the surface in like manner, produces the increasingly limited and the increasingly sense-conditioned forms of volition and desire. Concomitant with these faculties, especially with the conation, is a spiritual feeling which, when it accompanies more limited, more superficial and more sensible forms of consciousness and volition, becomes the sensible feeling that is so narrowly limited and so transitory. Thus there is, in the centre of the soul, as Ruysbroeck points out (*Mirror of Eternal Salvation*, chap. ix), an image of the most Holy Trinity. For him, as for many mystics and fathers, from St Augustine downwards, this created trinity of the human soul consists of memory, understanding and will. Without in any way desiring to reject or belittle this venerable image, I find myself better aided by a modified form of it, since the memory does not seem to me so fundamentally distinct a function or faculty as are the understanding and the will. The created trinity in the central soul consists, in my view, of the central ego—the ground of the soul, the synderesis and the cognitive and the conative faculties—the understanding and the will. The synderesis or the ground of the soul is an image of the Father, for from it proceed the two fundamental properties or functions of the soul, cognition or understanding and conation or will. The understanding is an image of the Son, the Eternal Wisdom, the will of the Holy Ghost, the Eternal Love. The procession of both from the ground is an image of the procession of the Divine Persons.

Now it is clear, I think, that a man's will is the most fundamental expression of himself. This primacy of will in the psychical life, the fact that conative activity is the most fundamental of all our psychical activities, has been greatly stressed by modern psychologists. Wundt, for example, regards " will as the central point of the psychical life " (Höffding, *Modern Philosophers*, trs. Mason, p. 6). According to Professor Höffding "there is an element of will in all psychic states " (*Modern Philosophers*, p. 282). He, of course, understands by will every kind of purposive or conative activity. But of these conations, will, in the usual sense of the term, especially the decision and orientation of the radical will, is the highest, most interior and most spiritual form. Therefore in all the highest, most interior and most spiritual activities of the soul, which are those with which mystical theology is concerned, there is doubtless present an element of will in the strictest sense. It follows, therefore, that of all our psychical functions or faculties the will penetrates farthest into, and is most deeply rooted in, the central ego ; or, if you prefer a less metaphorical expression, that will is the most fundamental and most representative aspect of the ego. M. Bergson supports this psychology when he teaches that it is " in an energetic decision of the will that ' the basal ego finds self expression,' and that in such volition the ego of the depths rises to the surface and asserts itself " (Höffding, *Modern Philosophers*, p. 282). That is the reason that certain mystics term the centre the apex of the will.

All our knowledge in this life—that is to say, all our natural knowledge—is conditioned by the images received from sense. Not natural but supernatural is the intuition or realisation of God as present in and intimately united with the apex, which is given in mystical experience. But although all our other knowledge is thus sense-conditioned, it is not so conditioned to an equal degree. We can, even in the natural order, live an interior life, spiritualising our knowledge by the contemplation of spiritual ideas, whence the particular images of sense are abstracted as far as may be and bringing into play our most interior and self-expressing faculties both cognitive and conative.

These preliminary remarks will, I hope, be sufficient to outline the psychology of the human soul as the subject of mystical experience. Further light and more detailed information will be supplied by our consideration of the mystical way itself—which is, from first to last, dependent upon and conditioned by the essential nature of the soul and on its consequent relationship to God. Nothing is laid down by St John of the Cross which is not logically consequent on his doctrine of God and the soul, and the understanding of the mystical way will therefore throw the clearest light on its Object and subject in their mutual relationship—or, to speak more accurately, on the relationship of the latter to the Former. The Being of God is the fixed and changeless, because Absolute, Reality, immanent in yet transcendent of the soul, with Whom the soul of man is in relation, and towards Whom that soul progresses in the mystical way.

CHAPTER V

THE RELATION BETWEEN THE SOUL AND GOD

THE FUNDAMENTAL PRINCIPLE OF THE MYSTICAL WAY

Jacob being departed from Bersabee went towards Haran. And when he would rest after sunset he took of the stones, and putting them under his head he slept. And he saw in his sleep a ladder standing upon the earth, and the top thereof touching heaven, the angels also of God ascending and descending by it: and the Lord leaning upon the ladder, saying unto him: "I am the Lord God." And when Jacob awaked out of sleep, he said: "Indeed the Lord is in this place and I knew it not. How terrible is this place! This is no other but the house of God and the gate of heaven." GENESIS xxviii.

O world invisible—we view thee,
O world intangible—we touch thee,
O world unknowable—we know thee,
Inapprehensible—we clutch thee.

. . . .

The angels keep their ancient places:
Turn but a stone, and start a wing!
'Tis ye, 'tis your estranged faces
That miss the many splendoured thing.
But (when so sad thou canst not sadder)
Cry!—and upon thy so sore loss
Shall shine the traffic of Jacob's ladder
Pitched between heaven and Charing Cross.

FRANCIS THOMPSON.

" There are different roads by which this end (apprehension of the Infinite) may be reached. The love of beauty, which exalts the poet; that devotion to the One, and that ascent of Science which makes the ambition of the philosopher; and that love and those prayers by which some devout and ardent soul tends in its moral purity towards perfection. These are the great highways conducting to that

96

height above the actual and the particular, where we stand in the immediate presence of the Infinite, who shines out as from the deeps of the soul."

PLOTINUS,
Letter to Flaccus. Quoted by Miss Spurgeon,
Mysticism in English Literature, p. 33.

MAN's relation to God differs fundamentally from that of infra-rational creatures. He is no longer the blind slave of the life impulse, or of instinct, though these play a far greater part in his life than psychology has, until lately, been prepared to admit. His soul is not merely the principle of his animal life, but a rational spirit. As such the human soul is not bound by the limits of the particular object, but is capable of generalisation. Man can, moreover, criticise his own impulses and desires and frame his own ends, rationally chosen, his free will being thus grounded in his rationality. Furthermore, his reason makes known to him the inadequacy of any finite object. His reason cannot, indeed, form any concept of the infinite—being essentially finite. It can only lead him to a negative knowledge of the infinite, as that which lacks the limitations inherent in every finite image and concept. To this good, however, he can reach out by his will. For the object of the will is good, and since reason apprehends the inadequacy of finite goods, the will cannot ultimately rest in such, but stretches out to infinite good. This infinite good is God, conceived in the negative-positive manner discussed in the preceding chapters. Therefore in this life the will is the supreme means of union between the human soul and God. The author of *The Obscure Knowledge* states this very clearly. "It is most certain," he says, "that in this life the union of the will is far more excellent and of higher worth than the union of the understanding, and it is better to love God than to know Him, because that which we can love with the will is much more than that which we can attain with the understanding. The reason of this may be gathered from a consideration of the respective modes of operation of the understanding and the will. They are completely different. When the understanding understands, it attracts to itself the object understood and forms an idea of it within itself, which idea it contains within itself. Since its capacity is finite, it reduces within its own limitations the object understood, even if in itself that object be infinite, even as the ocean is reduced and narrowed when it enters the Straits of Gibraltar. The will, on the

G

contrary, when it loves goes out of itself and is transformed into the object loved and is made one thing with it. The object loved is not therefore limited by it. From this we can see how different is our understanding of God in this life from our love of Him. We understand Him according to our own capacity; we love Him as He is in Himself " (*Obscure Knowledge*, chap. x). Similar is the teaching of Mother Cecilia. " From the limitation inherent in everything external there is," she writes, " no escape, unless the Divine communication find an abiding place in the heart, by which is meant *the intimate part of the will* or the essence of the soul. Since this was created by God after His own image and likeness, *it possesses an immensity so profound that it is like a bottomless well, or rather an ocean* in the which the deeper the soul sinks the farther is she from touching bottom, for she has a life grounded in the very life and essence of her Creator. . . . The will alone is permitted to love the soul's lord with a certain infinity in its love, due to the infinity of the object of its love, in Whom it loses itself completely " (*Transformation*, st. 1). " Love gives the soul . . . more of God than any other means " (*Transformation*, st. 11).

If man lived wholly or chiefly by reason, he would reach out to this supreme good. I do not mean that he would attain to the beatific vision of God, or even to mystical union with Him, for that is essentially beyond the capacity of unaided nature, but he would have a certain will union with God—a union such as we may suppose to be enjoyed by the souls of unbaptized infants. It is certain that man has no real satisfaction short of the attainment of infinite good. All lower satisfaction is merely seeming. Along every line of human activity there is this striving after the infinite—an ascent from the more to the less limited. Such is the way of knowledge, rising from a merely practical colligation and generalisation of the sense-presented facts of everyday life, to the apprehension of scientific laws and metaphysical principles. It is the same with the way of love—never to be satisfied with any limited object. Hence the cry of the mighty lover, St Augustine : " Thou madest us for Thyself, and our heart is restless until it repose in Thee." [1] The infinite good that is God is indeed the sole true happiness, and therefore the sole end of the human heart.

But we have already seen that God is not only the transcendent goal of creatures but is also immanent in the human

---

[1] *Confessions*, I. i.   Trs. Pusey.

soul, as the ultimate ground of the psychic life of man. As this life, being spiritual, is immeasureably higher than infrarational being and life, it is, to use a spatial metaphor, more deeply grounded and rooted in the Divine Being because more fully participant of that Being. Most deeply grounded in the Godhead, since it is most fully possessed and most fully representative of God, is the higher or spiritual life of the human soul, especially its root, the synderesis or centre. For that central life is freest of limits, and in it therefore the Unlimited is peculiarly present. Thus God dwells especially in the centre of the soul. Moreover, the powers of the soul are its instruments for dealing with creatures and with the images and concepts derived therefrom. Hence the powers—and the more so in proportion to their distance from the centre—that is, the more sensible and superficial they are—are farther removed from God than the centre and the highest powers that are most intimately rooted in it. Moreover we have seen that the will reaches deepest into this central ground. Therefore the will is for this reason also the chief means to union with God within the centre. Just now we saw that this was the case, because the will most completely transcended the particular in its outgoing search of unlimited good. But it is also true because the will reaches innermost into the central life, away and free from the superficial life that is conditioned and limited, immediately or mediately by sense images. This is, of course, the same fact regarded from different points of view, the same reality under two aspects. I will now quote the words of St John and his school on the presence of God in the centre of the soul. " We must remember," he says, in the *Spiritual Canticle*, " that the Word, the Son of God, together with the Father and the Holy Ghost, is hidden in essence and in presence, in the inmost being of the soul. That soul therefore that will find Him, must go out from all things in will and affection and enter into the profoundest self-recollection. . . ." Hence St Augustine saith : " I found Thee not without, O Lord ; I sought Thee without in vain, for Thou art within." (God is indeed immanent in external creatures —but as their being is less representative of His—participating less fully in His Being on account of their greater limitation— He is not so fully present in them as in the human soul that is capable of apprehending and willing an Infinite Good, and is as such made in His own image and likeness.) " God is therefore hidden within the soul, and the true contemplative will seek Him there in love." . . . " O thou soul . . . thou knowest now that thou art thyself that very tabernacle where He dwells, the secret chamber of His retreat where He is hidden. Rejoice, therefore, and exult, because all thy good and all thy hope is so near thee as to be within thee, or to speak more accurately that thou canst not be without it, ' for, lo, the kingdom of God is within you.' . . . What more canst thou desire, what more canst thou seek without, seeing that within thou hast thy riches, thy delights, thy satisfaction, thy fulness and thy kingdom ; that is, thy Beloved, Whom thou desirest and seekest ? Rejoice, then, and be glad in thy interior recollection with Him, seeing that thou hast Him so near. There love Him, there desire Him, there adore Him, and go not to seek Him out of thyself, for that will be but distraction and weariness, and thou shalt not find Him, because there is no fruition of Him more certain, more ready, or more nigh than that which is within " (*Spiritual Canticle*, st. 1). "We must remember that in every soul God dwells secretly and veiled in their substance, for were it otherwise they could not endure in existence. There is, however, a difference as regards this inhabitation between one soul and another, and a great difference it is. In some souls He dwells alone, in others not alone, in some pleased, in others displeased, in some as in His house, commanding and directing everything, and in others as a stranger in a house not His own, where He is not permitted to order or to do anything " (*Living Flame of Love*, st. 4). " By saying that the flame of love [*i.e.* God's infused love] strikes the deepest centre of the soul, it is implied that there are other centres in the soul not so deep. I must explain how this is so. We must realise, first of all, that the soul, being a spirit, has in its being neither height nor depth, neither a deeper nor a less deep portion, as have bodies that are possessed of quantity. Moreover, since it has no parts, there is no distinction of outer and inner, but the entire soul is uniform. Neither has the soul a centre more or less profound in a quantitative sense. It cannot be more illuminated in one part than in another, as are physical bodies, but uniformly in whatever degree of illumination it may possess, even as the air is uniformly illuminated whether in greater or lesser degree. In the case of material objects we term that their deepest centre which is the farthest to which their being and virtue and the force of their activity and motion extend, the point beyond which they cannot pass, nor can they be kept away from thence save by some obstacle which forcibly impedes them. We say, for example, of a stone when it is inside the earth, although not in the greatest depth thereof, that it is in some sense in its centre, because it is in the sphere of its centre, activity and motion. We do not, however, say that it is in its deepest centre, for that is the mid-point of the earth. That stone, therefore, still possesses virtue, force and inclination to descend until it reaches this ultimate and deepest centre, if only the obstacle be removed. When the stone reaches that centre, and no longer possesses in itself the capacity or inclination for further movement, we say that it is in its deepest centre.

"The centre of the soul is God. When the soul shall have attained to God to the utmost of its capacity it will have attained its ultimate and deepest centre in Him, which will be when it understands, loves and tastes God with all its powers" (*Living Flame of Love*, st. 1). We note, indeed, in this passage a change of idea—God being now regarded as the centre of the soul. The reason is that the centre or ground of the soul is itself grounded in Him, and that in the most intimate manner. It is therefore easy to pass from one concept to the other. In fact certain unorthodox mystics—*e.g.* Eckhardt—have actually confused the created centre or ground where God dwells, and where we find Him in mystical experience, with God Himself. The existence of this confusion should make us realise how intimately the centre of the soul, the very ego, is grounded in the Divine Being, though, of course, as a creature, infinitely distant from Him. I have already warned the reader against an exclusive understanding of the statements of the mystics, and our subsequent consideration of the transcendence of God has explained and stressed that warning. The mystic feels so intensely and so intimately the presence of God in the centre of his soul as the very ground of his selfhood that he is driven to use language which might suggest to the unwary the notion that the centre is itself divine. The Spanish mystics, however, are more careful to guard against such misunderstanding than were the German and Flemish mystics before them. Perhaps the clearest statement of the Divine immanence in the centre, or ground, of the soul, is the following passage from *Mother Cecilia*, in her comment on the lines :

> She (the soul) ascendeth to the empyrean heaven
> And lifteth the veil from her secret centre.

" We are to understand," she says, " by these words the force wherewith the soul is raised above all her faculties superior and inferior to her centre, which is meant by the empyrean heaven, where God dwells within her and where she has the fruition of Him as if in heaven. Hence some have termed the centre the heaven of the spirit. . . . Only he who has had the experience can believe the immensity of blessings that are revealed or hidden in this Divine heaven. He who knows only the grossness of man's exterior will never be able to understand that within the soul hidden beneath this shabby veil of mortal flesh there is contained an immense centre of boundless riches and glory. The senses cannot perceive nor the human intellect understand, nor can our reason judge how God dwells there. . . . This most profound and most sacred depth of the soul is the dwelling-place of God. In this Divine centre we are made in His likeness. Nothing can fill or satisfy this centre save God Himself. Until the soul loses herself in the immensity of God, she does not know or understand the wealth that she possesses within herself, nor does she obtain even an inkling of what this Divine centre really is in its substance and true nature. Verily, no living man exists, or has existed, who has comprehended the nature of this centre." . . . " The words ' And lifteth the veil from her secret centre ' are intended to make us realise how different is the state of such a soul from the condition of those who have not attained to the revelation of this centre. From these latter this centre is hidden by a veil so thick and dark that it not only hides the centre itself, but even the knowledge that they possess within themselves that hidden place. . . . If however a soul empties and purifies herself, she will be able to discover her centre and to plunge in the Divine immensity the emptiness of her very essence which none can fill or satisfy save God Himself. I am . . . treating here, of those who have wholly plunged themselves into their God and have discovered this immense place which they possess in themselves and in Him and have attained the riches aforesaid, and the other ineffable immensities. . . . They have discovered this empyrean heaven which is their most profound centre, whereon God fully smote and from which He has removed the dark veil of all that hindered this Divine communication " (*Transformation of the Soul in God*, st. 4).

Cardinal Newman, who realised so intensely the immanence of God in the centre of the soul as to term God " the true self, that better part of our being, of whom our very self is but the impersonal instrument and the servant," and who bade his hearers regard God " as enthroned within us at the very springs of thought and affection," termed this centre conscience. I cannot but feel this to be a misnomer. Conscience is surely but the discursive reason as perceptive of ethical truth. The possession of this perception is indeed a strong argument for the existence of God— but it is not therefore to be identified either with the intuitive perception of God or with the central ego. Both of these are deeper and wider than the ethical judgment. We cannot regard ethical perception as the sole or even as the supreme avenue of communication between the soul and God Who is revealed to us alike in His historical revelation and in our personal experience not only as Absolute Goodness but also as Absolute Beauty and Truth. It is indeed true that our closest union with God is effected through love, and that love is an ethical activity. The love of God, however, is far more than a morally good will. Still less is it identical with ethical perception which pertains to reason not to will.

God is therefore the end and goal of the human spirit, and He is immanent in the centre of that spirit as the ground of its being. Why then is man not in closer and more actual union with Him ? Why are we not normally conscious of God's Presence within our souls? On account, it may be replied, of the limitations of human nature. There is much truth in this answer, but it is inadequate. The only answer that is fully adequate is that given by the Catholic Church. That answer is simple—it is contained in one word : sin. Original sin, actual sin and their consequences : these and these *alone* separate the human soul from God. I will first discuss the theory of this separation and will then point out how it is realised in actual life. Original sin consists in the loss of a supernatural elevation of the soul (the state of original justice) whereby the essential limitation of created being was so removed by a supernatural being and life infused by God [1] and named by theology habitual or sanctifying grace that the soul was capable of a superhuman union with Unlimited Godhead, in emancipation from the creaturely limits that naturally exclude such union. When through Christ we are restored in baptism to the supernatural order of sanctifying grace, the potentiality together with a radical actualisation of this superhuman union with God is once

[1] Strictly speaking, a quality or habit.

more ours and continues ours until we wilfully lose it by grave actual sin. Actual sin is a deliberate turning of the will from God to creatures—aversion from God, conversion to creatures. When this aversion is complete, the sin is mortal, when partial, it is venial. Every sinful act is then the deliberate preference of some finite good to the infinite good. By this preference we erect that finite good into a barrier whose finitude shuts out from us the infinite good. It is not that God can ever cease to be actually present in the soul—but that the wrong will averts the soul from Him, cuts it off from will-union with Him. If through a truly invincible ignorance a man does not know God, he will be guilty of sin or imperfection whenever he deliberately prefers in his ethical choices the more limited to the less limited good. But it may be urged that it is impossible for any man knowingly to prefer a lesser to a greater good, much less a finite to an infinite good ; and that therefore sin is nothing but ignorance, as Plato maintained. Certainly there is an element of ignorance in all sin. It is true that nobody can choose a lesser good to a greater with attention fixed on this fact. He can, however, shut his eyes to the difference of value, because the lesser good is more pleasant for the moment. Furthermore, there is in fallen man a rooted tendency to prefer his immediate but limited pleasure as a separate individual to the universal or absolute good with which, or rather with Whom, he ought in reason to identify his own good. This tendency shows us that actual sin arises out of an infirm, indeed a depraved condition of human nature—the result, so the faith teaches us, of the fall, that is of original sin, and its consequences, still abiding even in the regenerate. This depravity may be reduced under two heads. There is, first, the rebellion of the lower and sensual desires against the spirit—the law of the flesh fighting against the law of the mind. " The flesh lusteth against the spirit." The soul is, as we saw, the principle of physical life and of bodily desires. These lower functions of the soul are in fallen man at variance with the higher, and are ever dragging him downwards and imprisoning him within the limits of the unspiritual, narrowly limited and therefore comparatively unreal creatures and their images, which are the proper objects of sensible life and desires. There is, however, a yet deeper deordination in the higher soul itself, the above-mentioned tendency to isolate the self from the Absolute and Universal good. This more spiritual deordination leads man to place his happiness in creatures of a more spiritual and therefore less limited character than the objects of the sensible desires though still wholly finite—for example, the gratification of intellectual or spiritual pride or ambition. Both these evils are manifestations of concupiscence. Concupiscence in the widest sense of the term is the limited and the selfish desire or volition due to the sense dependence of the embodied soul, working freely and limiting the soul. But for original sin this operation and potency of concupiscence would have been destroyed by the presence of supernatural grace uniting the soul with God. Original sin, " the lack of this superadded gift," has enabled concupiscence to bind the soul within the limits of selfish and sense-conditioned desires and apprehensions by which bondage and limitations it has been separated from the Divine Union. This loss of supernatural elevation and its concomitant deordination are due to the sin of the first man in virtue of the mysterious solidarity of mankind founded in their common humanity. Although the fact of an historic fall can be known by faith alone, lacking as it does all other evidence, the principle of solidarity through which that fall has operated as original sin is an undeniable fact of experience, and pre-eminently of mystical experience.

To the ultra-individualism of nineteenth-century speculation, whereby the individual was treated as a circle wholly closed, the doctrine of original sin was of necessity radically unintelligible. That ultra-individualism has, however, received mortal blows from every quarter. M. Bergson, for instance, insists on reproduction as a breach of that circle (*L'Evolution Creatrice*, 8th edition, p. 14). An exaggerated insistence on racial solidarity—indeed of the solidarity of man with the rest of creation—has succeeded the opposite exaggeration. Such an exaggerated solidarity is one of the dominant *motifs* of Romain Rolland's *Jean Christophe*—that novel so faithfully and so fully reflective of the modern Zeitgeist. Yet it is, as we have seen, in this fact of human solidarity—a solidarity constituted, moreover, by reproduction—that original sin is grounded. It is indeed the inherited nature of man, as fallen from and exclusive of its supernatural elevation by the grace-union with God. Considered in this light, the doctrine is in harmony with the conception of solidarity so dominant in modern speculation, is indeed its application in the religious sphere.

Moreover the deordination of human nature, its bondage to

concupiscence, are data of all truly religious experience, especially, therefore, of the experience of the mystic.

Concupiscence is idolatry in the strictest sense. For it is, essentially, the making of some limited good the end of life. It may indeed be that this limited good is of an altruistic nature—the good of one's family, country, or of mankind. If God be without personal fault unknown, and if these altruistic goods be chosen as the highest good known—this is an imperfect grasping after God. This service of other creatures as the final end of man is, however, always essentially irrational, because at the end of all a limit still remains. It is only rendered possible by an ignorance of God, which is itself the result of sin in others. Altruism is therefore an irrational and transitory compromise between the love of concupiscence, which prefers the limited good of the creature to the unlimited Divine Good, and the love of charity, which unites the soul to God by removing the barriers of self-will present in all love which rests in the limited creature as its end.

Even the briefest contemplation of mankind suffices to reveal how radical and how widely extended is this perversion of our will. Almost all men to the end of their lives, even if their will be radically united to God in the state of supernatural grace—are bound in undue bondage within the limitations of creatures. Vast multitudes live almost entirely on the surface of life—in the gratification of the desires of sense. Many have never unified their life at all by deliberate choice of any one good deliberately willed as the supreme end of life, but live, as it were, from hand to mouth, following in turn each narrowly limited desire. Of their higher spiritual faculties they know little, and are never, or hardly ever, recollected in themselves. Their life is most literally summed up by the words of the Preacher, "Vanity of vanities; all is vanity." Others perhaps have unified their life more or less completely by one aim, but that aim is very superficial and limited. It therefore only serves to bind them the closer within the limited. Of course there are moments of dissatisfaction, vague longings for something better. But the chains of habit bind fast—distractions are many—example is plentiful—there is little time for thought in the press of business or dissipation. The desire rises. It is put away. The cords are tightened around the soul. Others are on a higher plane, have chosen a spiritual and therefore more unlimited and more real good. These are happier, for there is more fulness in their life, greater reality in the object of their love, and its possibilities are not exhausted so quickly. Nevertheless the greater reality, and the more unlimited nature of their idol, roots that idol the deeper in their heart. Such souls—ambitious men, lovers of military fame, political power, literary or artistic success—are harder to convert and more likely to have fundamentally and deliberately averted their will from God than the former class. Then again, there are those whose idol is a fellow-being—a wife or child—or a group of fellow-beings, a party or a nation. These have indeed broken through a very strong barrier, have achieved a very large measure of emancipation from limits, for they have identified their good with a good higher, wider and more real than their individual selfhood—namely, the good of other spiritual beings. But there is always a limit, and with that limit disappointment. Nevertheless, souls who make human love their end are the readiest to turn to the love of God.

Since God is in the truest sense the natural end of the human soul, and since in the fundamental Divine Intention every soul was intended for supernatural union with God, there are, I think, few, if indeed there be any, who do not at some time or other feel at least a vague craving for an infinite good, that is in reality for Him, though they know it not themselves. Even in the most sinful, in the most self and sense-limited souls, in the depths below the threshold of consciousness, the central ego still craves for the Unlimited God. This central craving emerges into consciousness at times, as at least an indefinable yearning, an apprehension of, a craving after an unknown Reality that will satisfy the emptiness of the heart created for the Infinite. Souls gifted intellectually or spiritually feel this craving and apprehension most often and most keenly. This craving often involves an intuition of the Divine Presence—not the supernatural intuition of the mystic, which is an immediate fruition of His Presence, but the perception that there is an Unlimited Being other than the limited creatures in which the soul cannot rest. This intuitive perception may not be, usually is not, explicitly present in consciousness. It is rather the subconscious background of the craving for the Unlimited. It is the presupposition and the stimulus of that craving. Were not the presence of the Unlimited in some way manifest to the soul, the limited would not be thus felt as vain and unsatisfying. Moreover, this Presence is undeniably apprehended in and through that craving. Dissatisfaction with the limited is a search after the

Unlimited, and that search of the central conation involves a certain apprehension of its Object as existent. In many men this background intuition of the Presence of the Divine Being tends to become more or less explicitly conscious, an intuition concomitant upon or causing the will act. This intuition is, however, still indirect, the apprehension of the existence of an unknown Somewhat immanent in external creation or in the soul itself. It is often confused with some creature through whom Its presence has been revealed. Next to the man whose natural bent is religious—who has a religious temperament—the artist and the poet—both are fundamentally one, the media of expression alone being different—enjoy most strongly and most often this sense or intuition of God. But we all have some share of the religious temperament, and most of us some share also of the artistic or poetical temperament. For this reason the master-pieces of religious thought, of poetry and of art, so often seem to us like the realisation of vaguely apprehended potencies in ourselves.

This sense of the Divine presence in its lower and purely natural forms is so common that its reality has been, and is, admitted by many who are far from any faith that could adequately interpret its nature in terms of reason. Even such a stalwart sceptic as Professor Gilbert Murray has to admit its existence ; and is driven to *explain* it as a result of inherited herd-instinct ! (Lecture on Stoicism, concluding pages.) This intuition of the Divine Presence immanent in creatures appears in higher, clearer and more direct forms. Often it is an apprehension of a Presence that far exceeds the creatures wherein It is manifested as im-manent, and is nevertheless not clearly distinguished from them. Hence it is often misinterpreted intellectually in a pantheistic or quasi-pantheistic sense. At other times it is a clearer and a direct intuition of a Being wholly distinct from and infinitely transcendent of creatures, and Who is usually thus apprehended rather in the centre of the soul than in external nature. In this clearer and more transcendent intuition there is present, I believe, a supernatural element, an operation of grace, so that it is indeed the dawn of the truly mystical intuition of God. The lowest, most obscure and purely immanental intuition, on the other hand, I regard as wholly natural. In proportion as the immanental perception becomes a clear consciousness of the Divine Being present in, but other than, nature I am inclined to trace an increasing presence and working of grace—as I trace it, for instance, in much that is often termed nature-mysticism (see Chapter XIV). The progress from purely natural to purely supernatural intuition will thus correspond with the progress from the purely immanental to the clearly transcendental apprehension of God. This progress will be, of course, incapable of accurate determination from the external and empirical standpoint to which we are of necessity confined. Nevertheless there is an absolute distinction. There is a definite point, though we can never fix it, where the supernatural that is Divine grace supervenes on the natural operation of the soul, when a new principle is introduced. In the introduction of this new principle the transition from natural to supernatural differs essentially from the gradual increase and revelation of grace in mystical experience.

A passage of Lucie Christine's *Spiritual Journal*, truly remarkable for its clarity and beauty, describes this gradual rise of intuition from God immanent to God transcendent, from the purely natural level to the purely supernatural level. We have first a purely natural intuition, when her soul was filled with natural beauty in itself, when, as she tells us, " The first glimpse of the sea from the cliffs drew tears from my eyes. I often remained whole hours contemplating its immensity without being able to express what I felt." Then followed a level when the intuition was still that of the nature mystic—the perception of God immanent. But that apprehension was so clear that it surely postulated a co-operative working of supernatural grace. " I sought Thee, my God, in all things beautiful and in all things I found Thee. I asked Thee of the sea . . . Thou wast reposing in its depths . . . I met Thee in the impenetrable gloom of forests. I have felt Thee in the hidden travail of nature." Finally followed a purely supernatural intuition of God transcendent of His creation. " As the stars fade away in the light of the sun, so everything grew pale in the glance of God upon my soul ; *I gazed on sea and land and saw only God*" (*Spiritual Journal*, Eng. Trs., pp. 130-134). [1]

Concomitantly with the intuitional progress is the progress of the will-union which accompanies it, the volitional nisus towards

---

[1] Of course Lucie's soul was throughout in the supernatural order. The intuition was nevertheless simply natural in its earlier stages and could have been possessed by a soul in the order of mere nature. Not so with the higher levels.

God—a progress from a merely natural craving for unlimited good to the supernatural love of God.

I wish now to consider some of the forms of purely natural intuition and corresponding volition of the Unlimited. I will endeavour to point out their incapacity to admit the soul to the fruition of that Unlimited Good that in them is apprehended and desired.[1] When this has been made clear, I will pass on to the life of supernatural grace and show how, through that life of grace, this fruition is truly and fully obtained, a fruition which is manifest to the soul even in this world, in that higher form of the grace-life which is mystical experience. This discussion cannot fail to illuminate the positive relationship or union of the human soul with God—of which mystical experience is the most intimate degree possible on earth and the prelude of the perfect union of heaven.

Before, however, I speak further of the natural intuitions of God and volitions towards Him, that are manifested in the spiritual life of man, I must mention the more usual way by which theism and its consequent will attitude towards God are attained by the normal man who lacks supernatural faith. This is the way of discursive reason, of the rational arguments or proofs of theism. Such is the reasoning of the plain man, who from his knowledge of creatures argues the existence of a Divine Creator. A higher and more complete form of this reasoning is the intellectual or philosophic theism of the student and thinker who is led upward from generalisation to generalisation, till he catches a glimpse of the ultimate Unity. These theistic proofs of the discursive reason serve also to interpret the more obscure intuitions which would otherwise lack definite significance. Without this rational interpretation the lower intuitions would be of scant value. Moreover, whereas God grants the intuition of His Presence to those only Whom He chooses, the proofs of discursive reason lie open to all sane men of good will. The natural theology reached by the scientific or metaphysical ladder of discursive reason is often the precursor and occasion of supernatural faith. For this intellectual or philosophic theism arouses the will to seek union with God, since all knowledge carries with it the possibility of corresponding volition. This volition is often transformed by grace into true charity, as the natural knowledge of God is similarly trans-

---

[1] I will also take occasion to point out this incapacity of all kinds of higher spiritual life other than the religious.

formed into faith. But surely, *despite their sovereign importance,* I need speak no further of this rational knowledge of God and of the will-union arising therefrom. For the matter is amply treated in countless text-books and is obvious to Christian common-sense. Moreover, mysticism has little to do with discursive reasoning. It lies rather in the province of intuition, and to intuition I will therefore return. Of a nature different altogether from those conclusions of discursive reasoning, which it confirms and by whose aid it is itself often interpreted, is the intuition of the Divine Presence wholly or partially natural, which in various degrees of clearness and obscurity is an experience by no means uncommon.

Indeed all true lovers of nature possess some degree of this intuition, if only in its lowest and purely natural form. Perhaps the Divine Presence is less often felt at high noon, in the blazing light and scorching heat of a midsummer day, when the very multiplicity and wealth of natural phenomena and activities fill the soul, though then, indeed, it was that Richard Jefferies felt it most of all. It is perhaps felt least of all in winter, when the vital force of earth is fast bound, as within bars of iron, by cold and barrenness. But there are other moments when we are more intimately in touch with the life of nature. There is the early morning of spring, when the new-risen sun bathes the world with clear and cool light, when the birds are singing, and a soft breeze stirs the young leaves whose green is so exquisitely delicate. The grass is starred with bright flowers, the blue dome of sky is trellised around the borders with interlacing boughs of trees, woodland and hedgerow trees in new leaf, orchard trees bright with the splendour of pale pink and snow-white blossom, a scene such as that imaged by Dante for the earthly paradise. There is a bathe in the sea in the early morning, when the fresh sunlight glows on the white foam of the breaking billows whose energy seems to penetrate the body and fill the soul with the very life of nature, that life which is the luxuriant growth of the vegetation and the strength and swiftness of the untamed beasts of the field. Every detail of the scene is rich with a beauty that is sacramental of something beyond.[1] The white- or brown-sailed fishing-boats put out to sea one after the other and glide swiftly over the blue waters, violet horizoned, beneath a sky of paler and clearer blue

---

[1] Nevertheless on this purely natural level that farther something is still unknown. The sacraments of nature cannot as yet be fruitfully received.

hung richly with white and purple clouds. The subtle grace of their motion and form, their fresh colouring is in perfect harmony with the scene to which they lend that touch of specifically human significance which crowns and points the natural beauty, like a windmill or church spire in a landscape of fields and woodland. At such moments as these the soul is taken back into that primitive world when the entire life of man was in such harmony with Nature that every act, however simple, of human life was a communion with her life, and an expression of that life, and was invested thereby with a mysterious beauty, for it was a symbol of the Spiritual Reality of which Nature is at once a revelation and a veil. In that world of natural poetry Nature seemed sufficient for man, and his awful and irretrievable [1] loss of the supernatural was scarce felt. To that world, the world of Homer and the sagas, does the soul now return. At such moments physical nature is enough, for the soul is filled with beauty and life.

Indeed, Nature is then felt as a mighty aspiration after a life of unlimited fulness, an aspiration which bursts all bonds in a new freedom of unimpeded energy, as a prayer so ecstatic that it seems its own fulfilment. In that aspiration and prayer our heart also is rapt—it becomes our aspiration, our prayer, our hope, our striving and our present satisfaction. But reason intervenes, asking the question wherefore, inquiring the significance and the end of this rapture. Is it simply the life of nature ? Is the object of this prayer, this largely physical activity which passes so swiftly away ? No ; it is not that ; it is an unlimited good, an eternal good—the everlasting satisfaction of our entire being—it is God. It is, however, so far as this natural experience is concerned, the unknown God ignorantly worshipped. The experience cannot answer clearly the questioning of the mind. Ignorant even of its own true nature the intuition, for all its might, can find no way to its enduring fulfilment. On a spring evening, when the softness of the waning light on the fresh green, the pleasant mildness of the air, the delicate fragrance of the flowers and grass fill the soul with peace, it is rather a sense of an infinite presence behind these veils that is ours. Gently, almost passively, we long after an unlimited, all-satisfying Reality whose presence is dimly apprehended. But this gentler yearning is but the aspiration of the morning, mellowed and chastened. The prayer is the same ; the underlying presence vaguely felt is the same. The same presence and the same prayer

---

[1] *I.e.* by man's unaided powers.

are in the sound of the wind among the pines, in the murmur of the waves as they roll shoreward on a summer's day. They are in the light of the moon and stars, reflected in the river on a summer night, when the black leaves are rimmed by a margin of bright silver, when the willows cast strange shadows and the slender shapes of the poplars rise against a background of silver cloud. They are in the brilliant colours of sunset, in its gold, its flame, its emerald and in its rose-bloomed sky. They are in the still, turquoise lake of hyacinths that lies outspread beneath a heaven of chrysoprase, the new-born foliage of the beeches. The prayer, if articulated at all, is articulated as a longing to secure and possess eternally the reality underlying and manifested by these fair forms—an unending life, suggested by the young life of spring, an eternal peace veiled in the peaceful radiance of evening and moonlight—in a word, the God immanent in the becoming of natural life. This reality seems so near at such hours as to be all but in our grasp. We reach out to it. We imagine, perhaps, that it is itself the beauty presented to the senses. But we cannot lay hold on it. It is no visible loveliness. We clutch at phantoms, which vanish from the grasp of the soul as Casella in Purgatory from the hand of the living poet. As the Reality fades from our spiritual vision, keen is our realisation of the vanity and fleetingness of the sensible beauties that revealed to us Its presence. We know that the splendour and the rich life of spring and summer will yield to the barrenness of winter, that the tints will fade from the clouds, that the cherry blossom will die. We know, too, that our power to enjoy these things will soon pass away. A satiety of these sensible images will destroy it, exhausting our limited capacity with the multiplicity of diverse forms. The cares and business of life will snatch us from this contemplation, and before many years are past old age will make the renewed youth of spring and nature a mockery, until death blots it out for ever. Is not this the secret of the Nietzsche tragedy—the attempt to satisfy a longing for the infinite life of the spirit by that lower life of nature which first revealed the presence of the higher, unlimited life? Nietzsche sought to perpetuate the first moment of the Godward aspiration of the human soul—that moment of pure naturalism—with which Greek literature began, but which cannot afford abiding satisfaction to the human heart. This attempt to satisfy his hunger for life eternal and infinite by the life and energy of pure nature, and thus to go back on the spiritual progress of humanity,

H

resulted in a fruitless antagonism alike to the intellectual movement which had rendered this naïve naturalism impossible, and
to that revelation of the true spiritual life which is the essence
of Christianity.   The attempt to find the unlimited life in the
essentially limited life of nature was a self-contradiction.   To
seek the Superman was right, was indeed a spiritual necessity.
Since, however, the true Superman is the supernatural man who
has been raised by grace to partake of the life of God, to seek him
in a glorification of the natural man was to render his attainment
an impossibility.   The outgoing of Nietzsche after the fulness of
life was checked by the barrier which his own naturalistic conception of that life had set up.   The consequent struggle rent his soul
asunder.   This tragedy of Nietzsche is the inevitable tragedy of a
neo-paganism which would turn back to Homer, a world that has
known Dante, to Dionysus, a world that has known Christ.   This
inadequacy of naturalism has been stated with great force, clarity
and beauty by St John of the Cross.   In the fifth and sixth stanzas
of the *Spiritual Canticle* St John shows how creatures can only
point out a God Whom they cannot bestow.   " In the contemplation," he says, " and knowledge of created things the soul beholds such a multiplicity of graces, powers and beauty wherewith
God has endowed them, that they seem to it to be clothed with
admirable beauty and natural virtue, derived and communicated
from the infinite supernatural beauty of the face of God, Whose
beholding of them clothed the heavens and the earth with beauty
and joys.   Hence the soul, wounded with love of that beauty of
the Beloved which it traces in created things, and anxious to behold that beauty which is the source of this visible beauty, sings :

> Oh, who can heal me ?
> Give me perfectly Thyself.
>   Send me no more
>   A messenger
> Who cannot tell me what I wish.

As created beings furnish to the soul traces of the Beloved, and
exhibit the impress of His beauty and magnificence, the love of
the soul increases and consequently the pain of his absence. . .
As it sees that there is no remedy for this pain except in the
personal vision of the Beloved . . . it prays for the fruition o
His presence, saying : " Entertain me no more with any know
ledge or communications or impressions of Thy grandeur, fo
these do but increase my longing and the pain of Thy absence

Thy presence alone can satisfy my will and desire." This fruition lies not in nature—for it infinitely transcends Nature. We cannot apprehend and detain the Reality of which we are vaguely conscious, for it is wholly other than the outward forms that suggest and symbolise it. It is certainly true that the nature mystics have received an experience of God through nature, mystics such as Wordsworth and Richard Jefferies. This was, however, either a purely external apperception of a Reality not inwardly apprehended, or else, as I believe was certainly the case with Richard Jefferies, supernatural grace bore a part in the experience, which was thus raised to the rank of true supernatural mysticism.[1] To those, indeed, who are in a state of grace, and who are seeking God supernaturally in prayer, these passing intuitions of God's immanence in nature are, as it were, the occasion of an inward union with Him by the will union of prayer to which such experiences give rise. Apart from the working of grace, this sense of the Divine immanence only occasions vague and vain longings for an unknown God.

To the artist and the poet the sacramentalism of material nature as a manifestation and symbol of spiritual ideas, and ultimately of some incomprehensible spiritual good, is more apparent than to other men, and it is more deeply realised by them than it is by ordinary lovers of natural beauty. By the exercise of intuitive imagination, termed by Ruskin imagination penetrative, they seize on these inner spiritual realities, and so present their rendering of corporeal forms as to bring out this underlying spiritual and ideal significance. Of the vast multitude of detail, which in the actual phenomena of nature and human life distracts and overcrowds the mind of the observer, they select those features which are suggestive of the particular idea or spiritual reality which they desire to present. Hence the poetic description of a scene, or its pictorial representation, often moves us more strongly than the actual scene described or depicted. We see more in it than we ever did before, enter more deeply into its soul or spiritual significance, and receive suggestions of an infinite spiritual good or Being underlying and unifying all that we see and feel. Thus it is that art in its various forms, as also that unconscious art which constitutes mythology, conveys a higher, though a more indefinable and obscure, truth than is contained in the more definite teaching of physical science. Indeed, it is just

[1] See Chapter XIV.

because the truth of art, of poetry, of mythology is more spiritual, and therefore less limited, than the truth of physical science, that it is less susceptible of exact formulation.   Hence the destruction of a myth, if it be not replaced by some truer presentation of spiritual reality, entails a loss of truth.   Take, for instance, the case of a child taught to believe that the woods and fields around his home are peopled with fairies.   When he grows older that belief is shattered, those woods and fields are henceforth empty of their unseen inhabitants and he no longer feels himself surrounded in his walks abroad by the presence of these kindly and protecting spirits.   Suppose this vanished belief to be replaced, not by knowledge of the immanence of God in nature, and of the presence of the angelic hosts watching over the lives of men—perhaps also guiding the physical forces—but by the mere knowledge of the physical causes, principles and laws which are the subject-matter of natural science.   Such an one has lost truth by the exchange. He has, it is true, discarded a childish error, but with that error he has parted with a fundamental truth of immense significance, the truth that material nature is the habitation and expression of spirit.   His view of the Universe is now confined to its lower and material aspect,[1] that which is least real, because most narrowly limited and consequently most lacking in being.   Suppose that child to become a learned botanist.   He knows less of the trees and flowers now, when he can explain all the physical constituents and forces which have gone to their making, than he did when he believed that the fairies danced in the shade of the trees and watered the flowers with drops of dew.   He can now explain the mechanism of plants, but he has lost the knowledge he once possessed (expressed though it was in an inadequate and therefore erroneous form) of the spiritual reality which is their true soul the ground of their life.   A more extensive and a more accurate understanding of the body is poor compensation for ignorance of the soul.   The botanist's knowledge of chlorophyll and carbon, of the laws of growth and reproduction, and of the classification of orders and genera is abstract and unreal by comparison with that knowledge of the spiritual immanent in physical nature which was contained in the child's belief that the flowers feel and sympathise with its own feeling, and are the dwelling-places of friendly elves or beautiful fairies.   It was for this reason that Our Lord told us that we cannot enter the kingdom of heaven except w

---

[1] Blake's " single vision."

become as little children—that is, unless we return to the child's simple faith and personal apprehension of the spiritual reality underlying, indwelling and operative in the material universe. Our spiritual progress must therefore possess a somewhat circular character from faith through scientific and logical reasoning to a deeper faith, from a personal but narrowly limited apprehension of the spiritual, through theoretical study and practical handling of the material and its impersonal mechanism, to an even more personal but increasingly less limited apprehension of the spiritual. (*Cf.* Baron von Hügel, *Mystical Element of Religion*, vol. i., pp. 60-70.) This cycle is exemplified in the spiritual history of European civilisation. The Greeks began with a childish belief in Divine presences that indwelt the forces of nature. The universe was full of gods, their palace, nay, their very garment. The clear air was the abode of Zeus the All-Father, the sapphire waters of the sea were the realm of Poseidon, and in its waves, crested with white foam and penetrated with the bright sunlight, danced the graceful forms of the sea nymphs. Divine presences dwelt in the cool fountain and in the river swollen with the winter rains. In the green silence of the forest glade might be heard the soft footfall of the dryads, and in the wild passes of the hills the lonely traveller might meet, as did Philipides, the day runner, the awful yet kindly Pan. Such was the world of Homer, and such was still, in great measure, the world of Herodotus.[1] But this inadequate and crude expression of the spiritual was self-doomed, despite its exquisite beauty. It could not endure the light of a more mature reason. The moralist made short work of its immoralities, the natural philosopher discarded its anthropomorphic explanation of physical phenomena. Euripides and Anaxagoras replaced Homer and Hesiod. But the soul of man could not rest there. The new physical and mechanical explanation of reality was less true than the mythology which it had destroyed. It failed to account for just that which is most real and most ultimate in human experience. Hence a spiritualistic reaction was inevitable. Nor was it slow in coming. It began to make itself felt in Orphism and a little later in Socrates,[2] the first

[1] It must not, however, be forgotten that there was another and a very important aspect of Greek religion—that of the Cthonic deities and cults. The aspect emphasised above was pre-eminently the religion of the Achæans.

[2] Professor Burnet (*Greek Philosophy*, vol. i.) seems to establish successfully his thesis that the mystical element in the Platonic dialogues is essentially Socratic. He maintains, moreover, that Socrates was himself an initiate of Orphism.

great mystic of Europe. Though after his death it was checked for some centuries by the materialistic development of secular civilisation, it was never wholly destroyed. It was chiefly kept alive in the Dionysic-Orphic cults and in the mysteries of the more official Hellenic religion. At length the Christian revelation came, with its fulness of spiritual truth, and was received by all that was deepest in the soul of the ancient world. It was no longer loss but gain to disbelieve in nereid and hamadryad, in mighty god and beauteous goddess, when these crude beliefs were replaced by the doctrine of angelic powers at work behind the phenomena of nature, by the knowledge of Jesus, the all-perfect Man Who is also God Almighty, and of His immaculate Mother, so ineffably beautiful in the spotless purity of her soul and in the unimaginable splendour of its physical expression her assumed body, and above and in all these by the knowledge of God—goodness absolute, beauty absolute and truth absolute, present in all His creatures, material and spiritual alike, sustaining them in their being, co-operating in their working and manifesting in and through them His beauty and His truth, His wisdom and His love.

Although the truth of physical science and the truth of art are alike aspects of the Absolute Truth—that is, of God—the latter is the higher, deeper and fuller truth, and therefore far nearer to the Divine Truth and Being, which contains both eminently. We are beginning now to see this. We are coming to learn that the destruction of even the crudest superstition is not gain but loss, unless the spiritual truth conveyed thus crudely and inadequately by that superstition is preserved in a more adequate expression. We are beginning to realise that poetry and symbolism, music and painting, legend and parable contain more truth, tell us more of ultimate reality, bring us into a closer contact with that reality —in a word, give us more knowledge of God than do the exact definitions and clear concepts of mathematics and physical science. Indeed it is only in the light of the spiritual and sacra-mental vision of the universe which is reflected by art, though, as we shall see, adequately given and secured by religion alone, that scientific knowledge can possess its full value. It is only when we realise that all the principles and laws of matter are sacramental of a spiritual reality, are manifestations and operations of spirit, that we appreciate their true significance. As a result of that knowledge science itself becomes assimilated to poetry—no longer confining the soul within the limits of matter, but opening new avenues to knowledge and worship of the Divine Author of the facts and laws, which it is her province to discover and expound. Art, however, always retains her pre-eminence, for her apprehension and presentation of spiritual reality is fuller and more direct, her truth deeper and less limited, and her message is therefore a more adequate vehicle of the Infinite Reality and Truth that is God.

Nevertheless the artist cannot altogether free himself from the limited. He is unable to transcend the material image or symbol in which he must of necessity embody and present the spiritual and apprehend in its purity and immateriality the Divine Idea, underlying that material image, and, through that idea, the infinite Being of God, of Whom even the ultimate spiritual ideas are but aspects. Unless grace unite him to God, his soul is bound fast within the limitations of the corporeal images which he employs and he can never wholly transcend their physical beauty. The necessity for its perpetual mediation between his soul and the Divine Beauty debars him from the fruition of the latter. Art draws aside the curtains that veil the windows of man's sense-limited and self-limited experience. Through the windows thus unveiled by art the artist looks out over the wide spaces of the spiritual universe, bathed in the sunlight of God's creative and sustaining love, and over the storm-tossed waters of the deep and " perilous seas " of his own soul, lit by the soft moonlight of God's secret Presence. But Art is powerless to do more than this. She cannot open those windows so that the soul may go forth in freedom. The will is still imprisoned within the limits of the creature bound with the chain of its natural self-seeking, self-centred and self-impelled activity. So long as the picture is shown, and the music heard, the artist feels himself one with Infinite love, and the universe that It made, a freeman of infinity. The picture is left, the music is still. He goes home and torments his wife because the dinner has been badly cooked. Despite Blake, art is not religion. Not by art can man obtain the fruition of God, for which he was created. Hence is born " the pain that the sight of great beauty brings " (Pearse, *The Singer*).[1]

Blind and barren intuitions of God are also abundantly present in human love, in its passion and its sacrifice. The lower forms of love are, of course, simply instinctive and animal, but I do not

---

[1] Need I say that I am speaking only of the artist *qua* artist, the artist apart from religion. Far from excluding or hindering the effective union of religion, art often prepares the way to its reception.

refer to these.   In the higher forms of love the instinctive and animal elements are felt to be insufficient and are idealised more or less consciously.   The higher the love the greater is the idealisation.   Commonest and most typical is the idealisation of that love which is normally the only absorbing and passionate love in human life, the love of man and woman.   This idealisation is at root the transference to a created object, to a human beloved, of the soul's love of a perfect and by implication of an unlimited Goodness and Beauty, that are realised only in God.   Therefore this idealising love involves a certain intuition of a Perfect Object of Love—a Being Wholly and therefore Unlimitedly lovable.   This outgoing of the soul through the will to a perfect and therefore Absolute Goodness, to the Absolute Beauty is, however, deflected to the narrowly limited goodness and beauty of a fellow-creature.   The wholly lovable, vaguely apprehended is sought in a necessarily imperfect creature.   The Absolute and Altogether lovely Loveliness is sought in the beloved, to whom it is unwarrantably transferred by the lover in the idolatry of his love.   In vain is it sought thus.   The end of this search for the Unlimited in the limited is, of necessity, disillusion and disaster.   For the love of the Infinite cannot be satisfied by aught that is finite.   No created love can fill the boundless craving of the human heart for a love that is boundless.   If indeed the intuition and love of the Unlimited were self-conscious as such, this illicit transference of that intuition and that love to a human being could not be effected.   As, however, it is not thus fully self-conscious, the mistaken transference is made and bears in due season its bitter fruit.   Moreover, the greater the capacity and intensity of love in the lover, the more inadequate is the beloved, however noble and fair, to correspond with it and to satisfy it.   The higher, moreover, the notion or ideal formed by the lover of the Absolute Perfection that he seeks, the greater is his idealisation of the beloved, and the more, therefore, does the beloved fall short of that ideal and disappoint the expectation of the lover.   Truly is it said that love is blind, and blindest is the love of the noblest and deepest hearts.   This is the reason that poets and other artists are usually so unhappy in their loves and marriages.   They are really in love with infinite goodness and beauty.   Though they do not consciously identify absolute and infinite goodness with the goodness of a creature which would be a self-evident absurdity, they do this in practice by directing to the beloved their love of infinite goodness and by investing the beloved with that most lofty and most far-reaching—indeed, potentially limitless—ideal of goodness which they have formed. Ignorant that this is to be found and enjoyed in a personal self-communicating God, they seek it in a creature clothed by their love with perfections that belong only to the Infinite Creator. Of course the essential limits of the beloved soon disillusion them. But they repeat the error and replace the fallen idol by another. This is the profoundest idolatry and therefore the most cruel tragedy of the human heart. Sooner or later, indeed, the lover realises to his cost that human love cannot satisfy the soul's need. Either the beloved proves unworthy, or external circumstances prevent or cut short the fruition of their love. " The lover is unloved. The beloved does not love. The lover who is loved is sooner or later torn from his love." [1] It is in truth only the barrier of opposing circumstances that renders possible any long-continued illusion. Romeo and Juliet could not have remained at their height of idealising passion had not death overtaken them almost immediately.[2] But even then these poets and artists do not perceive the cause of their failure and they ascribe it to the essential tragedy and vanity of human life. Think only of Wagner's *Tristan und Ysolde*. The absolute mutual surrender of the entire being in love which dominates that opera is obviously such as no human being is adequate in himself or herself to inspire and return. The aspiration and need of the lovers for a Beloved wholly and everlastingly lovable, ignorant of its true object, took occasion from physical passion to idolise the object of that passion by its identification with that absolute Goodness and Beauty. In this case the tragedy arose out of the external limitations of circumstance ; but its coming was inevitable. Either the internal limitations of the beloved, or the external limitations imposed by circumstances, satiety or mutability must sooner or later shatter the idol into dust, dissolve the mirage that hid for a moment the desert waste and arouse the dreamer from his fair vision of bliss to a bitter awakening of disillusionment and tears. Hence the universal wail of lamentation that ascends from the pages of literature, that love cannot endure, that it perishes in the very hour of fruition. Why need I quote the poets in proof of this ? To cite innumerable passages would be a useless weariness. For the expression of this

[1] Romain Rolland, *Jean Christophe*, Eng. trs., vol. ii., p. 93.
[2] Compare Ibsen's treatment of " the law of change " in *Little Eyolf*.

sorrow I would but refer to Keats' odes on the Nightingale and the Grecian Urn—particularly to the latter, for its expression of the hopeless longing for eternal possession that dwells in the heart of love's most fervent rapture.   To the operation of this idolatry in actual life there is the eloquent testimony afforded by the life of Shelley.   Having caught a glimpse of " intellectual," that is of spiritual, of divine beauty, he vainly sought to embody it in the woman he loved.   For the inevitable result let us rather pity than condemn.   Dante, on the contrary, being a Catholic, indeed, a mystic, as well as a poet, learnt that no earthly woman can be the adequate embodiment of Perfect Beauty and Worth.   He therefore changed his Beatrice into a symbol of the Christian revelation and its grace, through which our love reaches its true goal.   Hence it is that his great poem, almost alone among the supreme achievements of literature, is not a tragedy of infinite aspiration, thwarted by limits and change, but a Divine Comedy of its eternal satisfaction in God.   Plato, indeed, had already expressed and explained the essential vanity of limited and mutable creatures, and had risen beyond them to the eternal ideas.   Most poets and artists, however, have preferred the lower way, as indeed has the modern age as a whole.   Hence it is that modern life and literature are so sorrowful, so disillusioned, so world-weary.

Neither can altrustic endeavour for the betterment of human life on earth avail to satisfy the soul's need, to provide it with a way of escape from the limits of creatures to the Unlimited, which it has dimly apprehended and for which it obscurely but deeply yearns.   It must, perforce, lack the intensity of individual human love, and like that love is wrecked by limit and its consequent mutability.   Even if these altruistic schemes were to succeed on a large scale—which they can never do in a world where the vast majority are self-seekers—they could not satisfy the soul hunger for the infinite.   Mill, with a fearless honesty deserving of the highest praise, confessed this bitter truth.   To anyone who has in the least felt that hunger for the bread of angels which religion alone can satisfy, the naïve belief of writers like Mr Bernard Shaw in this worldly progress, in socialism, in the universal diffusion of a purely intellectual enlightenment, is at once so pathetic, so ludicrous and so exasperating that the reader scarce knows whether to weep, to laugh or to be angry.   Nor, again, can our need of the unlimited be satisfied by pure ethics without religion. If non-religious morality breaks through some limits, it imposes others far more destructive of the soul's true liberty. It binds the love impulse with the iron chains of a loveless legalism and respectability. It either confines the soul within the limits of purely external duty or imposes a task which it can never perform. The barrier set by this external and legal ethics is often harder to remove than the more superficial and narrower limits of many sins—especially those carnal sins of all kinds, which this legalistic ethic treats as the worst of all, because the most obvious, and therefore the most opposed to external propriety. In reality the Bohemian, "the publican," often possesses a love and aspiration —however perverted and deformed—after infinite Goodness, which is wholly non-existent in the highly respectable Pharisee who condemns him. Modern philosophers and men of letters are apt to reject, even to make mock of, conventional morality. For instance, conventional morality is the object of attack and derision throughout the plays of such typical modern dramatists as Bernard Shaw, Galsworthy and Hankin. Am I, then, a Catholic, in agreement with this "advanced thought"? Do I also desire the destruction of conventional morality? Here a careful distinction is necessary, a distinction whose observance would enable Catholics to answer clearly and effectively the anti-moral teaching of many representatives of modern thought. Conventional morality is an equivocal term by which two distinct things may be understood. It may mean either the moral standard which is maintained by convention or moral practice motived by obedience to convention. In the former sense conventional morality, though grossly inadequate and to a large extent actually false, does indubitably contain a valuable element of ethical truth. To attack conventional morality thus understood is to attack truth as well as falsehood, to root up the wheat together with the tares. Conventional morality, however, when understood in the second sense, is sheer evil, a thing that is intrinsically base and mean, worse in many respects than immorality itself. The modern opponents of conventional morality have confounded the former with the latter in one indiscriminate condemnation. By investing conventional morality in the former sense with the odium justly due to conventional morality in the latter sense, they have confused the issues and won a cheap but empty victory. We therefore must keep clearly before us the distinction which our adversaries ignore. We must maintain strictly the moral standard of Christianity with which the standard of popular morality to some degree—*though but partially*—coincides. On the other hand we must wage unremitting warfare against morality motived by convention, by mere regard for good appearances in the eyes of our neighbours. Such a morality is the bondage of the human soul within extremely narrow limits. It is the positive exclusion of the supernatural, whereby our moral action and life are rendered a way of escape from the limited to the Unlimited, from the human to the Divine. Such respectable morality is therefore the destruction of Divine love. It is a form of the law of dead works opposed to grace, that law from whose bondage we were freed by Christ. For Christians to act morally from a motive of conventional respectability is simply to exchange the freedom of the Gospel, the liberty of the unlimited Godhead with Whom we are united by grace, for the old servitude of the merely natural and creaturely. As Scheeben points out (*Dogmatik*, French translation, vol. iii., p. 537), " the moral ends " of " a creature raised to the dignity of a child of God "—*i.e.* to the supernatural order of grace beyond the limits of nature—" are *quite different* to the moral ends of a mere creature." It follows from this that moral conduct motived by these lower and merely natural ends, and therefore conventional morality in the sense of morality motived by regard to convention, is transcended and abolished by the grace of Christ. The fulfilment of charity, which is a boundless energy, an unlimited fulness of life, not the limited and limiting obedience to the demands of convention and respectability, is the ethical principle of the true Christian, who is thus in the infinity of the former freed from the narrow limits of the latter, limits justly odious to the greater souled and wider minded among the pagans, who, however, are unhappily ignorant of the true way to their removal. But surely I need not labour the point. We have but to read the Epistles of St Paul, remembering that conventional morality— indeed all morality practised from a merely natural motive—of which morality motived by respectability is the most limited and limiting and therefore the lowest species—is the modern representative of the Pauline law. Then we shall fully realise that irreligious morality—above all, the hypocritical sham which is the modern social substitute for lost Christianity—is one of the closest and darkest dungeons wherein the human soul can be confined and debarred from the Divine infinity. For it is, as was said above, more limited and more limiting than many forms of positive sin and therefore more removed from and more opposed to God even than they. From this narrow confinement, from this spiritual dungeon we can be freed and brought into true liberty, not by the moral anarchy of the " emancipated " freethinker, which would be but an exchange of prisons—though an exchange from a narrower to a wider prison-house—but by the grace of God through Christ Our Lord, whereby we are made free of the Infinite and the Eternal in " that freedom in which Christ hath made us free." [1]

It may indeed be that by non-religious ethics is understood a striving after an infinite goodness, in which case it is the worship of the unknown God and is not really secular in character. But truly secular ethics, even in its noblest forms, must, as we have seen, be limited and therefore unable to satisfy the deepest craving of the human heart. This love must be directed to its true end and find its true goal, and no natural means can avail to effect this. No natural experience or activity is therefore able to render the human soul truly happy. It cannot free the soul from the limits of the creature to unite it to the infinite Good, the Creator. In other words, ideals divorced from God and treated as ultimates are thereby transformed into idols. Bernard Shaw, regarding ideals as ends in themselves apart from God, of Whom they are partial aspects and to Whom they are ways, recognises this and becomes an iconoclast (except indeed for the one remaining idol of social democracy). In this attack on ideals he is quite logical. Ultimately and logically a man must regard life from the stand-point of one of two Bernards—of Bernard Shaw, who believes in nothing,[2] or of St Bernard, who believed in God, in nothing apart from God and in everything in and for God, and to the extent in which it reflects God and leads to God. To ascribe absolute value to a creature, however noble, is to make that creature an idol, and sooner or later idols are discovered to be what they are—lifeless caricatures of the living God. If, however, the created ideal be regarded as a reflection of God, and a means to God, it is no longer an idol, but an image, for it is no longer regarded as

---

[1] For this ethical anarchism, while aiming at the transcendence of fixed ethical standards, succeeds in effect but in substituting for them a bondage within the highest desires or loves realised by the individual soul. Since the loves of the majority are selfish, the more limited good of individuals in this life is thus preferred to the wider good of society, and to the unlimited good of the fruition of God.

[2] Again except socialism. This exception is, however, inconsistent with his own point of view. It is arbitrary to overthrow all idols except one. Moreover, by nothing I mean here—nothing of objective value apart from the desire or life impulse of the subject.

something Divine in itself, but as a symbol of the one true God, to Whom it points a way. Against the veneration of images there is no sound objection, but idolatry stands self-condemned. The superficial resemblance between the two is great, but the reality is poles asunder.

It is not, of course, meant that all natural experiences and activities are equally remote from God, equally limited. Indeed, this is obviously untrue. The less limited their scope and object, and the more interior and spiritual the psychical operations involved, the nearer do they approach to God, and the more of His Being they represent and mediate. Indeed in the higher activities discussed above there is often present, as we have seen, the intuition of an unknown God and an aspiration towards Him. But all are ineffectual and ultimately unsatisfactory. For the limit is always there, the centre of the soul is never fully actuated and the intuition of an infinite reality is but a passing glimpse of an unattainable good.

The will, indeed, always preserves its intrinsic capacity for the apprehension of an infinite good—that is, of God, because this is essentially consequent on the possession of a rational spirit. Nevertheless this potential capacity can never be actualised in the natural condition of fallen men—that is, in the purely natural man not elevated by sanctifying grace. The lower functions of the embodied soul—dependent as it is for knowledge on the essentially limited data of sense—bind the spirit within the limits of the creature and drag down the will on its upward course to God.[1] Before the fall, as was pointed out earlier in this chapter, this was remedied by a supernatural quality in man, superadded to his natural gifts (the *donum superadditum*), whereby his will was so united to God that he was enabled to adhere to God and to be united to Him with his entire being, and that with a consciousness of his union.[2] The lower sense-conditioned knowledge and the lower desires were in complete subordination to this supreme activity of unitive love. This superadded quality was sanctifying grace, whose end is perfect union with God and full fruition of God in the beatific vision and the participation of the proper activity

---

[1] It is also true that even a disembodied spirit is naturally incapable of sharing the life of God or of possessing the beatific vision. Such a spirit would, however, naturally possess (except for the consequences of sin) a very high fruition of God.

[2] I presume that in the sinless soul of unfallen man the grace union with God amounted to the mystical union and was therefore conscious.

of God Himself. It has, however, pleased the infinite mercy of God to restore this sanctifying grace to vast numbers of the human race. The solidarity of mankind indeed entailed the common participation of all in its loss. This was, however, remedied by Our Lord's Incarnation and Redeeming death, which substituted among His members a new solidarity with Himself, for that solidarity with Adam, which was the ground of original sin. Through this solidarity we partake of His Spirit through the possession of sanctifying grace. As we have seen already, God is always substantially immanent in the soul and present in special manner to the centre. But the barrier of the soul's natural and sense-conditioned activities—indeed, the essential limitation of its creatureliness—prevented the fruition of that Presence. This fundamental limitation has been, however, destroyed by sanctifying grace. Thus the supreme barrier between the soul and God, indestructible by natural means, has been removed, so that, as long as the soul remains in grace and its concomitant charity its ultimate fruition of God and union with Him is secure. The possession of this restored grace has united to God by supernatural charity the ultimate and most fundamental will, and through that will the central ego or ground. In virtue of this new relationship and special union with God of the central self, God indwells or inhabits the soul after a peculiarly intimate manner, in which He does not and cannot inhabit souls in the natural order whose central selves are bound fast within the limits of their creatureliness, and in the almost inevitably consequent limits of a will actually averse from God.[1]

But the work of union is only begun, the Divine indwelling is still largely potential. The radical healing of the will and its radical union with God release indeed the soul from irremediable bondage to the limited, so that the limits of its love of creatures and occupation with creatures, above all, of its essential limitation as a created being, which is the ground of all other limits, are no longer an insurmountable barrier between it and God, debarring it wholly from supernatural will-union with Him and rendering the complete union, which is the true end of man, an intrinsic impossibility. Nevertheless, the soul is still actually occupied for the most part with the finite creature. Its activities are

---

[1] Still there may be, and doubtless are, souls in a state of pure nature whose will is united to God as far as is consistent with the limits of a creature not elevated to the supernatural union.

extremely external and limited, being still for the most part sensible or sense-conditioned. Its life is superficial. The soul has not turned its operations and its gaze inwards to the higher faculties and their centre, where it is united to God immanent. Moreover, the mainspring of its actions is still some limited end, usually selfish—that is, something more limited than its Divine End—the immediate pleasure of self as an independent entity, or something referred to that self as its end. All that habitual grace and charity have done is to subordinate these superficial and selfish volitions and occupations to a radical determination of the will not to defy and lose God by mortal sin in order to gratify them. Far other is the goal to be reached—the perfection to which the soul is called. Its gaze is to be wholly fixed on God—recollected in Him from the view of creatures *except* as seen in Him as manifestations and participations of His Being. It is thus to be, in Father Baker's phrase, wholly introverted. The will is to be so intimately united with God that it wills nothing except for His sake and because He moves it to that volition. It is true that each soul is called to a different degree of union in this sense, that the capacity of vision and will-union differs in every case, but that capacity, be it great or small, is to be wholly occupied by God and by creatures only as in and for Him. This goal is, of course, only attained fully in the beatific vision. Mystic union is a stage on the way—a stage in which, *at its highest perfection*, the perfect will-union is in substance already accomplished, and there is a veiled (not an open) constant or quasi-constant intuition of God's presence.[1]

Mystical union is essentially a high degree of sanctifying grace, involving its correspondingly elevated operation of actual grace, which degree and operation are normally manifested to the consciousness of their possessor, the grace being the mystical union, its conscious manifestation the concomitant intuition. As we shall see hereafter, mystical experience may be divided into transient operations and habitual states. The latter are high degrees and manifestations of habitual or sanctifying grace, the former correspondingly elevated operations of actual grace. The loftiest form of mystical experience, the transforming union essentially consists of habit and act. The habit of this union is

---

[1] This is the nature of the transforming union, the highest degree of mystical experience. The further discussion and explanation of this, as described by St John of the Cross and the interpreting treatises of Mother Cecilia, will be given later.

thus habitual grace in its fullest and highest earthly manifestation before it passes into glory at death, its act, the operation of that supreme degree of habitual grace, is the supreme operation of actual grace. Mystical experience is thus an essential constituent of the economy of grace as revealed to us in the Bible and in the teaching of the Church, an economy which may be summarised as a progress of grace through mystical union to glory.[1] *The way from sanctifying grace to beatific glory is one continuous road of increasing supernatural union* between the soul and God. Glory, the *lumen gloriæ*, as it is termed in theology, is thus but sanctifying grace in its fully unfolded flower—sanctifying grace the germinating seed of the *lumen gloriæ*. The Mystical union-intuition in its various degrees is the foliage and finally the opening bud of the same plant.[2]

In stanza 23 of the *Spiritual Canticle*, St John says : " It is not the betrothal of the Cross that I am speaking of now—that takes place, once for all, when God gives the first grace to every soul in baptism, I am speaking of the betrothal in the way of perfection, it is a progressive work. And *though both are but one* yet there is a difference between them. The latter is effected in the way of the soul and therefore slowly, the former in the way of God and therefore at once." Here St John teaches the essential unity of the way of grace. Only the first step, he says, is wholly God's work—to which we can contribute nothing— for God places us in the state of grace without any previous merit on our part. The perfection, however, of the supernatural work, begun without our co-operation, requires our co-operation, and is, therefore, a gradual process. Of this gradual process the mystical intuition-union is an essential part—a necessary stage of the supernatural growth of the soul, or, to speak more accurately, the union is so—for the conscious element of the union, the intuition, may perhaps in certain instances be dispensed with.[3] We have seen that the central depths of the soul with the roots of her spiritual functions are normally subliminal. Subliminal also is the ordinary supernatural union of the central ego and its radical functions with God through sanctifying grace. The ordinary soul in a state of grace has no direct consciousness of the special

[1] *Cf.* Scheeben, *Dogmatik*, French trs., vol. iii., p. 542.

[2] For the essential continuity of grace and glory see Fr. Terrien, *La Grace et a Gloire*, vol. i., pp. 99-101.

[3] *I.e.* By a special dispensation the mystic union would remain entirely subliminal—as are the earlier stages of the union of sanctifying grace.

I

union with God thus constituted.[1]   Only at a certain stage of this grace-union does the Divine Presence and Operation in the central depths emerge with and through these into consciousness.   The process of grace-union in the mystics is therefore from ordinary subliminal grace-union, through the conscious union-intuition of mystical experience—to the beatific union and open vision of heaven.   In the case of ordinary souls—that is, of the vast majority —the second stage is absent, and is replaced by purgatory.

There is thus but one and the same way by which all the saved must reach the fulness of Divine Union, one and the same progressive union of love through the operation of one and the same indwelling Spirit, a union which when it has reached a certain stage is the mystical union, normally revealed to consciousness in mystical intuition.   The superficial diversity between the spiritual experience of different souls only emphasises the underlying unity of the path to God.   The general principles of the way from ordinary grace to glory through mystical union or purgatory are identical for every soul that shall be saved. Far greater is the fundamental identity of the way of grace in the case of those who enjoy on earth mystical union.   For all the mystics the chief stages or degrees of the Godward ascent are the same.   There is but one summit to which the diverse ways of the spirit lead, and they pass through the same zones.   Though the mount of perfection may be climbed in this life by innumerable paths, they all begin in the tropical zone of vocal prayer and sensible sweetness, pass on through the temperate zone wherein lie the quiet pastures of affective prayer,[2] traverse the shady forest of infused contemplation, simple, loving and obscure, wind upwards across the barren soil and among the stern crags of the mystical desolation, until they reach finally the summit, clad in the perpetual snow of absolute purity, where there is nothing to impede the traveller's vision of the boundless firmament of the Triune Godhead.

But I feel that the reader must be rushing forward with objections—objections which are, I think, reducible to two—a

---

[1] Even the mystic below the final union of spiritual marriage, though conscious of the Divine union through grace, cannot be more than morally certain that he is in a state of grace, for the experience might be a purely transitory union effected, so to speak, from without by actual grace alone.   Still he is morally sure that it is more than this.

[2] Usually this prayer is reached by way of discursive meditation.   This may however, be replaced by a more affective continuance of vocal prayer.

lesser and a greater. I will take the lesser first. It may be urged that there is no uniform road to the Divine union. Are not all souls different ? Do not the various stages of prayer occur in varying order ? Did not, for example, St Teresa experience the prayer of quiet at the very commencement of her religious life, before she had yet acquired the habit of meditation ? But I have already admitted this obvious diversity of spiritual life between soul and soul. St John of the Cross fully recognises that every soul is led by a different path. " Devout souls," he tells us, " run in many ways and in various directions, each according to the spirit which God bestows, and the vocation which He has given, in the diversified forms of spiritual service on the road of everlasting life, which is evangelical perfection, where they meet the Beloved in the union of love, after spiritual detachment from all things " (*Spiritual Canticle*, st. 25). Indeed, in *The Living Flame of Love*, he even says : " God raises every soul by different paths. Scarcely shall you find one soul that in half its way agrees with that of another " (*Living Flame*, st. 3, § 12). This variety, however, does not involve a fundamental divergency. The many ways lie along one " road of evangelical perfection " ; the road of " spiritual detachment " and consequent " union of love." There may be many paths by which a peak in the Andes may be climbed—yet all will lead from zone to zone in due order—from the tropical zone of the valley to the Arctic zone of perpetual snow. That the zones of the spiritual ascent are not entered and left at the same point does not invalidate this fundamental principle. All paths up a mountain do not ascend as high in an equal distance. If the path is steep, the ascent is very rapid. If it winds much, or lies along a gradual slope, it takes a long journey to ascend an equal height. Natural temperament enables some souls to follow God's grace by a more direct way to contemplation, or to fuller union, than that taken by others whose radical will is as good as, perhaps better than, their own. Some souls have fewer obstacles than others to overcome and can reach full union with a lesser degree of passive purgation, or after a shorter stay in all or certain of the intermediate stages of the way, than is necessary for other souls. Moreover the zones of the spiritual life are no more sharply severed than are the zones of the mountain ascent. One zone passes gradually, often imperceptibly, into another. The zones are not regularly marked off at certain altitudes, as if drawn by compasses. At particular places, owing to some local accident, one zone may push into another and continue at an altitude chiefly occupied by a higher zone, or a higher zone may occur at an altitude chiefly occupied by a lower zone. If his path lie in that direction, the traveller's stay in a particular zone is unusually long or unusually short. So is it with the degrees of mystical prayer union. Moreover, in the spiritual life, God the all-powerful dispenser of His graces may, by anticipation, raise a soul temporarily into a higher zone of mystical intuition or contemplation than corresponds with its degree of will-union. In other words, a peculiar actual grace places the soul, so to speak, externally, above its state of sanctifying grace. This would seem to have been the case with St Teresa's first prayer of quiet. Such also I believe to be the explanation of the special illuminations, occasionally even ecstasies, that often accompany the first entrance into the mystical way, graces of prayer far in excess of the soul's degree of grace-union. We must also bear in mind that the souls in heaven do not possess equal degrees of glory, because their sanctifying grace is unequal. It follows, therefore, that grace does not become openly manifest as beatific glory at one and the same degree in all souls—unlike, e.g., water which always boils at one and the same degree of heat and barometric pressure. But it follows from this that the veiled manifestation of the life of grace, which is mystical experience, does not presuppose an identical degree of sanctifying grace, in all who first receive this experience. In other words, union does not become conscious as intuition at one and the same degree in every soul. The occurrence of mystical experience, though not arbitrary, but the manifestation of grace in a particular soul at a particular degree, presupposes different degrees of grace in different souls. It is like the line of perpetual snow which occurs at different altitudes in different climates.

Now, however, I have to face the greater difficulty, a difficulty divided into two heads. Have not souls reached the perfection of canonised sanctity without mystical graces ? Are not the majority of souls who are saved, saved without passing through the stages of the mystical union ? How then can it be maintained that these stages of mystical union are the necessary path of sanctifying grace on its way to glory ; the one way by which all must reach the beatific vision ? To the second objection I am but partially open. For I confined the progressive order of zones to the ascent of perfection in this life. When perfection is not

attained in this life the zones of prayer union omitted on earth
are not simply supplied beyond the grave. They are indeed
traversed after death in the substance of their progressive will-
union and progressive detachment from the limits of the creature.
This substantial identity is, however, presented under a diverse
form. The same work is effected by partially different means.
Nevertheless, I do maintain the substantial identity of the way
of perfection whether in this life or in the next, the one indispensable ascent from the hidden life of sanctifying grace through
the mystic purgation and union, ever substantially the same, to
the beatific vision. In so far, however, as I am thus open to the
objection that salvation is attained by the majority of the saved
without the mystical union, I have already answered that objection
by saying that purgatory is the equivalent of that union. For
purgatory is essentially the mystical purification of the will from
adherence to the finite, which with the mystics takes place more
or less perfectly in this life in certain negative stages of the mystical union. It is, indeed, true that sanctifying grace does not
positively increase by the post-mortem purification, as it does in
the purification of this life. Therefore it is that souls who have
had their purgatory here possess a higher degree of sanctifying
grace and, therefore, of heavenly glory, than those purged after
death, where there is no more temptation and therefore no more
merit. But the purification itself is essentially the same.[1] How
this is the case I will discuss at length when I speak in detail of
the nights of the soul. Moreover, the supreme degree of mystic
union, the spiritual marriage, is, as we shall see, but a foretaste
on earth of the beatific vision, and to the overwhelming majority,
including the majority of mystics, who have never reached it,
it is given eminently in that vision. Thus must all who are saved
tread the mystic way to union, the few here, the many hereafter.
The mystics are but the advance guard of the army of the elect.
They are the spies who have gone on ahead and entered before
death the promised land, to report somewhat of its bliss to their
fellow-travellers in the desert. For proof of their journey and
vision they bring us back a cluster of grapes such as never grew
in the vineyards of Egypt.

[1] To avoid misunderstanding I would point out that both death itself and the
vision of God in the particular judgment must be regarded as essential elements
of purgatory if it be thus identified with the mystical purgatory of earth.

[2] See Chapter XI., *passim*.

A certain modification of this statement is clearly required in the case of baptized infants, indeed of all who have not attained before death the *full* use of reason.   These souls are not at all, or but little, bound by the limits of a will-activity deliberately anti-supernatural and self-principled, averse from God and unduly converted to creatures.   This however it is that requires the painful purgation.   Therefore none or little purgation of this kind must be endured by such souls after death.   Must we therefore conclude that the mystic way, in its character of a gradual removal of limits, will be wanting.   Does a baby behold God's open vision the moment it passes from this life ?   I should myself be inclined to conjecture that such a soul will be exalted to that vision without pain, by a gradual unveiling of God with a concomitant removal of limits, attaining, for example, the knowledge and vision of Christ in His humanity before passing on to the vision of the Unlimited Godhead and to the unlimited life in Him.   If this be the case, my principle will hold good even of these souls although in a greatly modified form.   I confine myself, however, in this discussion to the case of adult souls enjoying the complete use of reason and speak solely of these, whose psychology is in some degree open to our understanding.

Since the mystic experience and way is thus a manifestation in this life of the principles which determine and constitute the condition of the saved after death, the study of mysticism should be of engrossing interest to every Christian soul.   Since life is so short and death so certain, we cannot but long for some knowledge of the life to come, beyond the bare statement of the revealed truth.   Or rather, we cannot but desire to attach some fuller and more concrete significance to the brief eschatological definitions of the Church.   We cannot take at its surface value the corporeal imagery of Scripture and religious art.   In fact, the educated modern Catholic finds this imagery far less helpful than his forefathers seem to have found it.   The conventional pictures of purgatory as a crowd of nude persons in a blast furnace, and of heaven as an assembly of white-robed persons seated on clouds and engaged in a perpetual sacred concert,[1] though consecrated by

---

[1] I do not mean to mock at these pictures, as artistic symbols, if they are depicted in sufficiently good taste, which indeed they never are in modern religious art, but only to consider their appearance to one who is not quite sure how far the Church intends them as a true representation of purgatory and heaven, and who, regarding the m as such, is justly irritated and amused.

traditional symbolism, are altogether inadequate for our meditation. In fact such picturing, if taken seriously, is in danger of causing a sense of unreality, and hence a feeling, if no more, of scepticism in regard to the life beyond the grave. Nothing is more helpful to rid us of such feelings than the knowledge that purgatory and heaven, especially the former, are not states wholly without analogue in this life. To know, for example, that St Catherine of Genoa while living and working in our human body, eating, drinking, sleeping and tending the sick, in a particular city many of us have seen, at a particular epoch of history of which all may read in the most prosaic history, experienced in its essential character the state of purgatory, and that St Teresa, also a human, indeed a very human, person, living in a Spanish convent about a century later, by entering into the mystical marriage, enjoyed, under a veil, that eternal union and fruition of God, which, unveiled, is heaven—renders purgatory and heaven realities, as they could never have been before.

The objector, however, will now fall back on the first part of the greater objection and will say : " According to you every canonised saint must have reached in this life the state of mystical marriage, that supreme state of union which you say follows the endurance of purgatory on earth. How then is it that there have been canonised saints who never enjoyed mystical prayer at all ? " Père Poulain, in his important text-book of mystical theology, *Les Graces d'Oraison*, maintains that almost all the canonised saints—apart from the martyrs—enjoyed mystical prayer, and in this judgment he follows Pope Benedict XIV. He also proves that this was so in the case of certain saints whose prayer is popularly supposed to have been ordinary. Therefore I should myself conclude from this weight of historical evidence that there is nothing to disprove the essentiality and the necessity of mystical union. Hence these saints whose inner life is unknown may be presumed also to have been mystics, and thus all canonised saints other than martyrs have been mystics. As for the martyrs, who have not previously attained heroic sanctity, was not their martyrdom itself their self-destroying purgation, especially if it was accompanied or preluded by interior desolation ? Moreover we may suspect that in a great many cases the martyrs, having once sacrificed themselves wholly for God by offering themselves to die, and having thus entirely detached their will from the limited, received in return the mystical

union intuition of God.   If the life of any saint in the calendar
might seem to have been active rather than contemplative, full
of reasoning and images, and thus very unmystical indeed, it would
be the life of Blessed Thomas More.   Yet he in early life had a
great longing—which never entirely left him—for the Carthusian
life, and when imprisoned in the solitary confinement of the Tower
he told his daughter : " Methinketh God maketh me a wanton
[*i.e.* a spoiled child] and setteth me on His lap and dandleth me "
(Bridgett, *Life of Sir T. More*, p. 367).   If this saying be not an
allusion to mystical experience, I do not know what it can mean.
Nevertheless it cannot be plausibly maintained that all the saints
have passed through the full purgation of the second night and
reached mystical marriage.   To this difficulty I reply with a
question.   Did all the canonised saints reach heaven directly
without any passage through purgatory ?   We know by the
infallible teaching of the Church that when beatified they are
already in heaven.   Can we say more than that ?   Certainly
St Ambrose held that every soul passes through a purgatorial fire
before entering heaven,[1] and although we cannot adopt this
extreme position, we may, I think, hold it true of saints who have
not in this life passed through the second night.

Neither need we be disturbed by the statement in the seventh
colloquy of *The Thorns of the Spirit*, a treatise written possibly
by St John of the Cross himself, that some souls are led all their
life long to God by vocal prayer and through vocal prayer attain
perfection and will-union.   For I gather from the context that
such vocal prayer is so full of aspirations as to be in truth a form
of affective prayer, a simple contemplation.   In fact, their vocal
prayer becomes in the end a vehicle of mystical prayer-union.
It is a question here of the machinery rather than of the substance
of prayer.

There is every reason to believe that those souls alone whom
God will raise to a high degree of beatific glory are effectively
called to perfection here on earth.   Countless souls have grace to
see and reject fully deliberate sins, who are left without light in a
life full of imperfections, to be purged hereafter.   Such will reach
their lower goal in the end, and were never intended for a higher
one.   The only real evil and loss is the deliberate refusal to corre-

[1] Père Tixeront, *Histoire des Dogmes*, vol. ii., p. 345.   Saint Ambrose, however,
seems to have admitted in another place that certain perfect souls would find in
this fire refreshment rather than pain.

spond with light given, grace received, perfection proposed. Even among those called to aim at perfection, there is an indefinite difference of degree according to the capacity of each. Of these latter St John of the Cross (*The Ascent of Mount Carmel*, Bk. II., chap. v.) says : " Though certain souls in this life enjoy equal peace and tranquillity in their state of perfection, everyone being satisfied, nevertheless some of them may be more advanced than the rest, in a higher degree of union, and yet all equally satisfied because their capacity is satisfied. But that soul which does not attain to that degree of purity corresponding with its capacity (which I take to mean the complete abandonment of its will to do the will of God as far as it perceives that will) will never attain true peace and contentment." In the opening chapter of Book II. of *The Obscure Night*, St John speaks of a proportion between the purgation of the soul and the degree of love (will-union) to which it is to be raised. Whether in his opinion souls raised to inferior degrees of love will have a further purgatory to undergo after death is not clear. I should be inclined to the view that however low a degree of glory be predestined to any soul, if that soul wholly submits its will to God's known will without *voluntary* imperfection, its purgation is complete. It is ready to be filled by God according to its utmost capacity, however scant. Such a constant obedience to the Divine will would, however, involve an earthly purgatory of detachment, and thus the mystical purgation, at least in a milder form. It would also leave that soul at death in achieved perfection—in fact, a saint, however unsuited for canonisation. Souls, however, who have not seriously aimed at perfection, though perhaps they never received a call to it, and are therefore exculpated by ignorance, must in reality fall constantly into voluntary resistance to God's known will in matters not commanded under pain of grave sin. Such souls would require a purgatory after death.[1]

We must observe also that the essential matter is not the conscious fruition of mystical marriage but the completion of the purgation, the perfect detachment of the will from limits by union with the Unlimited Godhead. The proposition which I maintain amounts, therefore, to this, that before a soul enters heaven it must have passed through a complete purgation from all selfish attachment to the finite, to creatures—a proposition which, far from being doubtful, is of faith. This complete purgation involves,

[1] For a further discussion, see Chapter XI.

however, either a purgatorial detachment and desolation on earth or a martyrdom such that it is its equivalent, or an equivalent purgatory after death.   But this earthly purgation is, as we shall see, a mystical state—a special manifestation of grace at a certain stage on the way to glory.   In it, however, the soul is not directly conscious of the Presence and Action of God.   Were it otherwise there would be no purgation.   Therefore it is clear that the essential and indispensable element of mystical union, as the way to beatific vision, is not the consciousness of God as the object of union but the union itself.   This union, when it reaches a certain stage, is usually conscious when fully actualised, although not directly so in the desolations.   Therefore the normal order, I should be inclined to think, the universal order, is that no soul reaches the second night or the full mystic purgatory without previous conscious union with God in the lower stages of mystical prayer.   This consciousness, however, is not the essential part of the mystical union and, even if He has not actually done so, God could dispense with it.   However this may be, we must be quite clear that the psycho-physical phenomena normally attendant on the earlier stages of mystical prayer are in no sense essential, and may indeed be completely absent.   As for visions and revelations, these, as we shall see, constitute no intrinsic part whatever of the mystical union.   They are purely adventitious graces, either given for the benefit of others or, as it were, ornamental concomitants of the mystical prayer-union itself.   But the gradually increasing will-union supernaturally infused, with its correspondent decrease and destruction of will attachment to the finite, is the one intrinsically necessary road to the beatific vision in every soul that is saved.   As the limits of our natural and selfish attachments and activities are progressively destroyed by the process of purgation, the Divine Action in the soul and God's indwelling Presence in and through that Action increases with the increase of sanctifying grace whose function it is to remove the limits of nature and sin and so to unite the soul in special union with God.   Thus does the Action of God in the soul through grace increase and the natural self-principled activity of the soul proportionately decrease.   When this process is completed and all limits have been destroyed, God through grace wholly possesses and moves the soul.   When the soul is thus wholly possessed and moved by God, the purgation is ended and the beatific vision is reached, or at least its earthly foretaste, the mystical marriage.

Mystical union (involving normally the consciousness of it) is therefore not an extraordinary grace beside the ordinary way to God, but an essential stage of that way. The only extraordinary characteristic of this mystical union and concomitant purgation is that it is given in this life, instead of in the next, when the vast majority of the elect will attain to it. A progressive supernatural union with God, begun in the first regeneration to the life of grace,[1] continued in the growth of that supernatural life, a growth hidden at first, later made manifest in mystical purgation and union, whether here in this life or beyond the grave, completed at last in the beatific vision of heaven—this is the common substance of the Christian life and of the mystic way, the fundamental principle, alike of Christianity [2] and of mysticism.

[1] Normally effected in baptism.

[2] Equally fundamental to Christianity is, of course, the accomplishment of this grace-union by incorporation into the mystical body of Christ the Incarnate Word of God, an incorporation effected by the indwelling of His Holy Spirit.

CHAPTER VI

VIEWS OF THE MYSTIC WAY

Twelve Aspects or Characters of the Mystic Way

(1) *Emancipation from Limits.*—I ascend to my Father and to your Father, to my God and to your God. I will come again and will receive you to myself that where I am you also may be.

(2) *Conversion from Creatures to God.*—Every one that hath left house or brethren or sisters or father or mother or lands for my name's sake shall receive a hundredfold and life everlasting. Blessed are the poor in spirit : for theirs is the kingdom of heaven.

(3) *Introversion.*—When thou shalt pray, having shut the door, pray to thy Father in secret. The kingdom of God is within you.

(4) *Detachment from Self.*—If any man will come after me, let him deny himself. For he that will save his life shall lose it, and he that will lose his life for my sake shall find it.

(5) *Conversion from Matter to Spirit.*—That which is born of the flesh is flesh : and that which is born of the Spirit is spirit. The hour cometh, and now is, when the true adorers shall adore the Father in spirit. God is a spirit, and they that adore him, must adore him in spirit.

(6) *Increase of Delicacy or Subtlety.*—Be ye wise as serpents and simple as doves. Blessed are the eyes that see the things that you see. Think not that I am come to destroy the law or the prophets ; I am not come to destroy but to fulfil. For I tell you that unless your justice exceed that of the scribes, you shall not enter into the kingdom of heaven.

(7) *Liberation.*—You shall know the truth and the truth shall make you free. The Spirit breatheth where he will. So is everyone born of the Spirit.

(8) *Unification.*—Martha, Martha, thou art careful and art troubled about many things. But one thing is necessary.

(9) *Purification.*—Blessed are the clean of heart for they shall see God. Now, you are clean by reason of the word that I have spoken to you.

(10) *The Attainment of Peace.*—Peace I leave with you, My peace I give unto you. Take my yoke upon you and learn of me and you shall find rest to your souls.

(11) *Will Identification with the Will of God.*—I came not to do my own will but the will of him that sent me. Thy will be done on earth as it is in heaven. Not as I will but as Thou wilt.

(12) *Progressive Attainment of Reality.*—Not by bread alone man lives. Labour not for the meat that perisheth, but for that which endureth unto life everlasting. I am the bread of life. Give us this day our daily bread.

The ever-increasing and in its later stages more or less conscious will-union with God affected positively by the increase of sanctifying grace and negatively by the gradual destruction of all limits within which the will and understanding are by their natural operation bound, the soul's escape " from every limit of nature and reason " [1] in its union with the Unlimited Godhead, may, as I remarked at the outset of this book, be regarded from various points of view. A few of these general aspects I will now discuss before dealing in detail with the chief stages of the mystic way as explained by St John of the Cross.

(1) *Emancipation from Limits.*

All the various aspects of the mystical way are grounded in its fundamental character as the way from the limited to the unlimited or infinite, a gradual emancipation from limits. Each separate aspect is simply an aspect or result of that escape from the limited to the unlimited. That fundamental character has already been discussed. We have seen how the soul of man by its reason and rationally directed will has a natural capacity for the infinite, even a certain need of the infinite and consequent aspiration thereafter.[2] This capacity was fulfilled by his first supernatural union with God, an elevation which *more* than satisfied the natural need and aspiration of the soul. Sin and its results have, however, confined man within the limits of creatures—as the ends of his will and the conditions of his understanding. These limits must be and by grace are, and by grace alone can be, transcended. Thus the life of grace is a gradual

---

[1] *Ascent of Mount Carmel*, Book II., Introductory Chapter.
[2] It has an exigency for a certain union with and knowledge of the Infinite God, though not for the beatific vision and union.

escape from limits. Hence the mystical union-intuition in which that life issues is this emancipation in an enormously higher degree. This freedom from limits by full union with the Unlimited is often spoken of by St John and Mother Cecilia as an immensity.

But a difficulty must now be faced. It will be asked : " Is not such a progress essentially impossible to the created soul of man ? How can a creature which is as such essentially limited escape all limits ? " The answer is that man's reason and rational will enable him to apprehend the existence of an unlimited good, and to strive after its attainment. The centre essentially possessed of this direction towards, and capacity for unlimited good, is thereby in an especial sense grounded in the Divine Being. This capacity and the grounding in God that is its cause endows the soul with a certain potential infinity. " The heart," says Mother Cecilia, " by which I mean the root of the will or the essence of the soul was created by God in His image and likeness. It possesses in consequence an immensity so profound that it is like a sea or bottomless well, wherein the deeper we plunge the less do we find bottom, and this immensity is due to the fact that the soul is grounded and lives in the very life and essence of its Creator " (*Transformation of Soul*, st. 1). " The soul, though clothed in a veil of miserable, mortal flesh, possesses in itself an immense centre, containing infinite riches and glory. In this divine centre we are like God and nothing can fully satisfy it save God Himself " (*Transformation*, st. 4). This centre is, as we have already seen, the root of the will and it is as such that it is thus unlimited. " The will," says the writer of *The Obscure Knowledge of God*, " goes out of itself and is transformed into the object of its love, so as to become one thing with that object, and therefore it does not limit that object " (chap. x). St John of the Cross speaks of this potential infinity of the soul when he says, in *The Living Flame*, st. 3 : " The capacity of these caverns "—the powers of the soul—" is profound because the object of which they are capable, namely God, is profound and infinite. Hence the capacity of the soul is, in a certain sense, infinite, and its hunger profound and infinite." When the union with God is complete, the soul is at once finite and infinite. " God," says Mother Cecilia, " has willed to communicate His Divine Being in such wise that His creatures are able to receive Him without limit, though not with the measure of His immensity as He knows it in Himself alone." " Blessed is the soul that possesses in itself the immensity of God through participation and union with Him." Though still indeed finite in its own essence, it is infinite in its eternal participation of the Unlimited, in its union with God. It is like a vessel closed at the bottom and sides, open at the top. Finite in itself, in its union with God and apprehension of God it is infinite. This mystery, this seeming paradox, is strictly parallel with the paradox that the soul created in time should be able to participate in eternity, and both paradoxes spring from the ultimate mystery of the co-existence of the creature with the Creator, of the finite with the infinite, of time with eternity, of the relative with the absolute. Any attempt to solve the mystery to the conceptual reason involves the rejection of one of its component elements, a solution that denies one of the factors of the problem to be solved. As we cannot comprehend God, neither can we comprehend this mystery. We can, however, have an intuitive perception of the two co-existent elements in the life of the soul, the finite and the infinite, the temporal and the eternal, and to reject this immediate perception because we cannot state it with entire conceptual intelligibility would be folly. Those therefore who possess mystic union or beatific vision are free from all limits and thus are infinite, while ever remaining in their essential finitude as creatures, because while remaining creatures they are united with God in the most intimate union and thus participate in His Unlimited Being. Moreover, the finite activities of the blessed, while still existing, and even the activities arising out of the Resurrection body, will, though limited, be no longer limiting, for they will be but an appanage and instrument of the unlimited Divine life, of which the blessed to the utmost measure of their capacity partake. This emancipation of the soul, from limits by the reception of the Infinite Being of God, constitutes the mystic way, whose goal is its perfect achievement in heaven.

(2) Conversion from Creatures to God.

When God grants sanctifying grace to the soul, He does not change or move so as to come and dwell where He did not dwell before. This would be an intrinsic impossibility, for the Divine Nature is changeless and immutable. When, therefore, Our Lord said : " We will come and take up our abode," He was using the language of appearances, as we do when we speak of the sun rising and setting. The entire progress in the way of grace, from the first infusion of sanctifying grace to the entrance into glory, is a change in our relation to God. Gradually the confining barriers, concepts and limited will aims and images, which separate our soul life from the infinite Godhead ever immanent in all creatures, are removed and destroyed. Since, however, where there are the fewest limits of non-being there is the greater participation of the Divine Being, God is most especially present when the limits are least. Hence He is especially present in souls emancipated from the limits of nature by sanctifying grace, and the greater the degree of this emancipation the fuller is the Divine Presence. Thus the increasingly full and increasingly intimate Presence of God in the soul, as the mystic path of perfection is ascended, is constituted by a progressive emancipation of the soul from the limits of creaturely attachment. The soul gradually turns towards God, first in the general direction of the will alone, later in all its volitions and in a conscious though obscure perception of His Presence. Sin and imperfection which are essentially aversion from God and conversion to creatures are destroyed, to be replaced by a life of communion with God and aversion from creatures, except in and for Him. This gradual conversion of the soul towards God— present in its centre—may be fitly imaged by a comparison drawn from the theatre. Until a few minutes before the curtain rises the stage is in complete darkness. The curtain alone is visible. The attention of the playgoer is therefore occupied by the orchestra, by the fittings of the auditorium and by the dress, the looks and the behaviour of the audience. These are far more interesting and more real than the monotonous curtain and the darkness behind it. This represents the ordinary knowledge of the soul in this life. The Divine Reality is hidden in darkness and apparent unreality, behind the curtain of a dogmatic system that seems a dreary and chillingly abstract system of merely verbal propositions and formulæ and of meaningless distinctions. The soul is occupied by the external world and its visible inhabitants. They appear so undeniably real, and religion so unreal. They are living, religion is dead. Interest centres in the beauties of nature, the decking of the world theatre, in a science that is practically useful, its warmth and comfort, in an art whose appeal is more or less confined to the senses, the music of the orchestra, in the superficial character and conduct of individuals and the fashions and current views of society, the audience around, their features and coiffures, their gowns and jewels. Later on, however, just before the play commences, the auditorium is darkened and the curtain alone stands out in brilliant light. The attention is turned by this from the auditorium and audience to the bright curtain, and through that to the stage beyond, with its approaching scenery and drama. In this altered condition is represented mystical experience, and most especially that most perfect mystical experience which is the transforming union. All the light of the soul now proceeds from the mystical intuition, which, however, is also the darkness of faith in a Divine Reality still veiled from open vision. The natural light of the soul's self-principled knowledge, the light derived from creatures, is now but obscurity. The false brilliance of the world, of its art and literature, its science and philosophy, its luxuries and amusements, its fashions and views, its codes and conventions, just now so dazzling and so inevitable, has faded into darkness before the approach of this Divine light, which, however, reveals nothing distinct. The illuminated curtain does not disclose the scenery behind it. There is now an entire conversion or reorientation of the entire psychical life, as there is of the attention of our theatre audience. The curtain of dogma and moral precept, formerly so dull and so uninspiring, alone glows with light in the darkness, and that radiant curtain is the portal of another world, a world of surpassing beauty and wonder. Soon the curtain rises in the theatre, the scene is disclosed and the drama begins. So is it with the mystic when he passes out of this life. Death lifts the curtain of the faith and discloses the open vision of Reality, at once the One and the All, God Himself.

Keep in mind those intermediate moments when the curtain is still lowered, but is alone brilliant with a light that draws the attention in expectant concentration to the stage beyond it, and to its approaching drama. They are an image of the veiled knowledge of the Divine Being which is mystical intuition,[1] and of the total conversion of the soul from the emptiness of creatures as they are in their limiting limitations to the fulness of the Divine Reality presented thus in the intuition which at once cloaks and reveals It.

(3) *Introversion.*

Another aspect of the mystical way is its progressive intro-

---

[1] Of course the comparison, like most other similes, is incomplete. The illuminated curtain discloses nothing of the scenery and actors of the play; the mystical intuition which is the perfection of infused faith does reveal the Presence, though not the nature, of God.

K

version. As we have already seen, God indwells and manifests Himself in a special manner in the central depths of the soul on account of their extreme freedom from limitation. Therefore the infusion of sanctifying grace is pre-eminently the constitution of a new relationship to God of *these central depths*, of a special union with God of the central ego, so that He is present, operates and manifests Himself in that centre after a new and peculiarly intimate fashion. Hence the process of conversion to God, which is, as we have seen, one aspect of the way of sanctifying grace and therefore pre-eminently of the mystical way, is also a process of introversion from the external world to those central depths wherein He is thus found. The attention, indeed the very life of the soul must be gradually detached from all things without and concentrated on itself (recollected in itself, as it is often said), this, however, not in egoism for the sake of the self, but for the sake of God there present and operative. Moreover, since the most superficial—that is, the peripheral—activities of the soul are the most limited, they cannot be so immediately the subject and sphere of the Divine Working through grace as are the most central and least limited activities. For they are through their greater limitation intrinsically incapable of so full a reception of the Divine Being and Operation. Hence as the soul advances in the mystical way its activities become ever less peripheral and more central. The superficial activities with their correspondingly superficial objects continuously decrease. Thus the entire soul life, at the outset almost wholly peripheral, becomes increasingly central—a conscious life of the centre increasingly united with the centrally present Godhead and increasingly controlled by that immanent Deity. As a result, prayer becomes ever more free from the surface activities and attentions conditioned by sensible images and becomes a contemplation of the unimaged Presence in the central depths. This is the gradual introversion of the way of grace through the continuous stages of mystical union. A certain introversion is indeed possible apart from grace by the use of natural reason. The most ignorant are the most superficial. The scientist and philosopher, and still more the artist, will and know at deep psychical levels with many limits removed. But the inner barriers remain as closely barred as ever. Grace alone can so introvert the soul as to free the central trinity, the ground of the soul, the radical cognition and the radical will from bondage, within the creaturely limits constituted by the ultimately sense-conditioned objects of natural knowledge and desire. Grace alone can set free the innate Godward tendency of the centre, so that it may become effectual and may reach its goal. I have already quoted from the first stanza of the *Spiritual Canticle* passages in which this introversion is described.[1] It is one of the most fundamental aspects of the mystical way.

(4) *Detachment from Self.*

Another aspect of the mystical process is the increasing destruction of selfishness. This does not mean that we are to seek the fulfilment of God's will, wholly prescinding from our own possession of the Divine union—a specious error condemned in Fénelon. It is true that certain saints have expressed a willingness to be deprived of God by eternal damnation, if it were to His greater glory. Such a supposition is, however, an intrinsic impossibility. The essence of damnation is the eternal separation of the will from God, the will's eternal rejection of God. But that rejection or separation is, of course, the absolute disjunction of our good, our will's end, from the will of God—a state of will intrinsically incompatible with a will to be damned for his glory—*i.e.* for the perfect fulfilment of His will. Thus true love of God is incompatible with willingness for the eternal will aversion from God which constitutes hell. Why then have the saints used language implying readiness to be damned for Christ's sake? The answer surely is that they were thinking, not of the essence of damnation —the eternal aversion from God—but of its secondary character of eternal suffering.* That they were ready to endure if only they might be united to God the closer by this supreme self-surrender. That, however, is not the condemned pure love that is willing to lose union with its object. For indeed it is of the very nature of love to seek union with the Beloved. No lover either in the natural or in the supernatural order can be satisfied with pleasing a Beloved absent and unpossessed. He demands the closest possible union, the most entire possession of the Beloved. The folly of a love so " pure " that it rejects union with its object for the joy that union would bring has been brilliantly exposed in the case of human love in that delightful, well-known comic opera, *Patience.* One could not find a more striking *reductio ad absurdum* of this false principle, a more convincing exposition of

[1] See Chapter V.

its incompatibility with the essential character of love. But the essential character of love is the same in the supernatural and the natural orders. It is equally incompatible with a saint's love of God not to will union with Him as it is with an earthly lover's love of a woman not to will to have her, if possible, in marriage.[1] Therefore it is of the nature of divine love, when pure in the true sense, to will the possession of God its Object by the closest possible union and, therefore, to will the beatific vision of heaven as being essentially that union. On the other hand, when love is perfectly pure, it is free from all selfish aim, because it seeks nothing outside of God, not even the joy which is inevitably concomitant upon conscious union with God ; therefore, not even the bliss which necessarily attaches to the beatific vision. Pure love loves God, not for the eternal joy of His eternal possession, but for Himself, and therefore for His eternal possession prescinding from the joy possession cannot but bring with it. If by an impossibility that possession brought torment instead of joy, pure love would will it notwithstanding. This is the true " pure love " as opposed to its condemned perversion ; this is the true unselfishness which is gradually acquired in the mystic way. Its nature can be abundantly illustrated from the sayings of the Saints. Dame Julian expressed it clearly when she said : " I choose Jesu to *my* heaven," St Catherine of Genoa voiced pure love when she thus addressed her Lord, when after communion He filled her with sensible sweetness : " I do not want that which proceedeth from Thee ; I want Thyself alone, O tender Love . . . O Love, art Thou perhaps intending to draw me to Thee by means of these sensible consolations ? I want them not : I want nothing except Thee alone " (Baron von Hügel, *Mystical Element of Religion*, vol. i., p. 280). Lucie Christine accustomed to express willingness to be deprived of glory for eternity, heard the Divine Voice saying : " I Myself am the glory " (*Spiritual Journal*, Eng. trs., p. 24). St Bernard said of love : " Habet praemium sed id quod amatur " [Its reward is the possession of the object loved] (*De Diligendo Deo*, chap. vii., pp. 72-73. Ed. and trs. by Edmund Gardner). The desire for this reward is essentially involved in the love itself. This true doctrine of pure love was summarised by St Augustine in the following words :—" Whoso seeks from God any other reward but God " (*not any reward but any reward out of God*

---

[1] Unless indeed a higher love supervene, or the marriage union would injure the beloved, neither of which is possible in the case of the love of God.

Himself), "and for it would serve God, esteems what he wishes to receive, more than Him from Whom he would receive it. What then ? Hath God no reward ? None, *save Himself*. This the soul 'loveth.' If it love aught else, it is no pure love " (St Augustine on Psalm lxxii. Quoted by Pusey in note to *Confessions*, iv. 4).

The true sense, therefore, in which love must be disinterested is that the soul must make this complete identification of its own good, its end, if you will, its reward, with God, not with any consolation or other gift received from God, but with Him in Himself alone. This " pure love " identifies the lover's good wholly and solely with its Object, and therefore must will the possession of its Object as its good and nothing beside that Object. This entire identification of the soul's good with God—the absolute unlimited good—is St Bernard's fourth degree of love, when self is loved solely for God's sake. This is a disinterested and pure love indeed, not, therefore, a love which excludes the desire of the beatific vision, but a love which involves that desire.[1]

The attainment of an entirely pure love, of perfect detachment from self-love, is the gradual change of isolated acts of pure love, into a continuous state in which no selfish activity of the soul continues to exist. This can only be attained at the close of the mystic way when the soul has been detached, not only from self as the end, but from self as the principle of her activity. This final and most radical detachment from self, involving the replacement of the self by God, as the ground and principle of the soul-life will be explained later, when I discuss the second night and spiritual marriage. Here let it suffice to have indicated this goal of the mystic way under its aspect of complete detachment from self. Enough has been said to emphasise the fundamental importance of this aspect without which any activity directed towards the attainment of the more unlimited and therefore more real realities that lie beyond the ordinary scope of our psychical life is not only barren but positively dangerous.

(5) *Conversion from Matter to Spirit*.

The mystic way is a gradual emancipation of the soul from the limitations of matter, by a progressive spiritualisation of its life. Matter, in its ultimate analysis, probably an electric energy,

---

[1] Nevertheless St Bernard thinks that this love will not be perfect till heaven is gained—nay more, the Resurrection of the body past—since these desires, right as they are, in some sense distract from the love of God (*De Diligendo Deo*).

differs from spirit by the lack of certain properties, or, from another point of view, by its reproduction and representation of the Divine Being under certain fundamental limitations which are absent from spirit. Therefore the process from the limited to the un-limited involves the ever-increasing transcendence of the limita-tions arising from matter. I do not mean by this that matter is itself finally abandoned. The entire Incarnational and Sacra-mental system, with its corollary, the Resurrection of the Body, affirms the unsoundness of this Platonic belief. But it does mean that the material ceases to confine with its limitations. In the Resurrection the material body will be the perfectly docile in-strument of the spirit. It will not, like our present body, condi-tion or limit the activity of the spirit. Now the spirit is incarnate. Then the flesh will be inspirited. This transformation is indeed the final and most perfect triumph of the soul, the third stage of its progress. First, the spirit is in bondage, though never *wholly* enslaved to the limitations of the flesh, unable to know or will anything that has not first been presented by the bodily senses. Under the action of grace, it attains an ever-increasing freedom from these bodily limitations, until at death it becomes wholly discarnate. It is true that even the most sensual, body-enslaved souls are freed from the body at death. We may, however, conjecture that their life beyond the grave is of a very feeble and semi-dormant nature. They have actualised their spiritual powers so little, have reduced the soul to so close a dependence on the body, that the spirit is now left in darkness of understand-ing and feebleness of will-energy, an all but empty shade, as the Greeks imagined the ghosts in Hades, and the earlier Jews, the dead in Sheol. The soul is indeed essentially immortal, and this involves some exercise of the spiritual powers, but that exercise is reduced to a minimum. If this condition endures only for a time it is the purgatory of sensual souls saved at the last—if for ever, their damnation.[1] This second stage, wherein the spirit is wholly separated from the flesh, was erroneously regarded by Plato as the highest and final stage. Last and highest of all is the third stage, when the body is restored, but the spirit is in such

---

[1] This is, of course, mere speculation—well grounded, I believe. All the damned receive back their bodies. In the case of these sensual souls we may believe that their bodies are left without power to supply due food—subject matter —to the spirit, which remains, therefore, in its impotence and inanity. And still less can the soul inspirit the body as in the Resurrection of the just.

full actualisation that its operation wholly dominates and, so to speak, absorbs the sensible operations and consciousness of the body.   The mystic way on earth is, of course, essentially the way from the first to the second stage, the gradual escape of the soul from bondage to the limitations of matter and sense, the substitution of the spiritual for the carnal man.[1]   For St Paul terms the natural life of the soul, the life of the old man, carnal, and its possessor the carnal man :   its opposite, the supernatural life, the life that is manifested in mystical experience, the life of the new, man spiritual, and its possessor the spiritual man.   He does so because the natural soul life of man is essentially bound by material conditions transcended only by the new " creature " of grace.   The soul can only become a free and matter-transcendent spirit by its elevation and possession by the Holy Spirit through grace.   Hence St Paul speaks indifferently of " carnal " and " psychic " for the matter-conditioned life of the unregenerate and reserves the appellation " spiritual " for the Spirit-quickened and therefore matter-emancipated life of the regenerate.

In its gradual emancipation from the limits of matter, the soul transcends first the limitations of the bodily senses and desires.   Then it transcends in the understanding the image-conditioned concepts and discourse due ultimately to sensible data, and in the will, attachment to those more spiritualised goods, which are, nevertheless, ultimately generalisations from the more external goods of sense—for example, ambition, desire of sensible consolations in religion and the like.   These attachments to less immediately material goods are classified by St John of the Cross under seven heads, which he terms the seven spiritual sins.   They are the spiritual counterparts of the seven capital vices.   Though many of these sins appear at first sight desires of spiritual goods, closer examination reveals them to be desires containing a material element, limitations of material origin.   These limitations are desires for particular selfish pleasures sensibly felt, pleasures of the lower sensible functions of the soul.

Of course certain spiritual sins have less of the material than others.   Spiritual pride may seem far indeed removed from sense and its pleasure.   Nevertheless spiritual pride is essentially a love and esteem for the ego as a limited being, apart from the universal

---

[1] There is, however, as we shall see later, a certain foretaste in the mystic way of the third or Resurrection stage.

good. But this limitation by the self and by its selfish good— for example, individual pre-eminence above others—is largely rooted in the material and sensible, in images and in image-derived concepts. Pride, though the sin of discarnate devils, is in man carnal in the widest sense. We must not confuse the psychology of the angels and devils, of which we know practically nothing, with the psychology of man in his bodily life on earth.

The progress of the understanding and of the will are parallel. While the will is being gradually detached from all limitations in its object, limitations due directly or indirectly to matter, the understanding, having first transcended the limits of images corporeal or imaginary, proceeds to free itself, or rather to allow itself to be freed from the limitations of even the most general ideas ; for even these most general and most spiritual ideas, in so far as they are distinct notions, are generalisations from ultimate sense data, and as such are rooted in the material, are limited by matter. Indeed, in human psychology the distinct and the limited are ultimately deducible to the material. Pure spirituality is the entire actuation of the soul to and in God, the one sole Unlimited. But it may be urged, though God is indeed pure spirit, is not this true of many creatures also—namely, the angels, even the fallen angels ? There may, therefore, be pure spirituality without union with God. All spirituality, I would reply, that is truly pure, is in closest union with God, as are the angels in heaven. Although the diabolic nature is indeed wholly immaterial, it is in many ways subject to, conditioned and limited by the material. Indeed, may not this limitation and confinement by matter, which must be agony to a discarnate intelligence, constitute one of the chief sufferings of the evil spirits ? To me this seems very probable. Thus is the mystic way an increasing emancipation of the spirit from the matter which conditions and confines its natural life on earth.

(6) *Increase of Delicacy or Subtlety (Delgadez).*

A subordinate aspect of this gradual dematerialisation of the soul is its increasing subtlety or delicacy (delgadez, as St John terms it). This epithet is employed by St John, both of the soul in its highest state of union and of the Divine Being, Who then consciously operates within it, having penetrated and taken possession of its central substance and its functions. (See

Mystical Marriage, chap .xii.) The meaning of this somewhat strange term is perhaps a little obscure at first sight, and its elucidation will amply repay careful study. The principle underlying the use of the epithet is, I believe, that the coarse is always the most limited and the most material. A coarse soul is conversant entirely or almost entirely with matter and material phenomena as such, not as embodiments of spirit, and therefore perceives only the most material and superficial aspect of experience, and is always arrested at the surface of things. Coarse humour, for instance, differs from refined or delicate humour by its greater limitation and externality. It does not penetrate so deeply below the surface. It is true that in ordinary usage the term " coarse " is confined to those who know and love only those absolutely material facts and aspects of life which are perceptible and lovable by the irrational beasts. If, and in so far as, a soul penetrates below these absolutely material and utterly exterior aspects, it ceases to be termed coarse. Such a soul, however, may still be confined to the more superficial regions of experience, without penetrating deeply in any direction and never attaining the truly spiritual. This soul is still essentially a vulgar soul, for coarseness is simply the highest degree of vulgarity, vulgarity in its greatest intensity. Coarseness is that condition of soul in which the will and perception are most narrowly limited and least penetrative. But there are other degrees to which the term coarse is not applied, where the limits are still exceedingly narrow. These lesser, but still very great, degrees of limitation constitute, if not coarseness, vulgarity. Vulgar souls of this kind are conversant only with pleasures and perceptions but one degree superior to those of the beasts. They still perceive and love only those things which belong to the surface of experience, which are almost wholly material, the obvious hard and brutal facts which possess an exceeding small degree of reality because so limited and exterior. If the coarse man judges all things by their direct relationship to sensual pleasure, the vulgar man applies the same standard somewhat more indirectly. His thought and will move within a narrow circle and they never pierce far below the surface. His psychical activities are essentially coarse, because essentially matter-bound, in their inability to escape these superficial limits and to attain the deeper reality that is farther removed from the senses.

In fact the essence of vulgarity, which is, after all, but another term for coarseness of soul, is extreme limitation and externality. To be very narrow-minded and shallow-minded is to be vulgar. If a man's soul is narrow in its sympathy and knowledge, but deep, he will be a bigot, but cannot be a vulgarian. Or again, if a man's sympathy and knowledge are wide, but more or less superficial—if they are really wide, they cannot be extremely superficial—such a man is not entirely vulgar, though still vulgar in proportion to his lack of depth. It is the union of narrowness with shallowness which constitutes perfect vulgarity. The vulgar man is incapable of any true intellectual or artistic activity or perception, for such perceptions and activities transcend the limitations of the immediately sensible. On such matters his views are but a parrot-like repetition of those current in his social environment. For the vulgar man science is valuable only as a means to tangible results and profit-making inventions. His notion of art is the provision of gaudy colours and jingling tunes for the grossest delight of the outer senses. To the beauty of nature he is blind, or at best he sees it but as a superficial pretti-ness, the utmost attainable by the physical senses *alone*. In religion, a man may indeed be saved by grace from vulgarity, while remaining vulgar in all other departments of life. True devotion pierces below the limits that constitute vulgarity. Otherwise his religion is but the utterance of resonant catchwords and the intoxication of hymn-singing.[1] Thus is vulgarity the confinement of the soul in the prison of the external aspects and the material objects that are immediately perceptible by sense. Refinement or subtlety, St John's delgadez, penetrates below the surface by transcending the particularity and limitations of the superficial and sensible fact, or appearance, or of the concept, thence derived. It reaches either by intuition or by thought, the more unlimited because more spiritual reality that underlies the immediate sense datum, the surface appearance, the particular and sense-derived concept. Refined and subtle souls are quick, therefore, to perceive the underlying identity of various particulars which are superficially different. If they effect this by intuition, they are men or women of delicate and subtle sympathies ; if by reasoning, they are quick-witted, acute, clever. This identity perceived by the subtle soul is not primarily one of material elements. The identities apprehended by the penetration of sensibility, talent and, in a higher degree, of genius, are spiritual

[1] And what hymns ? Consult our popular hymnals.

identities of principles and ideas. From the perception of spiritual identity arises that wide and comprehensive sympathy which accompanies delicacy of soul. Even the senses of the subtle soul are disciplined to perceive details, whether similarities or differences, that do not appear in the broad outlines and large characters which alone are perceived by the senses of grosser souls. This more acute sense-perception is due in such souls to their fuller perception of the significance and beauty of material objects— that is, to the deeper penetration which pierces below their superficial aspects. Subtlety or refinement is, therefore, essentially an aspect of insight, opposed to the spiritual blindness of those who can only see the superficial phenomena discernible by the senses. Genius is but a supreme degree of this subtlety or penetration, for the genius is a genius essentially because he perceives more clearly than others the inner likeness and kinship, the underlying identity of superficially unlike objects. This is the explanation of the fact, often remarked, that the supreme genius sums up his age, that his work is the full and final expression of all the forces which constitute his epoch, its aims, conscious or unconscious, its religious beliefs, its dominant ideas and interests, its moral preferences, its æsthetic canons, even its limitations, its ignorances, its prejudices—in short, that in him his age becomes fully self-conscious. Thus does Homer sum up the heroic age of Hellenic migration ; Euripides the rationalism and the newly awakened humanity of fifth-century Athens. Virgil is the voice of the Roman Empire, the *Divina Commedia* of the Catholic and feudal civilisation of the Middle Ages, Shakespeare of the Humanist Renaissance, while Monsieur Rolland's *Jean Christophe* represents the immanentism and natural vitalism of the present day. For the genius by his penetrative vision has more than any other broken through the barriers between himself and the general life of his epoch. Indeed his genius is essentially his free receptivity of the complexus of forces composing the " time spirit " that below the surface of divergent and conflicting individualties invisibly fashions, unites and directs the life and thought of his contemporaries. For these forces of which they imprisoned within the limits of the superficial, the individual, the local, are not at all or but partially conscious, are apprehended by this delicate, sensitive instrument, his subtle, and therefore widely perceiving and deeply penetrating, insight.

Delicacy or subtlety is thus clearness and penetration of

spiritual vision—" insight " ; vulgarity or coarseness is dimness of spiritual vision, a dimness which amounts in many cases to an almost total blindness. This blindness of vulgarity is at the opposite pole to mystical intuition, as indeed the vulgar man is of all men the farthest removed from the mystic. For the vulgar soul is the most limited, the mystic soul the freest from limits.

It may be objected that the most vulgar man, the bestial man of Aristotle and St Thomas [1] is not so guilty as the man or angel who uses his higher faculties, his less limited being, to exclude God by deliberate malice. Therefore on account of his greater guilt or aversion of will the malicious man, and even more, the fallen angel, is further removed from God and therefore from the mystic than the vulgar or bestial man. We need here a careful distinction. Since the soul of the vulgar man is confined within narrower limits, he participates less in God's Unlimited Being than the malicious sinner and a fortiori than Satan,* and is therefore further removed from God.   Since, however, his will has not been so deliberately averted from God in despite of knowledge, he does not adhere so fully and so firmly to the more limited good of his choice, as do the malicious sinner and Satan to their less limited goods. Although his prison is narrower, he is not bound so fast within it. He has *de facto* less of God, but that greater lack is not so much his own fault. Hence he has a greater capacity and more prospect of release from his narrower limitations and of future union with God than has the malicious sinner on earth, whereas Satan and a damned soul have no capacity for this release and union. Thus although those latter are not so far removed in being from God as the former, their removal is in another sense more complete, for their fuller being is more actively exclusive of the Divine Being than the scantier being of the vulgar soul, which does not oppose an equal resistance to fulfilment by God's self-donation. This is surely the ground of Gregory's dictum that " carnal sins are less guilty but more infamous than spiritual." [2] For guilt is the measure of a soul's deliberate self-confinement, disgrace the measure of the limitation within which the soul is confined. Therefore although in guilt that is in the intensity

---

[1] I regard this " bestiality " as the supreme degree of vulgarity beyond coarseness. What is said of vulgarity at its maximum is applicable in due proportion to lesser degrees.

[2] Quoted by Reade, *Moral System of Dante's Inferno.*

of bondage an evil spirit and among men a malicious sinner is the antithesis of the mystic, in the limitation itself, that is, in the scope of confinement—the lack of actual participation of God, the bestial or vulgar man is the antithesis of the mystic. From the cognitional standpoint with which we are at present concerned the field of vision of the vulgar man is narrower than that of the malicious, although it is less indisposed for possible future enlargement. Hence the vision of the vulgar man rather than that of the malicious soul or the evil spirit is antithetic to the vision of the mystic.

It is true that insight in one direction must usually be purchased by a temporary sacrifice of insight in other directions. To attain depth the soul must become less broad. In the end, however, the breadth is restored at a deeper level, attained not by wide knowledge of facts at a more or less superficial level, as in the case of the typical broad-minded man, but by apprehension of the spiritual unity underlying the superficial manifold. The real bigot, on the other hand, stops short too soon. He reaches indeed a deeper level and therefore a more unlimited reality than the more superficial, broad-minded man. But he is arrested by a spiritual pride and selfishness which prevent him from going deeper and reaching an even more unlimited reality and therefore exclude from his spiritual vision the true generality of the spiritual fact or principle which he has attained. When therefore the world abuses a religious soul as narrow-minded and bigoted, we have to discover whether that soul is really bigoted—that is, narrowed by the limitations of self-satisfaction—or has simply concentrated its activity in order to attain a deeper level, a principle of wider scope, at and by which it will be able to unify and embrace the manifold, superficially embraced by the broad-minded man of the world. We must, however, remember that in this life a truly religious soul—nay, even a saint—may only grasp *potentially* this universal character of spiritual reality. Seeing that various departments of more or less superficial activity or knowledge tend in practice to exclude souls from the depths of the spirit, he may on that account ruthlessly condemn them as essentially and necessarily limiting and therefore evil in themselves. Such an one fails to realise, though he must admit it theoretically, that even these superficial activities and spheres are in their positive being good. He equally fails to realise that vast multitudes are in the present order so ignorant of divine

truth and so temperamentally disposed as to be quite unable to
transcend them save, of course, in the general will aim necessary
to supernatural charity.   For these souls, much occupation with
these activities and spheres, despite their inevitable limitation,
is the best course possible, and, in proportion as the activities and
knowledge is question are more spiritual and unlimited, is increasingly good.   This want of realisation and consequent narrowness is not, however, due to any defect in the saint's principles
or way of life, or to any deficiency or limitation in the object
attained by him, but simply to the inability of any soul while in
this mortal flesh to actualise fully all potencies, to grasp all aspects
of truth, to draw all the logical inferences, to see the full significance of a truth attained.   This necessary limitation, which is
least existent in the greatest saints, does not alter the fact that the
saint and the mystic have grasped the one Unlimited Reality,
which gives its meaning and value to every activity and apprehension of any human soul whatsoever, however superficial and
limited that meaning or value may be.

Hitherto I have spoken of delicacy in its cognitional aspect
as penetrative insight free from the narrow limits of superficial
vision.   It has, of course, its corresponding conational aspect,
the delicacy of will, that loves and seeks the deep spiritual values
apprehended by the subtle understanding.   Thus delicacy or
subtlety (delgadez) is the state of soul, whether manifested in
knowledge or love, that penetrates deepest beyond the most
limited surface appearance or sphere of being, and attains the
more unlimited reality which underlies it.   The freer our psychical
operations are of limits the more are they conversant with the
interior and spiritual realities that underlie the complex manifold
of the external and material, the more delicate and more subtle,
therefore, are they, since they are not hindered, blunted and
diminished, and therefore coarsened, by the limitations of the
most superficial and the most particular objects.   " We must
bear in mind," writes St John, " that a thing is wide and capacious
in proportion to its delicacy, and the more subtle and delicate it is,
the more extensively does it diffuse and communicate itself "
(*Living Flame*, st. 2).   When finally the psychical operations
are immediately conversant with God, not apprehended under
any particular image or concept, but as the incomprehensible
Being infinitely transcending all created objects and yet intimately present to and immanent in them all in porportion to

their freedom from limitation, these operations are most subtle and delicate, fitly imaged by some very subtle, physical force, which by reason of its subtlety penetrates other substances, and is not confined by grossness of bulk or nature to a very limited [1] sphere of being and activity.

As we shall see later, the activities of a soul in the highest state of union are receptions of the Divine activity.   Therefore in describing the operation of such a soul St John speaks of the Divine activity or operation in that soul.   But it is plain that if delicacy or subtlety increases with increased freedom from limitations, the activity of God must be infinitely delicate or subtle, being excluded or confined by no limitation.   Everything, therefore that I have said of delicacy applies pre-eminently to the Divine operation, and indeed it is only by participation in that operation that the activities of the soul can attain to the perfect subtlety of entire freedom from limits.   " O thou delicate touch, thou Word the Son of God," writes St John, " that through the delicacy [subtlety] of thy divine Being dost subtly penetrate the substance of my soul and touching it delicately throughout dost absorb it wholly in Thyself in divine ways of delights and sweetness never heard in the land of Canaan nor seen in Teman. . . . Oh my God and my life, they only shall see Thee and shall feel Thy subtle touch who have made themselves alien to the world, and have made themselves subtle, for the subtle fits the subtle, and so shall they be able to feel and to enjoy Thee.   Such as those dost Thou touch with a subtlety proportionate to their condition seeing that the substance of their soul hath now been purged, purified and rendered subtle."   (All the natural limits of its activity have been destroyed that hitherto excluded it from the unlimited reception of the all-penetrating Unlimited.) . . . " Oh, once again and many times over delicate touch, Thou art the more strong and powerful, the more delicate Thou art, for with the force of Thy delicacy Thou dost undo the soul and alienate it from all touches of things created and dost appropriate it to Thyself and unite it to Thyself alone.   Thou dost leave within it an effect so delicate, that every touch of aught, high or low, seems coarse and impure " (because its essential limit is felt, excluding and debarring the soul's activity). . . . " The Word, that is the touch that toucheth the soul, is infinitely subtle and

---

[1] I mean limited qualitatively not quantitatively.   Grosser substances obviously occupy more space.

delicate. The soul is a wide and capacious vessel on account of the great purity and subtlety possessed in this state " (of supreme mystical union). " Ah then, O thou delicate touch, Thou dost infuse Thyself into my soul with such plenty and abundance proportionate to Thy subtlety and to the purity of my soul. . . . This divine touch possesses no bulk nor volume, for the Word that effects it is devoid of all mode or fashion, and free from all volume, form, figure or accident, whose nature it is to confine and limit substance. . . . Ah then, in fine, how ineffably delicate is this Thy touch, O Thou Word, seeing it is effected in the soul with Thy most simple substance and with Thy intimate Being, that is infinitely delicate, because it is *infinite* " (without limits) (*Living Flame*, st. 2). Thus in proportion as the soul is united to the unlimited Being of God by its reception and participation of His unlimited activity, the activity of that soul becomes delicate or subtle, for it penetrates and transcends all the limits of creatures passing through and beyond them to the Unlimited present in, through and beyond them all. This is well expressed by Mother Cecilia when she says that one of the effects of the mystical union is that " God renders increasingly subtle all the properties and activities of the soul . . . so that all things that might hinder it seem now devoid of substance " (*Transformation*, st. 16).

(7) *Liberation.*

> Patrata sunt haec mystice
> Paschae peracto tempore
> Sacro dierum circulo
> Quo lege fit remissio.

> [These things were done in type that day
> When Paschal tide had passed away.
> The number told which once set free
> The captive in the jubilee.]

These words are sung by the Church in her Whitsun lauds to commemorate the first indwelling of the Holy Spirit in the souls of her children. In remarking this numerical coincidence between the Jewish liberation of slaves in the Sabbatical year—that is, every fiftieth year—and the advent of the Spirit on the fiftieth day after Easter, she insinuates that the indwelling of the Holy Spirit and His work in the soul is essentially an emancipation of the soul from spiritual bondage. The mystical union-intuition is, as we have seen, but a manifestation of the life of grace and therefore of that Presence and Work of the Holy Spirit in the soul that is constituted by sanctifying grace. If, therefore, the ordinary life of grace with its secret indwelling of the Spirit be essentially a liberation of the soul, the mystical union must be the attainment of a far more complete liberty. Thus the mystical way is under another aspect a gradual emancipation.

No age has boasted a greater devotion to freedom than our own. We are impatient of all control, whether of Church, of State or of family, except, indeed, in war-time, when no servitude seems too great, no yoke too hard for the patient endurance of the peoples of Europe, who rush gladly in their millions to be butchered at the command of irresponsible cliques of statesmen. Such a slavery is indeed the fitting Nemesis of the false liberty of modern thought and life. But what then is true liberty? The prevalent confusion of thought, the strange mixture of anarchy and slavery, show the need of an answer, and our account of the mystical way urges me to attempt it. In its more superficial aspect, liberty is freedom to follow reason unhindered by external violence. In a deeper sense it is this same freedom to follow reason unhindered by the force of our own lower passions and desires. Bondage to the latter is, of course, a far worse slavery than any slavery to the former, since it confines the inner life of the soul, not merely its external manifestation. Everything, therefore, that enables us to follow reason [1] sets us free, everything that hinders us from following reason enslaves. No fallen man, however, can follow reason without the help of an external law and authority. Freedom from law and authority means slavery, for it involves more or less of inability to follow reason, an inability due in part to ignorance of what right reason prescribes, in part to the innate tendency of the fallen will to follow irrational affections. But every state being merely human, an assemblage of more or less sinful and ignorant men is in greater or lesser degree divergent from right reason, and may therefore, indeed often does, prescribe what is opposed to it. Such laws and commands truly enslave the subject who submits to them by hindering him from following in his conduct the dictates of reason. Nevertheless the slavery so incurred is far less than the slavery which would result from anarchy. Therefore the authority of the State must be maintained and obeyed, save where it plainly conflicts with the law

[1] When I say reason, I include superrational intuition.

L

of God or deprives the individual of some inalienable right—
that is, some power or possession necessary for the due operation
of a rational soul life.   Nevertheless this necessary evil may and
should be minimised by restricting the power and scope of the
State to such authority over the individual, as shall prevent one
individual from injuring another (the police and judicial function),
and shall secure to every individual equal opportunity to develop
his capacities in the fulfilment of his particular office (a limited
function of social reform and regulation).   Higher, less limited
authority can safely be entrusted to that society alone which has
been instituted by God Himself and endowed by Him with infallibility—namely, the Catholic Church—a society, moreover,
whose authority is based not on brute force, but upon the free
obedience of conscience.   By submission to the State the individual
soul is, or should be, freed from the bondage of irrational interference by his fellows, whether positive by aggression on his
rights, or negative by the refusal of the due opportunity which he
requires to follow out the vocation which his reason assigns him.
By submission to the Church, so that it be internal—that is, of
the free will—not merely external, for some natural end, or under
legal compulsion, the soul is freed from the imprisonment of a
radical aversion of will from the Unlimited God to the limited
creature.   This is, however, but a beginning.   If the soul wills
the close union with God which is the end of the mystic way, it
is not sufficient merely to perform or omit those acts whose
performance or omission the Church prescribes under pain of sin.
That soul must submit its will in all things to the will of God.
Thus alone can it be freed from all the limitations of creaturely
attachment.   In proportion as the soul effects this submission
or will-union it becomes ever freer to follow the voice of conscience illuminated by grace and later by mystical intuition,
a voice which tells her plainly that the infinite and Absolute
Divine Goodness is the only true end of her actions and life.   But
we have now traced freedom to a deeper source than that reached
by our definition of freedom as the unimpeded following of reason.
For we have shown that this following of right reason leads to
perfect will-union with God, and that this perfect will-union is
perfect freedom, because it is the complete emancipation of the
soul from the bondage of the limitations necessarily inherent in
creatures.   Wholly to submit, to inone the will with the will of
God is to become perfectly free, because it is the destruction

of all limits. For the will-union of love frees, in proportion as it releases the will from limited ends. The lowest and most limited are, of course, the animal desires, and the sensual man is therefore the greatest slave, or, to speak more exactly, his prison is the narrowest. Those whose will is set on more unlimited because more spiritual objects have a far more spacious prison-house. They are like a dethroned monarch allowed the range of an entire estate or island. Nevertheless their slavery is often more intense, their prison far more difficult of escape. For the very fact that the object of the will is now less limited makes it more satisfactory and more attractive to the entire soul. Hence the will of such a man is often more firmly attached to his less limited good than the will of the sensual man to his more narrowly limited good. Divine charity alone gives true freedom to the will, detaching it ever more completely from any and every limited good, and fixing it ever more closely on the unlimited Good. This is the freedom of the sons of God, led by the Holy Spirit of God Who is the eternal love of Absolute Goodness for Absolute Goodness. It is a freedom which is perfect obedience, obedience indeed to the dictates of reason, but essentially and primarily obedience to the Personal Will of God which the understanding supernaturally enlightened by grace and later by mystical intuition, recognises as the Supreme Good and End of creatures. In this life this higher and more complete obedience which is the supreme freedom is greatly assisted by obedience to earthly superiors and directors whose guidance on the mystic way is therefore most valuable. Even if these should err in the matter of their command, so long as sin is not involved, should order what is not in itself in most perfect accord with God's will, it is His will that the soul should obey for the sake of the general good thereby obtained of the destruction of the essentially limited and limiting self-will of the soul. Even tyranny and oppression are often used by God as instruments to effect the liberation of the soul from this inner bondage to limiting desires, and limiting self-will, a bondage incalculably closer and more powerful than any external slavery.[1] For self-will is the choice of a limited good which is immediately pleasurable to the soul, or more radically its own supposed good as apart from the Absolute Good. God's will which is identical with His being is the sovereign good of all, and therefore of the

---

[1] Nevertheless we ought to oppose tyranny because (1) it often does enslave the soul of its victims ; (2) it is always the spiritual ruin of those who practise it.

individual soul.   Therefore when self-will is destroyed, and God's will is perfectly chosen, the will is wholly free to attain its true good and end, which it has perversely sought from the outset. In the possession of this boundless Good it enjoys perfect freedom. As mystical will-union through love thus emancipates the will from limited ends, mystical intuition emancipates the spiritual consciousness or understanding from limited apprehensions. That intuition reveals the Unlimited as the ultimate and the solely adequate, the one complete and wholly evident Object of knowledge.   Thus in the highest sense is Our Lord's promise fulfilled when this sovereign truth revealed in mystical intuition makes us free.   The understanding that accepts as ultimate the particulars of sense is the most completely enslaved.   Understandings that are conversant with far-reaching hypotheses, first principles and spiritual ideas are in various degrees freer.   The understanding that enjoys direct intuition of God is truly free, for it has attained the Absolute Truth, the source and ground of all the more or less limited truths of created being.   In this life we cannot comprehend this Absolute Truth, for we cannot attain clear knowledge of the Godhead.   Therefore the understanding is not wholly free as it will be free in the beatific vision.   Faith, even in its highest degree and most complete infusion, the veiled intuition of the mystic, apprehends Absolute truth obscurely under a veil.   This veiled intuition is, however, an intellectual freedom beyond that possessed by any other man, even by the philosopher, who is bound by distinct concepts ultimately sense-derived and therefore limited, limited, moreover, in proportion to their distinctness.   By this double emancipation of the radical will and understanding the centre of the soul is set free to possess that perfect union and fruition of God for which it was created and sanctified, undetained by the limits of creaturely attachments and ideas.   Thus is the mystic way, the way, the only way, to perfect freedom.

(8) *Unification : Increasing Simplicity.*

We have seen that God is absolute unity and simplicity, because His infinite multiplicity is not exclusive but inclusive.   It was pointed out at the same time that as the scale of created being mounts Godward the unity increases, the internal organic unity which harmonises, subordinates and, so to speak, absorbs an ever increasing complexity or multiplicity. The same law holds good of the spiritual life of the individual soul. The need for unification both in practice and in theory, unification alike of will aims and of knowledge, is imperiously insistent in the soul of man. It exists even in the natural order when the mystic way is altogether unknown. In practical life a man must have one dominant aim, one dominant affection, if his life is to possess any degree of stability, if his work is to attain any degree of successful achievement. It is the same with speculation. The aim and achievement of the sciences is the unification of the data which constitute its subject matter. Philosophy attempts [1] to unify the first principles of all the subordinate sciences in one harmonious self-consistent view of reality as a whole. Art creates such sensible harmonies—that is, unifications—of form, colour or sound as will convey to souls duly attuned the spiritual and therefore more perfect harmony or unification which underlies the sensible and therefore more imperfect, because more exterior, unifications and harmonies. But it is only in the order of grace and in its sovereign manifestation, mystical experience, that this need of unification can attain full satisfaction. For in mystical experience the soul attains a supernatural union with the Absolute Unity of an infinite manifold, from Whom all multiplicity proceeds and in Whom it is all made one. Moreover, as the soul draws nearer to God and this union increases, its operations become more unified, because their subject matter is increasingly simple. In the earlier stages of the life of grace the soul's strength is not completely focused on God. The will is divided among many objects, not willed in order to God ; the consciousness is similarly distracted by a multiplicity of divers objects, unharmonised and mutually competing for the soul's attention. Even the soul's prayer-energy is divided among various images, by whose aid alone it approaches God, Who is now envisaged under one image, now under another. It is true that from the first there exists in the central trinity, the centre and the radical consciousness and the radical will proceeding from the centre, a unity of direction towards the unlimited, towards God. This unity, however, is not carried into act, but remains an unfulfilled potency, a beginning never carried out. The life of the soul is thus like the water of a fountain, which begins indeed to rise in one jet from the pipe, but

[1] An attempt which, as we saw, can never be completely successful (see chapter III).

is soon dissipated into a shower of separate streams and drops
pursuing each its own independent course. The energy of the
soul, instead of ascending undivided to God, is distracted among
the variety of creatures known and willed in and for themselves.
The mutually exclusive limits of these created ends and objects
split up the soul life and dissipate its force. All this ununified
and consequently distracting multiplicity gradually disappears
as the soul draws closer to God, as its union with Him becomes
more intimate and more continuous. Finally, nothing is willed
save in order to God, nothing contemplated by the understanding
in which He is not beheld. The soul's prayer is unified in one
direct obscure contemplation of God, and in one immediate direction and union of the will to and with Him. This principle is
plainly stated by St John in the sixteenth chapter of the second
book of *The Ascent of Mount Carmel*. " I say, therefore," such
are his words, " with respect to all these apprehensions and
imaginary visions, and other forms or species of whatever kind
they may be or images or *particular apprehensions of any kind* "
(*i.e.* distinct intellectual concepts about God), " whether false as
coming from the devil, or known to be true as coming from God,
that the understanding is not to perplex itself about them, nor
feed itself upon them ; the soul must not willingly accept them
nor cleave to them in order that it may be detached and naked,
pure and simple without particular mode or fashion of any kind,
which is the condition of the divine union. The reason of this is
that all these forms are never represented so as to be laid hold of,
but under certain ways and limitations ; and the divine wisdom
to which the understanding is to be united admits of no such
particular ways or forms, neither can it be comprehended under
any limitation or distinct and particular concept, because it is all
pureness and simplicity. However, if two extremes are to be
united together, such as the soul and the divine Wisdom, it is
necessary that they should meet under a certain kind of mutual
resemblance ; and hence the soul must also be pure and simple
not limited by, nor adhering to any particular concept and un-
modified by any limited form, species or image. As God is not
comprehended under any form or image or particular concept, so
the soul also, if it is to be united to Him, must not be under the
power of any particular or distinct concept." In short, the manifold of distinct and particular apprehensions must give place to a
unified though obscure apprehension of the God Who is Absolute

Unity. Thus is the mystical process a process from multiplicity to unity. This unity, however, is not a barren unity—a unity attained by the cutting away of all the constituents of experience save one, a unity like the unity of almost contentless units. The enemies of the mystical life regard its unity in this light, but that is their calumny. Within the unity there is an infinite variety of acts of will and of apprehensions, perfectly blended in one. As Baron von Hügel points out, the more wholly an object occupies and absorbs the attention of the soul, the more are all the soul's powers unified in a unity composed of a multiplicity of operations so subtle as to be subconscious.[1] When the Object is Absolute Goodness and therefore all-satisfying and all-absorbing, Absolute Unity, focusing in that unity all that is positive in the incalculable variety of created things, this unification of the soul is complete. Limits divide. Hence occupation with the limited is divided or externally multiple. The unlimited unites. Therefore concentration on the Infinite harmonises in one act all the multiplicity of the soul. On the other hand, the one act preached by the Quietists was a contentless or bare unity. That is why it was condemned by the Church. Here, as elsewhere, Quietism is the ape of true mysticism. For the Quietist imitates the external phraseology of mysticism, but fails to understand her inner spirit, to follow her real practice.

It is true that in the case of the individual soul the multiplicity of different interests and functions of which our soul life is composed is usually diminished as the soul draws nearer to God. The reason of this, however, is that this multiplicity was by reason of its externality exclusive, dividing and distracting. The inner substance, however, of these multiple external activities is not lost but fused in the interior unity of the mystical life. If, for example, a soul loses its love of art or natural beauty, it is because the inner substance or spiritual significance of these has been abstracted from the external form in which it was first conveyed, whose limits excluded other psychical activities, and is now possessed in a more spiritual and interior manner, in which the substance of each distinctive activity is one with that of the others, while subsisting in full unimpaired being. For the more spiritual is the more purely positive, though God alone is pure positivity, and therefore one spiritual being does not exclude another in the same way that one material unit excludes another material unit.

[1] *Mystical Religion.*

I cannot contemplate a beautiful painting and a beautiful land-scape in one and the selfsame contemplation.   The mystic can have the fruition of the spiritual realities, of which the picture and the landscape are the respective embodiments or sacraments, in one and the same contemplation, for both are but aspects of one spiritual or ideal reality, and only exclude one another when externalised on the lower plane of mutually exclusive material objects.   Since God is Absolute Unity, the activity of the God-possessing and God-possessed soul is unified in proportion to the degree of the divine possession.   Thus is the mystical way essenti-ally a Unitive way, and most completely unitive is that final stage known by this name.

(9) *Purification.*

The operations of the soul in mystical union are increasingly pure energisings to God, undistracted and undiluted by created images and ends.   This purity is a concomitant aspect of the soul's unification and of its release from limits, even as the Divine Purity is a concomitant aspect of the Divine Unity and the Divine Infinity.   The gradual purification of the soul will occupy us at great length hereafter.   Here I would but point out the general law that the increasing unification of the soul life and activity, together with their increasing emancipation from limits, involves their increasing purification from the multiple and limiting attachments to creatures that sullied the purity of the soul's concentrated force of Godward love.   In the second volume of *Modern Painters* Ruskin maintains that purity is essentially energy or life unimpeded.[1]   Spiritual purity is thus the energy or life of the soul unimpeded in its outgoing to God by the limits of created attachments immediately or mediately derived from sensible objects.   St John regards purity from this point of view in the twenty-fifth chapter of the third book of *The Ascent of Mount Carmel.*   Purity is there treated as the free actuation of the soul in and to God in a fulness of spiritual life not repressed and dis-persed by sensible attachments.   These attachments repress this Godward life and energy of the spirit by confining our psychical activities and life within the limits of the sensible and the created. They disperse that fulness of life by dissipating its energy among a multiplicity of objects.   The intention of the will and the appre-hension of the understanding, pure in source owing to their

[1] Vol. ii., chap. ix.

primitive unity, in man's innate Godward outgoing and need,[1] are defiled in their outward flow by attachments to creatures and to particular images and concepts which limit the will so that it no longer wills the Divine Union, and in which the understanding rests, so that it is held back on its onward course to the Absolute all-explanatory truth it would fain apprehend. This is the double impurity of sin and its consequences, in their twofold result of blindness of understanding and powerlessness of will. The work of grace in the entire mystic way is to get rid of these stains, not of sins alone, but of all undue will attachments and irrational acceptance of images and distinct concepts, as sufficient principles of knowledge. Of this present impurity of the soul in its undue attachment to the limited, and in its exclusive multiplicity thence resulting, and of the essential purity of its central being, we have a beautiful image in the tenth book of Plato's *Republic*. " Would you see the soul as she really is, not as we now behold her, marred by communion with the body and other miseries ? "[2] (Plato was, indeed, wrong in regarding this bodily incarnation as an evil or the cause of evil. The true cause is that the particular knowledge and desires due to the senses have through our lack of grace more or less closely imprisoned the soul in their limits so that it cannot as it ought, and in sanctified souls does, transcend these limits.) " You must contemplate her with the eye of reason, in her original purity, and then her beauty will be revealed. We must remember that we have seen her only in a condition which may be compared to that of the sea-god Glaucus, whose original image can hardly be discerned because his natural members are broken off, and crushed and damaged by the waves in all sorts of ways, and encrustations have grown over them of seaweed and shells and stones, so that he is more like some monster than he is to his own natural form. And the soul which we behold is in a similar condition, disfigured by a thousand ills. But not there, not there must we look. What then ? At her love of wisdom. Let us see whom she affects, and what society and converse she seeks in virtue of her near kindred with the immortal and eternal and divine " (that is, let us consider that inmost will-apprehension

---

[1] An outgoing and need completed and superabundantly gratified by supernatural grace and glory.

[2] On account of the long parenthesis I have taken the liberty of slightly altering the wording of Plato and his translator. But I have, of course, scrupulously respected his sense.

of man, rooted in his central self, wherein God is especially immanent, which is especially made after His image, and which, therefore, is ever directed to absolute truth and unlimited goodness—that is, to God—though in sinful souls out of grace this nisus is rendered ineffectual by the soul's bondage to the lower desires and images that are essentially limited). "How different she would become if wholly following this superior principle " (*i.e.* living an interior life, following reason and the will for absolute good) " and borne by a divine impulse " (this surely is fulfilled in sanctifying grace, and its consequence the indwelling and sanctification of the Holy Ghost) " out of the stream in which she now is, and disengaged from the stones and shells and things of earth and rock which in wild variety spring up around her because she feeds upon earth, and is overgrown by the good things of this life, as they are termed " (the sense-given particulars and desires). "Then you would see her as she is, and know whether she has one shape only or many, or what her nature is." The soul impure in its division among mutually exclusive, because essentially limited, attachments becomes pure in its unified actuation to and in the Unlimited Godhead, detached and therefore pure from all restraining and distracting limits. This gradual purification is, then, a fundamental aspect of the mystical way—the result of the progressive unification of the soul by its increasing union with God, Who is Absolute Purity, because He is One Simple Act unlimited and therefore indivisible.

(10) *The Attainment of Peace.*

An aspect of the mystical way grounded primarily in its unification, the aspect whose abuse has given its very name to Quietism, is a gradual attainment of interior peace, repose or quiet. In mysticism this repose or quiet is understood in two senses. There is first of all the repose that is the direct result of unity, and is opposed to the restlessness of divided aims and attention. If there is no unity of aim in life there can be no peace in that life— except a false and short-lived peace, when for a time the activity of the soul is concentrated on some one object. God, however, is the one only end that is wholly satisfying to the human soul. Therefore the soul that does not make God the supreme end of its life cannot have perfect and perpetual peace. If, indeed, a created end be a wide and lofty end—an object rich in content, and spiritual in nature—its deliberate pursuit as the supreme end of life, involving, as it must, the subordination to that end of all other ends and activities, will produce great and often long-continued peace, because it will so largely unify life, and the peace will be in proportion to the unity achieved. It may indeed be that, if that end of life is very high and wide, the soul may achieve a very great and on the whole permanent peace. Nevertheless its peace can never be perfect or wholly secure, because the end cannot be entirely satisfactory nor can the soul be sure of attaining it. Indeed the loftier the end is the surer the soul may be of its non-attainment. Moreover, if the end were attained, the soul could not enjoy for ever the prize of its struggle. Death at least would take it away. Those, on the other hand, who know that God is the supreme and sole satisfying end, and yet do not choose Him as the supreme end of their life, but will created ends irreconcilable with His will, can never achieve any measure of true internal peace. They cannot unify their lives by an end known to reason to be unsatisfactory. It is indeed a practical impossibility to achieve a complete unification of life around a created end, prevented as it is by its inherent limitations from affording satisfaction to all the desires and aspects of the soul. Hence there is a corresponding lack of complete repose or peace in all save those whose will is wholly fixed upon God. "The main cause," says Professor Höffding, "of fatigue and exhaustion in life is unrest and distraction of mind. We are influenced on so many sides that it is difficult for us to collect our thoughts ; we are drawn in so many directions that we find it difficult to focus our will on any one aim ; so many different and changing feelings are aroused that the inner harmony of the mind is exposed to the danger of dissolution" (*Philosophy of Religion*, II. iii., p. 120). We can see this truth writ large in states and civilisations. Only in proportion as there is one national aim is there national peace. A striking instance of this was seen at the outbreak of the late war. Such a unified aim is, however, never realised completely, seldom even partially. Hence a permanent state of internal strife, strife of classes and strife of parties. In proportion as a civilisation has before it one supreme end, or harmony of ends, it enjoys a satisfaction and a peace which, if perfect, would express it itself outwardly in external peace and union between the states who share in that civilisation, and which when present in any large degree expresses itself in the predominant peace and satisfaction and successful achievement of the individuals who partake in that civilisation. Mediæval civilisation possessed this unity in a very high degree.   Hence the high degree of inward peace, of spiritual certainty, security and satisfaction, and of unhesitating, joyous and mutually co-operative achievement attained by its members.   Because modern civilisation lacks this unity of end, or harmony of ends, Matthew Arnold's complaint is bitterly true of it :

> This strange disease of modern life
> With its sick hurry, its divided aims.
>
> Strong the infection of our mental strife
> Which though it gives no bliss, yet spoils for rest,
> And we should win thee from thy own fair life,
> Like us *distracted* and like us unblest.
>
> *The Scholar Gipsy.*

It was for this reason that Plato was so insistent on the need of unity both in the state and in the individuals composing it.

In the conception of Plato unity that is the organic unification of a multiplicity of functions is the principle of stability and internal peace.   The justice of this view is borne out not alone in the social organism, but in the life of the individual soul, especially in that spiritual grace-life with which we are here concerned.   As the soul unifies ever more completely its spiritual life and its prayer, that life is the achievement of an inward peace, and that prayer a prayer of quiet.   The soul is in a state of peace in so far as the will is unified by will-union with God.

Thus as the soul progresses in the way of grace and reaches mystical union, with that union increases her peace, for peace and union increase *pari passu*.   Moreover, the attention of the soul in prayer is progressively unified by increasing freedom from the distraction of limited and therefore diverse images and concepts. In proportion as this unification of attention is accomplished, and prayer becomes a simple attention of the will to God as the Unlimited Good, prayer becomes a prayer of peace and repose, peace from the mental strife and distraction of diverse apprehensions. In this sense, therefore, is the mystical way a growth in peace— an increasing absence of distracting desires and thoughts.   The consummation of the mystical way is also the perfection of peace, because it is the perfect union with the Eternal and the Unmoved. We can never rest in creatures because they all pass away, save indeed those found finally in and through God.   Since mutability is the universal law of this lower world, those who set their love on things here below set their love on things that pass or fail.   For such there can be no true peace.   As, however, the soul's union with God becomes closer and its will is fixed on Him alone, it is delivered from the dominion of change by this union and love of the Eternally Unchanging.   Even sufferings, trials and aridities cannot deprive the soul in the supreme mystical union of the inward peace that is the result of a central union fruition of the Immutable Deity.   In this state of perfect union the soul is like the ocean.   Whatever storms vex the surface, in the depths there is perpetual calm.   In this sense also is the mystic way a way of increasing peace.

The mystics, however, understand peace in another sense, that of passivity as opposed to action.   Here it is that Quietism erred by urging the soul to do nothing whatever in prayer, but simply to wait on God in absolute passivity.   But the orthodox mystics * use very strong language about the passivity of the soul in mystical prayer, one of whose stages is thence designated the Prayer of Quiet.   Their language is indeed so emphatic that at first sight it seems simply Quietistic.   It bears, however, a very different sense.   The orthodox mystics bid us cease to act only when God acts in our souls.   The Quietists tend, in proportion as they are complete Quietists, to bid every soul adopt passivity from the outset.   What is meat to the mystic may well be poison to the ordinary soul.   The Quietist position amounts to saying that because when your food is cooked you have but to eat it, therefore you must not cook it.   When the soul acting through and in obedience to grace has broken down to a certain degree the barriers of undue adherence to and occupation with the finite, when it has attained by simplifying its spiritual attention a certain degree of the unitary peace spoken of above, the peace due to absence of distracting multiplicity in prayer, it becomes conscious of God's grace at work in itself, of God's Presence in its centre.   It has then, of course, but to attend to that grace and Presence.   But until that time arrives, which is when God wills—for His grace works at no uniform or calculable rate—it must prepare for it by its own activity.   Moreover, this manifestation in the soul of the Divine Presence is but intermittent, at least until the highest stages are reached.   In the intervals activity even in prayer is as necessary as ever.   When, however, God speaks the soul must do nothing but listen, when He appears the soul must simply behold, when He gives the soul must do nothing save receive.   This is surely obvious, and this is the true meaning of the seemingly Quietistic passages of St John and other mystical writers. Far different is the Quietist teaching that the soul, at least in prayer, must never do anything save listen, behold and receive, even when there is nothing to be heard, beheld and received. This false generalisation of the mystical teaching on passivity makes common-sense into absurdity, truth into the deadliest of falsehoods. Let us not be surprised, therefore, if sayings of St John of the Cross are condemned on the lips of Molinos, since Molinos applies them with a scope and sense which St John, indeed any orthodox mystic, would have entirely repudiated.

Nevertheless, however we restrict the application of St John's teaching of passivity, it still requires careful attention if it is not to be misunderstood. If I am absorbed by complete attention to an object externally presented, I am in a state of passive receptivity, and the more completely absorbed my attention is, the more complete is the receptivity or passivity.[1] But that receptivity is itself an intense actuation or activity of the soul, a forceful exercise of attention. Indeed the greater and more complete the absorption of the entire soul by the object presented to it, the more intense is this psychical activity, of which, however, for that very reason the soul has no reflex consciousness. If, therefore, the soul is absorbed in the contemplation of God and in the reception of His divine action, it is then most intensely and completely actuated or active in its entire being, and has, nevertheless, no consciousness of that activity. We may indeed say, the greater the passivity the more intense the action. Moreover, in the earlier stages of the action of grace, when that action was as yet imperceptible, at least not immediately perceptible, God's Presence and action were therefore unperceived. This left the soul free to perceive its own action. When, however, God and His action become manifest, this manifestation so occupies the attention of the soul that it is increasingly unconscious of its own activity, though that activity has been in fact increased in the very attention that renders it imperceptible.[2]   The progress from

---

[1] Throughout this discussion I owe much to Baron von Hügel, *Mystical Element*.

[2] This conception of an activity so intense and so interior that it is rest from motion, understood as change even intellectual, is ultimately due to Aristotle, who posits it of the Godhead and terms it ἐνέργεια ἀκινησίας. Its incomprehensibility by our discursive reason, which is of its nature mobile, has led to its widespread but unjustifiable rejection.

activity to passivity is, therefore, to a great extent a change of consciousness, a change from consciousness of the soul's normal, more or less superficial activity with unconsciousness of the action of God in the central depths to a consciousness of the action of God in those central depths with a resultant unconsciousness of the soul's own activity. Consciousness of the soul's own activity at the surface has yielded to consciousness of a reception of God's action in the depths. For this change of consciousness is indeed due to a change in the character of the soul's activity itself. Before, that activity was a reaching out or search after a God wholly absent from perception. Now it is a reception of God present to consciousness. There is in the latter activity the repose and apparent passivity of fruition, in the former the restless activity of search. The change that has taken place is analogous to the change from the activity of hunting or cooking food to the comparative passivity of eating it. Alike in the obtaining and in the eating of the food there is activity, but of this activity we are more conscious when we are seeking or preparing the food, yet untasted, than at the time of the actual eating, when the food itself absorbs the attention,[1] rather than our activity in its regard, whereas before the contrary was the case. So is it in this mystical prayer in which the conscious activity of the search after the hidden God is replaced by the fruition of His revealed Presence. The consequent sense of passivity is heightened by the concomitant peace or repose in the former sense, the peace arising from the unity and freedom of the soul's action, when thus borne Godward by this lofty action of grace, indeed of God Himself through grace. The increasing passivity of the mystical way must not, therefore, be regarded, as it was favourably by the Quietist and is unfavourably by the Philistine, as an increasing idleness. It was only the limits which barred the conscious fruition of God from the former activity that rendered that activity conscious, and it is the consciousness of His Unlimited Being that now renders it partially at first, later wholly unconscious, since the soul is in this unlimited good wholly unified and absorbed. Therefore when the mystic union is fully achieved the soul is established in peace, and that for the three reasons that have just been mentioned. There is repose from distracting multiplicity, freedom from mutability, and the peace of unselfconscious reception of the

---

[1] For the purpose of this illustration I suppose the food to be the engrossing object of our desire and thought !

Divine influx. St Catherine of Genoa has well expressed this achieved peace of the supreme union. " The state of this soul," she says, " is then a feeling of such utter peace and tranquillity that it seems to her that her heart and all her bodily being, and all both within and without is immersed in an ocean of utmost peace, from whence she shall never come forth for anything that can befall her in this life, and she stays immovable, imperturbable, impassible. So much so that it seems to her in her human and her spiritual nature both within and without, she can feel no other thing than sweetest peace. And she is so full of peace that though she press her flesh, her nerves, her bones, no other thing comes forth from them than peace." [1] Thus does the mystic way establish the soul in peace, the fulness of that peace promised to men of good-will, the peace which the world can neither give nor take away.

(11) *Will Identification with the Will of God.*

If we would consider the mystical way from a point of view simpler, more personal and more practical, we should regard it as the ever-increasing identification of our will with the will of God, which is itself but the more personal way of expressing the gradual identification of our good with the Absolute Good. To break through the limits attaching to all created activities and ends and to make the unlimited that is the infinite and absolute goodness our end is to identify our soul life and our will with the Divine life and will. All who are in a state of grace have made a fundamental choice of the Divine Will as their supreme end, but the mystic carries this out actually in every activity, interior or exterior, however unimportant it may seem. To identify our will, our good, our very life with God involves a participation in the Divine will, good and life—that is, in God Himself, Who is His will, His good and His life. The mystic is secure from failure, for his will is a Will that cannot fail. He is in harmony with all things save sin, because all except sin is the product of God's will, and the operations and mutual interventions of creatures are ordered by His will. Therefore all these are now in perfect accord with the will of the mystic, working together for his good, who wholly loves God. Even the sin of others, as he well knows, is powerless to harm him, for it cannot frustrate God's Almighty

---

[1] *Vitae Dottrina*, xviii., quoted by Miss Evelyn Underhill (*Mysticism*, p. 518), who believes it to be authentic.

Will. His entire will identification with the will of God is itself the destruction and reparation of his own sins. It is, moreover, universal charity, for God's will, now by participation his, is love of His entire creation. The mystic realises his unity with all creatures in his union with God their one source and ground. Hence he feels himself in love with them all, a note in their universal harmony, their fellow-member of one Divine kingdom which is an externalisation of God's Will and Being. All creatures, even the soulless elements, are his brothers and sisters, and all things are his indeed, his because they are God's and he is now wholly of and in God. Moreover, this will identification is untroubled peace, because it involves perfect and joyful resignation and acceptance of God's dispositions for himself and others. It is unity, because there is no longer distraction in his ends and activities. It is power, because God now works unopposed through him, and the feeblest instrument, if an unresisting instrument, in His hands can accomplish wonderful things. It raises his soul above the dominion of change, of care, of loss, of injury from others. This ever-increasing participation in, and union with, the Divine Will and Life is spoken of by St John as a transformation of the soul in God and a deification of the soul. This language I will discuss later when I deal specifically with the final stage of mystical union as taught by St John. All that I wish to insist on here is that the very essence and the sole test of progress in grace, and later in the mystical way, is the identification of the will and hence of the activities and the life of the soul with God's will, activity and life—that is, with God Himself.

(12) *Progressive Attainment of Reality.*

We may finally envisage the mystic way as a gradual attainment of Reality. It is here that great caution is required. Many modern writers on mysticism misinterpret the doctrine, that God is the ultimate reality, in a pantheistic sense, as if created things were merely unsubstantial phenomena of one underlying Divine Substance, and therefore unreal in the sense of being an empty illusion, *maya*, as the Hindus term it. The ordinary non-mystical Christian, however, is apt to fly to the opposite extreme, and to regard creatures as fully real and all creatures as equally real. The truth lies between these two extremes. All creatures are certainly real, for they exist. Any attempt to deny this is self-

condemned. So far we must go with the plain workaday man.
But they are not real in the sense that God is real. For their
being is not self-subsistent, but rooted in His being and Will.
Therefore their being compared to the fulness of His absolute
self-dependent Being is not being. Regarded as ultimately self-
sufficient or self-existent entities, they are indeed illusion and
vanity. Moreover, though they are all real, they are not all
equally real. Even the plain man will admit that dreams and
fancies and optical illusions have existence, therefore reality, but
that compared with the objects of the normally working and
correctly functioning senses they are unreal, because they have
so much less being. The closer a creature approaches to God
the more being it possesses, because its being is less narrowly
limited. Here we are, then, back at the old refrain of the entire
chapter—I might say of the entire book—Unlimited Being—
Absolute Reality, fulness of Being self-existent : more limits—
less being, less reality : fewer limits—more being, more reality.
What ultimately differentiates matter from spirit ? Matter has
more limits, therefore less being, less reality : spirit has fewer
limits, therefore more being, more reality. Hence the Eastern
doctrine of *maya*, false as a philosophy, is the inaccurate transcript
of a profound truth underlying the entire mystical way. Created
being though not simply illusion, sheer unreality, when compared
with God and therefore in regard to the exigencies of the rational
soul capable through grace of the fruition of God, is illusion,
is unreal. Catholic mysticism—that is, simply Catholic faith
in its highest intensity—links together the West and the East.
It touches with one hand the hard-headed, practical, but somewhat philistine Western, the man of affairs who prides himself on
his full recognition and successful manipulation of plain facts,
the obvious realities of this world in which he lives. With the
other hand it touches the Buddhist devotee who kneels on the
pagoda steps to recite his rosary of disillusionment, a rosary whose
paters and *aves* are the repeated condemnation of all earthly
experience as nothing but " sorrow, misery and trouble." [1] The
Western man of business rejects or misunderstands, the Buddhist
wholly rejects the mediating truth of Catholicism with its message
to both and its proffered satisfaction to the spiritual needs of
both. The narrowness of the human mind will not contain an
all-comprehending truth, unless circumstances peculiarly favour

[1] See Fielding, *The Soul of a People*, p. 157.

and a special grace be granted. But the truth is comprehensive all the same.

If an important function of mysticism be thus a realisation of the comparative unreality of the creature, its lack of being when being is understood as the Divine fulness of being without lack or limit, and especially of the unreality of the more narrowly limited, superficial and sensible spheres of creation, it is the function of common-sense to insist on the reali⁴y of creatures, and especially of the more limited and more immediately sensible creatures. Catholicism, as we have seen above, insists on full acceptance of the reality demanded by common-sense and also of the comparative unreality discovered by mystical intuition, and it is in virtue of this twofold acceptance that Catholicism mediates between the "pure" mysticism of the Buddhist that denies the dicta of common-sense, and the "pure" common-sense of the Western philistine that rejects mysticism as a mischievous absurdity. Castlereagh once characterised the Holy Alliance as "sublime mysticism and nonsense." Catholicism may be aptly described as "sublime mysticism and common-sense." [1] In this combination of mysticism and common-sense, of the denial and the affirmation of the reality of creatures, and consequently of their rejection and acceptance lies the peculiar genius of Catholic Christianity. Hence also the double attitude of the Church towards this worldly knowledge and endeavour, towards "enlightenment and progress" whereby she seems at once to bless them and to ban them, because in truth she receives and rejects them—receives them as positively good because real, rejects them in so far as they exclude by their comparative unreality the attainment of fuller and higher degrees of reality, and above all, the attainment of the Absolute Reality of God. Outside the Church we find to-day mysticism running riot in the denial of all validity to the common-sense beliefs of mankind, of all reality to the objects of sense perception and of discursive reason. We have already discussed an instance of this denial of common-sense in Miss Evelyn Underhill's "superior" attitude to the unenlightened plain man who believes that if he sees a brick wall he really is in contact with such an object existing outside his own perception. Thus does non-Catholic mysticism seek to

---

[1] Hence the welcome of Aristotelianism in the Middle Ages, for of all philosophies that of Aristotle shows the greatest and the most openly avowed regard for the dicta of universal common-sense.

transcend common-sense and its sphere by the rejection of both. It would fain reach heaven by denying the existence of earth. For lack of support it falls and lies prostrate on the despised ground, absorbed in the contemplation of "dissipated tabbies" and "sooty trees" (Miss Evelyn Underhill, *Practical Mysticism*).* Catholic mysticism, on the other hand, transcends common-sense and the world of common-sense by the acceptance of both as real and valuable in their own place and degree, as the starting-point of the soul's journey to God. With her feet thus firmly planted on the earth, her eyes endure to look upon the sun, and her view is among the stars. At the other extreme are innumerable multitudes who explicitly or implicitly deny the reality, or at least the superior reality, of the spiritual. Both extremes are offended by the Catholic *Weltanschauung*. Both can find in Catholicism acceptance and reconciliation. But in the meanwhile the " mystic " is apt to disdain Catholicism as crude and material-istic, the "plain man " to regard it as fantastic and superstitious, an obstacle to the material progress of mankind. I cannot here illustrate this point, and must be content with asking my readers to test for themselves whether this double acceptance of mysticism and common-sense, of the reality and the comparative unreality of creatures (the latter varying in degree according to their limitation and consequent distance from the unlimited Godhead), be not the fundamental characteristic of Catholicism determining the Catholic attitude to human experience and conduct in all their manifold aspects.[1]

Surely I have now removed all danger of pantheistic mis-apprehension of my thesis, that the progress from union with creatures as they are in themselves and from activity bounded by creatures to union with God and activity in God, is a progress from non-reality to Reality, to the ultimate Reality, which in the created non-realities is the source and ground of whatever degree of reality they possess, to the Reality, that is so real, that all else *by comparison* is unreal. This, therefore, is the mystic scale of

---

[1] Hence it is that the Church's attitude seems under certain aspects and to certain temperaments so brutally realist and even materialistic—*e.g.* in her wide use of Roman law, her stern and suspicious examination of all claims to special sanctity or supernatural favours, and in a " somewhat business-like " dispensa-tion of the sacraments ; under other aspects and to other temperaments so "fantastically " other-worldly—*e.g.* in her preference for the material overthrow of a nation to the commission of sin, her thronged pilgrimages to the place where a peasant girl saw a vision.

values : the nearer to God—that is, the more of His being there is represented in any creature—the greater its reality, therefore the greater its value ; the further from God—that is, the less of His Being there is represented in any creature (as matter represents less of God than spirit), the less its reality and therefore the less its value. Thus in *The Ascent of Mount Carmel* St John maintains the superior value of sense impressions to imaginary pictures constructed by the combination of sense data, on the ground that the former possess more reality than the latter (*Ascent*, II. xii.). The truth of the mystic way is thus the direct opposite of the popular notion of it. Far from being a progress from the more to the less real, from the concrete thing to the empty abstraction, it is a progress in the opposite direction, ever adding degrees of reality, greater fulness of being, as limits, which are negations of reality—that is, of being—are gradually transcended, in the ascent to the infinite. There is nothing ultimately negative in the mystical way, which is a process of ever-increasing positivity, as God the all Positive without any negation, because without any limit, is ever more fully attained. Nevertheless this positive process has of necessity its negative aspect. The elimination of limits involves the elimination of much that is positive in which those limits inhere. Later, all that is positive in creatures is indeed restored in a higher way, when their limits no longer come between the soul and God. Till, however, that stage is reached, a stage on which the soul enters when the night of purgation is passed, and which is fully completed in the resurrection of the body, the negative process is essential. It constitutes the dominant characteristic of the beginning of the mystical way, reappears later with far greater intensity, and is never wholly transcended in this mortal life. It is the subject matter of two of St John's treatises—both unhappily incomplete—*The Ascent of Mount Carmel* and *The Dark Night of the Soul*. This negative way, therefore, will require a very close study. Such a study, however, could not have been profitably undertaken until the positive character of the mystical way had been made clear. Otherwise the reader could hardly have failed to receive the false impression that St John's negative way is ultimately negative or nihilistic. It is, on the contrary, the destruction of the limits which kept the soul from the fruition of unlimited good, temporary rejection in the interest of possession, No as the inevitable way to the perfect Yes.

CHAPTER VII

THE NEGATIVE WAY

Joy, joy.   There is nothing, nothing . . .
Oh infinite happiness.

JEAN CHRISTOPHE,
English Translation, vol. i., p. 90.

Hark to the Alleluia of the bird
For those that found the dying way to life.

FRANCIS THOMPSON.

Where is the land of Luthany ?
Where is the tract of Elenore ?
I am bound therefor.

" Pierce thy heart to find the key ;
With thee take
Only what none else would keep ;
Learn to dream when thou dost wake,
Learn to wake when thou dost sleep.
Learn to water joy with tears,
Learn from fears to vanquish fears ;
To hope, for thou dar'st not despair,
Exult, for that thou dar'st not grieve ;
Plough thou the rock until it bear ;
Know, for thou else couldst not believe ;
Lose, that the lost thou may'st receive ;
Die, for none other way canst live.
When earth and heaven lay down their veil,
And that apocalypse turns thee pale ;
When thy seeing blindeth thee
To what thy fellow-mortals see ;
When their sight to thee is sightless ;
Their living, death ; their light, most lightless :
Search no more—
Pass the gate of Luthany, tread the region Elenore."

FRANCIS THOMPSON,
The Mistress of Vision.

THE verses of Francis Thompson, so hauntingly beautiful, but at
first sight so obscure, with which I have prefaced this chapter are

but the poetical expression of that Via Negativa of mysticism of which St John of the Cross is the clearest and most uncompromising exponent. St John has devoted to the negative way two treatises, or rather, as he intended and regarded them, two portions of one treatise—namely, *The Ascent of Mount Carmel* and *The Dark Night of the Soul*. His teaching on this subject has often been grossly misunderstood, as also has its ground, already discussed, the negative knowledge of God. The misapprehension has been in both cases to regard what is relatively negative as absolutely negative. In order the better to avoid this misapprehension I have emphasised already the essentially positive character of mysticism. I have pointed out that the mystical way— or rather the way of sanctifying grace of which the mystical union-intuition is a stage—is a progress from less to greater positivity, from the comparatively unreal to an ever fuller reality. For the creature contains qua creature a negative or unreal element, and it is for this very reason that the Uncreated Being of God cannot be known through any created concept, since every such concept involves a limitation and therefore a negation which is infinitely distant from pure positivity. But it plainly follows from this that union with God must involve the progressive rejection of creaturely limitations, and that alike in the cognitive and volitional aspects of the soul's activity. Until the soul is wholly free from the limitations of finite aims and concepts, it cannot fully receive the unlimited Being of God. This gradual process of detachment from the limited is called by St John the Night of the Soul. " I call," he says, " this detachment the night of the soul . . . which consists in suppressing desire and avoiding pleasure : it is this that sets the soul free, even though possession may be still retained " (*Ascent*, I. iii). "The soul must of necessity —*if we would attain to the divine union with God*—pass through the dark night of mortification of the desires and self-denial in all things. The reason is this : all the love we bestow on creatures is in the eyes of God mere darkness, and while we are involved therein, the soul is incapable of being enlightened and possessed by the pure and simple light of God, unless we first cast that love away. . . . The affection and attachment which the soul feels for the creature renders the soul its equal and its like— the greater the affection the greater will be the likeness. . . . He who loves the creature becomes vile as that creature itself, and in one sense even viler, for love not only levels, but subjects also the lover to the object of his love." [1]   Both these reasons amount to this, that attachment to the limited for its own sake involves the limitation of our love with the limits of its object, and this limitation debars the soul from free and full love-union with God, the Unlimited Good.   This is perhaps stated somewhat more clearly in the immediately following paragraphs.   " He who loveth anything beside God " (*i.e.* not in order to God) " renders his soul incapable of the pure divine union and transformation in God, for the vileness of the creature is further removed from the greatness of the Creator than darkness is from light.   All things in heaven and earth are nothing in comparison with God. . . . All created things with the affections bestowed upon them are nothing, because they are a hindrance, and the privation of our transformation in God, just as darkness is nothing, and less than nothing, being the absence of light.   And as he who is in darkness comprehends not the light, so the soul, the affections of which are given to the creature, shall never comprehend God.   Until our soul is purged of these affections we shall not possess God in this life in the pure transformation of love, nor in the life to come in clear vision. . . . The whole creation, *compared with the infinite being of God,* is nothing, and so the soul, the affections of which are set on created things, is nothing, and even less than nothing before God, because love begets equality and likeness and even inferiority to the object beloved.   Such a soul, therefore, cannot by any possibility be united to the infinite being of God, *because that which is not can have no communion with that which is* " (*Ascent,* I. iv).   That is to say, a soul bound by the negation-limits of the creature, and thus deprived of being by its lack of being, and that in the exact measure of that lack of being cannot be united with the Unlimited, cannot receive the fulness of Absolute Being.

This doctrine is expressed in a later chapter in a series of apparent paradoxes which sum up St John's teaching on the negative way.   The student of mysticism will do well to bear them in mind —for they go to the root of the matter.

" That thou mayest have pleasure in the All, seek pleasure in nothing.   That thou mayest know the All, seek to know nothing.

" That thou mayest possess the All, seek to possess nothing.

" That thou mayest be the All, seek to be nothing.

" When thou dwellest upon anything, thou hast ceased to cast thyself upon the All.

[1] *Ascent,* I. iv.

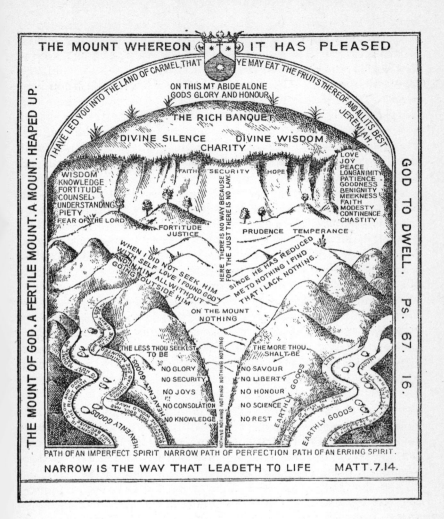

" Because in order to arrive wholly at the All, thou hast to deny thyself wholly in all.

" And when thou comest to attain the All, thou must keep it without desiring anything.

" Because, if thou wilt keep anything with the All, thou hast not thy treasure simply in God."

These lines, with some others to the same effect, were placed also by the saint below a curious diagram with which he prefaced *The Ascent of Mount Carmel.*   I reproduce this diagram here as it stands in the original, save that I have translated the Spanish and Latin into English.

We remark first that there are three ways set before the soul. Of these the right-hand path, that of the goods of earth, leads wholly away from the ascent of the mountain—that is, from God. The left-hand way, that of the goods of heaven,[1] does indeed lead to the summit, but by a slow and circuitous route.   The central way—the narrow path—leads thither directly and speedily.   It is marked by one significant word oft repeated—nada—nada—nada—nada—nada—nothing—nothing—nothing—nothing—nothing.   It is the path of utter rejection.   But is not this sheer nihilism ?   Does not this terrible nada fully justify St John's severest critics ?   This is too hasty.   Before rushing at conclusions, let us consider the matter in the light of what has been already discussed and quoted.

First note well that nada is but the way—not the goal.   The goal is, as the above-quoted verses emphasised, the very opposite pole to nothingness—namely, the All, that which is the positive being of all things, God Who is eminently all that creatures are, without the negation inherent in creatureliness.   The goal of St John is not a negative Nirvana.[2]   How infinitely positive and rich is the goal to which St John would bring us will be better realised when we come to discuss in detail the higher stages of the mystical union.   But at least we know already that it is the very opposite of nonentity.

The next point to which attention must be called is that Our Lord teaches in substance the same doctrine of the negative way that is expressed with such terrifying force by St John.   " Blessed are the poor in spirit "—*i.e.* those detached from worldly goods—

---

[1] *I.e.* spiritual things that are not God Himself.

[2] Whether Buddha's Nirvana was negative or positive is a vexed question which I do not wish to discuss here.   The probability is that it was negative.

the " goods of the earth " of St John's right-hand path. " Blessed are the meek," those who have utterly rejected self-aggrandisement in opposition to and at the expense of the universal good. " Blessed are they that mourn." " Blessed are they that suffer persecution." " Lay not up for yourselves treasures on earth." " If any man come to me, and hate not his father, and mother, and wife, and children, and brethren, and sisters, yea, and his own life also, he cannot be my disciple." " Every one of you that doth not renounce all that he possesseth cannot be my disciple." " For he that will save his life shall lose it : and he that shall lose his life for my sake [that is, for God's sake—since Christ's sovereign claim is the consequence of His Divinity] shall find it." " He that findeth his life shall lose it, and he that shall lose his life for me shall find it. If any man will come after me, *let him deny himself,* and take up his cross and follow me." " Amen, Amen, I say to you, unless the grain of wheat falling into the ground die ; itself remaineth alone. But if it die, it bringeth forth much fruit. He that loveth his life shall lose it ; and he that hateth his life in this world keepeth it unto life eternal." Nor can it be said that we are reading into these words of Our Lord a later asceticism. It is present in their obvious meaning. It may also be remarked that the most modern and most independent of higher critics, Dr Schweitzer, insists on this " world negation " in the teaching of Jesus, a negation which is, he points out, in conflict with the " world acceptance," forced into the Gospel by Protestant theology.[1] St Paul echoes the hard sayings of his Divine Master.

" It remaineth that they also who have wives be as if they had none : and they that weep, as though they wept not : and they that rejoice, as though they rejoiced not : and they that buy, as though they possessed not : and they that use this world, as though they used it not." " The things that were gain to me, the same I have counted loss for Christ. Furthermore, I count all things to be but loss for the excellent knowledge of Jesus Christ

---

[1] See his *The Quest of the Historical Jesus,* especially the concluding pages (pp. 400-401, English translation). The author's one-sided emphasis on eschatology does not invalidate the force of this testimony to the evangelical character of Catholic renunciation of the world.

Dr Schweitzer has since given practical testimony to his conviction of this " world-negation " in the teaching of Jesus. For he has abandoned his position in the world of European scholarship to become a medical missionary in Africa. He has thus, indeed, left all to follow a Christ whose Divinity he disbelieves.

my Lord : for whom I have suffered the loss of all things, and count them but as dung, that I may gain Christ." It is therefore evident that we cannot reject the teaching of St John of the Cross without at the same time rejecting the teaching of Christ, the doctrine of the Cross. St John has but worked out the significance and the logical necessity of the Gospel teaching. Human nature may and does shrink from the cross. But we cannot, therefore, deny the force of St John's reasoning. If we wish to be made one with God, we must be detached from the finite. The life of grace is the progress from the life of nature self-centred and bounded by the limitations of the creature to the full supernatural participation (to the utmost measure of our capacity) of the un-limited Being of God, a participation that is a life God-centred and God-principled. To draw near to one terminus is of necessity to depart from the other. If our life is to be supernatural, it cannot be merely natural. If it is to be for God, in God and of God, it cannot be for self, in self, or of self, for the creature, in the creature, or of the creature. If it is to be a participation of the unlimited, it cannot be confined and conditioned by the limits of creatures. The vessel that is bound for the ocean cannot remain in the harbour or even in the estuary. The butterfly cannot come forth into the freedom of the air until the caterpillar, with its earth-bound life, has been destroyed and buried in the tomb of the chrysalis. So long as we are attached to some finite idea or image, or to some finite aim, so as to adhere to that idea, image or aim for its own sake—as a final value in our spiritual life—we are not free to pass beyond it to the infinite life of God. We must remember also that it is not the enjoyment of created goods, but the adherence of the will to those goods, not the use of created images and concepts, but the resting of the soul in them, that is condemned. Only in so far as possession and use inevitably cause adherence of will or understanding are such possession and use to be rejected. When and in so far as attachment is destroyed, the soul may safely use and enjoy created goods and ideas. They will then help it to pass through and beyond them to the infinite and will themselves be rightly valued and used. " He has greater joy," says St John, " and comfort in creatures if he detaches him-self from them ; and he can have no joy in them if he considers them as his own. For selfish attachment is a bond that chains the soul to earth and suffers not breadth of heart. He acquires also in this detachment from creatures a clear comprehension of them.

. . . For this reason his joy in them is widely different from his who is attached to them and far nobler. The former rejoices in their truth, the latter in their deceptiveness ; the former in their best, the latter in their worst conditions ; the former in their substantial worth, and the latter in their seeming and accidental nature through his senses only. For sense cannot grasp or comprehend more than the accidents, but the mind, purified from the clouds and species of the accidents, penetrates to the interior truth and worth of things, for that is its proper object. Now joy as a cloud darkens the judgment, for there can be no rejoicing in created things without the attachment of the will, just as joy cannot exist as a passion without habitual selfish attachment of heart. The negation and purgation of this joy leaves the judgment clear as the sky when the mists are scattered. The former, therefore, has joy in all things, since he has no proprietary pleasure in them, and it is as if all were his own : and the latter, in so far as he regards particular things as his own, loses that universal joy in all things. The former, whilst his heart is set upon none of them, possesses them all. . . . The latter, while in will attached to them, neither has nor possesses anything ; yea, rather created things have possession of his very heart, for which cause he suffers pain as a prisoner " (*Ascent*, III. xix). In this passage we have a clear exposition of the true meaning and of one important value of detachment. To be detached from creatures is to possess their positive being without bondage within their negative element, their limitation, and to pass in and through this to the infinite ground of their being. It is also to apprehend the spiritual reality externalised and symbolised in the material object.[1] In the twenty-third chapter of the third book of *The Ascent* St John tells us that the use and enjoyment of sensible things is profitable to the mystic if he rise from them to God, and he emphasises this teaching in the twenty-fifth chapter. " As to the eye," he says, " now purged from all joy in seeing, the soul receives joy, directed to God, in all that is seen. . . . As to the ear, purged from all joy in hearing, the soul receives joy a hundredfold, and that most spiritual, directed to God in all that is heard, whether human or divine. The same observation applies to the other senses when purged." [2] In other

---

[1] Material in the widest sense. A distinct idea is material in so far as it is an abstraction from material images.

[2] *Cf.* St Ignatius, *Spiritual Exercises*, Fourth Week, A. 7.

words, the true function of creatures is sacramental. They are
to lead us inwards or upwards (as you choose to symbolise the soul
movement) to their Divine ground and source. If we follow this
attraction, the soul finds rest and joy; if we remain attached to
the external and the particular, satiety and weariness will be our
portion.   To be attached to or *to desire* creatures, not as channels
to God, but as ends in themselves, is to be bound in and by their
creaturely limitations.   For the love of the will rests in a limited
object and thus is, as we have seen, impeded or altogether prevented from passing onward to the perfect will-union with God
that is the goal of the mystical way, indeed of the life of grace.
The cognitive function of the soul is bound in like manner within
their limitations, within distinct ideas, and cannot escape to the
free intuition of the Unlimited God unknowable by distinct ideas.
Moreover, any one desire deliberately entertained, however slight
its subject matter—that is,the adherence of the will to any creature,
however trifling in worth as apart from God—is sufficient to effect
this bondage within the limited which prevents the soul from passing onward to full union with God.   The will is not wholly directed
to God, wholly made one with His will, for it wills some object
other than and besides God and His Will.   Therefore the perfect
union with God, which is the end of the mystic way, can never be
attained so long as any deliberate desire remains, however insig-
nificant be its object.   " All voluntary desires," says St John,
" whether of mortal sins . . . or of venial sins . . . or of imperfections only must be banished away, and the soul that would
attain to perfect union must be delivered from them all, however
slight they may be.   The reason is this : the state of divine union
consists in the total transformation of the will into the will of God,
so that there is in the soul nothing contrary to the divine will.
But if the soul cleaves to any imperfection contrary to the will of
God, His will alone is not done, for the soul wills that which God
wills not.   It is clear, therefore, that if the soul is to be united in
love and will with God, every desire of the will must first of all be
cast away, however slight it may be ; that is, we must not deliberately, and knowingly, assent with the will to any imperfection. . . .
Does it make any difference whether a bird be held by a slender
thread or by a rope ? Although the cord be slender the bird
will be just as bound, as by the rope, so that it cannot fly. . . .
This is the state of the soul with particular attachments, it
never can attain to the liberty of the divine union, whatever

virtues it may possess. Desires and attachments effect the soul as the remora is said to effect a ship, that is but a little fish, yet when it clings to a vessel it effectually hinders its progress " (*Ascent*, I. xi).

In the opening chapters of the first book of *The Ascent* St John analyses with great psychological skill the effects of desire, desire for creatures as ends in themselves. He shows how such desires fatigue, torment, darken, pollute and enfeeble the soul. He calls these effects the positive evils of the desires. The desires fatigue the soul because they demand first one thing, then another, and yet are never satisfied. They torment the soul by the keen cravings they awake and by robbing it of its strength. They darken the soul in several ways. They overcloud the perception so that the soul cannot attain a true view of reality nor receive the supernatural wisdom of God. They deprive the soul of clear judgment, leading it blindly in the wrong direction. Finally, they so dazzle the soul with the false glamour they cast upon their objects, that the spiritual vision cannot penetrate beyond these objects to the true Object of Love. They pollute the soul by staining the purity of its life, of its Godward nisus with the multiple stains of their unworthy objects, whose images are impressed on the understanding. They enfeeble the soul because they divide the unity of its life and will among a manifold of " trifles," and this distraction of spiritual energy is, of course, its diminution (*Ascent*, Book I., chaps. vi-xi). In all these respects, some of which have been discussed in detail in the last chapter, their action is diametrically opposed to that of the Divine Love which is the substance of mystical union. The evil effects of the desires have indeed been fully realised outside the pale of Christianity. The evil of desire, the commonplace of Buddhism, the basis of the pessimism of Schopenhauer, and strange as it may seem, was a fundamental principle of the practical philosophy of Epicurus. It is, however, plain that desire is of the very essence of life. Activity must always be motived by desire for some end. Hence it was that Schopenhauer, together with that school of Buddhism whose Nirvana is extinction, denounces life itself as evil. Christian mysticism, on the contrary, sees that the evil lies not in desire as such, but in desire for particular objects, for creatures which cannot, owing to their essential limitations, satisfy the need of the soul for perfect—that is, unlimited—happiness. We have already seen that there is more of positive being in some creatures than in others.   Therefore desire for the creatures that have more positive being is less harmful than desire for those that possess less positive being, because in the former there is more positive good to satisfy the soul.[1]   Those creatures, however, which have the least positive being are those whose enjoyment and use involves the most exclusive possession.   As their positive being increases, the exclusiveness of possession necessary for their enjoyment tends to decrease in proportion.   The better goods, those possessed of a high degree of positive being—intellectual truths, moral qualities, friendship and love, the beauties of nature and art [2]—do not thus depend on exclusive possession.   My knowledge of a truth in no way excludes others from knowledge of the same truth.   My possession of moral qualities helps instead of hindering the possession of these qualities by others.   My enjoyment of a landscape or of a work of art does not prevent its enjoyment by others.   Many persons can read the same book, see the same picture, enjoy the friendship of the same friend.   Love indeed does involve a large element of exclusive possession.   That element, however, is grounded in, and attached to, the lower or physical constituent of love.   None but the father and mother can share their love of their children, because the physical relationship of parenthood is absent.   The mutual love of husband and wife excludes the participation of a third party for a similar reason.   These physical conditions, however, are but temporary limitations—limitations confined to human life on earth.   They do not belong to the essence of love.   Love when it is full grown to the maturity of the spiritual and the eternal, knows no more the exclusions which are but the swaddling clothes of its earthly infancy.   In heaven the mutual love of the elect infinitely surpasses the deepest earthly love of man and wife, or mother and child.   Nevertheless "they do not marry nor are given in marriage." *   Therefore the more of positive being, the less the limitation, and consequently the less the exclusion.   Therefore also the greater and the deeper—that is, the more spiritual—our love, our charity, the more universal will it be, and the more

---

[1] This supposes the force of desire to be equal in both cases. If, as often happens, the desire for the less limited goods is stronger than desire for the more limited goods, the former desire is the more harmful, because more exclusive of charity.

[2] Yet these latter require more exclusion than the former goods. A particular work of art can only be accessible to a comparative few. The beauties of nature are often visible solely to those who can afford time and money to visit them.

complete will be its rejection of the exclusiveness which springs from the limitations of the finite.

Exclusive possession is, however, obtained by money and measured by money. There are goods that are entirely or almost entirely to be obtained for money, goods, therefore, which are wholly, or almost wholly, dependent for their use on exclusive possession. Such, for instance, are articles of food and clothing, houses, estates, motors, horses, yachts and the like. Of such goods, there are those that are necessary and those that are superfluous, luxuries. The former cost so little that they are, or rather could be and should be, within the reach of all men. They are also the goods that Our Lord has promised to those who seek first His Kingdom. The latter, though capable of good use, have on the whole an evil effect on their possessor, by binding him in the chains of their exclusiveness. There are other goods which cannot be obtained without money, but cannot be obtained by money alone. Such goods are, for instance, works of art, which require for their right use and choice good taste as well as the means to purchase them; friends whom we cannot buy for money and whose society nevertheless we often cannot enjoy unless we have sufficient means to afford them hospitality; a happy marriage, which is indeed beyond all price of gold, and nevertheless requires a certain income. One sure test of a vulgar man is his attitude towards this second class of goods. The vulgar man only values works of art for their price, and friends as proofs of wealth and means to further wealth, and he measures matrimonial success by the income of the bride. I have pointed out already that the vulgar man, the opposite pole to the mystic, is the man who lives entirely on the surface, entirely captive to the most external and material, and therefore the most limited, objects of desire. Now it is just these objects that are valuable by a money value, because of their complete exclusion of common possession, an exclusiveness which itself is constituted by their extreme limitation. Hence the vulgar man is the man who measures everything by money and who therefore aims primarily at the first class of goods and at the second class only in so far as they are dependent on money and reducible to a monetary standard. These goods of the second class vary indefinitely in the degree of their dependence on money for their enjoyment, and the measure of their independence of money is the measure of their true value because it is the measure of their freedom from limits and therefore

N

of their positive reality and of their spiritual significance. As they ascend in this scale, they approach ever more closely the goods of the third and highest class, those that are altogether independent of money for their enjoyment. Such are intellectual and artistic capacities, moral virtues and, above all, religion. "The gift of God cannot be purchased with money," nor will money help us to possess it. The poorest may be a saint. It is indeed true that there is a degrading poverty which hinders the knowledge of religious truth and the attainment of virtue. This is the poverty that is neither holy nor blessed, the poverty that is directly caused by sin,[1] and which God hates. The poverty of the East End slum is not the poverty of Nazareth nor of the saints, but an abomination to be abhorred, and to the measure of their opportunities eradicated, by all good men. That moral and spiritual goods are not as much in the reach of the labourer as of the prince is due, in so far as it is the case, to a social disease arising directly from the sinful materialism of a godless civilisation. Poverty of the type lauded by Christ and the saints, far from being an obstacle to the possession of the highest goods, is, at least in the will, an essential prerequisite for their acquisition.

Thus to the mystic, as well as to the vulgar man or the complete materialist—they are two different names for the same person—money is the measure of values, but in the reverse way. The vulgar man values goods in proportion to their dependence on money—that is, in proportion to the exclusiveness of their possession, and that in turn is in proportion to their externality and materiality, to their limitation. The mystic values them in proportion to their independence of money—that is, in proportion to the inclusiveness or community of their possession, and that in turn is in proportion to their inwardness and spirituality, to their freedom from limitation.

Hence it is that the saints felt the need to get rid of possessions by a voluntary poverty. Only thus could they free themselves from the limits of particular things and particular desires, and from the evils resultant on those limits, to find God the infinite Good in all things, and to possess and enjoy the positive being or goodness of all things as sacraments of Him. Such was the joyous poverty of St Francis.

Hence also the mystic replaces the desire for those creatures

---

[1] I mean by the sin of society, and especially of the plutocrats who organi society.

whose possession by one is in greater or lesser degree exclusive
of their possession by others, by the supernatural love-longing
for the Unlimited God, Whose possession is rather increased than
diminished by the participation of other souls. Dante in the
Purgatorio has expressed very beautifully this inclusive character
of the love of God, having especially in mind the love of the
blessed in Heaven. He has asked Virgil why a certain spirit
had bidden men fix their desire where there was no need of exclusion of partnership. Virgil replies :

> Perchè s'appuntan li vostri desiri
> Dove per compagnia parte si scema,
> Invidia move il mantaco ai sospiri.
> Ma se l'amor della spera suprema
> Torcesse in suso il desiderio vostro,
> Non vi sarebbe al petto quella tema ;
> Chè per quanti si dice più lì nostro
> Tanto possiede più di ben ciascuno,
> E più di caritate arde in quel chiestro.

> (Because your aspirations are directed thither
> (to worldly advantages) where by participation
> some part is lost, envy sets in motion
> its bellows upon your sighs. But if love
> for the most exalted sphere turned your
> desires upwards, you would not have in your
> breasts that fear (of diminution of portion) ;
> for the more persons there are by whom
> "Ours" is said up there, so much the more
> of good does each one possess and so much
> the more is there of holy Love burning
> in that cloister.)

Dante demands further explanations which Virgil proceeds
to give :

> Quello infinito ed ineffabil bene
> Che è lassù, così corre ad amore
> Come a lucido corpo raggio viene.
> Tanto sì dà, quanto trova d'ardore :
> Sì che quantunque carità si estende
> Cresce sop'essa l'eterno valore
> E quanta gente più lassu s'intende,
> Più v'è da bene amare, e più vi s'ama,
> E come specchio l'uno all 'altro rende.

> (That infinite and ineffable Good,
> which is yonder on high, speeds to love
> (*i.e.* to unite Himself with the souls that

are filled with it) even as a sunbeam is drawn
to a translucent body.   It bestows itself
in proportion to the warmth (of love) :
so that in whatever measure Love extends,
the more does the Eternal Worth increase
upon it.   And the more spirits there are
on high yonder who love, the more there are
to love perfectly and the more do they love
each other, and as a mirror one reflects
back (the love) to the other.)

Purgatorio, xv. 49-75.

The mystic in proportion as he has climbed the mystic ladder
has already attained this heavenly love whose freedom from
limit rejects all exclusiveness.

Another effect of attachment to particular goods, or of exclusive possession, is the reference of these goods to self as an
altogether independent centre, hostile at least in potency to all
other individuals.   It builds up a wall around the soul whereby
it is cut off from other souls and from God.   Detachment from
this exclusive possession and from desire for such possession unites
the soul with others in a common charity and with God who is
sought, known and loved in all things.   St John, however, goes
further and demands of the mystic detachment even from moral
and spiritual goods as ends in themselves.   It is here that mystical
theology demands a higher asceticism than is required of those
not called to the mystical union.   The reason is that these highest
goods, though not valuable by money, nor exclusive of a common
possession, contain as creatures a finite element by which the
soul is limited so long as they are regarded as ultimate values
or ends in themselves.   So long as the understanding and will
are bound by this finite element they cannot pass onward to the
mystical union with the infinite Being of God.   But, it will be
urged, all cannot solely seek the Uncreated Good, nor even the
highest created goods, all cannot be detached even from exclusive
possession and from desire of the lower goods.   The order and
well-being of society demand not only attachment to the higher
creatures, but also private ownership and a pursuit of material
aims.   This is true, and for that very reason St John addresses
his book to the friars and nuns of the Carmelite reform.   The
majority of mankind cannot be actually free in this life from the
love and desire of created goods for their own sake, or even from
the *exclusive* possession of such goods.   They can, however,

and indeed should, be potentially or radically free by making a constant choice of God before all things and by a constant rejection of any and every created good that cannot be possessed, not only without positive sin, but without any degree or kind of opposition to His known will in their regard. Moreover, they must aim, in proportion as God by His grace gives the requisite light and strength, at a progressive detachment of will from all created goods and at a correct valuation of such goods. They should prefer the more unlimited, more real and more spiritual, and therefore less money-valuable goods, to the more limited, less real and less spiritual, and therefore more money-valuable goods, and should increasingly love all and every creature because and in the degree of its relation to God.

St John recognises differences of vocation based on differences of spiritual capacity. "That soul," he says, "which does not attain to *that degree of purity corresponding with its capacity* will never obtain true peace and contentment, because it has not attained to that detachment and emptiness of its powers which are requisite for pure union with God." [1] "Note," he says, as he enters on the discussion of the active night of spirit, "that I now address myself principally to those who have already begun to enter into the state of contemplation, *since in dealing with beginners a somewhat laxer treatment of this matter is requisite*" (*Ascent*, Book II., chap. vi).[2] Elsewhere he bids his readers bear in mind that the negation of spiritual goods demanded in the second and third books of *The Ascent* is not applicable to beginners who have need of such (*Ascent*, Book III., chaps. xii., xxxviii). By beginners are meant all who have not yet entered into mystical contemplation. The majority of souls, however, are not intended to attain on earth to mystical union with God, and they therefore do not require, and are indeed incapable of, the detachment indispensable to mystics. Even those who have this vocation are not called to an equally high degree of union, and therefore, not to an equally high degree of detachment. It is, I think, true that St John, like most spiritual writers, failed to realise sufficiently the spiritual incapacity and the narrow limitations of the average man. He would not, I think, have agreed that vocations to

---

[1] *Ascent*, Book II., chap. v.

[2] This is my own translation and understanding of the passage, which, I must warn my readers, differs from that adopted by David Lewis.

mystical union are few and rare.[1] Nevertheless he does explicitly recognise the principle of vocation. Only the few are called—here I think St John would probably have taken an erroneously optimistic view—to the detachment requisite for mystical union, or at least for its more advanced and continuous degrees. The majority, though they must be fundamentally detached, are rather called to serve and find God in scantier measures and by more indirect ways which involve secular activities, and the possession and desire of creatures. St John tells us that we must not abandon meditation till we have obtained its positive substance. Then only do its limitations hinder our ascent to God. This principle holds good universally. Until and unless grace enables us to dispense with creatures [2] and to rise above their limitations to a more immediate union with God and that as our continuous life exercise—and but few [3] are so called—we must not reject, but use aright the creatures God has given us as His vestiges and ministers ; we must not eradicate but subordinate desires and loves for particular objects. A due proportion must, however, be observed. None should fix his choice on the creatures that are lowest in the scale of being, on the most superficial activities, on the most exclusive and material, and therefore the least real goods. A life absorbed or dominated by such goods and activities is the vocation of none. It would, for instance, be clearly irrational for a merchant to bestow such love on his trade as an artist might legitimately bestow on his art, for art is more spiritual and therefore more real and more God-like than trade. As Baron von Hügel says truly, there is need both for detachment and for attachment. The higher, however, the spiritual life, the greater the proportion of detachment, the less the proportion of attachment. It is simply a matter of vocation, and, as we have seen, St John admits vocation in principle, though probably failing to realise the full consequences of his admission. A time must, however, come when all the saved will be wholly detached from creatures by death and purgatory. Then, however, there will be no merit in the detachment, because we cannot help being detached. Attach-

[1] Nevertheless they are, I am sure, far more plentiful than is commonly thought, and will be increasingly common in the future. Everything points to a coming " age of the spirit " in the sense of a wide diffusion of mystical graces and calls (see Lucie Christine).

[2] As ends in themselves as apart from God—and actually to a very large extent.

[3] I mean few by comparison with those who have no such vocation.

ment will be no longer in our power. Hence those who do not detach themselves while they still have the power of attachment will not attain the same high degree of beatific union in heaven as the saintly few who detach themselves from creatures while yet on earth. Nor need we suppose that the ultimate actual detachment from creatures will be equal in all who enjoy the beatific vision. It must, however, reach a very high degree to render that vision possible, a degree so high that no deliberate desire remains for any creature taken apart from God. Only the pure in heart shall see God. Therefore the souls who die unduly attached to the particular, to the limited—that is, to the creature *qua* creature—cannot reach heaven till they have passed through the night of detachment, in death which strips from them all their possessions, even to the very body ; and in purgatory which purifies with its searching pain the denuded and lonely soul that now possesses nothing but God and nevertheless cannot yet possess Him. Therefore the principle of the mystical night holds good of every soul that is saved, but is not fully applicable to all in this life. I do not mean that even in death and purgatory the detaching loss and suffering are equal in all souls, or necessarily equal to that endured by the saints on earth. They are, however, identical in essence and, up to a certain degree, that requisite for the lowest grade of beatific vision, equivalent in amount. But, it may be urged, the suffering of purgatory expiates positive sin, and there is no sin in failing to go beyond our spiritual capacities. To this I reply that every soul in grace is by that very fact capable of sufficient detachment in this life to live primarily for God, and to choose on the whole the better part in dealing with and valuing creatures. It is capable of refusal to fix so strong a desire on any creature as to choose that creature before the known will of God on its behalf, even if that will bind not under sin. Suppose any soul perfectly faithful to conscience, however unenlightened. It would infallibly be led onward in ever-increasing light and strength to a degree of spirituality and detachment which, if not that of the saints, would at least be that of truly religious, unworldly people, whose enjoyment of creatures never involves bondage to the desire of any, and who seek God before and in all lesser aims. In communities where faith is strong, as in mediæval Europe and in modern Ireland, Brittany and the Tyrol, the general level of unworldliness—that is, of detachment from creatures and attachment to God as the supreme end of life—is enormously higher than any conceivable by those acquainted only with the materialistic civilisation of Western Europe to-day.[1] What will be the ultimate fate of souls who have lived without God in the world, total slaves to creatures, but who have apparently lacked all opportunity of doing otherwise, is an unrevealed secret. Perhaps such never attain the beatific vision. If they do, they will surely pass through a purgatorial detachment of great severity. The purgatorial and the satisfactory aspects of purgatory need not be inseparable. Souls that die in bondage to the finite cannot be united to God without a process of detachment involving suffering, and that even if their state of undue attachment was the fault rather of their environment than of themselves. And after all, would not the witness even of their extremely unenlightened conscience have been sufficient, if heeded, to carry them far beyond the point they actually reached? However this may be, it is surely clear that either in this life or beyond the grave every soul must be detached from all adherence of will and understanding to the essentially finite creature if it is to be united in supernatural union of love and knowledge to the infinite God. All the souls that are deified by the beatific union and vision of God must reach this infinitely superhuman goal by the negative way, must pass to the Divine dawn through the dark night.

This process of detachment must always involve keen suffering. Pleasure is the inevitable accompaniment of the unimpeded exercise of our natural activities, of the free action of the life-impulse. Bodily pleasure accompanies the unimpeded activity of bodily functions, spiritual pleasure the unimpeded activity of psychical functions. Disordered activity, whether actually sinful or merely imperfect, is a going forth of the soul to a limited object, to the rejection total or partial of God, the unlimited Good, and this going forth is accompanied by pleasure. But the repression of a natural activity is accompanied by pain—physical or psychical —according to the nature of the activity repressed or impeded. Therefore the deliberate repression of an activity by the will, in order to the avoidance of undue adherence to the limited, is accompanied by pain, or, rather, pain is an inseparable aspect of such repression. It is true that the limitation of this undue adherence must itself cause pain, pain far greater because far more interior and spiritual than the pain involved in the repression of the adher-

[1] Catholic Ireland though geographically part of Western Europe is, thank God, spiritually poles asunder. Long may it remain so.

ing activity. Nevertheless, unlike the latter, the former pain is not felt immediately, because the limit involved in the undue adhesion is not reached immediately, whereas the soul is immediately sensible of the instrumental limit of its repression. Nor only is the repression painful ; the pain itself is often a further repression of outgoing activity. For pain renders the sufferer wholly or partially impotent to energise physically or psychically, as he otherwise would. The process of detachment or mortification is therefore essentially painful. Often, as, for example, in disease, the pain-repression is not willed. If, however, the will accepts submissively the involuntary pain-repression, that pain-repression is thereby rendered voluntary. The pain-repression in which mortification consists, whether freely caused or freely accepted, is a destruction of the superficial activities that hindered the free activity of the inner self, of the limited activities directed to creatures that impeded the unlimited activity directed to God. Pain purifies, because, when freely caused or accepted, it destroys the barrier of superficial and selfish activities that the soul may be free to find God in its central depths. If man were sinless, purgative pain would be unnecessary for him. His lower and more superficial activities would not then interfere with or exclude, but would wholly subserve, the central activity of communion with God. So it was with Our Lady on earth ; so is it and so will it be with the saints in heaven. It is indeed true that Our Lady suffered, and, above all, supreme was the suffering endured by the All perfect and infinitely Holy humanity of Her Divine Son. But voluntary suffering has another function than that of individual purgation. It expiates the sins of other men. The sinful going forth of a man's will to the limited brought a disharmony into creation and offended against that extrinsic glory of God which creation should by its goodness set forth. This Harmony could not be restored, and creation duly show forth God's glory, save by a voluntary repression by man of his will activity, when such repression was not of itself necessary to avoid sin or to purify the individual soul. Such service of pain-repression man must render. But he could not by himself do this, since any such repression that a sinful individual or race might make must fall short of his or their sinful volitions against the will of God. Even a sinless man could not have repaired the disorder of his fallen nature, could not have balanced the sinful rebellion of the human nature of which he partook. Only the God-man could make such redeeming expiation by becoming himself the Head of the human race.   In person sinless, in nature one with sinful humanity, indeed its Head, He bore our sins.   He could thus expiate sins not His own in virtue of the spiritual solidarity of mankind, whereby the sin of one member can be balanced and redressed by the voluntary pain-repression of another.   Through this expiation made by Him Who alone could make it was restored the prefect balance of God's satisfied justice in regard to the human race and the full measure of His extrinsic glory for which that race was created.   Our Lady and the saints in virtue of their mystical solidarity with Christ, their head, have been able to partake in some measure of His expiatory suffering, to share His victimhood.   Since expiatory suffering is grounded in two fundamental mysteries, the essential opposition between sin and sinful humanity and the Divine holiness, an opposition not to be removed by a merely extrinsic pardon, and the solidarity of mankind with our sinful first parent on the one hand, and with the sinless Humanity of Christ on the other,[1] its nature and operation are beyond the investigation of human reason.   It is thus a truth rather to be believed by Christian faith, felt by religious experience and seen by mystical intuition, than to be explained and justified by reason.   This expiation effected by suffering, while connected with its function as the purgation of the individual soul, transcends that function.

In this discussion of the negative or purgative way, it is the more individual purgative aspect of suffering with which we are concerned.   This purificatory suffering is aptly symbolised by the figure of the cross.   The upright of the cross figures the central motion of the soul to God the supreme good.   The cross beam figures the superficial activities directed towards creatures that cross and thwart this Godward motion.   On the cross of their conflict is nailed the soul that persists in the search after God. For this contradiction results inevitably from the internal disharmony of man's fallen nature, in conjunction with its external disharmony with its environment, a disharmony also due, as faith teaches, to the effects of sin.   But this very conflict becomes the means of sanctification.   If the soul persist in the

---

[1] This solidarity with Christ, though possessed by all men in so far as all men are intrinsically capable of sharing the redemption of Calvary, is, unlike our physical solidarity with Adam, fully effected or actualised in those who are regenerate into the order of supernatural grace, a regeneration by which we are incorporated, whether we know it or not, into the mystical body of Christ, redeemed humanity, and thus are, in Pauline phrase, "in Christ."

Godward movement, despite the constant efforts of the lower selfish desires, aided as they are by its external environment, that movement is strengthened by the opposition endured and overcome, until at length it forces all the lower motions into subservience to itself. The pain-repression involved in the process purifies the soul of its limited activities and desires and sets it wholly free for perfect union with God. I do not mean that this conflict exhausts the significance of the cross in the soul's life. As we saw above, it does not. It is, however, one, and that a fundamental, aspect of the cross.

We must, however, always bear in mind that no activity or desire is sacrificed as bad in itself, but only as impeding the higher life and love. When union with God has been fully achieved, all that was positive in the lower desires and activities of human life is achieved with and in it. Then, also, much may be safely restored that had in the process towards union been rejected. This restoration will be complete with the bodily resurrection, and its correlative the new heavens and earth. Then the lower, even the physical, activities and their accompanying pleasures will subserve the Divine union, and God, being all in all, will be found in all the activities that will make up the complete life of glorified humanity. From these will indeed be absent the lowest, most limited functions of this life, such as eating, sleeping and reproduction. For these activities are essentially relative to this earthly life, too essentially limited to co-exist with the beatific union with the Unlimited. Those physical activities and pleasures will, however, persist which even on earth are channels of spiritual values—for example, the activities and pleasures of sight and hearing. There are thus three stages on the way from the limited to the unlimited, in Hegelian language, a thesis, an antithesis and a synthesis.[1] The thesis is the positive use and enjoyment of creatures as good in themselves ; the antithesis the destruction of their limits by a temporary detachment from them ; the synthesis is the recovery of the limited in the unlimited—no longer limiting by its limits. The thesis is represented by naturalism, or paganism; the antithesis is represented by asceticism and by Christianity as manifested on earth, when the supernatural is destroying the bonds that nature would impose on its free action ; the synthesis

---

[1] Here, as in vol. i., chap. iii., I find this terminology of great practical utility. Indeed the thesis, antithesis and synthesis in question is substantially identical in both passages. Need I repeat, I am no Hegelian for all that !

is the completely triumphant supernaturalism that receives and subsumes the natural as its instrument and receptacle. This final stage begins indeed on earth, but its fulness is reserved for the world to come. I have termed it the Resurrection stage. We may perhaps understand the process better if we consider it under one aspect alone, the æsthetic. The thesis is then physical beauty, the beauty of Greek sculpture, of the Venus of Milo and the Hermes of Olympia. The antithesis is spiritual beauty, achieved at the expense of physical, the beauty of the saintly soul burning in a body marred, often crippled, by asceticism. It is the beauty that radiates from the worn countenance of a desert hermit, the beauty of early stained glass.[1] The synthesis is spiritual beauty united with a physical beauty which is wholly the expression of the spiritual, the beauty of the Resurrection. It is the beauty of our assumed Mother and Queen. In that beauty the flesh is glorified beyond our utmost dreams in the stainless purity of entire subservience to the spirit. The beauty of the Hellenic Aphrodite as expressed by the supreme sculpture of ancient Greece is sheer ugliness by comparison with that unimaginable beauty which adorns the Immaculate Mother of God.

The Resurrection stage, which is the synthesis of flesh and spirit, of natural and supernatural, of created and Divine, is partly manifested even here on earth in certain concomitants and consequences of mystical union, which are an earthly foretaste of heaven. Fragrant odours emanate from the bodies of saints miraculously incorrupt, melodies are heard sweeter than our sweetest music, visions are seen wherein are landscapes of ravishing beauty, garments of exquisite shape and tint, jewels burning with a glow of rich colour beyond that of earthly gems, and wherein walk the forms of saints, even of friends, arrayed in superhuman loveliness.[2] St John has, I believe, this Resurrection synthesis in mind—I mean its first beginnings on earth in the passages such as that where he speaks of the pre-eminent enjoyment of all things seen or heard possessed by the truly detached (*Ascent*, III. xxix).

No positive being of the creature is, therefore, finally lost by

---

[1] Christian art fluctuated between antithesis and synthesis, and finally relapsed at the Renaissance into the mere thesis and became pagan once more.

[2] See St Teresa, *Autobiography*. Doubtless the proximate cause or means of all these phenomena is purely subjective and natural, not, therefore, their first or ultimate cause.*

detachment. It will be restored later, now no longer a barrier between the soul and the infinite, but a door wide open to the Infinite. In and through the limited the unlimited will be manifest. God will be All in all. For the mystic this begins even in this life. He finds God in the beauties of nature and art, instead of being detained and barred from Him by their limits. The soul, therefore, possesses all things, because it possesses Him in Whom are all things, and, as St John points out in the Canticle, is all things, since He is eminently their positive being. " When the soul," says Mother Cecilia, " truly possesses and knows God and is transformed in Him, she possesses eminently all things, just because she is not attached to any of them, *in so far as it is a creature, and in particular*, as are the souls who have not tasted the immensity of God." " The soul, by her possession of God, possesses all things after the fashion most similar to Him." "Having nothing, yet possessing all things." Thus does St Paul describe souls truly detached. It is but the creaturely limitations of creatures that such souls have rejected—though the process has required much rejection of creatures themselves for that end. Now they possess all creatures again in a higher and altogether positive way. " All things are yours "—that is, theirs who have nothing—in and for its own limited and limiting self apart from God ; all things received in and with Him Who is the All. Now dawns that morning knowledge of creatures in God spoken of by St John. For now the mystic realises the truth discussed in a previous chapter that the positive Being of creatures is God reflected in them, and their creatureliness a negation of being ; so that apart from him they are like accidents without a substance. The attachment that is opposed to detachment once fully destroyed, a new attachment which is compatible with detachment, because it is attachment to the positive substance of creatures alone—that is, to God *in* them, and not to their creaturely limits—comes into being to be perfected with the perfection of Divine love and therefore of detachment itself in the beatific vision and its complement the resurrection. The imperfect law of Sinai, the stone engraven ministry of death, proclaimed Thou shalt not. The perfect law of Christ, the ministry of life written in the heart, is no longer Thou shalt not, but thou shalt, thou shalt love with thine entire being.

---

[1] It is true that this positive precept is found even verbally in the old law. The new law is not without its anticipation in the old. It has, moreover, retained the negative decalogue of Sinai. But the emphasis has been completely reversed.

In this difference is shown the imperfection and transience of denial and rejection, the perfection and finality of affirmation and acceptance.   Sacrifice, mortification, detachment, this is the way, not the goal.   The goal is the achievement of fulness of life, of entire reality.   How negation is the way, the only way, to this goal I have sought to indicate.   Such indication is all that is possible.   In the deep things of the soul experience alone gives true knowledge.

CHAPTER VIII

THE ACTIVE NIGHT

To the deep, to the deep,
Down, down
Through the shade of sleep,
Through the cloudy strife
Of Death and of life ;
Through the veil and the bar
Of things which seem and are,
Even to the steps of the remotest throne,
Down, down.

Through the grey, void abysm,
Down, down
Where the air is no prism,
And the moon and the stars are not
And the cavern-crags wear not
The radiance of Heaven,
Nor the gloom to Earth given
Where there is one pervading, one alone,
Down, down.

SHELLEY,
Prometheus Unbound, Act II., scene iii.

The flight of the alone to the Alone.   PLOTINUS.

THE night of purgation is divided by St John into parts.   In the second chapter of the first book and in the second chapter of the second book of *The Ascent of Mount Carmel* he speaks of three nights.   The first night is detachment from the things of the world of which I have already spoken at length in the preceding chapter. St John calls it the night of sense.   It is the Active Night of sense. The second night he calls the night of faith.   It is the detachment from all spiritual realities less than God Himself—the Active Night of the Spirit.   The third night is evidently a passive communication of God to the soul, and therefore part of the mystical process. I believe that by this third night is meant the Passive Night, chiefly but not exclusively the Passive Night of the Spirit.[1]   Immediately after this night follows " union with the bride which is the wisdom of God."   In the second passage where three nights, or more strictly three parts of one night, are mentioned, he says : " When these three parts of the night *have been passed* . . . God illuminates the soul supernaturally with the ray of His Divine Light . . . which is the *beginning* of the perfect union which ensues *when the third night is over*."   Are the three nights finished before the beginning of the supreme union, or is only the perfection of that union deferred till then ?   Is this perfect union, spoken of as the union with the Divine bride, the beatific vision, or the highest degree of mystical union, termed the transforming union, and spiritual marriage ?   I believe that no absolutely certain answer can be given.   St John's language is extremely obscure, perhaps not altogether consistent.   Indeed there was, I think, a fluctuation in his own mind.   In one sense the night lasts till death so that even the transforming union is included in the third night. On the other hand, the " beginning " at least of the " perfect union " and therefore part of the " union with the bride " takes place in this life, and thus at least the beginning of that union is the transforming union on earth.   Yet we are told that the union in general and in the second passage that even its beginning takes place when the three nights are passed.   Therefore the transforming union is in some sense at least not part of the third night. Indeed elsewhere St John distinctly terms the transforming union day.[2]   Moreover, as we shall see, the passive night is essentially constituted by a beginning of the perfect mystic union.   Therefore I think that it is most conducive to clearness if we identify the passive night with the third night, and regard the transforming union as the dawn of the supernatural day following.   On the other hand, we must not forget that it is but the dawn, with its dim lights and lingering shadows, and that it therefore belongs also to the night.   Here as elsewhere we need to bear in mind that our clear divisions cannot adequately represent the imperceptibly graduated process which constitutes the mystical way.

[1] Bride is here used, not bridegroom, on account of a reference to the story of Tobias.

[2] *Ascent*, Book II., chap. xiv. *ad fin*.

Hence the obscurity and hesitation of St John's language. In these two chapters alone does St John speak of three nights, and they are therefore somewhat anomalous. Elsewhere he speaks consistently of two nights—the night of Sense and the night of Spirit. If, however, we consider his actual teaching rather than his terminology, it is plain that there are four distinct nights discussed by St John—namely, the Active Night of Sense, the Active Night of Spirit, the Passive Night of Sense, the Passive Night of Spirit. The Active Nights constitute the purgation accomplished by the soul's own will, of course with the assistance of Divine grace. The two Passive Nights constitute the deeper purgation effected in the soul by the mystical experience itself— that is, by immediate Divine action in the soul that has reached a certain degree of sanctifying grace ; the effect on the soul of the special relationship with God constituted by certain stages of the mystical union. The Passive, unlike the Active, Nights are not an ascetical preparation for, or accompaniment of, the mystical union, but are themselves constituent parts of that union. It was apparently the intention of St John to treat of the four nights in a work composed of four books. The title of the work was to be *The Ascent of Mount Carmel,* and the two later books, whose subject would be the passive purgation, were to receive the subtitle of *The Dark Night of the Soul.* As it is, the work has come down to us in the form of two distinct treatises—both unfinished. Both, however, take the form of a comment on one and the same mystical poem—the exquisite lyric beginning " *En una noche escura* " (" In a dark night "). Moreover, in the work as it stands we have references to the first book of *The Dark Night* as the third book of *The Ascent of Mount Carmel.* The original plan has on the whole been adhered to. *The Ascent of Mount Carmel* deals with the active night or purgation, *The Dark Night of the Soul* with the passive night or purgation. The first book of *The Ascent* treats of the Active Night of Sense ; the first book of *The Dark Night,* of the Passive Night of Sense ; and the second book of *The Dark Night,* of the Passive Night of Spirit. The discussion, however, of the active night of spirit is not confined to the second book of *The Ascent,* but occupies also an unfinished third book, which, moreover, includes matter belonging strictly to the Active Night of Sense. St John's treatment of the active night of spirit required the discussion not only of the purification of the understanding by faith, the subject of the second book of *The Ascent,* but also of the purification of the memory by hope and of the will by charity, the subjects of the third book. But the purification of the will includes its purification from the desire of worldly goods, and thus the saint was led to return upon his discussion of the active night of sense. Moreover, the treatment of the active night of spirit includes a discussion of the position to be adopted by the mystic towards the phenomena of the passive night of sense, and thus a treatment of that night from the active standpoint. Hence certain chapters of the second book of *The Ascent* cover the same ground as certain chapters of the first book of *The Dark Night* (chaps. xii., xiii., xiv. and xv. of *The Ascent*, Book II., and chaps. ix. and x. of *The Dark Night*, Book I). There is clearly a certain confusion in the arrangement of St John's treatises, owing to a conflict and overlapping of the principles on which that arrangement is based. Nothing is harder than to arrange a treatise on mysticism where there is such a lack of sharply defined boundaries.

St John says of the three nights of chap. ii. of *The Ascent* that they are parts of one night. By this is meant that they are aspects of one fundamental principle, that of purgation or detachment, the principle discussed in the previous chapter. It should also be noticed that the nights do not follow in chronological order. It is, of course, obvious that the active night of sense is the first to occur in the spiritual life. Every Christian must be to some extent in that night if he is even attempting to lead a Christian life. For this night is simply the practice of mortification with regard to the things of earth. It is also obvious that this night cannot entirely end till death. So long as man possesses his earthly body he is in some danger, however slight, of yielding unduly to the desire of bodily and worldly goods and pleasures. " I chastise my body," wrote the Apostle who had ascended to the third heaven, " lest, having preached to others, I myself should become a reprobate." Nevertheless, when a certain stage in the spiritual life has been reached, the mortification of worldly and sensual desires becomes secondary in the Christian life. The soul is so eager for spiritual satisfaction that it has almost wholly ceased to value the goods of earth. Henceforward the purgation is primarily a spiritual purgation, the detachment of will and understanding from adherence to spiritual and supernatural goods that are not God Himself, and which the soul is tempted to seek and value for their own sake. What these are we shall consider when we come to discuss in greater detail the Active Night of

Spirit. This Active Night of Spirit also continues of necessity to the end of life, for there are always secondary spiritual goods intended by God as means to union with Himself in which the soul is tempted to rest as ends in themselves. Prominent among these are certain phenomena concomitant upon the mystical union. Hence the active night of spirit is, in its later stages, contemporaneous with the mystic union, and therefore with the two passive nights which are stages of that union. Only when this union has reached its final earthly stage does the active night of spirit fall into the background of the spiritual life, since its main work has been accomplished. Since, however, this final stage is of extreme rarity even among those who attain to mystical prayer, the active night of spirit is one of the predominant features of the spiritual life of the majority of mystics.

That portion of the mystical experience which constitutes the first passive purgation known as the passive night of sense occurs at a stage in the spiritual life when the active night of spirit is predominant. In dealing with it the mystic needs to practise the principles of the active night of spirit. Therefore St John treats of it from this point of view in *The Ascent of Mount Carmel*, when he is discussing the active night in detail. The second passive night, that of the spirit, begins far later in the mystical way and is of far rarer occurrence. Its working is such as to leave the soul powerless to do aught but endure in passivity and patience. It occurs, therefore, when the active night of the spirit has achieved already the greater part of its work. Hence it finds no place in *The Ascent of Mount Carmel*. The two passive nights will be discussed in their place in the mystical way. The remainder of this chapter will be devoted to a discussion of the active night of spirit as treated by St John in the second and third books of *The Ascent*.

Of the Active Night of Sense—that is, detachment from all sensible and material goods, and the mortification and rejection of all desire for such—nothing further need be said. I have already discussed it in the last chapter when explaining the principle of detachment.

The Active Night of Spirit depends essentially on the Negative knowledge of God, which has been already discussed in my chapter on the Divine Transcendence. It is the detachment of the soul from all spiritual objects and concepts that are distinctly apprehensible by its natural or supernatural activities in this life, and which are therefore essentially limited, and in virtue of this essential limitation infinitely distant from the unlimited Being of God.   We have, however, already seen that this detachment does not apply in the same sense to the mysteries of Christ, since the Sacred Humanity and its mysteries are in personal union with the Infinite Godhead.   By this detachment from the limited the substance of the soul and its fundamental powers are set free to receive the Being and Operation of God.   The manner in which this is to be effected in the understanding forms the subject of the second book of *The Ascent*, in the memory and will, the subject of the third book.   The quintessence, however, of St John's teaching is contained in his account of the purgation of the understanding. With relentless logic St John rejects all rest in the limited, even in limited presentations of Divine truth.   All such must, he says, be set aside by the mystic.   By faith alone can he attain the immediate and supernatural knowledge of God, which is the goal of his understanding.   Faith and love are indeed the two great means of mystical union.   It is by faith that the soul is united with God through its cognitive aspect or faculty, as it is by love or charity that the soul is united with God through its conative aspect or faculty.   Faith, as Catholic theology teaches, is an infused supernatural gift whereby we are enabled to believe without doubting whatever God has revealed.   If we could understand—that is, if we could grasp the internal coherence of the truths of revelation, together with their coherence with the totality of human experience—there would be neither need nor scope for faith.   It is, however, of the essence of revealed dogma to belong to a sphere that transcends the limited operations of the human understanding. They are, as it were, bridges between the finite and the Divine Infinity, between the comprehensible and the Divine incomprehensibility.   They touch the comprehensible, for otherwise they would be meaningless formulæ.   But at the other extreme they merge into the incomprehensibility of the Divine Being, wherein also they are united at a point beyond the reach of our understanding.   We may picture the dogmas of revelation as streams that take their rise in the firm dry land of the limited and comprehensible world, which is the proper sphere of the human understanding, but flow onwards till they meet unseen in the ocean of the Godhead.   It is the work of faith to reach this Divine Ocean by following the streams of dogma.   Faith, therefore, cannot rest in aught that reason can comprehend.   It either rejects such pre sentations of Divine truth, or if, as in the case of the Incarnational dogmas, it accepts them, it passes in them and through them to the infinite Being therein revealed and found. It is indeed true that reason also leads the soul to a knowledge of the Divine incomprehensibility. Reason cannot, however, bring the soul into living contact with it. Supernatural faith can alone lead the understanding to this union. By faith we accept and adhere to truths concerning the work and Being of God which we cannot understand, and so pass beyond the intelligible to grasp the Unintelligible Unity whence these truths proceed. "Faith," says St John, "teaches us what the understanding cannot teach by the light of nature and of reason, being, as the Apostle saith, 'the substance of things to be hoped for.' And though the understanding firmly and certainly assents to the doctrines of faith, yet it cannot discover them, for if the understanding discovered them there would be no room for faith, and though the understanding derives certainty from faith, yet it does not derive clearness but rather obscurity" (*Ascent*, ii. 6). "As God is darkness to our understanding, so faith also blinds and darkens our understanding" (that is, it removes the clear ideas which are essentially and necessarily limited). "Thus by this means alone—that is, faith— God manifests Himself to the soul in the Divine Light, which surpasses all understanding, and therefore the greater the faith of the soul the more is that soul united to God. This is the meaning of St Paul when he said, 'He that cometh to God must believe that He is,'" (that is to say, he must grasp a Being whose nature is in this life wholly incomprehensible). "Such an one must walk by faith, with his understanding blind and in darkness in faith only, for in this darkness God unites Himself to the understanding, being Himself hidden in it" (*Ascent*, ii. 9). This Johannine teaching brings home to us the meaning of that pregnant scriptural definition of faith as "the substance of things to be hoped for." For faith is a possession or apprehension of the Divine Being that will be seen in heaven and cannot be apprehended by the distinct concepts of human reason. Nothing seen even intellectually can be the substance of that which we hope for in heaven—namely, the clear knowledge of God. If the unveiled or clear knowledge of God is what is hoped for, faith—that is, the obscure or veiled apprehension of God—is the substance of it. What can be seen— that is, clearly conceived—by human reason cannot be that substance, but must of necessity fall infinitely short of it. That substance must therefore be an apprehension which is not distinct understanding, and this is supernatural faith. Hence it is that faith must be a gift supernaturally infused. No natural principle could be adequate to cause such an apprehension of the Divine Being as is the veiled substance of that beatific vision, which is itself a participation of the Divine self-knowledge and therefore of God Himself. As grace to glory, so is faith to beatific vision. When sanctifying grace is present in the soul the understanding is emancipated from the limits of natural knowledge and raised to a supernatural apprehension of the transcendent Godhead. This apprehension is faith.

At first this apprehension is mediate, is, indeed, simply that supernatural grasp or apprehension of God beyond the limits of natural reason which is involved in firm assent to His supernatural Self-revelation, through the teaching of the Church. As faith deepens, the apprehension of God through faith becomes increasingly stronger and more immediate. A direct apprehension [1] of the Godhead incomprehensible to our reason, but the supernatural Object of faith, is imprinted on the central depths of the soul, on the root of the will that grasps God by love. The cognitive element of mystical experience is the apprehension of faith exalted to an immediate consciousness or intuition of the veiled Being of God present to and in the soul. Now that the soul has left behind it comprehensible notions of God and His Revelation, it receives and grasps firmly this incomprehensible Divine Presence of which in mystical experience it is thus immediately conscious. Nevertheless this conscious and immediate apprehension of the Godhead is still the obscure knowledge of faith, the adherence of the spiritual consciousness or understanding to an unintelligible and therefore a hidden Being. So must it remain as long as life endures. Perhaps certain saints have, as St John maintains,[2] enjoyed a momentary fruition of God in which faith is superseded by a Divine light that is a transitory and imperfect gleam of the light of glory. This, however, is not mystical intuition, which is but faith enormously deepened and strengthened. It is true that Mother Cecilia says (Trans., st. 11) that in the highest mystical experience " a supernatural light " is added to faith. She even says that the soul no longer needs faith now that it knows by this

---

[1] It may be termed, if you will, an idea, but it is an idea that is not positive and clear, but negative and obscure.

[2] Ascent, II. xxiv.

Divine experience and participation of the Divine Being (*Trans.*, st. 12). This language is, however, contrary to St John's more accurate teaching. St John speaks of mystical knowledge " as illuminated faith " indeed, but nevertheless as faith. Moreover, the conscious aspect of the mystical union is plainly identified with Faith when St John says that " this obscure, loving knowledge which is Faith serves in this life as the medium of the Divine Union, as the light of glory serves in the next life as the medium of the clear vision of God " (*Ascent*, ii. 24). The author of *The Obscure Knowledge* also admits no light intermediate between that of faith and glory, save an actual and therefore a passing light by which the soul understands special mysteries (ch. i. 3). This light is that by which intellectual visions are effected, and is not the mystical intuition whose object is no particular mystery, but the veiled Godhead incomprehensible by any concept or distinct knowledge. The supernatural light mentioned by Mother Cecilia must not therefore be regarded as a new and higher mode of knowledge superadded to faith, but as an extraordinary intensification of faith which renders it a vivid and immediate intuition of the unintelligible Godhead.

St John tells us plainly in *The Living Flame* (st. 4) that till death the veil of faith abides. Moreover, we gather from Mother Cecilia that the highest flashes of mystical insight are those in which we realise most fully the Divine Incomprehensibility.[1] It is indeed true that an extraordinary intellectual insight into the reality, necessity and internal coherence of certain revealed mysteries—for example, the Blessed Trinity—is often given to those in the highest stages of mystical prayer. Such insight, however, serves only to deepen the sense of the infinity and unintelligibility of the Divine Nature. This indeed is the meaning of the extraordinary paradox of *The Obscure Knowledge* that the supreme effect of faith is the knowledge that God is not anything cognisable by human knowledge. The highest mystical knowledge of God is like the unseen embrace of lovers in a dark room The depths of the soul are felt to be embraced by His unintelligible Presence. Not till death releases the understanding from its bondage to the data of sense as the sole ultimate source of distinct ideas will the darkness pass away and the light of glory illumine the soul to see the face of God. St John indeed compares faith to the pitchers carried by Gideon's soldiers wherein were hidden

---

[1] *Transformation*, stanzas 1, 4, 6 and 10.

lamps. " So," he says, " faith, of which these pitchers were a figure, contains the Divine light—that is, the truth *of what God is in Himself*; and at the end of this mortal life, when the work of faith is done and the pitchers broken, the light and glory of the Deity therein hidden will shine forth " (*Ascent*, ii. 9).

The work of the active purgation of spirit is therefore the progressive deepening of faith by persistent refusal to rest in or accept any distinct knowledge concerning God and His mysteries. The first class of apprehensions to be rejected are sensible phenomena of a religious character. St John forbids the soul to rest in these, even if caused by God, for otherwise it will be detained by the sensible appearance, instead of passing onwards to grasp by faith the spiritual reality inapprehensible of sense or reason. He also treats these external sensible manifestations as the lowest media of Divine communication. For since the immediately sensible is the most limited and particular of all our apprehensions, it contains the minimum of reality and is thus the least adequate presentation of the Ultimate Reality. Since the time of St John the progress of psychology has underlined his warning against these sensible visions, auditions and the like by bringing home to us the subjective element inherent in all such. Whatever their ultimate cause, they are always conditioned and largely constructed by the subjective consciousness or subconsciousness of the recipient.[1]

Huysmans, in his *Vie de Ste Lidwine,* points out that the saint's visions of the other world are in close relationship with the Flemish sacred art of her period, the fifteenth century. The visions of St Mechtilde are like the illuminations of a mediæval Missal or Breviary, whose glowing colours and conventional designs are faithfully reproduced. Indeed I am certain that such a dependence of the form of mystical visions on the art and literature of the seer's epoch and entourage would be found to hold good universally. There is also abundant evidence that such visions and other sensible experiences are largely conditioned by the objects of devotion used by their recipient. A striking instance of this is afforded by the stigmatic scourging of Gemma Galgani,

---

[1] Throughout the following discussion I treat together sensible and imaginary visions and auditions, though these are separated by St John. It is impossible to demarcate the two classes of phenomena. Though the former seem more objective than the latter, both are largely subjective, the former often to a greater degree than the latter.

the passion mystic of Lucca. Of this scourging a witness wrote :
" If you wish to form some idea of it, recall to mind the great
crucifix . . . *before which Gemma was in the habit of praying. She
was like that.* The same livid marks, the same torn-open gashes
in the skin and flesh *in the same parts of the body, equally long and
deep* and equally horrifying to behold " (*Life of Gemma Galgani*,
by Fr. Germano, English trs., pp. 68-69). Who can doubt the
existence here of an element of autosuggestion ? Equally indicative of subjectivity is the fact that no revelation or vision wholly
precedes the external growth of devotion to its object. No father
of the desert ever saw a vision of St Joseph. Indeed in this same
Life of Gemma we find that her visions of Blessed Gabriel of the
Dolours did not begin until she had read his life, and that even
then the visions were preceded by a sense of his invisible presence
(*Life of Gemma Galgani*, pp. 40-41). Moreover, no special revelation has ever made known a dogma of faith to a soul that had
never learned that dogma from human instruction. No devout
Sufi or Buddhist ascetic has ever been informed by a vision or
locution of the truth of the Christian religion. Sudden conversions to the Catholic Faith, like that of Mother Digby, Superior-
General of the nuns of the Sacred Heart, are only apparent exceptions. In these cases no new truth is added by revelation to the
previous knowledge of the recipient. The will is supernaturally
moved to accept a truth or teaching authority already known to
the intelligence. Such miraculous conversions are, in fact, but
the gift of supernatural faith bestowed with an extraordinary
intensity.

Moreover, the various visions and revelations granted to different saints of the incidents of Our Lord's life and passion are often
in mutual contradiction. Many, too, have been the demonstrable
illusions even of canonised seers. St Vincent Ferrer proclaimed
with certainty in the fifteenth century the immediate Parousia.
St Elizabeth of Schonau [1] and Bl. Hermann Joseph received
detailed revelations as to the relics of the Cologne virgins which
history cannot possibly accept as genuine. Yet their sanctity
and therefore their sincerity are equally beyond dispute. Instances and arguments could be multiplied indefinitely. I think,
however, that I have said sufficient to bring home the large subjective element present in these concomitant phenomena of
mysticism. There is indeed no reason to suppose that any sensible

---

[1] Although never canonised, she is generally accepted as a saint.

apparition or other similar manifestation is substantially objective (except, of course, from the scriptural appearances of Our Lord's Risen Body. which belong to a category apart). On the other hand, we must beware of the opposite extreme, the denial of all objective validity and cause to these sensible or quasi-sensible phenomena. Such a position would render a very large portion of the mystical experience even of so great and so eminently sane a mystic as St Teresa simple illusion. It would condemn the Church for the institution of such feasts as the stigmatisation of St Francis and the transverberation of St Teresa's heart.[1] It would leave unexplained the indubitable existence of much verified prophecy (confined, I believe, to private affairs [2]), of wise counsels and warnings, and of spiritual consolation and instruction given by means of visions and still more of locutions. It would not explain why the strenuous efforts of infidel psychologists to produce by suggestion phenomena such as stigmatisation have only obtained a very partial success. No one has yet been able to give a consistent explanation of the psycho-physical phenomena of any genuine mystic on *purely* subjective lines. A comparison of the phenomena of Gemma's life with the laws of hypnotic suggestion laid down by Hudson in his *Psychic Phenomena* is sufficient to show that the former do not conform to the latter. There is no space to work out details here. I can but take a few instances. Gemma's director bids her pray for the cessation of the external stigmata. She does so ; they cease. Suggestion, plainly suggestion. Gemma's director strongly desires their appearance before a certain doctor, and Gemma knows of this desire. They do not appear. Why has the suggestion now failed ? Gemma makes a novena for recovery from an illness to Blessed Margaret Mary. She is miraculously cured. By Bl. Margaret Mary ? No, by Blessed Gabriel of the Dolours. Suggestion would surely have evoked the former, not the latter healer (p. 45). The devil appears full of blasphemies and obscenities. Are these the subconscious self-suggestions of a girl so innocent that she did not understand the meaning of the foul speeches (p. 183). Again we are told by Hudson (*Psychic Phenomena*, p. 130, and elsewhere) that the presence of two contradictory suggestions confuses the patient of a hypnotic ecstasy and restores normal consciousness. Yet we find in Gemma's ecstasies long colloquies with Our Lord

[1] Univeral Calendar, 17th September. *Pro aliquibus locis*, 27th August.
[2] *Cf.* Fr. Thurston, *The War and the Prophets*, pp. 112, 118.

in which she pleads for mercy for a sinner (suggestion of mercy). He for a long while refuses mercy and demands the rigour of justice (suggestion of punishment without mercy). Yet Gemma is not confused nor awakened from her ecstasy. We are told, moreover, by Hudson (*Psychic Phenomena*, p. 133) that the most fundamental and strongest autosuggestion is the instinct of self-preservation and self-benefit in the natural order. Now this instinct cannot attain its end by a course of life which is the crucifixion and destruction of nature, a fertile source of ill health, and which often leads to the premature death of the body. Yet such is the course urged on Gemma by her locutions. How can autosuggestion thus act in the teeth of the most fundamental autosuggestion ? If, indeed, on other grounds we disbelieve the existence of the God of theism, the Divinity of Jesus, the survival of the saints in another world, the reality of angels and of devils, it is reasonable to ascribe these phenomena despite all the lacunæ in the explanation to a purely natural cause, to the working of autosuggestion and the suggestion of other men, trusting to further investigation to fill those lacunæ and to complete the proof. If, however, on other grounds we do believe in these objective realities, we have good reason to reject the *purely* subjective explanation, which is so insufficient, and to accept the presence of an objective element and cause in these phenomena and their production. These psycho-physical phenomena, therefore, are neither purely subjective nor purely objective. The external causes, God, a saint, an angel, an evil spirit produce them only through certain subjective and largely hypnotic and autosuggestive workings or functions of the soul. After all, even in the experiments of the hypnotic psychologists there is a large element of external suggestion, the suggestion of the operator. Yet this can produce at most phenomena analogous to those of Christian mysticism, but by no means identical, indeed but a faint reflex of the latter. Does not this point to the need for a supernatural or at least a preternatural influx or suggestion to effect the enormously more significant and more wonderful phenomena so often concomitant upon mystical experience ?

We should bear in mind that the relations between the psycho-physical phenomena of mysticism and the supernatural operation or cause are indefinitely various and complex. We cannot possibly treat all such phenomena as equally objective and Divine, or equally subjective and self-caused. Baron von Hügel in his admirable discussion of the psycho-physical aspect of mysticism in *The Mystical Element of Religion*, a discussion where the general lines along which the truth is surely to be found are clearly laid down and proved, points out the necessity of careful distinction between different cases. I believe, however, that for the better evaluation of the psycho-physical aspect of mysticism we may group such phenomena on three levels from the point of view of objective validity and Divine causality. There is first the level of pure subjectivity. We find here a class of phenomena without any special Divine causation, due entirely to the abnormal psycho-physical temperament of the mystics. These phenomena are often purely pathological, the results of physical breakdown. Their sole spiritual value lies in their utilisation by the mystic, and even this is at times wanting. Among these we must place the hysterical phenomena of St Catherine of Genoa's final illness, the yellowing of her skin, her arbitrary and shifting moods, tastes and distastes, her hyperæsthesia, her hallucinations and morbid quietudes, also such extraordinary phenomena as were manifested in the diseases of St Lidwine and in the lives of the Cistercian nun, St Lukardis (see Bl. von Hügel, *The Mystical Element of Religion*, vol. ii., pp. 52-55), and of St Christina Mirabilis, whose external behaviour amounted to sheer mania. On this level I would place phenomena due to a purely human suggestion, phenomena which the observance of St John's rules would render impossible. Such would be the wholly illusory revelations of St Elizabeth of Schönau and Bl. Hermann Joseph about the Cologne virgins, and the astronomical pseudo-revelations given to St Frances of Rome which were suggested by the current beliefs and occasioned by the blameworthy curiosity of her confessor (see Poulain, *Les Graces d'Oraison*, chap. xxi., pp. 350-351). On the second level are those phenomena that are the natural effect of a supernatural cause. Very many, probably the majority, of visions and locutions belong to this level. An instance of a vision on this level is, I believe, the vision of a ceremonial marriage with Jesus which often inaugurates the entrance of the soul into the highest state of mystical union. The objectively real entrance of the soul into that union gives rise to the subjective vision. An instance of a revelation at this level would be St Vincent Ferrer's illusion of the imminent end of the world. This was probably his subjective mistranslation of a true intuition that the mediæval and Christian world order was in process of rapid dissolution, and that the pagan

Renaissance and semi-pagan Reformation were close at hand to in-augurate a new era of naturalism. Among the phenomena of this second level must also be placed the psycho-physical effects of mystical prayer—for example, the external psycho-physical pheno-mena of ecstasy, including levitation and the stigmata. For of such phenomena it may safely be affirmed that they are the natural effects of supernatural causes. Granted a certain degree and quality of spiritual will-union and absorption in God, of concentra-tion on His Presence, these psycho-physical phenomena follow by the natural operation of psycho-physical laws. The passion stig-mata of St Francis, of Gemma Galgani and of other ecstatics were thus the natural effect on the body of a powerful supernatural influx of loving compassion into the soul. When in obedience to her director Gemma resisted this influx by a violent withdrawal of her contemplation, the stigmata did not pass beyond the pre-liminary stage of premonitory symptoms (*Life of Gemma*, p. 144). If many of these phenomena cannot be reproduced by natural suggestion, it is because the force of natural suggestion is too weak. A supernatural suggestion or impulse of Divine origin is required to make such an impression on the body. Nevertheless there are many of these phenomena which can be reproduced wholly or partially by the natural suggestion of other human souls or by autosuggestion.

St John himself admits in principle this explanation of second level phenomena in *The Living Flame of Love* in a passage of great importance. This passage, hitherto incompletely presented, I translate immediately from the Spanish text of the Edicion Critica. " If at any time," he says, " God permits any external effect of a spiritual wound of love to appear in the bodily senses, the wound is manifested externally after the fashion of the interior wounding. This happened, for example, when the Seraph smote St Francis. When his soul was wounded by love with the five wounds, after that very fashion was their effect communicated to the body, for the wounds were imprinted also in the body, which itself was wounded, even as they had been imprinted on the soul when wounded by love. It is indeed God's usual way " (does not modern psychology justify us in regarding it as a law of the supernatural order, or rather as a law that belongs to and proceeds from the harmony of the two orders of grace and nature ?) " not to bestow any favour on the body that he has not primarily and principally wrought in the soul " (*Living Flame*, st. 2).

This principle is exemplified abundantly in the history of miraculous cures.   Our Saviour healed the sick soul of the paralytic as a precedent condition to his bodily cure.[1]   Faith was miraculously infused into Gabriel Gargam when receiving communion at Lourdes, and only afterwards was his physical cure effected. The vast majority of these cures should therefore be regarded as belonging to this second level of psycho-physical phenomena. They are natural effects of a supernatural cause, the natural effects on the body of a psychosis itself produced by a supernatural operation.   Not the least part of St John's greatness as a doctor of mystical theology is his clear distinction between these external and physical embodiments and effects of Divine grace by which the multitude set such store and in which they rest content, but whose value has been so tremendously discounted by the observations of modern psychology, and the inner spiritual substance which is beyond the reach of a psychological science which confines itself to the study of the external psycho-physical phenomena.   The concomitant phenomena of ecstasy are treated in this way by St John.   He sees in the external physiological phenomena nothing but the natural effects of physical weakness, and of the natural incapacity of the soul's lower functions to endure the special operation of God in the inmost centre.   " As the sensual part of the soul is weak, without any capacity for the strong things of the spirit, they who are in the state of proficients " (*i.e.* who have reached a certain state of mystical experience), " by reason of the spiritual communications made to the sensual part, are subject therein to great infirmities and sufferings, and physical derangements, and consequently weariness of mind, as it is written : ' the corruptible body . . . presseth down the mind.' . . . Here is the source of ecstasies, raptures and dislocation of the bones which always happen whenever these communications are not purely spiritual ; that is, granted to the spirit alone as in the case of the perfect.   In them these raptures and physical sufferings cease, for they enjoy liberty of spirit with unclouded and unsuspended senses " (*Dark Night*, ii. 1).   In other words, the soul is then able to energise freely Godward in its centre and its radical functions, unhindered by the peripheral body-informing and sense-dependent

---

[1] There are perhaps exceptions where for a particular purpose a miracle was wrought on an unbeliever—*e.g.* the restoration of Malchus' ear.   But after all we do not know that Malchus' soul did not then receive a gift of conversion and faith.   Moreover, St Luke implies that the ear had not been wholly severed.

functions through which the soul chiefly energises in the ordinary course of natural life. It is in the passage from one energising to the other, from a soul life mainly peripheral to a soul life mainly interior and central, that the sensible functions are thrown out of gear by the introversion of the soul, or more truly by the result of that introversion its closer relationship to God and His more potent and more manifest activity in its centre. We must, however, remember that ecstasy, in the usual acceptance of the term which we find in most mystical writings, contains always two and often three distinct elements, which elements differ enormously in worth and in objective reference. There is the mystical union itself, in the degree termed ecstasy. This is, of course, purely and directly the supernatural work of God. Then there are the physiological accompaniments, such as anæsthesia and rigidity. These are natural effects of the extraordinary spiritual energising, the concentration of the entire soul in and on God. These effects are identical with those consequent on hysterical and hypnotic alienations (*cf.* Padre Germano, *Life of Gemma Galgani,* English translation, pp. 395, 396 and 413). Then there are often present in mystical prayer, especially in ecstasy, visions of sensible images, locutions of audible words. These are no essential part of the mystical union, and are caused in part by Divine action, in part by the autosuggestion of the subconscious self. The respective share of each factor can only be known, if at all, from the nature and value of the content of the visions or locutions. Hysterical ecstatics also see visions, composed and caused solely and entirely by their own autosuggestion, and therefore never rising above the miserable level of their own mentality. It is a pity that the word ecstasy is used indiscriminately of these three elements separately, and of all together. The ecstasy St John regards as a passing weakness is the second element. The first merges in a higher degree of union. The third is not peculiar to the ecstatic degree of mystical prayer, and to it is applicable all said in *The Ascent* of particular visions and revelations. Of these three elements the first alone is to be sought and accepted for its own sake by the mystic, and that and that alone is purely supernatural.

There is, however, a third level at which the content, that is to say, the significance of the psycho-physical phenomenon, of the vision or locution is such as to prove or suggest that even the psycho-physical form is not wholly subjective, but has been

externally caused by God or by the Sacred Humanity, by Our
Lady, or by some angel or saint, although the materials out of which
it is constructed are still subjective and are drawn from the
storehouse of subconsciousness. For instance, the history of
the apparitions at Lourdes fully warrants us in ascribing even the
external vision of Bernadette in its general features to a direct
communication by Our Blessed Lady, though given through the
mode of images taken from Bernadette's subconsciousness.
Another instance of this level would be the revelation of the
Sacred Heart to Bl. Margaret Mary.[1]   I should also be inclined
to place on this level the apparitions of Blessed Gabriel to Gemma
Galgani mentioned above.   Gemma was, I think, truly *en rapport*
with the saint, though he could only make his presence known
through the subjective and subconscious workings of her soul
which formed for him, as it were, a body and a voice.   If no psycho-
physical phenomena belong to this class and level, many of the
greatest mystics and saints were victims of unmerited delusion,
even granted the objective validity of their mystical union.   For
the entire or at least the greatest worth of their visions has often
consisted precisely in their objective validity on the psycho-physical
and phenomenal plane, not merely as being effects or concomitants of the mystical union.   If, for instance, Bernadette had not
been in especial communication with Our Lady and had not received an authentic message from her, she would have been under
a cruel delusion, even if God were really placing her soul in mystical
union with Himself.   It is in his denial of the existence of this
third level that we must part company with Baron von Hügel,
who is otherwise so valuable and reliable a guide in these still
very obscure matters.   On all levels, however, there is a subjective element present in these psycho-physical phenomena.
Otherwise we should attain in this life that open vision of spiritual
and divine realities as they are in themselves which has already
been shown to be impossible.   At the first level this element is
everything; even at the third it plays an important part.   Moreover, the three levels cannot be sharply distinguished.   Each passes
over imperceptibly into the other.   They are indeed simply three
categories under which it is possible and convenient to group
roughly the multitude of indefinitely varied and complex phenomena under discussion, phenomena wherein the subjective, the

---

[1] I mean the substance of that revelation.   I should not care to commit mysel
to belief in every promise in detail.

naturally objective and the supernaturally objective elements are almost inextricably blended. In individual cases the presence of a trans-subjective element must be affirmed or denied, and its degree and value must be estimated (often this can never be done with any certainty or accuracy) solely by the ethical and spiritual content and significance of the psycho-physical phenomenon in question.

The subjective element of these psycho-physical phenomena is not peculiar to the mystic, but is found also in the hysterical patient, in the hypnotic subject and in the lunatic. We have seen already how hysterical or hypnotic in character are the first level phenomena. There is often, indeed, no difference whatever in the phenomenal presentation between the visions of the hysterical or hypnotised subject and those of the saint, and there must always be an element common to both. The existence and necessity of this common element has indeed been clearly expressed by Myers in a canon which should be carefully borne in mind in any discussion of this psycho-physical aspect of mysticism. "It may be expected," he lays it down, "that supernormal vital phenomena will manifest themselves as far as possible through the same channels as abnormal or morbid vital phenomena, when the same centres or the same synergies are involved" (*Human Personality*, Abridged Edition, p. 255). This canon he proceeds to develop in one of the most valuable passages of his book.[1] He shows that since the supernormal (I should correct, the supernatural) works through the same depths or functions of the soul which are affected by abnormal and morbid psychoses such as hysteria, there must be a phenomenal element common to both classes of experience. The difference lies in the spiritual significance or value, or, as St John would term it, the substance—a criterion which is obviously external to the sensible phenomenon, and which cannot be grasped or applied by the soul that rests in that phenomenon in and for itself. These phenomena therefore *qua* external sensible phenomena are valueless.[2] Any value they may possess is due to an underlying spiritual communication made by God or by an angel or saint through their means. To rest in the sensible appearance

---

[1] I speak of its substantial meaning. With its details I am far from agreement. In my summary I have translated his meaning into the terminology adopted in this book.

[2] Except in the comparatively rare cases of third level phenomena. Even then the worth of the external phenomenon can only be determined by the consideration of its spiritual significance and power.

P

as such, in the glowing colours, sweet odours or musical notes, the element shared by the visions of the opium smoker, the hypnotic subject, the spiritistic medium and the madman, and to accept that as intrinsically valuable and Divine, an adequate manifestation of God, would obviously be the ruin of true spirituality, of the life that is essentially *interior*. On the other hand, we must, as has been pointed out above, avoid the opposite error of regarding such phenomena as always wholly subjective, even in their cause, however valuable be the spiritual significance or substance conveyed. Such an error is indeed identical in principle with its opposite extreme. In similar fashion it judges the inner substance by the outward form, making the external phenomenon the standard of value and resting the understanding in that. It is now evident how utterly opposed true mysticism is to the counterfeit mysticism which seeks and revels in extraordinary sensible phenomena, and which is indeed, as Baron von Hügel points out, the very essence of modern spiritism or occultism.

In his discussion of the active night St John proceeds to reject all images formed naturally by our understanding, as is done in the exercise of discursive meditation. These, though useful as a stage on the way, must finally be rejected, for if we rest in them we cannot attain to the Divine Being wholly inexpressible by images derived ultimately from sense impressions. The abandonment of this discursive meditation by means of sensible images is decided by the gift of a higher contemplation, passively received. Its discussion, therefore, belongs to the passive night of sense—and only to the active night in so far as the soul is able to follow or resist the Divine attraction to rise higher, to reject or accept the Divine gift.

St John proceeds to reject imaginary visions produced supernaturally, and that on the same principle on which he rejected the more external and therefore lower physical phenomena. These " imaginary " visions do not differ in principle from sensible visions and have therefore already been discussed together with them. Since, indeed, the so-called sensible visions have been shown to be subjective in their mode, if not in their cause, the reader may ask what difference there is between them and these " imaginary " visions. The difference is merely this, that whereas the former appear to possess objective existence in the physical world, to be apprehended by the senses, the latter do not. Yet they also seem to be spiritually trans-subjective, the perception by the imagina tion [1] of a reality and operation external to the soul. But the difference between the two classes of phenomena lies only in this appearance. The presence of trans-subjective validity may be equal or greater in the " sensible " visions and locutions, though normally this is not the case, since God prefers the more interior mode of communication.

Here St John sets himself to resolve a difficulty—namely, the Divine purpose in sending distinct apprehensions which must be rejected. He answers the objection by means of the principle used elsewhere to determine the right use of image worship by the mystic. Like images, these sensible or imaginary apprehensions are intended to lead the soul beyond them, being accommodations to the nature of an embodied spirit, excitants to a devotion which must transcend its stimulus. Their true substance is an obscure and loving apprehension of the incomprehensible Deity underlying the clear forms presented to the imagination. This apprehension and love union is given to the soul in the very moment when the "imaginary vision" enters the imagination. If the soul binds itself within the limits of the external appearance, by attachment to that appearance for its own sake, this substance is lost at least in part, for the soul cannot grasp the Unlimited Godhead, by loving faith, if and in so far as it clings to and rests in the essentially limited image. In view of the soul's weakness the external vision is sent to arouse it to grasp the inward Divine substance infused through love. The soul, aroused by the vision, opens to God its inmost will and selfhood in the act of supernatural love and apprehensive faith thereby excited. This enables it to receive more immediately and more fully the Divine Being Whom it finds and possesses in proportion to its freedom from limiting attachment to creatures. For this purpose was the vision sent, not to be the cause of a new self-limitation of the soul by attachment to its created and limited form. [2] The function of these supernatural visions is thus analogous to that of the mysteries of the Incarnation discussed already. It is, however, only analogous, for these images and apprehensions have not been brought like our Lord and the sacraments into an essential relationship of

[1] I mean, of course, the image-retaining and image-forming function of the soul, not imagination in the vulgar sense.
[2] St John not only explains this at length in this part of his book, but again in the twelfth chapter of Book III. he repeats the same doctrine with some further amplification.

peculiar intimacy with the Divine Being. They are bare symbols and no more.[1] Hence to pass through them is to pass beyond them and to forget them, not to pass deeper into them, as is the case with the Incarnation and its extensions. It is at this point that St John discusses the visions and revelations of the Bible. Of his profound treatment of this very difficult matter I will speak elsewhere.[2] He then proceeds to the purely intellectual or spiritual apprehensions of the soul. These he subdivides into several classes. As I know from bitter experience, it is by no means easy for the reader who comes to *The Ascent* for the first time to form a distinct notion of the differences between these. Moreover, they are not all treated alike. Some are integral portions of the mystical experience itself, and therefore in them the soul may rest. Others, distinct concepts of various kinds, do not belong to the experience, and these, like all the lower and less real because wholly or partially sensible apprehensions already discussed, are to be rejected. St John speaks first of intellectual visions which forms the subject of the twenty-fourth chapter of this second book. These are of two kinds. The former are visions of corporeal things made visible by a purely intellectual light supernaturally infused. As an example of these St John mentions the Apocalyptic vision of the new Jerusalem. These visions, however, obviously involve a sensible element, which element is surely constructed out of materials already present in the subconsciousness, as are the imaginary and sensible visions They may therefore be reduced to the same category as the two former. The other kind consists of clear visions of spiritual substances—" namely, the Divine Essence, angels and souls " which require " a light that is termed the *lumen gloriæ*." In other words, St John is speaking of the beatific vision of heaven. He adopts the view that an open vision of the Divine Essence, similar in principle to the beatific vision, has been, though very rarely granted to saints in this life, and he instances St Paul's vision of the third heaven. It is, however, more than doubtful whether such a vision has been or could be given to a soul still embodied in this mortal flesh. The passage is rather an interesting speculation than a solid contribution to mystical theology. Indeed in the older text of St John this passage has been so severely Bowdle

[1] The third level phenomena, however, approach the Incarnational mysteries of which, indeed, they are, so to speak, the outermost fringe.

[2] See Chapter XIII., "The Mystical Interpretation of Scripture."

ised as to leave the saint's meaning somewhat obscure. Of the
first importance, on the contrary, are the words which immediately
follow. "Though in the ordinary course," St John writes, "these
visions cannot be clearly and nakedly seen with the understanding
in this life, they may nevertheless be felt in the very substance
of the soul through the instrumentality of a loving knowledge
together with most sweet touches and unions. . . . These are the
end I have in view in writing, the divine embrace and union of
the soul with the divine Substance. . . . In this loving and
obscure knowledge God unites Himself with the soul eminently
and divinely. For this loving obscure knowledge, which is faith,
serves in a manner in this life as means of the divine union, as the
light of glory hereafter serves for the clear vision of God." This
passage is, as I have already pointed out, indubitable evidence
of what St John understood by faith—namely, an intuition of the
Godhead present in the centre of the soul, but veiled from all clear
conception, and therefore the substance of the beatific vision hoped
for hereafter. St John, returning to the intellectual visions of
corporeal objects, points out that from the very fact that their
subject-matter is created they are wholly inadequate as apprehensions of the Godhead, and therefore to be rejected. In the
twenty-sixth chapter St John speaks of supernatural "knowledge
of pure truths," which, he says, "consists in seeing with the understanding the truths of God, or of things or concerning things which
are, have been, or will be." Of this knowledge there are two kinds.
One of these is a knowledge of the Divine Being through one or
more of His attributes, whose meaning is realised with a depth and
fulness impossible to our natural understanding. For instance,
the soul has a sudden and powerful realisation of God as supreme
love or justice. Such knowledge is no distinct concept, but an
obscure though very vivid intuition infused into the soul. It is
not a knowledge of the Divine Being in Himself, but in a special
relationship to creation,[1] and is therefore a veiled and indirect
apprehension of the Godhead. Moreover, the attributes being
"unclosed" (see chap. iv.) are not themselves distinct concepts, but incomprehensible in their Divine infinity. Therefore
these apprehensions pertain to the mystical faith-intuition of
which they are a special, transient and inferior form.[2] St John

[1] More accurately of creation as in a special relationship to Him.
[2] For a series of these special apprehensions of the Divine Attributes see *The
Visions of Blessed Angela of Foligno* and the diary of Lucie Christine.

speaks of them here as "divine touches." Being part of the mystical intuition-union, they are, of course, to be received, not rejected. The second kind of knowledge of pure truths is a knowledge of created beings. This class includes a knowledge of natural truths supernaturally infused, as God might infuse a knowledge of secular science or philosophy into a saint that he might pass an important examination. St John instances the wisdom of Solomon. In this class are also comprised such graces as prophecy and the discerning of spirits, knowledge of distant events, or of the state of particular souls. All such graces are obviously granted for some end external to the soul's union with God through sanctifying grace. They are graces termed in theology *gratis datæ*. Such were the graces which the Corinthian converts overvalued, and to which St Paul bade them prefer charity, the true bond of union between the soul and God. St John speaks strongly on the great danger of delusion in these matters. "Let the director," he says, "guide his penitent quickly past this, *not making a mountain out of a molehill*, because it is of no help to him on the road to the divine union." Yet such occult phenomena are the utmost rewards aspired to by modern spirit ists, and the most desirable fruits of sanctity in the eyes of the multitude. Truly the active night of detachment is here carried to its furthest point. This supreme detachment is, however, perfectly logical, and indeed a striking manifestation of that supernatural common-sense which is known as the infused virtu of prudence, and which alone can guide the soul in safety along these Alpine precipices of the spiritual life where a false step may lightly precipitate it into the abyss.

On the other hand, we should remember that, when the sub stance of the mystical union has been attained and firmly grasped these more exterior phenomena—even the corporeal-imaginar visions—lose their danger. When the Resurrection synthes begins first to manifest itself, as it does in the higher degrees of union, the limits of such phenomena cease to detain the sou which passes in and through them to the unlimited Godhead. St Teresa's visions of jewels and music, of landscapes and of he friends in a strange beauty, may perhaps be accepted as instance of this, unless indeed we are to regard her practice as opposed to the teaching of St John, which should not lightly be presume I prefer to believe that this great mystic had entered in part into the final synthesis when these created, indeed sensible, goods

longer limit the soul, but arouse it on the contrary to a new fruition
of the Unlimited Goodness with Which it is in such close union.

Chapter twenty-seven is devoted to revelations—which are
again subdivided into two kinds. The former is the Judæo-
Christian revelation, finally closed at the end of the Apostolic era.
No new addition to that revelation is to be expected, and no
revelation of this kind can therefore be ever claimed by the
Catholic mystic. Outside the Church, however, there have been
many who, like Swedenborg, have claimed special revelations
against or beside the teaching of the Church. All such stand
self-condemned.* It may perhaps be thought that Catholics are
in no danger of being led astray by them. In our time, however,
there is so much false mysticism, or rather, perhaps, falsely interpreted mysticism, that even a Catholic mystic may be led to
accept alleged revelations that are out of harmony with the teaching of the Church. Even a Catholic mystical writer so fundamentally sound as Coventry Patmore toyed with strange Gnostic
fancies as to sex principles, and was greatly influenced by Swedenborg.[1] The second class of revelations are " Private revelations."
The subject-matter of these revelations often consists of private
matters concerning the recipient or his environment. Sometimes
they are special illuminations concerning some point of the public
revelation, a supernatural insight or vivid apprehension of some
mystery of faith. These are, as St John points out, not revelations in the strict sense, since they contain nothing not already
known in virtue of the public revelation. To this class belong
the intellectual visions [2] of the Blessed Trinity such as were granted
to St Ignatius and to St Teresa, and which normally accompany
the transforming union. Often, however, these private revelations,
or illuminations of the mysteries of the public revelation, contain
additional details concerning the mystery thus revealed—for
example, the Passion visions of St Bridget and Anne Catherine
Emmerich—or command special devotions, as did the well-known
revelation made by Our Saviour to Blessed Margaret Mary concerning the Sacred Heart. Of these private revelations some are
purely intellectual, especially those which are illuminations of

[1] See Miss Spurgeon, *Mysticism in English Literature*, p. 49 ; also Mr Meynell's
Life of Francis Thompson.
[2] Hence St Teresa's "intellectual visions " are not synonymous with those
so called by St John, which are, as we saw above, either (1) the beatific vision
anticipated or (2) visions of absent corporeal objects.

revealed dogma, and in particular the intellectual visions of the Blessed Trinity which accompany the supreme mystical union. These are, of course, the highest and the most Divine, because the least limited.   These revelations, however, are for the most part, as St John himself says, " expressed by words, figures and similitudes."   That is to say, they are expressed through the media of sense-derived images.   They are therefore in great part reducible to the kinds of extraordinary apprehension already discussed. This is an instance of that cross division that is inevitable in mystical theology whose subject-matter is not an orderly series of distinct facts, but one and the same obscure reality seen from various aspects which blend one into another.   The elaborate divisions and subdivisions of *The Ascent* give the reader a false expectation of a real distinction between all these, whereas they are often but different ways of regarding the same experience.   Here St John is discussing the same psycho-physical phenomena as he has already dealt with, but from a more interior point of view. He is considering no longer the external form but the intellectual knowledge conveyed, the revelation of truth to the understanding.[1] This knowledge or revelation as expressible in intellectual concepts is more spiritual, and therefore more real and more valuable, than the material images, but since and in so far as it is distinct, and comprehensible by clear ideas of the intellect, it is infinitely less than the spiritual substance, the Divine Self-communication which underlies both alike.   It is therefore to be rejected.   Especially to be rejected is new knowledge, additional to the dogmas of faith—for instance, new details revealed concerning these dogmas. Indeed even the dogmas of faith themselves, concerning which the soul receives an especial illumination, are not to be believed in virtue of that illumination, but solely in virtue of the teaching of the Church.[2]   For the ground of supernatural faith can only be the teaching of the Church, not the private illumination, however self-evident it may seem.   St John's caution is fully justified by the indubitable fact that the distinct details concerning mysteries of faith revealed to certain mystics are simply imaginative picturings of that mystery.   Nevertheless it is undeniable that the Church and her theologians have valued and admitted in practice private revelations.   St John's rejection may therefore seem

---

[1] Moreover, the external form is at times wanting and the revelation is purely intellectual (see above).

[2] *Ascent*, chaps. xxvii., xxix.

opposed to this practice. The rejection, however, which St John demands is in order to the mystical union. From a more exterior point of view, in order to help other souls, for the better accomplishment of the external work of the recipient or for the general good of the Church, such revelations ought sometimes to be received and used, as, for instance, the revelation requiring devotion to the Sacred Heart. Nevertheless the internal rejection or detachment must be present if the soul is to pass onward to the mystical union. We must also bear in mind that the Church never has accepted, nor can accept, any private revelation as authentic. She can approve of such revelations as useful, pious and as probably from God, but she cannot propose them to our belief as His certain revelation. To do so would be to add to the revealed depositum which is entirely beyond the power of its guardian and interpreter. Even if the Church institutes a devotion or feast in consequence of a private revelation, her ultimate authority is not the revelation but the theological certitude that such a devotion or feast is in harmony with the public revelation. Hence we are not bound in faith to believe that the private revelation was Divinely given, though of course there is the very strongest presumption of this. Still less are we bound to believe in the accessory details of that revelation, which details contain indeed in all probability a subjective element. As a Catholic I am bound to believe that the devotion to the Sacred Heart is orthodox and laudable. I have every reason to believe that its revelation to Blessed Margaret Mary was the work of God. I am, however, in no way bound to accept the last promise, if in my private judgment I regard that promise as erroneous or at least as misleading.* St John has good reason to insist in this matter also . on the danger of illusion.

Before passing on I should like to take this occasion to point out how ill-founded is the modern objection to the finality of the Christian revelation. It is thought that a progressive revelation never complete would be in greater harmony with a universe of change and progress. The answer is that the dogmas of the Christian revelation are of such infinite depth and scope that their significance can never be exhausted. No advance in knowledge, secular or religious, can outgrow them ; no process of development, however long, can be adequate to express their entire meaning. Because these dogmas are in immediate relation to the infinite their significance is infinite. There is no need of new doctrines. The

Divine revelation is adequate to the religious needs, theoretical and practical, of all races and of all ages. Man can discover nothing of ultimate Reality not contained explicitly or implicitly in the Christian revelation as infallibly proposed to our belief by the Catholic Church. Any theological teaching that is really outside the depositum, and in so far as it is outside it, is a negation of some portion of the fulness of the depositum due to the exaggeration or one-sided development of one aspect of it. Any such additional revelation, therefore, instead of adding to our knowledge of divine truth, would limit that knowledge and would thus cramp instead of expanding the soul. Thus the finality of the revealed deposit is our safeguard against doctrines which, while professing to impart new knowledge of religious truth, in reality limit the knowledge already possessed by the negation, at least implicit, of some portion of it.[1]

The ensuing chapters of this second book of *The Ascent* deal with locutions. These are divided into three classes—successive locutions, words formed by the mind itself so as to appear the words of an objective *interior* voice, which locutions are, of course, to be rejected ; formal words, which are phenomenally at least objective—that is to say, which appear to proceed from a source exterior to the soul, but which are most probably objective if at all, only in cause, being subjectively formed like sensible visions, and which are also to be rejected ; and substantial words, which in form are akin to the formal words, but which produce a spiritual effect, filling the soul with new consolation, peace, strength and spiritual life, indeed effecting in the soul what they signify. Since these locutions produce this quasi-sacramental effect in the soul, filling it with virtues and graces, they are to be accepted as direct aids to the Divine union.[2] St John closes the book with a chapter on divine impressions on the will and, deeper still, on the substance of the soul. These impressions are a portion of the mystical union itself and obviously closely akin to the " touches of union " described in the twenty-sixth chapter as the first class of pure truths. They differ, however, in that they are not primarily impressed upon the understanding or spiritual consciousness, but

[1] God could, of course, reveal more truth than He has revealed *potentia absoluta*. Having regard, however, to man's actual constitution and condition, the revealed depositum including all its implications exhausts all the RELIGIOUS truth which he is capable of receiving. A revelation of secular truth while possible would be rather pernicious than valuable.

[2] Locutions have been already discussed with visions and revelations.

are unions of the will or the central substance which is the apex of the will, and are received by the understanding only through an overflow from the will or its apex. The former touches of union were sudden intuitions of the Divine Being through some attribute supernaturally impressed on the understanding. These latter touches of union are sudden inflammations of love wherein God unites Himself to and is received in the will, or even in that inmost depth of the self in which the will itself is rooted. That is to say, the difference between these two kinds of transitory union is that in the former the cognitive element greatly predominates over the volitional and affective elements; in the latter the contrary is the case. Since these impressions are a portion of the mystical union to which the entire way of the soul has been directed, they are not to be rejected, but conceived in a complete passivity, in which the only activity of the soul is reception. The third book is devoted to the active purgation of the memory by hope and of the will by charity. St John's teaching concerning these purgations considers from another aspect the progressive detachment from sensible and spiritual goods already discussed. Incidentally phenomena pertaining to the highest mystical union are spoken of to the great confusion of the reader who imagines himself concerned only with the way of purgation. As was pointed out above, the nature of his subject-matter forbids the strictly scientific exposition which St John aims at. In *The Canticle* and *The Living Flame* such a method is not even attempted. The result here is much cross division, and the result of this is in turn so complex a programme that the treatise breaks down under it in the middle of this third book.[1]

Nor can we regard the memory as a primary faculty like understanding and will. It is really a subdivision of the cognitive faculty. Its perfecting virtue, hope, is similarly subordinate to faith. Moreover, hope does not unite the memory with God as faith and charity do the understanding and will. Its work is rather to destroy memory, as far as the spiritual life is concerned, by making the soul " forget the things that are behind " in its constant expectation of the eternal life to come. This, indeed, St

---

[1] Despite the discovery of a small **fragment** which would have been inserted at a considerable distance from the present conclusion, I cannot agree with the editor of the Edicion Critica that *The Ascent* was ever completed. It is far easier to suppose the discovered fragment specially written with a view to later insertion, than the unnoticed absence of a large portion from all the existent MSS.

John points out.   I have already expressed my belief that for the inner trinity of understanding, memory and will, should be substituted another trinity of the substance or ground of the soul, the will, the cognition.   The last is in the mystical union, rather intuition than understanding in the usual sense.

The purgation of the will by love from all rest in created goods is but the other aspect of the detachment of the understanding from creatures.   St John's treatment introduces no fresh principle, and is simply a searching criticism of the world's values, indeed of all created values, in which the illusion and emptiness of all creatures as ends in themselves is remorsely laid bare.   Incidentally the exasperating pettinesses of the class stigmatised by Huysmans as " devots " and " bigots " are exposed with a merciless hand.   If anyone ever knew the weaknesses of the " good " it was St John.   In discussing image-worship he throws out the illuminating suggestion that the reason why miracles are worked at one image or shrine rather than another is simply the special faith and devotion of the worshippers.   " It is certain," he says (I quote again a hitherto unpublished passage), "that the image is not the cause why God so acts, for that in itself is no more than a piece of painting, but rather our devotion to the saint depicted and our faith in him.   If, therefore, you had the same devotion, and faith in Our Lady when worshipping before one image as when worshipping before another . . . or even . . . without the use of either, you would receive the same favours " (iii. 35).   It is, unhappily, a psychological impossibility for the vast majority to have an equally intense devotion and faith in all places, or even in all churches alike, and hence the necessity for special shrines and miraculous images.   St John's explanation is striking in its boldness and penetration.

Two other remarks are needed on St John's inculcation of rigid detachment from particular *objets de piété*.   The first is to note that he expressly permits attachment to such in the case of beginners—that is, in reality of the great mass of the faithful.   But this is to concede by implication that we cannot expect from the majority of Christians in this life the detachment of a mystic.

We should also remark St John's express disapproval of ugly religious art.   The usual image of our modern churches, being as it is an offensive caricature of the Sacred Subject which it represents, indeed, to use Huysmans' strong but perfectly justifiable language, a blasphemy against the Divine Beauty, would have met with nothing but repudiation from our saint. Lack of ornament and poverty of material are one thing, positive ugliness another. Detachment does not and should not involve a tolerance of the milk-and-sugar images, the glass-eyed idiocies so dear to the average modern Catholic. Shortly afterwards *The Ascent* ends abruptly in the middle of a warning against the indulgence of " sensible delectation " in sermons, a demand for a self-denial somewhat less heroic than many others of the active night !

Whether any more was written we cannot tell. A few scraps have been found that would have come somewhat later in accordance with St John's scheme. That is all. Enough has certainly been written to explain and emphasise the Saint's teaching on the active purgation or night. I hope that I have succeeded in interpreting his doctrine correctly. It is now time to proceed to the mystic experience itself, including as it does the two passive nights.

APPENDIX

Throughout *The Ascent* St John insists on the danger of diabolic counterfeits of the Divine work. His demonology knew no hesitations. To many modern readers this will seem a defect. The devils and their doings are apt to appear unreal, grotesque products of superstitious terror. I would call their attention to the following points :—

(*a*) There is a specific class of madness which consists in the belief of the patient that he is obsessed or possessed by an evil spirit—a species so well marked as to have received the name of hystero-demonopathy (James, *Varieties of Religious Experiences*, p. 501, footnote). Such a label is obviously no explanation. The mental physician takes account of the psycho-physical phenomena of madness. In so far as these phenomena are due to a physical cause—for instance, to a defect or injury of the physical mechanism of the soul—that cause also falls within his purview. If, however, the ultimate cause be of the spiritual order, and the defect or injury of the mechanism of the brain but the concomitant or result of the psychical evil, that cause lies beyond his province altogether, at least as it has hitherto been understood. For the method of the mental doctor has been to approach and to handle the psychical through the physical. To-day, indeed, we are witnesses of a change, of a growing tendency to treat mental diseases by psychical methods. The general adoption of these methods may well lead to a revision of the popular views on such matters as possession.

(b) Our Lord assumed the reality of diabolic possession and practised exorcism. Indeed this formed a prominent feature of His ministry. We cannot logically escape this fact by vague language about epilepsy and madness and retain our faith in the Incarnation. How should God Incarnate mistake madness for demoniacal possession, or if He did not make that mistake, how should He go through the solemn pretence of an exorcism known to be an empty farce, or at best a means of suggestion based on a known falsehood ? There is clearly no help for it. Either we must accept demoniacal possession or deny Our Lord's Divinity as it is believed by the Church. Huxley saw this dilemma and pressed it home on the half-hearted Victorian Christians who, in denying the former, while accepting the latter, tried to combine two incompatible positions.

(c) No one can accuse Mr Clement Webb of believing anything against his private judgment, because he is compelled to do so by ecclesiastical authority. Nevertheless in his Wilde Lectures on Natural Theology he sums up the question of the existence of non-human evil spirits in the following terms :—" That evil *is* present in the human will is not deniable.   If, then, the presence of evil in the human will is not incompatible with the ultimate sovereignty of a good God, the presence of evil in finite wills other than human is not incompatible with it, and would in no way increase the difficulty, though it may not diminish it.   From Plato to J. S. Mill there have not been wanting thinkers who could not otherwise interpret the facts than by such an admission. . . . We cannot suppose with our present knowledge that the pre-human world was free from what we commonly call evils (*e.g.* from animal suffering), the existence of which in God's world constitutes for us a problem. . . . The recognition of an evil will or wills in the world by which our environment has been injuriously affected, in the same way as it undoubtedly is affected by evil human wills, would, while not affording any assistance to us in answering the ultimate question of the origin of evil, yet remove any additional difficulty due to the assumption we are nowadays so apt to make without hesitation that, while moral evil is explicable in so far as its possibility is involved in the existence of free will, moral evil can exist only in human wills, and that the environment of humanity must be attributed wholly, if at all, to God and in no degree to the operation of finite wills other than human. The supposition that it may be in part attributed to the operation or be consequential upon the operation of such finite wills, suggested by Plato and others, is not to be ruled out because such a supposition has in the past been presented in an unacceptable form " (*Studies in the History of Natural Theology*, pp. 99-101).

If, then, it is not intrinsically unreasonable to believe in evil spirits, we need not shrink with the timidity now all too common, even among orthodox Catholics, from proclaiming our assent to the infallible teaching of the Church that such beings do in fact exist. But if they exist, it is most probable that they should act on men in various ways, and the Church teaches us that they do so. Modern investigation of telepathic and hypnotic phenomena has abundantly proved the influence exerted by one human soul on another, the power of mental suggestion. If this suggestion is exercised very strongly and continuously the patient's will becomes more or less completely subject to the will of the operator. Suppose this suggestion to be exercised by an evil discarnate spirit, we should have an obsession or, in extreme cases, a possession of the human spirit by this evil spirit, and the effects of this obsession or possession would in some instances extend even to the body. Especially would the mechanism of the nerves and brain be thrown out of gear by this potent obsessing or possessing suggestion exercised upon the soul to whom it belonged, and this would in turn cause the phenomena of mania, hypnosis and nervous breakdown. This explanation of possession by suggestion is quoted by M. Joly in his *Psychology of the Saints* (Eng. trs., p. 110) as that advocated by Père Bonniot. " In the one case," writes Bonniot (*i.e.* possession), " the devil acts upon the subject, in the other the experimenter, and this is about the only difference between the two cases." " Possessions are cases of hypnotism, in which the evil spirit plays the part of hypnotiser." Such a conception of diabolic possession quite removes the grotesqueness attaching to the notion of a devil lodged inside a human body and brings possession within a class of phenomena whose existence is indubitable and whose psycho-physical characteristics are well known.[1]

---

[1] I should also explain by such a permanent suggestion-contact the presence of Mary in the soul vouchsafed to her great servant and preacher, Bl. Louis Marie Grignon de Montfort.

It also renders full justice to the objective reality of the possessions recorded in the New Testament. That similar cases do exist even to-day is well attested by the evidence of spiritistic investigators and of missionaries, and is indeed admitted by the scientific recognition of hystero-demonopathy. Such considerations as these should make the reader of St John realise that his acceptance of demonology, or diabolic mysticism, as it is sometimes termed, if perhaps requiring modification in detail, is fundamentally sound, and is as justified by the evidence as it is demanded by the teaching of the Church. It is true that St John is chiefly concerned with lesser phenomena than possession —namely, with diabolical counterfeits of various concomitants of mystical prayer. The mystical prayer-union itself being the operation of God in the central depths accessible to Him alone is, as St John often points out, entirely beyond the reach of diabolic imitation. If, however, the existence of the greater be admitted, no one will boggle at the existence of the less. On the other hand, there is no doubt that St John, like all his contemporaries, saw diabolical operation where it was absent. We have seen that a large class of supernatural phenomena—for instance, visions—are objective in cause, subjective in mode. Often, however, these phenomena are purely subjective in cause and mode alike and are then purely natural. St John would have been unduly inclined to ascribe such cases to an objective evil cause—namely, the devil. That is, however, no reason why we should go to the opposite extreme and deny that such an objective evil cause ever sets the subjective phenomena in motion. Such a denial would be unwarrantable, improbable and opposed to the universal teaching of Catholic theologians.

CHAPTER IX

MYSTICAL EXPERIENCE PREVIOUS TO THE NIGHT OF SPIRIT

When the sun was setting a deep sleep fell upon Abram and a great darksome horror seized upon him.

The word of the Lord came to Abram by a vision, saying : " Fear not, I am thy reward exceeding great." Genesis xvi.

Jacob remained alone and behold a man wrestled with him till morning. Jacob asked him : " Tell me by what name thou art called ? " He answered : " Why dost thou ask my name ? " And He blessed him. Genesis xxxii.

By degrees I passed from bodies to the soul, which through the bodily senses perceives, and thence again to the reasoning faculty, to which what is received from the senses of the body is referred to be judged ; Which finding itself also to be in me a thing variable raised itself up to its own understanding . . . withdrawing itself from those troops of contradictory phantasms that so it might find what that light was whereby it was bedewed, when without all doubting it cried out " That the Unchangeable was to be preferred to the changeable," whence also it knew That Unchangeable . . . and thus with the flash of one trembling glance it arrived at That Which Is. . . . But I could not fix my gaze thereon ; and my infirmity being struck back, I was thrown again on my wonted habits, carrying along with me only a loving memory and a longing for what I had, as it were, perceived the odour of, but was not yet able to feed on.

ST AUGUSTINE,
Confessions, Book VII. xxiii. (Trs. Pusey).

Since mystical experience is an increase and manifestation of sanctifying grace, it does not differ essentially from the hidden life of grace in the souls of all the just. Throughout the entire process from grace to glory no new principle is introduced. Hence the mystical union-intuition involves no such introduction of a new principle. It is but a development and unfolding of a principle already present.   Whereas the infusion of sanctifying grace in our regeneration is a new creation, the mystical way is but the growth of that new creature, mystical experience a concomitant manifestation of the new life thus growing.   Mystical union in its conscious aspect is the experience of God Present and Active in the soul through the new relationship constituted in principle and potency by the first infusion of sanctifying grace.   As the Divine Union becomes more intimate, the Divine Action more potent and more prevalent over the merely human self-principled life of the soul, that Union and Action become gradually manifest within the field of consciousness.   We have therefore no reason to expect any distinct line of demarcation between the ordinary life of grace and mystical experience or prayer.   The latter succeeds to the former gradually and imperceptibly, as dawn to the darkness of night, youth to childhood, spring to winter, friendship to mere acquaintance.   If we search the writings of the mystics for some definite criterion whereby to distinguish between all states of mystical prayer and all forms of ordinary prayer, we shall fail to find it.   It is true that there can be no confusion between ordinary prayer and well-marked mystical states.   But it is impossible to state clearly where ordinary prayer ends and mystical experience begins.   The latter gradually develops out of the former.   At first the indwelling Presence of God,[1] constituted by the operation of grace uniting the soul and its faculties with the Godhead, is manifested very faintly, almost imperceptibly, for a very brief space and at rare intervals.   Gradually the manifestation becomes more clearly marked, endures longer and occurs more frequently.   Finally, in a semi-conscious form, the manifestation endures permanently in the ground of the soul.   As the old man, the natural and limited soul life, decays, the new man, the supernatural participation in the unlimited life of God, is gradually manifested.   It is manifested at first when the soul has deliberately turned to God in prayer, and is therefore called a state of prayer.   But since the work of grace is to turn the soul Godward as grace increases in the soul, the entire activity of that soul gradually becomes a Godward turning, a union with Him, therefore prayer.   Finally, when the central functions of the soul are

[1] More strictly an inhabitation of God in His Third Subsistence or Person the Holy Spirit. Petavius, following many of the early fathers, and himself followed by Scheeben, is not content with the mere appropriation to the Holy Spirit taught by most modern theologians.

continuously turned Godward and the soul is conscious of their union with God, the soul is always in prayer. Indeed we should remember that every soul in grace is always in an unconscious habitual prayer by the very fact that the will is united to God as its supreme end. We speak, indeed, of mystical union as prayer, and we do not usually give that name to the entire spiritual life of a soul in grace. In principle, however, both are prayer at diverse degrees, since prayer is a conversion to God and union with Him, and this conversion and union are fundamentally identical in all stages of the life of grace. This essential identity of the life of grace through its manifestation in mystical experience to its consummation in beatific vision would forbid us to expect any sudden change from one stage to another. Nor, as a rule, is this the case. It is true that in certain souls the first manifestation of grace is sudden. This, however, is the exception, not the rule, and is probably due to the fact that some special obstacle hid the secret growth of grace till it had reached a degree far beyond that when it usually begins to be felt. This obstacle is suddenly removed by some extraordinary actual grace or external occurrence, as a tower whose foundations have been long undermined falls suddenly in a gale of unusual strength. I know that certain mystical authors attempt to establish the sharp distinction here deprecated. Père Poulain, for instance, defines mystical prayer in contradistinction to ordinary prayer, as a prayer which we cannot acquire by our own efforts, not even faintly nor for a moment.[1] Can we then acquire of ourselves the least degree of prayer that proceeds from sanctifying grace ? Surely this is impossible. The form of our prayer is indeed our own work, but its hidden principle is the infused grace of God. When mystical prayer begins, this hidden principle has begun to determine the form of our prayer. We need no longer formulate our prayer by a laborious search composition and rejection of ideas and images. Grace gradually dispenses with these and directly moves the soul Godward and unites with Him the radical faculties, especially the will. As the action of grace—that is, of God through grace—increases the work of the faculties becomes increasingly that of attentive receptivity—that is, they become passive in relation to the Divine action received, while increasingly active in their absorbed attention and reception of an activity so supernaturally intense. The multiplicity of images and distinct concepts also gradually gives place to a unity of

[1] Poulain, *Les Graces d'Oraison*, chap. i.

simple attention to the Divine work, to a unified absorption of the soul in its Divine Object, the understanding in obscure faith-intuition of God, the transcendent, unintelligible *Reality* and the will in love of that Divine Being.   In a process so gradual, where are we to set up well-defined boundaries ?   How are we to mark off sharply one state from another ?   " I cannot pretend," writes Professor James, " to detail to you the sundry stages of the Christian mystical life. . . . I confess that the subdivisions and names which we find in the Catholic books seem to me to represent nothing objectively distinct " (*Varieties of Religious Experience*, p. 408).   It is indeed impossible to give entire assent to this dictum.   Certain stages markedly different in character can be clearly discerned on the mystical way, or, as I would rather express it, on the way of sanctifying grace.   Certainly we cannot fix the exact point where one stage ends and the next begins.   Neverthe-less each of these stages in its fulness presents a character of its own, perceptible even to us, who only know it externally through the study of books.   It is the same here as it is with the four seasons. No one could possibly confuse a typical winter's morning with a typical spring morning, or a typical summer's day with a typical day of autumn.   We have only to recall first a walk through the fields in July, then a similar walk on a fine day in September, to recognise in the former summer, in the latter autumn.   On the former occasion summer manifested itself in the air, saturated with light and heat, scented and murmurous, and in the rich and vigorous life all but visible in the grass, flowers and leaves.   On the latter the crisp sharpness of the air, the mellowness of the vegetation and the softness of the sunlight told us plainly that the Earth's life blood, which in summer had coursed so lustily through her veins, was now being poured out, and that the grave of winter awaited her ; in a word, that it was autumn.   But we cannot say that till such-and-such a day it was summer, after such-and-such a day it was autumn.   Such an accurate delineation can only be made from the purely abstract point of view of the calendar, which fixes arbitrary boundaries between the four seasons.   There i often an autumn day that is succeeded by many days of summe and is but a forerunner of a season not yet fully come.

Still less can we fix the bounds of even the more marked stage of mystical experience—for example, the prayer of quiet ecstasy the night of spirit and mystical marriage.   Nevertheless thes stages are as objectively real and as plainly distinct in characte as are the four seasons. The minor subdivisions, on the other hand, so copiously multiplied by those modern theologians who wish to construct a mystical theology, as minutely scientific as the dogmatic theology of the school, and the moral theology of the casuist, serve only to darken knowledge and to confuse the mind. They are wholly absent from the pages of the great mystics, such as St John, and the less the student of mysticism concerns himself with them the better for him.

In Father Germano's *Life of Gemma Galgani* [1] we find a typical list of these divisions taken from Scaramelli. As he gives them there, the successive stages of the mystical way are Mystic Recollection, Spiritual Silence, Contemplation or Quiet, Mystic Sleep, Spiritual Inebriety, Flame of Love, Thirst and Anguish of Love, Mystic Espousals (by this is meant mystical marriage). Of these many are simply subordinate phenomena attendant on several different stages of mystical union. For instance, the Flame and Thirst of Love belong in a higher degree to mystical marriage than to the lower stage where they are here placed. This error of excessive schematism is pointed out by Père Poulain in the thirtieth chapter of *Les Graces d'Oraison*. There he tells us that the systematisers have sometimes numbered as many as fifteen degrees of mystical prayer, obtained by this false method of reckoning sub-phenomena common to more than one degree of union as being themselves distinct degrees. My own view is that it is best to recognise five stages of the mystic way, in which quantitative increase of union has issued in a qualitative difference distinctly cognisable. Nevertheless, since each stage in turn passes over into the next, they are incapable of exact delimitation. Out of these five stages or degrees of mystical union three are positive, two negative. The first stage is the Passive Night of Sense, the negative entrance into the mystic way. Then follows Quiet. Quiet is subdivided by St Teresa into two degrees, Quiet and Full Union (*Autobiography, The Interior Castle*). These are, as Père Poulain points out (chap. xxx), merely one and the same form of mystical prayer experienced at two different degrees of intensity. Since these sub-degrees thus lack qualitative difference, their distinction must be predominantly artificial. After Quiet follows Ecstasy. This is treated by Père Poulain as the third subdivision of Quiet, Quiet at its fullest intensity. I incline, however, to believe that Ecstasy is rather a foretaste of the spiritual

[1] Chap. xxii.

marriage to come, effected primarily in the will, while Quiet is effected primarily in the spiritual consciousness. St John does not discuss the distinction between these two or three stages. Then follows a negative stage, the Passive Night of Spirit. After that ensues the final stage, the Mystical Marriage, including as its inception its imperfect form, termed by St John the Spiritual Betrothal. It will be useful, therefore, to bear in mind these four or five degrees, paying no heed to the useless and unjustifiable sub-divisions above mentioned, and always remembering that even these merge into each other so imperceptibly that it is impossible to fix between them any clear demarcation.[1]

We must also bear in mind that when we attempt any description of mystical states we are trying to express purely spiritual realities in language drawn from sensible phenomena, a language of symbols. The very titles of certain mystical states or degrees are symbols—for example, the dark night and mystical or spiritual marriage. The more advanced and therefore the more purely spiritual the state or experience, the more symbolic must the description be, for the description must then be furthest removed from the reality. But it is obvious that the same symbols will apply equally well to different states. Different degrees of love will, for example, be described by the same symbols of fire and wounds, different degrees of intuition by the same symbolism of light or darkness. This makes it a very difficult, often an impossible, task, for us who lack the experiences to be compared to distinguish them by the external symbolic and therefore altogether inadequate descriptions of mystical writers. One and the same description will often fit different degrees, since it is really but an indication, not a description at all. A striking illustration of this can be obtained by comparing the order of stanzas in the earlier and later versions of the *Spiritual Canticle*. In the second version, the only one printed previously to the Edicion Critica, stanza 22 is devoted to an account of the mystical marriage, and all the following stanzas to stanza 39 inclusive are concerned with that state. In the earlier version, however, stanza 22 is the 27th stanza. Out of the stanzas 22 to 35 of the later version no less than ten occur in the earlier before the stanza which introduces the mystic marriage, and are therefore applied to earlier stages of mystic

[1] Such a clear line of demarcation is most of all to be found in the case of the night of spirit, but even there is far from absolute.

experience. Yet the prose descriptions attached to each stanza are substantially identical in both versions. This, then, is another reason why it is lost labour to attempt to give so exact a definition of the different stages that their boundaries can be accurately delineated. Only of the more important and well-marked degrees, and of these only of each at its height and fulness, can such indications be given as shall enable their differences to be in some measure suggested. To fix the boundaries of states which develop one into the other, and which are of their very nature so indescribable, is a sheer impossibility.

The inutility must now be patent of any attempt to distinguish where the ordinary prayer of hidden grace ends and the mystical prayer of grace manifest, at first so dimly as to be all but imperceptible, begins. The higher stages of ordinary prayer have been sometimes termed acquired contemplation, mystical prayer being distinguished as infused contemplation. *The Obscure Knowledge of God*, for instance, adopts this distinction, which is, however, absént from any of the indubitably authentic works of St John. Contemplation is itself defined as " the intuition of an object without discursive reflection." In this contemplation " the substantial nature of the object has been abstracted from its accidental properties and from its material embodiment." I have translated by intuition the Spanish phrase, " consideracion de simple inteligencia," literally " regard of simple knowledge." The author evidently understood by contemplation the occupation of the understanding by a simple apprehension without discursive reasoning or sense-derived images. This contemplation when natural is, he says, " acquired by the diligent and careful work of the soul, the fruit of long and intense meditation." When supernatural it is " due to a supernatural light infused by God into the soul, which is now moved by God with a supernatural movement " (chap. i). It is, however, obvious that this distinction being causal, not phenomenal, is no criterion. We are left in ignorance when a particular contemplation is the fruit of our past activity and when it is the work of God in the soul. Such a criterion is, however, attempted. " The most certain criterion," says this writer, " of supernatural and infused contemplation is that we do not enjoy it whenever we will to do so, nor does it cease at our will and pleasure. On the contrary, it comes when God wills and ceases at His good pleasure, God bestowing it and taking it away when He wills and deems good to do so." Such a criterion is, however, nugatory.

There are many forms of purely natural perception that are more
or less out of our power to exercise at pleasure. An illuminating
insight into natural truth is not ours when we will. It often
comes to us suddenly and unexpectedly, in a flash. Æsthetic
appreciation is most variable. The same beauty of art or nature
will at one time absorb the soul with admiration, at another leave
us cold and indifferent. Indeed the tendency of modern psychology has been to show that the intellectual insight of the philosopher or scientist, and the æsthetic insight of the artist, which
when extraordinarily intense become the insight of genius, are
usually manifested suddenly, often as if externally infused after a
long train of apparently fruitless study or practice. The ideas or
perceptions of conscious activity have accumulated gradually in the
subconsciousness and have there combined together to form a new
idea or perception, a new insight or apprehension of reality, which
then becomes suddenly conscious. Therefore suddenness and apparent externality are no criteria of supernatural working. Indeed
our author proceeds to remark : " It is true that as a general
rule He (God) gives this to those who persevere in the practice of
prayer and of the acquired natural contemplation, rewarding the
soul for her labours with this infused supernatural contemplation."
It is not indeed the case that a sudden irruption into consciousness from the subconscious depths of the soul disproves
supernatural action. This Professor James himself admits.[1]
Nevertheless such a sudden irruption is no proof of such action.

Our author, however, proceeds to invoke another test, and says
that in supernatural contemplation the soul enjoys an absolute
certainty of the reality of the Divine object of that contemplation.
This criterion is valid, unless we are to declare mystical experience
a delusion, which we have no more right to do than we have to
declare æsthetic or moral experience, or even sense experience
itself, a delusion. In the earliest stages, however, as we shall see
from St John's account of the night of sense, the contemplation is
so dim as to be almost imperceptible. In that case this certainty
is absent, for there is no *strongly impressed* object to cause it. We
are therefore still left without a criterion which would justify
the drawing of a hard and fast line between acquired and infused
contemplation. Acquired contemplation is the gradual super-
session of discursive meditation through sense images by a unified
attention of the soul to an obscure apprehension or intuition of God

[1] See introductory chapter.

as transcendent of all distinct images and concepts, which attention is an operation of love, as the obscure intuition or negative apprehension is an operation of faith. But this process is itself the work of grace, through infused love and infused faith, and is therefore the result of a supernatural activity making use of our natural faculties and working in accordance with their laws. At first this unified prayer requires laborious efforts on the part of the soul to exclude images and multiple notions and to concentrate first on some one distinct notion and finally on the negative apprehension or obscure intuition of God as the transcendent unintelligible Object of love. So long as this labour of the faculties occupies the field of consciousness the contemplation seems to be wholly acquired. When, however, the working of God through grace becomes fully conscious, and our own activity, now trained in concentration and detachment, becomes the obedient servant or passive receptacle of that supernatural activity, the contemplation seems to be wholly infused. In reality, it was not wholly acquired before, nor is it wholly infused now. The infused contemplation is largely the fruit of the acquired concentration and detachment which have enabled the soul to become conscious of the infused activity of God through grace and its concomitant faith and charity, which was, however, present unconsciously from the beginning. If it be asked why we cannot regard the entire process as the natural work of the religious sense of man, as the perception of the artist is the work of his æsthetic sense, the answer is that no merely natural activity could produce an experience whose supernatural character, *when that experience is fully developed*, is indubitable to the soul that possesses it. It has, moreover, been already shown in the introductory chapter, and confirmed by the admissions of modern psychologists of the subconscious, that mystical experience is the experience of an objective superhuman Reality, which objective Reality was identified with God. Therefore, even if mystical experience or contemplation were a purely natural activity of man, its object, at least, is the supernatural Godhead. The Deity, however, is essentially a living force, indeed a pure act, not a dead and passive object. Therefore when the soul in mystical experience possesses this immediate apprehension of God and communion with Him, it is in immediate communion with an Activity by comparison with Which it is passive. Therefore in this immediate communion between the soul and its Divine Object the activity must rather be the activity of God in the soul than of the soul towards God—although the latter is not thereby excluded.[1] Hence the activity whereby the human soul thus apprehends God immediately in mystical contemplation cannot be its own natural activity, but must be the supernatural activity of God received in and through its own activity rendered by grace obedient and receptive to the Divine influx. Furthermore, if the object of the soul's experience is supernatural—that is to say, wholly transcendent of the connatural object of the functions of the human soul—the experience of that Object must also be supernatural, the supernatural working of God in the soul through grace.[2] But this supernatural operation is present before the soul is conscious of it, and the natural activity of the soul continues even when the supernatural has come to dominate the field of consciousness.

If another argument be desired to prove the gradual development of mystical experience out of the hidden working of sanctifying grace, we should notice that Père Poulain, indeed the entire school of modern systematic mystical theology, interpolates between discursive meditation and mystical prayer two degrees of natural or acquired contemplation, as its operation is increasingly unified and its object increasingly general and obscure. These are termed affective prayer and the prayer of simple regard. Now, as Père Poulain has himself clearly demonstrated, St John's Passive Night of Sense is the passage to the lowest form of positive mystical prayer, the prayer of quiet, and indeed the first beginning of that prayer. But St John, who treats of this night in three distinct places,[3] always regards it as the passage from discursive meditation, which it supersedes and destroys. Therefore, according to St John, the night of sense follows meditation directly and thus includes in some way or other the acquired contemplation of affective prayer and the prayer of simple regard. That is to say, St John's mystical prayer or infused contempla-

---

[1] In a sense this is true of all created activity in its relation to the pure Act of the Divine Being. Nevertheless when the immediate activity is terminated wholly by creatures it is not true in the same immediate sense, as is the case when the supernatural apprehension of God is the immediate object of a creature's activity.

[2] Faith also, of course, forbids this naturalism. I am giving above natural arguments on behalf of the teaching of faith, to prove the necessity of a Divine operation to effect mystical contemplation. Only through the faith, however, can we possess *absolute* certainty that this Divine action through grace is essentially—that is, qualitatively—different from the Divine concurrence requisite for the activity of all creatures.

[3] *Ascent*, Book II., chaps. xiii., xiv. and xv. ; *Dark Night*, Book I. *passim* ; *Living Flame*, st. 3.

tion includes the two stages of acquired contemplation. When we read St Teresa's description of the Prayer of Quiet, as given in her *Autobiography*, we are struck with its resemblance, or rather its identity, with the state of prayer described by other writers as the acquired prayer of Simple Regard. Moreover, St John himself treats of this early contemplation as at once acquired and infused. In the Second Book of *The Ascent* St John regards primarily the active or acquired aspect of contemplation, whereas in the first book of *The Dark Night* its passive or infused aspect is treated. But in *The Ascent* he discusses both aspects conjointly. In chap. xiv. (Book II.) he speaks of the general knowledge of contemplation as a continuous habit acquired by many acts of discursive meditation. "Many acts of this loving knowledge" (acts of discursive meditation) ". . . by long use attain such a continuance that a habit is formed in the soul . . . by the soul's labour of meditation in particular acts of knowledge . . . there has been formed in it the habit and substance of a general loving knowledge"—*i.e.* contemplation. But in this very chapter he describes this general knowledge as a Divine light entering the soul, and tells us that this light places the soul in a species of oblivion wherein time is transcended. He says that "such a soul is united in heavenly knowledge," is "supernaturally raised into supernatural knowledge." "This supernatural knowledge of contemplation" (chap. xv). Further in this fifteenth chapter St John insists in the plainest terms on the passive and infused character of this contemplation. "God communicates Himself passively. . . . This reception of the light that is *supernaturally infused is a passive understanding*." In these chapters, therefore, the same contemplation is described as both acquired and infused; as acquired since it is the effect of operations of the psychic powers under the influence of grace and in the reception of grace; infused as being a new, higher and modally different operation and reception of that grace. The active and passive elements of the psychosis are now changing their mutual proportion and perceptibility. Hence this contemplation may be rightly regarded either as acquired or as infused, though in its lower degrees it is predominantly felt and described under the former aspect, in its higher degrees under the latter. In this wise, as meditation fails, its task accomplished, prayer, as its operation grows ever more unified and its object an ever more general, obscure and negative apprehension or intuition of God, passes gradually and imperceptibly, without the introduction of any new principle, through the night of sense into the prayer of quiet, from a state in which the acquiring work of the faculties occupies the consciousness of the soul to a state in which the soul is predominantly conscious of the activity of God.

When first the soul becomes conscious of a supernatural working, that working is felt as negative, as a force that constrains the faculties of the soul, so that they are more or less unable to produce a multiplicity of diverse acts of will, of sense images or of distinct concepts.   No positive working is yet felt in understanding or will but this negative constraint alone, which demands and supplements the active detachment of the soul from these multiple and distinct activities.   For this active detachment is required if the soul is to correspond to the passive detachment of which it is now conscious.   That is why this passive night of sense is partially conterminous with the active night of spirit and is discussed from that point of view in *The Ascent of Mount Carmel*.   The limited activities of the discursive reason and of volitions directed to particular ends have been so destroyed by grace-aided detachment of will and concentration of thought, that the working and, through the working, the presence of the divine Being, especially immanent in the soul, is manifested in consciousness as a powerful drawing of the soul away from the limited and therefore divided activities of multiple will acts and clear concepts, an abstraction that becomes at times a total inhibition of these acts and concepts. The soul is, however, still free to resist this negative working, which is, moreover, only manifested when the soul is in actual prayer.   There are, as I said above, three passages where St John describes this night of sense.   The first of these is contained in chaps. xii.-xvi. of the second book of *The Ascent*, where St John gives instructions for the active correspondence of the soul with the negative working of God.   The central discussion is the first book of *The Dark Night*, which is devoted to the Passive Night of Sense.   A large portion of this book, however, is occupied with a description of the spiritual evils of which this night is the sole cure, forms of selfishness which this night removes, limits from which this night alone can release the soul, so that it may go forth to the Unlimited Reality that is its God.   The third passage is to be found in the third stanza of *The Living Flame*, where the saint makes a long digression on the emptying of the faculties of distinct and therefore created objects, and takes occasion to rebuke directors who hinder the soul from following the Divine attraction to mystical prayer.   This night he calls the night of sense, because its primary effect is to free the spirit from bondage to its lower operations, which proceed from sense data and are conversant with particular objects at least ultimately sensible.   So long as the soul is held fast in these activities it cannot turn inwards to the central spiritual operations and powers in which God manifests Himself to it.   The destruction of these sense-caused limitations is thus called by St John the subjugation of sense to spirit, and its supernatural accomplishment the night of sense.

In *The Dark Night* St John prefaces his discussion of the night of sense by an account of the faults that are to be purged by it. These he reduces under seven heads, which he terms the seven spiritual capital vices (deadly sins, as they are popularly but inaccurately termed), which are analogous to, in fact extensions of, the seven capital vices as ordinarily understood.   In his treatment of these St John's genius for descriptive psychology finds full play. As an example of this I will quote certain traits from his portrait of spiritual pride.   " When beginners," he says—by beginners he means all who have not yet reached the night of sense—" become aware of their own fervour and diligence in their spiritual works and devotional exercises, this prosperity of theirs gives rise to secret pride . . . because of their imperfection ; and the issue is that they conceive a certain satisfaction in the contemplation of their works and of themselves.   From the same source, too, proceeds that somewhat vain, at times entirely vain, eagerness to speak before others of the spiritual life, and sometimes as teachers rather than learners.   They condemn others in their hearts when they see that they are not devout in their way.   Sometimes also they say it in words. . . . Some of them go so far that they will have none good but themselves, and so at all times, both in word and deed, fall into condemnation and detraction of others. . . . Sometimes, also, when their spiritual masters, such as confessors and superiors, do not approve of their spirit and conduct . . . they decide that they are not understood, and that their superiors are not spiritual men because they do not approve and sanction their proceedings.   So they go about in quest of someone else, who will accommodate himself to their pleasure, for in general they love to discuss their spiritual state with those who, they think, will commend and respect it.   They avoid, as they would death, those who destroy their delusion with the view of leading them into a safe way, and sometimes they even hate them.   Presuming greatly in themselves, they make many resolutions and accomplish little. They are occasionally desirous that others should perceive their spirituality and devotion, and for that end they give outward tokens by movements, sighs and divers ceremonies. . . . Many of them seek to be favourites of their confessors ; the result is endless envy and disquietude. They are ashamed to confess their sins plainly, lest their confessors should think less of them, so they go about palliating them, that they may not seem so bad. . . . Sometimes they go to a stranger to confess their sins, that their usual confessor may think they are not sinners, but good people. And so they always take pleasure in telling him of their goodness, and that in terms suggestive of more than is in them : at the least, they wish all their goodness to be appreciated " (*D.N.*, Bk. I. ii). The mystic is a realist, not only in his knowledge of God, but of man. Though he realises as none else the greatness of the human soul, no psychological novelist possesses clearer vision of its foibles and pettiness.

It may be urged that spiritual pride is a sin that concerns the depths of the soul rather than the relation of sense to spirit and is not, therefore, fit subject matter for the night of sense. But this pride, in the form described above, largely consists in petty conceits and vanities that are concerned rather with the soul's external life than its inmost substance. Moreover, the fact that the passive night of sense is ordained to purge the seven spiritual vices proves that its proper subject matter is not the most external, peripheral and carnal sins, which require no *mystical* purgation, since they must be purged as a precedent condition to any degree whatever of mystical prayer, but the sins which take their rise in the more external and sensible aspects of the spiritual life, and are therefore intermediate between the former sins and the central selfishness of the ego as a distinct individual which can only be purged by the more interior night of the spirit. The other spiritual vices are spiritual avarice, love of many and valuable *objets de piété*, spiritual luxury, impure motions of the flesh, resulting from sensible sweetness in devotion, anger, the nervous reaction after the excitement of spiritual sweetness has passed, which is sinful in so far as it is yielded to by the will, and also an unquiet and impatient zeal against one's own faults, or those of others, spiritual gluttony, the desire for sensible sweetness in devotion for its own sake, envy— that is, jealousy—of the spiritual progress of others, and spiritual sloth, which shirks and omits spiritual exercises when they cease to afford sensible consolation.

With the eighth chapter of the first book of *The Dark Night*
St John comes to the night of sense itself. He first notes that this
night is of common occurrence and has therefore been described
in many spiritual treatises. This statement is the disproof of
Père Poulain's contention that St John was the first to discuss the
night of sense.[1]

The first and most striking characteristic of the night of sense
is the withdrawal of all sensible sweetness in devotion, which is
replaced by aridity. This aridity extends to a positive incapacity
for meditation. " God leaves them in darkness so great that they
know not whither to betake themselves with their sensible im-
aginations and reflections. They cannot advance a single step in
meditation as before, the inward sense now being overwhelmed in
this night and abandoned to dryness so great that they have no
more pleasure or sweetness in spiritual things and exercises as
they had before, and in their place they find nothing but insipidity
and bitterness " (chap. viii). Such aridity and incapacity, however, may also be caused by ill health or lukewarmness. St John
therefore gives certain criteria by which the presence of this
purgative aridity may be detected. " The first is this : when we
find no pleasure or comfort in the things of God, and *none also in
created things.*" The second test and condition necessary for
belief that we are in this purgation is that " the memory dwells
ordinarily upon God with a painful anxiety and carefulness, the
soul thinks it is not serving God, but going backwards, because it is
no longer conscious of any sweetness in the things of God. In this
aridity, though the sensual part of man be grea ly depressed, weak
and sluggish in good works, by reason of the little satisfaction
they furnish, the spirit is, nevertheless, ready and strong." This
test excludes not only lukewarmness, but "mere ill health, for the
latter has no tendency in itself to cause this seeking of the will
after God." St John says *mere* ill health, because God may often
use ill health as a means to this purgation. " The third sign . . .
is inability to meditate and make reflections and to excite the
imagination as before, notwithstanding all the efforts we may
make ; for God begins now to communicate Himself, no longer
through the channel of sense . . . in consecutive reflections . . .
but in pure spirit, which admits not of successive reflections, and

---

[1] If a good modern treatment of this night be desired, it will be found in Dom
Lehodey's excellent *Voies d'Oraison Mentale*. A translation is published by
Gill, Dublin, *The Ways of Mental Prayer* (1917).

in the act of pure contemplation, to which neither the interior nor the exterior senses of our lower nature can ascend." St John enters deeper into the cause of the above-mentioned aridity. "The cause of this dryness is that God is transforming into spirit the goods and energies of the senses, and since the natural senses and operation are incapable of spiritual things, they are left dry, parched up and empty ; for the sensual nature of man is helpless in those things which are purely spiritual. Thus, since the spirit has been tasted, the flesh becomes weak and remiss ; but the spirit, having received its proper nourishment, becomes strong, more vigilant and careful than before, lest there should be any negligence in serving God. At first it is not conscious of any spiritual sweetness and delight, but rather of aridities and distaste because of the novelty of the change. . . . Because the spiritual palate is not prepared and purified for so delicious a taste until it shall have been gradually disposed for it in this arid and dark night, it cannot taste of the spiritual good and pleasure, but rather of aridity and distaste, because it misses that pleasure which it enjoyed so easily before. . . . The spirit, though at first without any sweetness . . . is conscious of strength and energy to act because of the substantial nature of its interior food, which is *the commencement of contemplation* dim and dry to the senses. This contemplation is secret and unknown to him who is admitted into it, and with the aridity and emptiness which it produces in the senses it usually makes the soul long for solitude and quiet, without the power of reflecting on anything distinctly or even desiring to do so. . . . This contemplation is so delicate that, in general, it eludes our perception if we have any special desire or anxiety to feel it, for . . . it does its work when the soul is most tranquil and free from care ; it is like the air which vanishes when we close our hands to grasp it " (chap. ix).

The meaning of this difficult passage seems to be this : God now begins to infuse into the understanding or spiritual consciousness a veiled intuition of Himself, as the transcendent Being present in the soul.[1] This intuition is at first so faint that it is not directly perceptible. It draws, however, the activity of the soul

---

[1] In the earlier stages of mystical experience the intuition is so dim as to lend support to those who maintain that it is rather a negative idea of God supernaturally impressed, than an intuition of His present Being. This explanation is certainly inadequate to the higher stages. It is surely an error to postulate without necessity any break of continuity in the development of mystical experience.

from the peripheral energies, conversant with sensible data, to the central and more spiritual functions, which by reason of their greater spirituality, and therefore reality, are in closer relation to God, and the immediate subject of sanctifying grace, and to and in which through that grace He is especially present in His special operation which is Himself. The result of this introversion is that the soul, particularly when most exposed to the Divine action —namely, in prayer—finds its peripheral activities, such as the formation of images and distinct concepts, impeded if not wholly inhibited. It is left with one simple and interior energising through the will towards the Divine intuition which attracts it. Since, however, that intuition is still so weak as to be entirely or almost entirely imperceptible, the soul finds little or no satisfaction in it and misses its former meditations and sensible sweetness. Meanwhile its release is being effected from the limited external activities which hitherto were barriers against God, and against the more spiritual central activities in and through which it is being brought into closer and more immediate relationship with God. The spiritual faults also which are rooted in these limited activities are being purged away through the destruction of their ground. It is, however, possible for the soul to resist this Divine working by a vain struggle to continue meditation. Indeed many directors ignorant of mystical theology forced their penitents to do this. Against such is directed St John's impassioned diatribe in *The Living Flame*. His indignation is the greater because he regards any hindrance occasioned to the mystical union of a soul called to that union by God " as a greater hurt, grief and stain than the troubling or *even the loss* of many souls of the common type." " It is as though a portrait of most excellent and delicate painting were daubed by a coarse hand with ugly and coarse colours. The damage thus inflicted would be greater and more notable and more lamentable than would be the entire obliteration of many portraits of indifferent execution." This spiritual aristocracy parallels the intellectual and moral aristocracy preached with such ardour and convincing logic by Ibsen in *The Enemy of the People*, and is the counterpart and fulfilment of Nietzsche's natural aristocracy of supermen. It is, however, in full accord with the universal order of nature, according to which innumerable hosts of inferior species subserve a few, indeed, ultimately, one supreme species, and of human society where a very small minority of gifted souls stand out above the vast

R

multitude of the commonplace and the average. It is also in accord with the theological principle that it was the peculiar elevation of Our Lord's sacred Humanity that lent infinite value to His most trifling action, and with the well-grounded opinion that Our Lord was incarnate and died, more for the sake of His immaculate Mother than of all the rest of humanity together. This spiritual aristocracy in St John intensifies his wrath against directors who seek to detain these choice souls within the narrow limits of discursive meditation, and makes him all the more eager with instructions to souls in this night of sense to follow instead of impeding the Divine attraction. He is urgent with these souls to cease vain attempts to meditate. To attempt meditation is a useless weariness in which the soul can find no satisfaction. All the good that can be obtained from such meditation—that is, all the knowledge and love of God to be extracted from this exercise— has been already obtained. Otherwise this night would not have come on. All the positive being—that is, all the participation of God—contained in its reasonings and images has been assimilated by the soul, and now only their essential limitations, the external husks, remain, spiritually indigestible, because simply negative of fuller reality. Henceforward these images and concepts can but hold the soul back in its prayer by their limits, when it is being drawn inwards to a more unlimited participation of ultimate reality by a closer and more immediate union with God. To redigest food already digested, to retrace a journey when the goal has been reached, are images of the folly of the attempt to return to discursive meditation when the time for it has passed by. Those who act thus, says St John, are " like a man who does his work over again, or who goes out of a city that he may enter it once more, or who lets go what he has caught in hunting that he may hunt it again. Their labour is in vain : for they will find nothing " (*O.N.*, i. 10).

Such souls, therefore, must replace meditation by a courageous and patient self-abandonment to the Divine operation. They must cease to attempt in prayer the active use of their faculties and must passively receive the contemplation which God is infusing. " Let these souls," says St John, " be quiet and at rest. . . They will do enough if they keep patience and persevere in prayer doing nothing therein ; all they have to do is to keep their soul free, unembarrassed and at rest from all thoughts and all knowledge . . . contenting themselves simply with a loving and calm

attention to God " (*O.N.*, i. 10). It is true that this attentive
receptivity itself involves a fuller and intenser action. That
action, however, is no longer a conscious effort of reasoning and
imagination, but a unified, simple and therefore imperceptible
attention to God and reception of His Action. If the soul perse-
veres in this attitude of patient receptivity, the intuition of the
Divine Presence emerges by degrees more clearly into consciousness. " If they," says St John, " who are in this state knew how
to be quiet, to disregard every interior and exterior work without
solicitude to do anything, they would have in this tranquillity and
freedom from care a most delicious sense of this interior refection "
—*i.e.* the obscure intuition of the transcendent Being of God
present in the soul. This intuition is apparently at first felt
simply as an interior peace or tranquillity. To strive to fix the
thought on any distinct concept or image disturbs this delicate
peace. For it is, as we saw, to exclude the fulness of the pure and
spiritual Divine communication, by the limits of distinct notions
and sensible images, or rather of vain attempts to achieve them
and to destroy its unity by the distraction of these mutually
exclusive particular objects. The nature of this infused contemplation is further explained in *The Living Flame*. " In the contemplation of which we are speaking, by means of which God is
infusing Himself into the soul, there is no need of any distinct concept nor for acts of understanding made by the soul. In one
simple act God is communicating light and love together to the
soul—namely, a supernatural, loving knowledge, which we may
call a warming light, for this light gives out the heat of love. This
knowledge is confused and obscure to the understanding because
it is a contemplation, and contemplation is (as St Dionysius tells
us) a ray of darkness to the understanding. The result is that the
love in the will corresponds in its manner to the knowledge in
the understanding. For as the knowledge infused by God into the
understanding is general and obscure without any distinct knowledge, so also does the will love generally without distinction of
any particular object apprehended." " At times in this subtle
communication God communicates Himself to one faculty more
than to another, striking that faculty with greater force, for at
times more knowledge is felt than love, and at other times more
love than knowledge ; at times it is all knowledge and no love,
at others all love and no knowledge " (*Living Flame*, iii. 10). We
should gather, however, from the concluding chapter of *The*

Obscure Knowledge that the union of the will, rather than the union of the understanding, is primary in the earlier stages of mystical prayer. To obtain without personal experience an idea of the nature of this mystical intuition is impossible. As soon might a blind man obtain an idea of colour. It is a peaceful and loving intuition or sense of a Presence within the soul, the Presence of a Being that is not created being of any kind, the transcendent and Absolute Godhead. It is the intuition of the veiled presence of a Reality altogether unlike, wholly transcendent of the world of creatures, a Reality by comparison with which that world is felt to be unsubstantial and unreal. But, after all, to say this is but to give an indication of an experience essentially incommunicable.

All this while we have gradually passed out of the night of sense and have emerged into the dim dawn of positive mystical experience. We are now discussing a state of conscious union with God, a union whose immediate term is no longer a creature, but the Godhead. In this union God is present to the soul as a lover to the beloved in a room that is completely dark. His presence is felt, but He is altogether invisible. As the mystical union progresses the Divine presence draws closer and closer, but the darkness is not dispelled. It is as though the lover, first felt as present at a distance, had drawn near and had enfolded the beloved in a close embrace. But his face is hidden to the end.

The world experienced in mystical prayer is a new and a strange universe. Souls who have entered it, even in the very transitory and very feeble contacts of the earliest stages of mystical prayer, are like beings who have come up to the surface of the sea from the submarine depths. Down in those depths is a faint greenish light, through which loom the weird, indistinct shapes of uncouth fish or of those more grotesque sea-monsters that appal us in aquaria with their fearsome ugliness. Bunches of matted and formless seaweed cling to the chilly rocks. When first the daring inhabitant of the sea-floor emerges from the water it enters a new world. The sun burns overhead and fills the air with heat and radiance. Above the sapphire expanse of sea flashing and shimmering with gold and jewels of sunlight there stretches a vast canopy of softer, clearer blue, that is bounded only by the wide circle of a horizon girdled by snow-white masses of cloud, as by a chain of distant Alps. But the new-comer, dazzled and bewildered, has to replunge speedily into the congenial gloom of its native home. It cannot see clearly the magnificent scene before it, for its organs are adapted to submarine life. It has therefore but a general confused and obscure consciousness of light and air. Not unless its organs were transformed and its abode in the upper world made permanent could that submarine being distinctly perceive and fitly handle its new environment. Man's soul, however, is in its central being made for the upper world of eternity, where God is the sun, and where the horizon is never reached. Into this eternity the soul now begins to enter. As the mystical union progresses, the soul's visits to the sphere of its eternal life become more frequent and more prolonged, until finally the centre abides habitually in this Divine world of Reality and truth. But not until its faculties have been wholly adapted to its environment, which cannot be till their bodily energising has been destroyed by death, will the soul be able to dwell with its whole self and without intermission in the eternal life, which is union with God, nor until that day will it see clearly a Reality which in this mortal life can but be felt as a dazzling light destroying by its impenetrable brilliance all distinct vision. Or to vary the image, the divine Sun in respect for the feebleness of mortal sight is hidden behind the soul's negative knowledge of its unintelligible transcendence. From behind this darkness rays of Divine truth and love are shed on the soul, even as we see at times the surface of the sea ruddy with light that issues from behind a black cloud.

St Teresa in her description of the prayer of quiet (*Autobiography*, chap. xiv.) makes it consist primarily in the love-union of the will. " The will alone is occupied in such a way that without knowing how it has become a captive. It gives a simple consent to become the prisoner of God." " The memory and the understanding come and go seeking whether the will is going to give them that into the fruition of which it has entered itself." Nevertheless we read a few lines farther down that " the understanding is now working very gently and is drawing more water than it drew out of the well," and she adds that " some little knowledge of the blissfulness of glory is communicated " to the soul. She further explains this knowledge to be a consciousness of the Presence of God in the soul. " This satisfaction," she says, " lies in the innermost part of the soul, and the soul knows not whence nor how it came ; very often it knows not what to do, or wish, or pray for." It is evident that St Teresa is speaking of approximately the same state of prayer as that into which St John has led us through the night of sense.   The next stage discussed by St Teresa, the prayer of union or full union, is but a completion and accentuation of this prayer of quiet in which the entire soul is dominated and constrained by the mystical union.

It will be well to call here to mind what was said earlier of the inmost ground of the soul (see Chapter V).

This is the central substance or ego into which plunge or from which proceed two channels, the cognitive faculty, or the understanding, as I should prefer to say, the spiritual consciousness and the conative faculty that is the will.   These functions are, however, in reality but aspects of the central ego.   Since the latter reaches deeper than the former, the central substance is, we saw, often termed the apex of the will.   In these earlier stages of mystical prayer the limiting barriers of the natural activities of the soul have so far been broken down that the divine Being present in the soul both by omnipresence and in virtue of the soul's special relationship through sanctifying grace—a relationship now far more intimate—is manifested from time to time in the depths of the soul.   The Divine manifestation takes as it were a transient possession of the centre, and thence as the possession grows stronger this Divine manifestation pours out through the two channels of will and understanding or spiritual consciousness. Nevertheless in all these earlier stages previous to the night of spirit the manifestation is only transient and the Divine possession of the soul is so to speak an external grasp.   The central barrier remains intact—namely, the independent selfhood or self-centredness which imprisons the soul life in its essentially limited selfness—now indeed almost wholly subordinated to God the All, but not yet destroyed, that He may be all in all.   The activities of the soul are still fundamentally rooted in self, not in God. That is why the Divine action can be as yet but transient in its manifestation and *in a certain sense* external.   These manifestations of God in the soul become indeed ever more powerful. When the state known as ecstasy is reached the will is seized by the fire of God's love, and through this violent inflammation of the will the soul is so possessed by God that it can no longer duly perform its peripheral functions through the bodily senses.   These fail during the ecstasy, and thus arises that state of bodily trance which is the subject of such admiration to the crowd, until indeed it is realised that this outward phenomenon can be produced by other and more material causes.   Of all this St John says very little. He is too intent on the goal of the mystical way to linger over these intermediate stages. It is, however, to this stage of ecstasy that we should especially apply certain passages in which St John speaks of Divine *touches*. Sometimes indeed these touches are acts of that supreme habitual union called mystical marriage. There are, however, others which belong to earlier stages. These Divine touches are primarily in the will—where the will touches God as the present Object of an infused love, in which His Presence is apprehended. If the intuition of the understanding at an earlier stage is fitly represented by the sense of the lover's presence in a dark room, this touch is like a grasp in the darkness of his garment or hand. Mother Cecilia speaks of these touches in the opening pages of her treatise on *The Union of the Soul with God*. " The soul now feels in itself the loving, Divine touch." I think, moreover, that we should also refer to ecstasy St John's description in the second stanza of *The Living Flame* of the wound of love, in which the soul seems pierced by a fiery dart, and of which St Teresa's external wounding by the Seraph was a physical manifestation. This, however, is rather a concomitant phenomenon than an essential constituent of ecstasy. An ecstasy—does not the very name call up the thought of a union with God of unthinkable elevation and intimacy?[1] Yet it is not the highest union possible on earth, though doubtless the highest reached by the majority of mystics. A more fundamental transformation has still to be effected, a far closer union contracted. As a night of passive purgation was the entrance to these lower degrees, these transitory and more external states of union-intuition, so also another and a far more terrible purgation is the entrance to the supreme union permanent and most intimate. Only the soul that is wholly dead to self, to the natural life centring round self and conditioned by the limited activities proper to a creature, can obtain the fulness of life unlimited, which is a participation of the life of God Himself, the life in which " I live no more but Christ liveth in me." We have reached thus the night of spirit.

[1] Its literal meaning is a being (standing) out of oneself.

CHAPTER X

THE PASSIVE NIGHT OF SPIRIT

Cum Christo confixus sum cruci.
Anima crucifixa, mortua, et sepulta.

THE ordinary Christian no doubt imagines that the sole evil from which the soul must be purged before it is fit to enter heaven is that evil because God-resisting and therefore deordinate will which constitutes sin. For him the destruction of self means merely the eradication of selfishness in the popular sense of the term. For the Buddhist and the pantheist, on the other hand, the destruction of self means the annihilation of the individual, or rather of the connected sequence of psychoses constitutive of the soul or ego.[1] The pantheist may indeed say that the ego will be absorbed in the All or the Absolute—but by this he means that its individual separate being will cease and in some unintelligible way its content will pass into the Absolute, because the individual self was always illusory, a transient mode of one underlying reality. It seems to me that the true conception of the destruction of the self lies between these two extremes, here as always a *via media*. That which is destroyed is more than such volition as is actually sinful, and less than the substance of the soul, the individual ego. It is rather the natural life of the soul that is destroyed, its present mode of action, the activity that proceeds from the self as independent of God, and which is therefore limited by the limitations inherent in all created activity. To describe in full the transformation of the soul into God, such as I understand it from the writings of mystics, would be to anticipate my account of the goal of the mystic way. This much, however, I must try to make clear. The self as an independent centre and source [2] of psychical

---

[1] For the Buddhist there is, strictly speaking, no self, but either a chain of interlinked phenomena, or mere illusion veiling either nothingness or undifferentiated thought without subject or object (see Vallee Pousin, *Le Buddhisme*, passim).

[2] Of course this independence was never more than relative.

life must be destroyed, and must be replaced by a self that is a receptacle of the Divine life and activity. One and the same individual soul substance endures throughout the process, for this created substance, as such infinitely distant from the uncreated Being that is Absolute or Pure Being, could never become part of that Being, and if it were annihilated there would be no subject of the Divine Presence and Operation. Nor, again, is the activity of the created soul destroyed, for this activity is inseparable from the being which is its ground. It is, however, destroyed, as independent of the Divine action, and is changed into a reception of the Divine action. The limitations essentially concomitant on the natural activity of a creature are destroyed by a participation in the infinite activity of God, which participation is, however, received through the created activity of the soul. It may be objected that sin is the only barrier between the soul and God. This objection has already been anticipated and answered. I will, however, briefly summarise here the reply already given. The statement that sin is the sole obstacle to union with God is only true if sin be understood as including all its consequences, and among these the consequences of original sin. For the result of original sin has been the confinement of the soul within the limits of its natural capacity and the natural activities conditioned by that capacity. These natural activities are indeed neither sinful nor even imperfect within the purely natural order.[1] They are, however, essentially limited, since they proceed from the natural selfhood of the creature and are conditioned by creaturely limitations. They are therefore obstacles to the supernatural union of the soul with the infinite Being of God, and are thus deordinations and imperfections in souls raised to that union by sanctifying grace. For their essential limitation bars the soul from that excess of all limits in free union with God which it is the work of grace to effect. They are therefore termed by the mystics stains, maculæ, that befoul the supernatural purity of the soul, which is perfect receptivity of the Divine action within itself, and perfect union with God through that perfect receptivity. These stains must therefore be purged away before that purity can be achieved. But this natural life and these natural activities are, as we saw, grounded in a natural selfhood essentially limited and therefore exclusive of the supernatural union with God, and

---

[1] Nevertheless these activities if left alone without any help of Divine grace *inevitably* lead to imperfection and to sin even in the natural order.

the supernatural participation and reception of His divine life and activity. Therefore that selfhood must be destroyed in order to attain the fulness of the supernatural union.[1]   This selfhood, which is our natural life as opposed to, and as resisting, the infused supernatural life, is in Pauline phraseology termed the animal or psychic man as opposed to the spiritual or pneumatic man. This terminology emphasises the fact that the natural selfhood is a bondage within the limitations which arise from the sense data that are the ultimate conditions of our natural psychical activity, limitations which resist and exclude the unlimited Divine activity infused by God into our souls through supernatural grace. For St Paul the Psyche means the soul as the informing principle of the body and as dependent upon the body. This term psyche, however, is all but absent from the Epistles. St Paul prefers to term the lower life of the natural man, the life that proceeds from his sense-conditioned soul, " Sarx "—that is, " flesh." This term emphasises the essential dependence of man's purely natural life upon the data of the bodily senses. By the Pneuma, on the other hand, St Paul means the soul when and in so far as it is emancipated from bondage to the natural limitations due to sense, the limitations which condition and constitute the merely natural life of the " flesh," by its supernatural elevation and motion by the indwelling Spirit of God, which elevation and indwelling is a supernatural union with the unlimited Being of God whose divine operations it now freely receives. Often, however, the term Pneuma denotes for St Paul the Divine Spirit, as indwelling, informing and impelling the human soul, and by this inhabitation and impulsion effecting its release from the lower self-proceeding and sense-conditioned life to the freedom of full participation of the life of God. Both meanings coalesce in the notion of a new *divine* life of the soul received supernaturally from the indwelling Spirit, a life in strong contrast and opposition to the old natural life which was purely human and creaturely alike in its principle and its end.[2]   It is this contrast between the two lives that St John has in mind when

---

[1] *The Cloud of Unknowing* identifies sin with the natural selfhood. " Thou shalt always feel sin . . . a lump thou wottest never what betwixt Thee and Thy God : *the which lump is none other than thyself.* For thou shalt think it oned and congealed with the substance of thy being, yea, as it were, without departing ' (separation) (chap. xliii).

[2] For a full account of this Pauline doctrine and terminology, see Père Prat *Théologie de St Paul*, vol. ii., Book II., chap. i.

he designates the "habits and properties of man" as opposed to "the virtue and properties of God" as "in the highest degree imperfect" (*Living Flame*, st. 1) and the subject matter of the mystical purgation. " Perfect spiritual life," he tells us, "which is the possession of God by union of love, is obtained by the mortification of all vices and desires and of the soul's *entire nature.* . . . We must bear in mind that what the soul here terms death is the entire old man—namely, the use, occupation and filling of the powers, memory, understanding and will with the things of this world, and, moreover, creaturely desires and tastes. All this is the exercise of the old life, which is the death of the new life, which is spiritual, wherein the soul cannot live perfectly until the old man is wholly dead. . . . In this new life which is the attainment of perfect union with God . . . all the desires of the soul and its powers in their affections and operations (that in their own nature were the death and privation of that spiritual life) are changed into divine. Moreover, seeing that each living thing, according to the philosophers, lives by its activity, the soul, since it now possesses its activities in God on account of its union with Him, lives the life of God, and thus it has changed its death into life—that is, its animal life into a spiritual life. . . . Thus is the soul dead to all that was its own, which was its death, and alive to all within itself that is God" (*Living Flame*, st. 2). If possible, Mother Cecilia is even more explicit than St John. " Resolved into nothing," she writes, " *and with her selfhood consumed* " the soul " is changed and converted into the Being of God . . . by grace and love and by a certain Divine participation" (*Transformation*, st. 2. *Cf.* st. 16).

This destruction of the natural extra-godly activity or life of the soul, of the self as independent of God,[1] and exclusive of the full Divine union, is substantially effected through the passive night of spirit. I say substantially, because a certain limiting activity that is not the reception of God's activity, that is not actual union with Him, must remain so long as the sensible functions of the soul continue, informing and operating a body that is not, as will be the glorified body of the Resurrection, the perfectly docile instrument and adequate expression of the soul. Nevertheless the radical change is effected in and by this night of spirit. In this night, St John tells us, " I went forth *out of my scanty*

---

[1] Of course the independence is itself God's gift and cannot be independence in the strictest sense.

human operation and conduct to a divine operation and conduct"
(*i.e.* a reception of God's unlimited operation)—"that is my
understanding went forth out of itself, and from human and
natural became divine ; for united to God in that purgation, it
understands no more by its natural force, but by the Divine
Wisdom to which it is united.   My will went forth out of itself,
becoming divine, for now, united with the divine love, it loves
no more meanly with its natural strength, but with the energy
and pureness of the Divine Spirit.   Thus the will acts now in the
things of God, not in a human way, and the memory is equally
transformed in eternal apprehensions of glory.   In fine, all the
energies and affections of the soul are by means of this night and
purgation of the old man renewed into a Divine temper and
delight " (*O.N.*, ii. 4).   All the central psychical activities are to
become receptacles of the Divine activity, for thus are we made
"partakers of the Divine Nature."   But this cannot be till the
radical selfness that is the principle of our selfish independent
activities is destroyed, and the inmost ego becomes a term or
receptacle of the Divine action instead of a principle of natural
extra-divine action.   This effected, the psychical faculties and
activities become channels and recipients of that Divine action, as
St John here describes them.   This is the work of the second night.

We have seen how hitherto the Divine Action has been progressively destroying the more external and therefore the more
limited and limiting activities of the natural man, the old Adam.
Undue occupation with the peripheral functions, desires for
worldly goods as ends in themselves, bondage to the limited
images and concepts drawn from creatures, all these have gradually
passed away.· God has already manifested Himself in the depths
of the soul as a force of love in the will and an obscure intuition
in the understanding, and these manifestations have become more
frequent and more powerful.   Now at length the time has come
when the natural activities of the soul, its desires and its thoughts,
that were not from and for God, but the expression of its self-will
as independent of Him, fail and become impossible.   The force
of the Divine action in the soul has so weakened the natural selfhood which is the principle of these purely natural and human
activities that this selfhood is more or less impotent to produce
them.

"God," says St John, "now denudes the faculties, the affections and the senses spiritual and sensible, interior and exterior

leaving the understanding in darkness, the will dry, the memory empty, the affections of the soul in the deepest affliction, bitterness and distress " (O.N., ii. 3).   " The Divine ray of contemplation, transcending as it does the natural powers, striking the soul with its divine light, makes it dark, and deprives it of all the natural affections and apprehensions which it previously entertained in its own natural light.   Under these circumstances the soul is left not only in darkness, but in emptiness also, as to its powers and desires, both *natural* and spiritual " (O.N., ii. 8).   " As God is now purifying the soul in its sensual and spiritual substance, its interior and exterior powers, it is necessary for it that it should be in all its relations empty, poor and abandoned, in aridity, emptiness and darkness " (O.N., ii. 6).   The soul " cannot pray or give much attention to divine things.   Neither can it attend to temporal matters, for it falls into frequent distractions, and the memory is so profoundly weakened that many hours pass by without its knowing what it has done or thought, what it is doing or is about to do " (O.N., ii. 8).   God has so intimately united Himself with the centre of the soul, and his action there is so potent, as to suppress the natural activities which proceed from a self that is not entirely united with Him, wholly receptive of Him.   " The soul is made to suffer from the failure and withdrawal of its natural supports and apprehensions which is a most distressing pain. It is like that of a person being hung or suffocated and thus hindered from breathing " (O.N., ii. 6).   " The soul can do so little in this state ; like a prisoner in a gloomy dungeon, bound hand and foot, it cannot stir, neither can it see or feel any relief " (O.N., ii. 7).

The agony of solitary confinement in a narrow oubliette, where there is no room to lie down or stand upright, is but a faint image of this spiritual bondage and suffocation.

The alienation of the soul from the things of earth in this ligature of its functions is at times so great that the soul " looks upon itself as if under the influence of some charm or spell, and is amazed at all that it hears and sees, which seem to it to be most strange and out of the way " (O.N., ii. 9).   " For this night," he tells us, " is drawing the spirit away from its ordinary and common sense of things, that it may draw it towards the divine sense, which is a stranger and alien to all human ways " (O.N., ii. 9, *loc. cit.*).   In this passage St John is introducing a further conception to explain the ligature, or rather a new standpoint from which to view it—namely, the introduction of the soul into a new environment, the world of Divine Reality. Since, however, it is naturally adapted to the lower world of creaturely activities and objects, it is at first altogether unable to correspond with the new environment, to receive freely the new Divine life. Hence the impotence of ligature. It is as when one who has grown up in the narrowly limited surroundings of a sheltered home in a quiet country village is suddenly brought into the vast world of a populous city, as when some new realm of knowledge opens out before the intellect of an individual or of a society, or as when the dormant heart of a youth or maiden is awakened by the compulsive touch of first love to a new life enormously wider and fuller than the old. In all these cases there must be at first a sense of impotence, ignorance and confusion. Former landmarks are obliterated, former habits of thought and feeling, former ways of action are destroyed. The soul cannot orientate itself in the new world into which it has been thrown. This passing confusion, this temporary impotence, are, however, no true loss or retrogression. They are simply the inevitable concomitants of the sudden acquisition of new spiritual wealth, of the new step forward. In like manner the ligature of this night of spirit is no true loss and destruction of the good hitherto possessed by the soul, but the necessary failure of the narrowly limited life of nature at the entrance into the soul of the infinite fulness of the supernatural life of God. When that entrance has been completely effected the loss of the lower life will be felt no more, for its entire value will be found again in the new life Divine.

For the present, however, this infusion of the Divine life is not complete, the Divine work has not yet been fully achieved.

The barrier of the egoistic anti-supernatural principle remains as yet undestroyed. Powerless to produce any longer the natural activity that springs from it, this principle of separate selfness is still able to exclude the complete surrender of the entire soul to God, and therefore its full union with Him. It has been shewn that the creature apart from its representation of the Divine Being is mere negation, or limitation. Here there is fully manifest this creaturely limitation of the self, the creatureliness of the self standing apart from and resisting and excluding the unlimited Reality that is being given to the soul. The soul is conscious of its central ego, normally subliminal, as impervious to the Divine action, and as excluding by its essential limitation the reception and fruition of God. Had there been no sin or imperfection, this creaturely limitation would have been from the first overcome and transcended by an absolute obedience to the motions of the indwelling Spirit, a complete receptivity of the unlimited Action and Being of God in and through the soul. The result of sin, however, has been to render this created selfness opposed to the Divine action, and exclusive of it, a nature that resists and combats grace. As such it is now felt as a barrier between the soul and the Being of God, a limit which the soul cannot as yet overpass to enter into the Unlimited. Nevertheless it is, as we saw above, already too far destroyed by the Divine action to be able to act as the free principle of a natural soul life, the life of the old Adam. So the soul finds itself deprived by the barrier of independent selfness of the desired fruition of the Divine life of God, and deprived by the Divine action of the natural life which it has hitherto enjoyed. The soul is conscious simply of the barrier between itself and God, a barrier that appears for ever insurmountable, as indeed, so far as the soul's natural capacity is concerned, it is.[1]

It may indeed be asked why the Divine union was felt before when the soul was less pure than it now is. The answer is surely contained in what was said above. The inferior and more external action and manifestation of God was felt and enjoyed while the radical selfhood remained entire, because that inferior and more external action and manifestation was compatible with the existence of this fundamental barrier and limit. Now that the Divine action is higher and more interior, the radical selfhood is an obstacle to it, and until it is destroyed it prevents the soul's fruition of the Divine union and operation. Nor would the soul be any longer satisfied with those inferior degrees of Divine union. It needs now a more unlimited participation in the Divine life which it cannot possess as long as it is confined by the fundamental limits of its natural selfhood. Those limits have therefore become to it a prison of darkness and pain. "The darkness now endured by the soul is so profound, so terrible and

---

[1] *The Cloud of Unknowing* speaks of this spiritual suffering and purgation constituted by a consciousness of the selfhood between the soul and God. "All men have matter of sorrow, but most especially he feeleth matter of sorrow that wotteth and feeleth that he is. All other sorrows be in comparison but game to earnest. . . . For he findeth evermore his wotting and his feeling, as it were occupied and filled with a foul, stinking lump of himself. This sorrow cleanseth the soul, not only of sin, but also of pain that it hath deserved for sin" (chap. xliv).

so very painful, because it is felt in the depths of the soul's substance, and therefore appears a substantial darkness " (*O.N.*, ii. 9).

Apart from God the creature is nothing, because created being is so essentially limited as to be *by comparison with God* nonentity. Now the soul feels this negation of the infinite Divine life as constituting its very self. In reality it is only by this supernatural consciousness of the nothingness of its natural and independent selfhood, realised thus by means of the mystic union to which that selfhood is the final and the supreme obstacle, that this extra-godly limiting selfhood can be destroyed. But the soul at the time cannot perceive this. Nor can it perceive that the stifling of the natural activities, and the sense of its independent selfhood, as excluding the Divine life and preventing the Divine union, are themselves the effect of a more intimate and more potent union or working of God which is no longer content with those more external and transitory manifestations that left in being the fundamental principle of the natural, selfish, extra-godly and therefore essentially limited life. The soul is also conscious as never before of the actual sins in which that life has issued, their utter opposition to God and to the Divine life which He communicates.

" When the rays of this pure light strike upon the soul in order to expel its impurities " (everything that opposes or excludes the Divine action in the soul is an impurity), " the soul perceives itself to be so unclean and miserable that it seems as if God had set Himself against it and itself were set against God (*O.N.*, ii. 5). " Now the dim and divine light reveals to it all its wretchedness, and it sees clearly that of itself it can never be other than it is " (*O.N.*, ii. 5). " While the divine purgation is removing all the evil and vicious humours "—the self-seeking and self-impelled activities—" which, because so deeply rooted and settled in the soul, were neither seen nor felt, but now in order to their expulsion and annihilation are rendered clearly visible in the dim light of the divine contemplation, the soul—though not worse in itself, nor in the sight of God—seeing at last what it never saw before, looks upon itself not only as unworthy of His regard, but even as a loathsome object and that God does loathe it " (*O.N.*, ii. 10). " Indeed the soul at the sight and consciousness of its own misery, imagines itself to be lost and all its good to have perished for ever " (*O.N.*, ii. 9). This apparent abandonment of the soul by God is according to St John " the greatest affliction of the sorrowful soul in this state." This abandonment appears to the soul certain, so certain, that anything the confessor may tell it to the contrary is ascribed to his misunderstanding of its state (*O.N.*, ii. 7). It even appears final, a foretaste of eternal damnation. The soul now feels an appalling loneliness, alone with a self that excludes God. St Teresa in her less scientific and less complete account of this state in the twentieth chapter of her *Autobiography* insists on this awful loneliness. "God," she says, "then so strips the soul of everything that, do what it may, there is nothing on earth that can be its companion. . . . No consolation reaches it from heaven, and it is not there itself ; it wishes for none from earth, and it is not there either ; but it is, as it were, crucified between heaven and earth, enduring its passion."

St John also speaks of this agonising darkness as a warfare of two contraries, the impurity of the soul, this natural God-excluding selfness, and its limited activity, with the sinfulness that has been its result, and the divine contemplation—that is, the Divine action in the soul now so greatly increased and so deeply penetrative. This "suffering and pain . . . comes from the meeting of two extremes, the human and the divine : the latter is the purgative contemplation " (the divine action in the soul), "the human is the soul itself " (the soul as the principle of extra-godly activity self-principled and selfish). "The divine strikes upon the soul to renew it and to ripen it, *in order to make it divine,* to detach it from the habitual affections and qualities of the old man to which it is closely united, cemented and con-formed. The divine extreme so *breaks up and undoes the spiritual substance* " (the soul as excluding the divine action, and existing apart from God in its own limited creaturely mode of being and acting), "swallowing it up in a profound and deep darkness, that the soul at the prospect and sight of its own wretchedness seems to perish and waste away, by a cruel spiritual death, as if it were swallowed up and devoured by a wild beast. . . . For it must be buried in this grave of a gloomy death that it may attain to the spiritual resurrection for which it hopes " (*O.N.*, ii. 6). Else-where he writes : " The virtues and properties of God being in the highest degree perfect, arise and make war within the soul on the habits and properties of man which are in the highest degree imperfect " (*Liv. Fl.*, st. 1). In this encounter the weakness of the soul suffers terribly. "The pain of the soul comes from its natural weakness moral and spiritual; for when this divine

S

contemplation strikes it with a certain vehemence, in order to strengthen it and subdue it, it is then so pained in its weakness as almost to faint away. . . . Sense and spirit, as if under a very heavy and gloomy burden, suffer and groan, in agony so great that they would welcome death itself as a relief and a benefit " (*O.N.*, ii. 5).

We may summarise these sufferings of the night of spirit as four negative effects of the Divine action :

(1) The failure of the natural activities proceeding from the natural selfhood now being destroyed by the Divine action.

(2) The sense of the absence of God excluded by the limitation of the natural selfhood as yet unconsumed.

(3) The consciousness of the vileness and weakness, indeed the lack of positive being, of that limiting and excluding selfhood.

(4) The painful opposition between the Divine action and the selfhood which it is destroying.

These four effects constitute the primary purgation of this night. St John enumerates precisely these four in *The Living Flame*. " At this juncture " (during the second night) " the soul suffers in the understanding a deep darkness " (the first effect, the ligature of the interior powers proceeding from a ligature of consciousness), " in the will aridity " (the result of the ligature) " *and conflict* " (the fourth effect), " in the memory the consciousness of its miseries " (the third effect), " and in its very substance the soul suffers utter poverty and dereliction " (the second effect) (*Living Flame*, st. 1). That these four effect are the results of one and the same divine action in the depths of the soul, we have already seen. Thus the night is not an accumulation of divers pains unrelated to each other, but the effect on the soul of one Divine operation through grace, when that operation has attained a certain degree of intensity. It is clear that the spiritual agony caused by this fourfold operation must be unthinkably terrible. St John turns to the complaints of Jeremia to express it, but it is in truth inexpressible. Each of the four effects by itself must be painful enough. What then must be the agony of the four together ? Moreover, this night endures for years (*O.N.*, ii. 17). During this period there are indeed intermissions in which, " by the dispensation of God, the dim contemplation divested of its purgative form and character assume

that the primary elements, that they may enter into the composition of all natural substances, should have no colour, taste
or smell peculiar to themselves, in order that they may combine
with all colours, tastes and smells, so the spirit must be simple,
pure and detached from all kinds of natural affections, actual and
habitual, in order that it may participate in liberty and breadth
of spirit in the Divine wisdom, wherein by reason of its purity
it tastes of the sweetness of all things in a certain pre-eminent
way. Without this purgation it is altogether impossible to feel
or taste the satisfaction of all this abundance of spiritual savours.
For one single affection remaining in the soul, or any one particular
object to which the spirit clings either actually or habitually, is
sufficient to prevent all consciousness, fruition or participation in
the subtlety and intimate sweetness of the spirit of love, which
contains within itself all sweetness eminently " (*O.N.*, ii. 9).
The darkness thus destroys all the limited objects and activities
of the understanding which constituted and conditioned its
natural operation. The ligature or suspension of all its natural
activities effects this directly, while the lack of the former mystical
fruition of God removes the adherence of the understanding to
His lower and more limited communications.

The reader will naturally wonder how a soul whose understanding is thus deprived of its natural activities can accomplish
its duties. St John would, of course, have admitted that the
ligature does not prevent the soul from performing, though
without pleasure, the duties of its state, of whatever nature those
duties may be. The requisite activity would be given either by
(1) a suspension of the ligature as far as was necessary for the
purpose ; or (2) the substitution of a supernatural operation of
God taking the place of the natural activity required for the
performance of the duty. The second alternative is stated explicitly by St John in *The Ascent*, Book III., chap. i., where,
however, he seems to be speaking of mystical marriage, when,
as we shall see, the natural activities have become receptions of the
Divine operation. What is there said is, however, applicable
to the ligature of this night.

When its limited natural activities have been thus purged
away the understanding becomes a receptacle of a divine intuition,
in and through which it unites itself to and is conscious of the
positive being of all things as contained in and known by God
without being any longer imprisoned by their creaturely limits.

" The characteristic of a spirit purified and annihilated as to all particular objects of affection and of the understanding is to have no pleasure in or knowledge of *anything in particular*, but abiding in emptiness and darkness, *to embrace all things in its grand comprehensiveness*, that it may fulfil mystically the words of the Apostle, ' having nothing and possessing all things ' " (*O.N.*, ii. 8).   " The spirit which is still subject to any actual or habitual affection or *particular knowledge, or any other limited apprehension*, cannot taste the delights of the spirit of liberty, according to the desire of the will " (*O.N.*, ii. 9).   " The reason is," continues St John, " that the affections, feelings and apprehensions of the perfect spirit, *because they are divine*, are of a different nature and order to those which are natural, and so surpass the former that they cannot be possessed either actually or in habit till the former have been annihilated, for they are two contraries which cannot co-exist in one and the same subject " (*O.N.*, ii. 9).   In other words, a divine understanding or consciousness replaces the old natural and limited consciousness of the soul, and this can only be effected by the destruction of that old natural understanding.   This Divine understanding is a participation or reception by the soul's understanding of God's Understanding or Consciousness of Himself and of all things in Himself.   St John here terms it " a certain Divine light, most lofty, surpassing all natural light, and not naturally cognisable by the understanding.   If, therefore, the understanding is to be united with this light and *to be made Divine* in the state of perfection, it must first of all be purified and annihilated as to its natural light, which must be brought actually into darkness by means of this dim contemplation " (*O.N.*, ii. 9). " This night is drawing the spirit away from its ordinary and common consciousness of things, that it may draw it towards the divine consciousness which is strange and alien to all human modes of consciousness " (*O.N.*, ii. 9).   In the passages above quoted St John speaks of a purgation of the affections as well as of the understanding, as effected by the darkness.   The affections, however, belong to the volitional aspect of the soul.   The reason is that the darkness does purge the will indirectly by removing its limited objects.   The direct purgation of the will is, however, the fire of unsatisfied love.   This fire entirely consumes the natural self-principled, self-impelled and self-directed and therefore essentially limited volition, which it replaces by itself, a super natural, unlimited love, God-infused and God-impelled and God directed ; indeed the participation and reception by the will of the Divine will wherein God loves Himself and all things for Himself.[1] " This love," says St John, " now partakes somewhat of the perfect union with God " (it is indeed the commencement of that union), "and thus participates in its properties, which are rather operations of God than of the soul itself, and are received passively by the soul, though the soul has to give its consent. The heat, force, temper and passion of love, or burning, as the soul terms it, are solely the love of God, Who is entering into union with the soul " (*O.N.*, ii. 11).

In this wise, through the consciousness and the will, is destroyed the natural selfhood which was the principle of that natural cognition and volition which by their essential limitation opposed and excluded the unlimited Divine operation in the soul. The purgative action of God in the soul is negative in its destruction of natural modes of consciousness and volition alike in things human and divine, but positive as being the increase of a supernatural life and activity, infinitely transcending our natural life and activities.

The darkness being negative passes away when the night is over, but the fire remains, deprived of its painfulness. When the barrier of the natural selfhood has been demolished and the operations of that selfhood eradicated, the divine contemplation no longer causes the negative darkness, a consciousness of the barrier that excludes it, but replaces or rather restores the consciousness that had been temporarily inhibited, deified now by the removal of its natural limits which prevented the free operation of God in and through it. The Divine intuition no longer blinds by reason of the stains of a natural self-moved consciousness, but since these have been purged away it floods the soul with its light. It is true that until death removes the veil of our corporeal life that light is indistinct, like a brilliant light shining full on to closed eyes. Nevertheless the darkness has passed, and the understanding is as conscious of the change as is one who goes with his eyes shut from a dark room into the glare of the noonday sun. The Divine love no longer lacking its satisfaction on account of the barrier of the selfhood between the soul and the supernatural intuition of God's Presence, is no longer a source of anguish, but of ineffable delight. While the night lasted the soul did not

---

[1] These participations being the participations of a creature have their created bases—infused faith and love and their root sanctifying grace.

participate in the Divine understanding, save in such wise that its natural understanding was destroyed and the self-barrier alone left in full consciousness. Hence its participation in the Divine love was but the torment of a mighty longing unfulfilled. Now that the night is over the soul participates in the Divine knowledge and love, with no other obstacle save that of bodily life and its sensible functions which, being peripheral, do not prevent this Divine Union which is accomplished in the central depths. " Since the understanding is enlightened," says St John, " with a super-natural light, the human understanding becomes divine, being made one with the Divine understanding. In the same way Divine love inflames the will so that it becomes nothing less than Divine, loving after a Divine fashion, being united and made one with the Divine will and the Divine love. The memory is affected in like manner ; all the desires and affections also are changed divinely according to God. Thus the soul will be of heaven, heavenly, and rather Divine than human " (O.N., ii. 13). All this is effected by the divine operation which purged the soul by darkening the understanding and inflaming the will. St John figures the purgation of this night by fire consuming fuel. First all moisture is expelled and then the fuel is blackened and dried, and then that blackness is itself destroyed. " Finally," he continues, " the fire having heated and set on fire its outward surface, transforms the whole into itself and makes it beautiful as itself. The fuel under these conditions retains neither active nor passive properties of its own, except bulk and weight, for it now possesses in itself the properties and operations of fire. It is dry and dries, it is hot and gives heat, it is radiant and emits radiance. In such wise must we reason concerning this Divine fire of contemplative love which before it unites and transforms the soul into itself purges it of all its contrary qualities " (O.N., ii. 10). Elsewhere St John expressly identifies this fire with the Holy Spirit. " Before this Divine fire of love has entered into the substance of the soul and unites itself thereto by the complete and perfect purgation and purity thereof, this flame, which is the Holy Ghost, wounds the soul, destroying and consuming the imperfections of its evil habits. This is the work of the Holy Ghost, Who thereby disposes the soul for its due union and transformation into God by love. For the flame which unites itself with the soul, glorifying it, is the very same which before assailed and purified it, just as the fire which penetrates the fuel is the very same which formerly assailed and wounded it with its flames, purging it of all its filthy qualities until it had so disposed it with its heat that it could enter into it and transform it into itself " (*Living Flame*, st. 1).

Contemplative love expresses the double aspect of the Divine operation in this night as intuition in the understanding (a negative intuition, however) and as love in the will. The intuition, first negative, then positive, and the love, first painful, then delightful, are one divine operation, even as the cognitive and volitional faculties are one in the unity of their common ground, the individual ego. Through the purgation of these fundamental functions the inmost centre of the soul, the root and ground of both, has been purged of its limited natural egoism, and through their participation and reception of the Divine activity, the Divine knowledge and love, it has become the receptacle and term of the infinite Being of God revealed in His twofold action as united in a special manner with the soul. The one divine operation, that in the night was darkness in the understanding and painful longing in the will, is now light in the understanding, though veiled as long as earthly life endures, and unitive love in the will, and in the affections, a heat that warms without pain. It is aptly symbolised by electricity. Electricity operates in three ways, as motive force, as heat and as light. All these three are but aspects of one electric energy. So is this operation of God, motive energy in the will, the heat of an ardent spiritual passion in the affections, these two forms being specially related, as are also volition and affection, and in the understanding a supernatural illumination. This is true also of the ordinary working of grace. Indeed this electric symbolism is applicable to the natural psychology of the human soul, in which the soul energises in these three ways and should, if its life be well ordered, be able to convert readily one form of energy into another—for instance, a perception of truth into action, an emotion of pity into self-sacrifice. This triple energy of electricity is nevertheless a symbol most peculiarly apt to illustrate the triple effect, when the second night is past, of the one simple and indivisible operation or union of God in and with the soul, after it has purged the soul through its faculties and by this purgation has transformed and taken full possession of the inmost centre.[1] But we have now left the purgative night behind and

[1] The reader may perhaps object that after speaking hitherto of two fundamental faculties or aspects of the soul—namely, cognition and volition, constituting with their ground the created Trinity—I now speak of three, adding affection

entered almost imperceptibly into the mystical union which is the highest possible in this life, that state of transformation into God which has received the name of spiritual or mystical marriage. Before I discuss this state further I have to consider in my next chapter a question which must have arisen in the mind of an attentive reader of this account of the night of spirit—namely, the relationship between this mystical purgation and the purgatory which awaits after death the vast majority of souls that die in the love of God.

APPENDIX

Throughout my discussion of the second night I have followed St John in treating it as a more or less continuous and clearly characterised stage of the mystical way. We must, however, always bear in mind that, as can be gathered from that which St John himself tells us, this continuous night is experienced only by those who are to be raised to the permanent habit of the transforming union. There are, however, many mystics who are not raised so high in this life, far more, indeed, than those who are. For these the purgation, which in its fulness and continuity constitutes the second night, is tempered both in its intensity and in its mode of occurrence. " God," St John tells us, " admits ' such souls ' at intervals into this night of contemplation or spiritual purgation, causing his sun to shine upon them and then to hide its face. . . . These *morsels* of obscure contemplation are never so intense as in that awful night of contemplation of which I am now speaking and in which God purposely places the soul, that He may raise it to the Divine union "—(*i.e.* the permanent transforming union or mystical marriage) (*Dark Night*, ii., chap. i). In the case of these souls the selfhood is gradually worn away, though never in this life so completely destroyed as in the greater mystics of whom St John writes, by more or less brief accesses of purgative contemplation, alternating with positive fruition of the mystical union intuition in its positive form. In these accesses of purga-

---

or spiritual feeling. But affection should not be regarded as so primary or so distinct a faculty or aspect as cognition and volition. It is a concomitant of both, but is particularly attached and subordinate to the will or conation as indeed heat is specially related to motive energy, though accompanying also cognition as heat accompanies light (see Chapter V).

tive union God works on the soul after the fashion described in the preceding chapter. His work, however, is not so complete, because the negative-seeming union does not endure till its full work has been accomplished in the complete destruction of the limiting selfhood. Nevertheless this intermittent and less intense purgation is one in principle with the continuous and complete purgation, one and the same union and operation of God working in the same way.

Moreover, since even the continuous purgation admits of intervals, no strict demarcation can be made between the inferior intermittent purgation and the second night in its complete and continuous form. The former tends to pass over into the latter. The reader must not therefore be surprised if in the actual experiences of mystics it is often difficult to trace the successive stages of the mystic way as laid down by St John. Those stages are, nevertheless, substantially present in the manner and degree peculiar to the individual mystic. In the spiritual life of those mystics who have passed through all the stages and have reached the *fulness* of the permanent transforming union they are all present, and are more or less clearly marked, as indeed they must have been in St John's personal experience. I must emphasise, however, the word *fulness*. The study of mystical biographies has led me to conclude that St John has been too absolute in his apparent teaching that the entire second night must always be passed through before *any measure* is granted of the transforming union. The transient gift of the act of that union, which constitutes the spiritual betrothal, often precedes the end of the second night. Moreover, a certain degree of habitul union in which God is continuously manifested as possessing the centre of the soul (see Chapter XI.) is granted to certain mystics in alternation with the negative and purgative union of the second night. The reason is that the barrier of natural selfhood has been sufficiently destroyed to permit of that Divine possession and penetration of the central ego which is of the essence of mystical marriage, but has not been so entirely destroyed as to permit of that conscious possession being altogether permanent. Hence certain intervals of the second night of purgation are requisite to complete the entire destruction of the natural selfhood. This I believe to have happened in the case of Lucie Christine. On the other hand, the *fulness* of the transforming union as it is described by St John and by Mother Cecilia, with its permanence of conscious Divine possession, requires the previous complete destruction of the selfhood. Therefore in such cases the second night is wholly ended when the soul enters the transforming union. These cases, however rare, are those in which the second night and the transforming union are alike manifested in their intensest, most perfect and therefore most characteristic forms. It is, however, obvious that for the purpose of the theoretical student of mysticism, of the "mystologist," the more intense, more perfect and more fully characterised forms of mystical experience, in which the progress of the mystical union is more clearly distinguishable, are to be preferred as the subject matter of study to weaker and more indefinite forms. To these, therefore, I confine this study, following thus the method of St John himself.[1]

---

[1] Among modern mystical biographies the experience of the night of spirit endured by Sœur Gertrude Marie, a nun of Angers, is in very close correspondence with the theoretical description given by St John. In her case this night was exceptionally well marked in its chronology and exceptionally continuous. (See *Une Mystique de Nos Jours*, by her confessor, the Abbé Legueu, pp. 98 *sqq.*) This mystic was raised to a supreme degree of Divine union, but the natural narrowness and pettiness of her intelligence unhappily necessitated a translation of her mystical experience into a somewhat irritating and monotonous series of images and concepts derived from her narrowly limited understanding and imagination. Fr. Hecker, the founder of the Paulists, died at the end of a long-continued night of the spirit.

CHAPTER XI

PURGATORY AND THE PASSIVE NIGHT OF SPIRIT

O Pain, Love's mystery,
Close next of kin
To joy and heart's delight,
Low Pleasure's opposite,
Choice food of sanctity
And medicine of sin.

. . . .

Thou sear'st my flesh, O Pain,
But brand'st for arduous peace my languid brain,
And bright'nest my dull view,
Till I, for blessing, blessing give again,
And my roused spirit is
Another fire of bliss,
Wherein I learn
Feelingly how the pangful, purging fire
Shall furiously burn
With joy, not only of assured desire,
But also present joy
Of seeing life's corruption, stain by stain,
Vanish in the clear heat of love irate.

. . . .

Leaving the man, so dark erewhile,
The mirror merely of God's smile.

COVENTRY PATMORE,
Pain.

Christopher came out of that state broken and scorched, but saved.
He had left Christopher and gone over to God.

ROMAIN ROLLAND,
Jean Christophe, Eng. trs., vol. iv., p. 366.

In iis quae de Purgatorio determinata non sunt ab Ecclesia
standum est iis quae sunt magis conformia dictis et revelationibus
Sanctorum. S. THOMAS.

(Quoted in title-page in English translation
of *Treatise on Purgatory*.)

EVEN if St John had omitted all reference to purgatory in his
discussion of the night of spirit, the thoughts of his reader would

inevitably have been turned in that direction. The night of
spirit is obviously a purgatory, and moreover like the purgatory
after death, it is at the same time a satisfaction for any temporal
punishment that may be due to sin. Nay, its satisfaction is more
potent, since its sufferers can merit by their free acceptance of the
terrible pains of this night. St John, however, has explicitly
referred to purgatory. At the end of the sixth chapter of
Book II. he writes of those placed in this second night. "They are
purged in this life after the fashion that souls are purged in the life
to come,[1] for *this purgation is that purgation* which must be under-
gone after death. The soul, therefore, that passes through this
night either enters not at all into purgatory (*lit.* that place) or is
detained there but a very short space, seeing that one hour of this
night is far more profitable than many there." Personally I should
maintain that the soul which has entirely passed through the
second night and has reached the mystical union that lies beyond
it does not enter purgatory at all, since its purgation has been fully
accomplished. Be that as it may, there can be no question that
St John teaches the substantial identity of the spiritual night and
purgatory, that one and the same spiritual operation is accomplished in both alike. In the tenth chapter St John says that we
" learn by the way how souls suffer in purgatory." It is true that
in the twelfth chapter St John distinguishes between "the loving
dark and *spiritual* fires " which purge the soul in the night of
spirit, and the " dark and material fires " of purgatory. We must,
however, bear in mind that the Church has deliberately refused,
explicitly at the Council of Florence, and at Trent implicitly, by
her definition of the dogma of purgatory wherein there is no mention of fire, to define the existence of material fire in purgatory.
This opinion of St John is obviously not the expression of his own
experience, but is simply his adherence to the common opinion of
theologians. If we can see no sufficient reason to posit material
fire in purgatory, we are perfectly free to disbelieve its existence.
If therefore we adopt a view of purgatory in which its operation
is fully accounted for by an immaterial fire, there is no need to
introduce another material fire which is thus otiose. *Entia non
sunt multiplicanda præter necessitatem* is a sound philosophical
maxim of application in this matter. Moreover, purgation by a

---

[1] Literally " in hell : inferno " ; but the context, as indeed the most elementary
principles of Catholic theology, makes it plain that St John is speaking of purgatory
—considered as a species of temporary hell, or as in locality adjoining hell.

spiritual suffering, which is so inevitably symbolised by the material image of fire that no other image would symbolise it equally well, would sufficiently account for and would fully justify the general tradition of the existence of fire in purgatory.

Just such a view of purgatory will be ours if we accept its substantial identity with the night of spirit. This identity could be established by examination of the purgatorial operation of the second night, its scope and mode. The result of such an examination would be the conviction that this earthly purification is the same in principle with that which all souls must endure as the necessary condition of entrance into the beatific vision of heaven. This work has, however, been already done for us by a mystic who may be truly styled the doctress of purgatory. The best treatise on purgatory ever written is that of St Catherine of Genoa. It is unhappily a patchwork of the saint's utterances on the subject, pieced together after her death, and it has suffered severely from interpolation.[1] Hence it is ill arranged and in places inconsistent. Indeed one paragraph, even one sentence, is sometimes inconsistent with itself. Moreover, many of the sentences are expressed so loosely that their exact meaning cannot be made out, the natural result of writing down from memory sayings remembered only in their general drift. Nevertheless this little treatise contains the most profound conceptions and the most illuminating views of purgatory anywhere to be found. A series of lightning flashes lays bare its depths, not indeed to the imagination, but to the intelligence, and still more to the spiritual intuition of the reader. St Catherine's account of purgatory possesses a convincing realism lacking in the imaginative accounts of other writers and seers. With her there is no material imagery, save for a few similes which are presented as similes, not as descriptions. This short treatise is a spiritual vision which penetrates behind symbolism and reveals the essential nature of the purification after death. St Catherine's doctrine is derived from her mystical experience in this life. She tells us this herself. " This holy soul, yet in the flesh, found herself placed in the purgatory of God's burning love, which consumed and purified her from whatever she had to purify, in order that after passing out of this life she might enter at once into the immediate presence of God her Beloved. *By means of this furnace of love she understood how the souls of the faithful are placed in purgatory.*" Her

---

[1] See Baron von Hügel, *Mystical Element*, vol. i., Appendix.

account is not, therefore, simply that of her own mystical state, the night of spiritual purgation, transferred arbitrarily to purgatory. On the contrary, her insight into that purgation was at the same time an insight into the nature of purgatory, because it was an insight into the essential character of the purification necessary in order to full supernatural union between the soul and God, and therefore the common principle of both purgatories, the mystical purgatory here and the purgatory which awaits us hereafter. This is the only vision into eschatological realities possible to us on earth, an insight into the nature and conditions of union between God and the soul, whether that union be effected before or after bodily death. Heaven, purgatory and hell and the various spiritual states of the souls incarnate on earth are essentially constituted by the relationship of the soul to God, either the positive relationship of union, or the negative relationship of separation. Anything not necessarily arising out of this relationship is merely a concomitant, not an essential constituent, of any of these states. Therefore to know the relationship of souls to God is to apprehend the fundamental principles of eschatology.

In virtue of such knowledge—the knowledge of personal experience—St Catherine describes the nature of purgatory. Examination of her description establishes its identity with St John's description of the night of spirit. A brief comparison between the two accounts will therefore enable us to share not indeed St Catherine's insight into the substantial identity of the mystical and eschatological purgatories, but the intellectual conviction of that identity to which that intuition gave birth.

We saw that one of the two chief effects of the Divine action in the night of spirit was a fourfold negative effect on the soul through the spiritual consciousness. The first of these was the complete ligature of the natural functioning of the faculties, a spiritual imprisonment or stifling. This ligature is mentioned in several passages of St Catherine's treatise. The souls " can remember nothing," she tells us, " of themselves or others, whether good or evil. . . . They are incapable of thinking of themselves " (chap. i). Here indeed she explains that the ligature is due to the absorption of the souls in the Divine will, but that is itself but an effect or aspect of the Divine action within them and thus is reducible to the cause of that ligature assigned by St John —namely, this Divine operation itself. The ligature is in St Catherine's thought carried so far that she even maintains that the souls in purgatory " do not know that their sufferings are for the sake of their sins, nor can they keep in view the sins themselves " (chap. i). Without adopting an opinion so opposed to the general sense of Catholics that it seems clearly an exaggeration, of statement at least, we can accept the main truth which underlies it—namely, that the souls have no longer a psychical activity conversant with the particular or limited as such—that is, with the creature as apart from God, which would thus come between them and God.

In the last chapter of the treatise is a detailed account of the ligature. This indeed (as Baron von Hügel points out) was spoken by St Catherine only of her experience on earth, not of purgatory. It was, however, applied to Purgatory by the compilers of the treatise, which is a proof that they recognised its substantial applicability to Purgatory. Moreover, as we have seen, ligature is mentioned in other chapters whose reference is directly purgatorial. I will therefore quote a few paragraphs.

" I see the soul," she says, " estranged to all things, even spiritual, which can give it nourishment. . . . It has no power of tasting anything temporal or spiritual by will, by understanding, by memory, so that I can say : ' This thing pleases me more than that other.' My soul is, as it were, *besieged* in such a manner that all spiritual or bodily refreshments are cut off. . . ." The soul " goes on, removing everything which might feed the inward man, and *besieges itself* so straitly, that not even the least particle of imperfection can pass without being spied out and rejected with abhorrence." " I remain," adds the saint, " in my prison." To St Catherine indeed that prison is this world and the chain is the body. This, however, is accounted for by the fact that the natural selfish activities to be destroyed in the night of spirit are *ultimately* due to the limitation of the soul by its sense-conditioned activities, from which it can only be set free by the action of sanctifying grace.

We may remark here that the effect of the night of spirit which consists in a ligature of the sensible activities of the soul is effected in a completeness impossible in any but this worldly state, by death itself, which destroys even those most external activities, such as bodily sight and hearing, which continued during the night of spirit. This ligature, therefore, has no existence in purgatory. A certain ligature, however, does continue in purgatory, a ligature of the more spiritual operations of the soul which

T

proceed from the purely natural principle of the ego as apart from God. Moreover, the Divine operation in the soul does not restore the substantial worth of the sensible activities until the obstacle constituted in the centre of the soul by the effect of their limitations has been fully purged away.

The two effects next discussed in my account of the second night were the soul's consciousness of abandonment by God or, to put it in another way, of His absence, and of the worthlessness or rather the positive evil of its natural selfhood, as being simply an obstacle excluding God. These effects are partially expressed by St Catherine in her simile of a covered object. " It is," she says, " as with a covered object. The object cannot respond to the rays of the sun, not because the sun ceases to shine—for it shines without intermission—but because the covering intervenes. Let the covering be destroyed, again the object will be exposed to the sun, and will answer to the rays which beat against it in proportion as the work of destruction advances. Thus the souls are covered by a rust—that is, sin " (as is clear from what has been already said, sin must be understood in a very wide and deep sense)—" which is gradually consumed away by the fire of purgatory. The more it is consumed, the more they respond to God their true sun ; their happiness increases as the rust falls off, and lays them open to the Divine ray " [1] (chap. ii). " The souls of the faithful are placed in purgatory to get rid of all the rust and stain of sin that in this life was left unpurged " (chap. i). This purgation is a gradually decreasing consciousness of the limited imperfect activities of the natural independent self, as the obstacle excluding the soul's free union with the infinite Being of God. St John also makes use of this very simile of rust. " This contemplation," he says, " is also purifying the soul, undoing or emptying or consuming in it, *as fire consumes the rust and mouldiness of the metal,* all the affections and habits of imperfection which it had contracted in the whole course of its life " (*O.N.,* ii. 6). In the fifth chapter St Catherine again refers to the rust of sin.

The third chapter has been entitled " Separation from God is the greatest punishment of Purgatory." Chapter six is

---

[1] According to Baron von Hügel we have here a conflation of two distinc similes : the uncovering of an object to the sunlight, and the removal of rust by fire (*Mystical Element of Religion*, vol. i., pp. 443-444). Both, however, represen the same spiritual operation.

devoted to the simile of the loaf of bread. The vision of God is the bread, the absence of which causes the hunger which torments the souls in purgatory. In the eighth chapter we read: " It appears to me that the greatest pain the souls in purgatory endure proceeds from their being sensible of something in themselves displeasing to God " (this I understand of the extra-Godly selfhood as explained above) " and that it has been done voluntarily against so much goodness " (the deordination of that undue attachment of the soul to the creature which hinders its free union with God is the result of sin because it was first caused by original sin, and because it would have been entirely destroyed by the Divine action through grace had it not been for actual sin and culpable *imperfection* resisting Divine grace). . . . They know the truth and how grievous is any obstacle which does not let them approach God." In chapter nine we are told "the soul finds itself stopped by sin," and the treatise speaks of "this sense of the grievousness of being kept from beholding the Divine light." [1] Of the pain caused by the clash of the two extremes the imperfect extra-godly self and the Divine Action, St Catherine has no explicit mention. It is, however, implied in my opinion by the ninth chapter of the treatise.

The thought of the saint is, however, fixed primarily on the purifying fire of unsatisfied love in the will—which is pre-eminently the fire of purgatory. Her account of this is largely identical with that of St John. In the third chapter St Catherine speaks of the " fire of love, which draws " the soul "to its end with such impetuosity and vehemence that any obstacle seems intolerable." In the same chapter, indeed, she says that "there springs up within them a fire like that of hell." This likeness can only be in respect of its painfulness and of its causation by the absence of God. The fire of hell is not a fire of love. In the marvellous sixth chapter this fire of longing love is hunger after the Divine Bread. Elsewhere we read that it was God who kindled that fire of love which consumes every imperfection there is to be consumed (chap. ix). And again she speaks of " that operation of His

---

[1] In certain places some external punishment rather than the inordinate self-limitation of the soul, or indeed anything inherent in the soul, is regarded as the obstacle. This is, however, due to the correction of some theologian whose purgatory was merely a satisfaction without any intrinsic purification. According to Baron von Hügel, the ten final chapters of the *Trattato* are chiefly the work of redactors. We can, however, utilise them where, as in my quotations, they agree with the teaching of certainly authentic passages.

pure and simple love which God works in us ; wherein he penetrates and burns the soul " (chap. xii). These statements indeed belong to chapters referring directly to the purgation of this life— but their correspondence with statements in the purgatorial chapters is obvious and serves to bring home to us the identity of principle in the two purgations. In the ninth chapter, indubitably purgatorial, the saint discusses this fire at greater length. God, she says, " imparts a certain attractive impulse of His burning love, enough to annihilate " the soul, " though it be immortal ; and in this way *so transforms the soul into Himself,* its God, that it sees in itself nothing but God " (this is obviously the end rather than the process of Purgatory, for that process was effected through ligature and sensible dereliction), who goes on thus attracting and inflaming it, until He has brought it to that state of existence whence it came forth—that is, the spotless purity wherein it was created. And when the soul, by interior illumination, perceives that God is drawing it with such loving ardour to Himself, straightway there springs up within it a corresponding fire of love for its most sweet lord and God . . . it finds itself stopped by sin, and unable to follow the heavenly attraction—I mean that look which God casts on it to bring it into union with Himself : and this sense of the grievousness of being kept from beholding the Divine light, coupled with that instinctive longing which would fain be without hindrance to follow the enticing look— these two things, I say, make up the pains of the souls in purgatory." This central passage plainly affirms the two main constituents of purgatory to be precisely those of the second night—the obstacle between the soul and God, and the unsatisfied love-longing for God. This is repeated in another passage where we are explicitly told that the instinct by which the soul " is kindled and the impediments by which it is hindered constitute its purgatory " (chap. xi). This is another instance of the perfect agreement between the passages which refer to the purification of this life—such as the above—and those whose reference is directly to purgatory, an agreement which led to the editors' confusion between the two, a confusion which is itself one of the strongest proofs of my thesis. The love-longing and its obstacle constitute St John's " *dark night of loving fire,*" the fire that purifies in the darkness (*O.N.*, ii. 12). In the tenth chapter the Saint compares the action of the fire on the souls to that of material fire on gold. The fire burns away, she tells us, the dross of self. " Gold," she says, " which has been purified to a certain point ceases to suffer any diminution from the action of fire, however great it be ; for the fire does not destroy gold, but only the dross that it may chance to have.   In like manner the Divine fire acts on souls : God holds them in the furnace until every defect has been burnt away, and He has brought them each in his own degree to a certain standard of perfection.   Thus purified, they rest in God without any alloy of self, they become impassable because there is nothing left to be consumed."   " If in this state of purity," she adds, " they were kept in the fire they would feel no pain, rather it would be to them a fire of Divine love, burning on without opposition, like the fire of life eternal."   In this passage, apparently an interpolated conflation of two genuine sayings, there is a difficulty as to the character of the fire.   What is this fire here apparently external to the soul ?   Not a material fire, for that could not become a fire of Divine love.   On the contrary, it is evidently the fire of love-longing infused by God which is in the saint's mind.   For this fire does continue when purgatory is over, though no longer painful, since it is fully satisfied.   We cannot doubt that such was the idea of St Catherine. The expression of that idea, however, has been obscured and confused by an attempt to conciliate it with the popular teaching of an external medium of torment.[1] Alike in purgatory and in the second night, God acting on the unpurified soul is its torment, not, of course, in Himself, but through the unpurified selfhood that excludes Him and resists His action, as in the beatific vision and in mystical marriage He is its joy and satisfaction.   This interpretation is central to the true understanding alike of St Catherine's view of purgatory and of that substantial identity between purgatory and the second night which it is the aim of this chapter to establish.   Its correctness is witnessed by the passages on the fire of love which I have already quoted.   The language of St Catherine's treatise is almost verbally reproduced by St John with a twofold reference to purgatory and the second night. " We learn," he says, " by the way, how souls suffer in purgatory. The fire, though it were applied, would have no power over them if they had no imperfections for which they must suffer, *for those are the matter on which that fire seizes ; when that matter is consumed there is nothing more to burn.*   So is it here " (in the second night), " when all imperfections are removed, the suffering of the soul

---

[1] This confusion was apparently present in the Saint's authentic saying.

ceases, and in its place comes joy " (*O.N.*, ii. 10). He has just established for the Night of Spirit the identity of the fire of purgation with the fire of union. As regards the object of purgation St Catherine's treatise is inconsistent. It contains passages which tend to make purgatory a mere satisfaction, the soul being already free of guilt (*e.g.* in chs. iii. and ix). These passages, however, are opposed by others far more central to the treatise, in which the object is regarded as the purification of stains that exclude the soul from the full union with God.[1] Surely we should regard the passages which speak of purgatory as a real purification of the soul as the genuine dicta of St Catherine. Otherwise her entire treatise would lose its meaning. The contradictory statements are but bungling attempts to reconcile her teaching with the more external and infinitely less spiritual conception of purgatory popular with influential schools of theology.[2]

The stains or rust to be purged away are sometimes spoken of as sin, sometimes as defect, sometimes as bad habits. But their true character is the common root of all these, is that limited extra-godly selfhood which I have already dwelt upon at such length. This is stated explicitly in the tenth chapter of the *Treatise*. "The soul cannot be annihilated so far as it is in God " (*i.e.* in so far as its life is a participation of His infinite life, its activities a reception of His Divine activity), "but only in itself ; and the more it is purified, so much the more it annihilates self, till at last it becomes quite pure and rests in God. . . . Purified, they " (the souls) " rest in God without any alloy of self ; *their very being is God.*" What St John states more or less implicitly is here stated with an explicitness beyond possibility of mistake. Thus alike in its twofold purgatorial operation and in its object, purgatory as understood by St Catherine is one with the night of spirit as described by St John.

[1] In chap. ix. *one and the same sentence* contains both views. It tells us that when God " beholds the soul in the purity wherein it was created " He purifies it with the fire of love " until He has brought it . . . to the spotless purity wherein it was created." We have here an obvious instance of the work of a clumsy redactor. St Catherine could not have held these two absolutely irreconcilable notions.

[2] According to Baron von Hügel, the corrections of the compilers may be referred to three heads : (1) no guilt is purged in purgatory ; (2) the punishment of purgatory is not truly purgative but *merely and solely* vindictive and satisfactory ; (3) it is therefore static, not progressive, the soul being equally pure from first to last (p. 448). My own examination of the *Treatise* had already led me towards this conclusion.

Our conclusion as to the substantial identity of both is supported by the consideration that mystical union, including its purgative degrees, is but a stage in the development of sanctifying grace on its way to become glory. In all the saved sanctifying grace must, as we saw, follow in substance the same development to the same goal. Therefore it must effect a purification identical in its operation and object with the mystical purgation. This purification, however, is purgatory. Therefore purgatory and the mystical purification are essentially one and the same purification.

There is thus a unity and continuity in the process of sanctification on both sides of the grave. It is, of course, true that there is in purgatory no increase of sanctifying grace. This fact, however, does not mean that the purgatorial process is not an effect of sanctifying grace and is therefore in no sense whatever a sanctification. It is, as we have seen, like the mystical night on earth, a destruction by God, especially immanent in the soul through grace, of the natural selfhood which opposes full union with Himself. As this barrier is destroyed, sanctifying grace penetrates and takes possession of the soul, thereby bringing the soul into complete subjection to God, and thus rendering all its life and activity, indeed its inmost centre, the receptacle of the Divine Life and Being which is God Himself. Therefore purgatory undoubtedly sanctifies the soul in the sense of rendering it wholly penetrated by grace and obedient to grace. On the other hand, the soul in purgatory is no longer free, like the mystic on earth, to escape the purifying pain by resistance to the Divine operation. Therefore, unlike the latter, he does not merit by his submission to the process, and since he does not merit, his sanctifying grace does not increase in amount as it does in the mystical night. When the soul emerges from the mystical night, not only is it wholly possessed by grace and by God through grace, but that grace and the degree of glory that must correspond with it hereafter have been enormously augmented during the purification. When, however, the soul emerges from purgatory, no such augmentation has taken place. For that soul the purification has been the perfect penetration and possession of his soul by a grace whose positive amount or degree has remained the same throughout.[1] Imagine a man possessed of a high degree of musical or dramatic sensibility but incapable of its expression. Suppose him to be

[1] See von Hügel, vol. ii., p. 243.

gradually given complete power of expression, though his degree
of æsthetic sensibility remains the same.   This supposition will
illustrate for us the sanctification of purgatory without increase of
sanctifying grace.   The soul's capacity of participation in the
Divine will and knowledge, in the life of God, the fundamental
relationship of the will to God, its strength of love, or rather its
power of receiving the Divine love, the depths to which that soul's
knowledge can penetrate the Divine Being, these are the same when
that soul leaves as when it entered purgatory.   Their actualisation,
however, hindered hitherto by the natural selfhood destroyed in
purgatory, and which was perhaps very slight at death, has now,
when the work of purification has been fully accomplished, become
full and continuous.   This is the perfect accomplishment of the
work of sanctifying grace, the complete sanctification of the soul.
It is clear, therefore, that the difference between this life and the
next as regards the positive augmentation of sanctifying grace
leaves unaffected the continuity of the sanctifying process, regarded
as the progressive possession of the soul by God through the gradual
destruction of the obstacles to that possession.   This gradual
purgation of the soul from its natural selfhood and its results is
one continuous process in which death usually occurs at an early
stage, owing in great measure to failure to correspond with grace.
But this is not always the case.   The mystics have reached before
death stages usually reserved for the life to come.   From the
mystics, therefore, we can learn something of the nature of these
later stages.   This knowledge enables us to look forward to our
own personal entrance into these stages after death as a journey
not by a road wholly unknown, but along a way already trodden
here on earth by a small band of pioneers.   Surely it is just that
knowledge which makes all the difference.   When we are faced
ourselves with death, or when our dear ones are laid in the grave,
great indeed is our painful longing for some information about the
life beyond the tomb, and our abhorrence of that dark abyss of
ignorance which hides the world of the departed.   We trust that
our dear one is saved and hope for our own salvation.   We have
every ground in the majority of cases to think that he or she is in
purgatory and that we shall be placed there ourselves on leaving
this world.   Purgatory, however, is only too often but a name.
Because we cannot imagine its conditions, it is a terror of the darkness, often so vague as to be all but a complete unreality.   The
conclusion just reached should do much to make it a reality, and

to satisfy this longing for knowledge of a state in which many whom we love are now, where we expect ourselves to be hereafter. Certainly it provides no sensible picture, for there can be no sensible picture of a spiritual state. Nor does it give us that intimate knowledge of the purgatorial purification which can be possessed only by those who, like St Catherine of Genoa and St John of the Cross, have had personal experience of the mystical purgation. It does, however, give us indications, however inadequate, of the nature of purgatory, ideas which enable our understanding to apprehend to some slight degree at least its reality and necessity. We come also to understand, as never before, that to the just the life beyond the grave is but the fulfilment of this present life, the fructification of a plant sown here below. We realise that our dead in purgatory have not passed into a state almost unknowable to us who are left on earth, for we know that it is the state which souls have passed through here on earth. To know this is to know that the two worlds of time and eternity are divided more sharply by baptism[1] than by death, that life eternal has already begun on earth, for some even consciously. In the light of this knowledge the after-life will no longer seem, as at times we are tempted to regard it, a picture cast by the magic lantern of imagination and desire on the emptiness of the void. Rather will it be to us the one solid reality that underlies the comparative nonentity of this material world, a reality whose complete manifestation is indeed reserved for the life to come, but which has been manifested even in this present life, and of which the mystics have possessed before death an experience which for most of us is delayed till death is past. The realisation of this truth robs death of its bitterest terror—the terror of the unknown.

APPENDIX

Before I pass on to the chapter which deals with mystical marriage I would say a word on a matter which must have occurred to some at least of my readers—namely, the likeness which cannot fail to present itself between the dereliction of the

---

[1] Not always the sacrament. For many the supernatural life begins with a baptism of desire, and what exactly is requisite for that baptism is known with any certainty to God alone.

second night and the dereliction of Our Lord on the Cross.   On this subject, so deeply mysterious, there can be no certainty nor even confident opinion.   We can but make conjectures which we know to be utterly inadequate and quite probably false.   Such conjectures, however, may help us to realise, as perhaps we had not previously realised, the depth of dread mystery which constituted this central Passion of Our Lord, a passion in comparison with which His physical passion in all its horror and cruelty was as nothing.   My conjecture is then this, that Our Lord's Human Soul was temporarily excluded from the fruition of His personal Union with God by the obstacle consciously realised, not, indeed, of personal sin, imperfection or natural selfhood, such, of course, being non-existent, but of the sin, imperfection and natural unregenerate or grace-resisting selfhood of fallen humanity as a whole, with which humanity Our Lord as the second Adam had mystically identified Himself.   In virtue of this identity, that mass of sinful, God-excluding selfhood came between Our Lord's Human consciousness and the Godhead with Whom His Humanity was personally one, and by its limitation shut off His Soul from Its Divine fruition.   Moreover, in virtue of this same identification Our Lord's Soul would, we may conjecture, have so experienced the essential and necessary opposition between God and this sinful selfhood with which Our Lord had in some sense identified Himself as to be conscious of a Divine dereliction.[1]   Since, however, Our Lord was one Person with God, full fruition of the Godhead was His right.   By abandoning that right in this freely assumed dereliction He satisfied as Our second Head and Representative for the rebellion against God of our first head and representative. If this conjecture be true, the dereliction of Our Saviour was not indeed like Purgatory, substantially identical with the second night, but was analogous to it.   By means of that analogy we are able to contemplate the surface at least of a mystery whose depths are perhaps impenetrable by any created intelligence.

[1] In this passage I follow, as I believe I am at full liberty to do, those theologians, though the minority, who teach that during our Lord's dereliction His Human Soul did not enjoy the Beatific Vision.

CHAPTER XII

THE TRANSFORMING UNION: OR MYSTICAL MARRIAGE

His pale, wound-worn limbs
Fell from Prometheus, and the azure night
Grew radiant with the glory of that form
Which lives unchanged within, and his voice fell
Like music which makes giddy the dim brain,
Faint with intoxication of keen joy.

" Sister of her whose footsteps pave the world
With loveliness—more fair than aught but her
Whose shadow thou art—lift thine eyes on me."
I lifted them : the overpowering light
Of that immortal shape was shadowed o'er
By love ; which, from his soft and flowing limbs
And passion-parted lips, and keen, faint eyes
Steamed forth like vaporous fire, an atmosphere
Which wrapped me in its all-dissolving power,
As the warm œther of the morning sun
Wraps ere it drinks some cloud of wandering dew.
I saw not, heard not, moved not, only felt
His presence flow and mingle with my blood
Till it became his life, and his grew mine,
And I was thus absorbed, until it passed,
And like the vapours when the sun sinks down,
Gathering again in drops upon the pines,
And tremulous as they, in the deep night
My being was condensed.

SHELLEY,
Prometheus Unbound, Act II., sc. 1.

Jam hiems transiit, imber abiit et recessit. Flores apparuerunt in terra nostra: vox turturis audita est. Surge, amica mea, speciosa mea, et veni.

Dilectus meus mihi, et ego illi, qui pascitur inter lilia.

Et resurrexit.

Ego vivo, sed jam non ego, sed vivit in me Christus.

299

Not immediately on emerging from the darkness of the second
night is the happy soul introduced into the fulness of blazing light
which is that final stage known as the mystical or spiritual marriage or as the transforming union.   The rays of the divine Sun
are tempered to its weakness by the mystical Betrothal. This
betrothal differs apparently from mystical marriage by its inter-
mittence and by a certain rebellion which still persists of the
powers of sense (*Canticle*, st. 17, note). Its positive character
is a foretaste of the marriage to come. It is essentially a state
intermediate between ecstasy and mystical marriage—the act of
the latter without its permanent habit (see below).   It is
indeed probable that souls not called in this life to the transforming union obtain this betrothal without having fully passed
through the night of spirit.   The scope of this work does not
demand my lingering over this intermediate stage.   My object is
rather to give the reader some indication of the final stage of the
mystical way, the fullest and most perfect form of the mystical
union, the marriage itself.   Here above all is it essential to bear
well in mind that we cannot possibly understand what such a
state is in its inner being to those blessed few who have experienced it themselves.   With far better reason might an old bachelor
who had never fallen in love hope to present an adequate description of that experience, and its crown, betrothal and marriage.
It would be ludicrous to suppose that such an one could describe
the sensations of the lover or the beloved, could reproduce the
little nuances of speech, so charged with hidden meaning, the
gestures and tokens that at once express and conceal the avowal
of love and its return, could make his readers enter into the fears
and hopes, the sorrows and the joys of that most intimate union of
human hearts.   Infinitely more ludicrous would it be for me to
undertake to initiate my readers into the secrets of the spiritual
marriage wherein the Divine Lover is united so intimately with
the soul for whose love He has paid so dear.   Even if a writer
possessed the experience himself, as St John of the Cross possessed
it, and St Teresa, when she wrote her *Interior Castle*, he could not
reveal that experience to others who have never enjoyed it themselves. *Secretum meum mihi*.   If that innate desire of self-
expression which is an integral part of human nature should urge
him to speak or write his love story, he could but pour forth
metaphors and images infinitely inadequate to the reality.   This
indeed is largely true even of human love, infinitely more true of

Divine. St John, who in his writings on the purgative way attempted a more or less scientific exposition, abandons even the attempt when he comes to write of the final union. He falls back on art pure and simple, and clothes the experience he would fain reveal with a rich garment of sensible figures. He paraphrases that inspired poem of spiritual passion, that treasure-house of luxuriant oriental imagery, the Song of Songs.

If this be so, is not this chapter self-condemned ? Were it not better to close the book with that silence which is the most eloquent expression of the inexpressible ? Such silence must indeed close every effort to follow the soul on her Godward flight. It should, however, be the silence not of blank ignorance, but of thoughts that lie too deep for words, or, more truly, of intuitions that lie too deep for clear concepts, of a vision overwhelmed by the veiled revelation of the infinite. It must be the spiritual counterpart of that silence, sung by the poet, of Cortez and his band when first from the brow of the Darien peak they beheld the waters of an unknown ocean far stretching to the western horizon. Such a silence can only be ours if we can ascend some peak of thought or insight from whence we catch a distant glimpse of the ocean which awaits the souls of the elect, the boundless and fathomless ocean of the Triune Godhead. An attentive study of the descriptions of the transforming union given by such mystics as St John will be the spiritual mountain peak, from whence we may view that ocean, or, if you prefer another simile, the promised land outspread from Dan to Beersaba, whose fertile valleys and pastures green, with their refreshment of cool streams, shall be our eternal dwelling-place if we are faithful till death. Even the purely external indication afforded by such study will be sufficient, not, indeed, to tell us what is perfect union with God, whether in the unveiled vision of heaven or in the faith-veiled transforming union of earth, but to make us realise its existence, *that it truly is*, and that it infinitely exceeds all that our study can hint. This is the value of external schematic notions which are at best but a diagram representing the skeleton of a living body. The diagram makes us aware of the existence of the living reality and indicates to us its infinitely pre-eminent possession of all that is of positive value alike in the diagrammatic representation and in that which we clearly apprehend by its means. The external knowledge of the complete mystical union which we may gather from the mystical writers should leave on our souls an impression which may be symbolised by the impression received by Crusoe from his discovery of the footprint in the sand. That footprint indicated to him the presence in his island, hitherto imagined as inhabited only by plant and animal life, of a being of a superior order. Even so will the study of the mystics' description of the transforming union reveal to us the presence in human experience of a union with God so intimate that we could not otherwise have dreamt of its possibility. It will make us realise the existence of spiritual planes attainable here on earth, of a Divinity that has been man's possession even before death, which had hitherto been wholly unsuspected. If my discussion of mystical marriage helps to effect this for even one reader my labour will have been amply rewarded.

The state of spiritual marriage has been treated by St John in the above-mentioned paraphrase of the Song of Songs—*The Spiritual Canticle of the Soul*—and in *The Living Flame of Love*, which latter treatise is almost wholly devoted to it. It is also the subject of Mother Cecilia's treatises entitled respectively *The Transformation of the Soul in* (*to*) *God* and *The Union of the Soul with God*, although she only once gives it the name of spiritual marriage. It is on these treatises that my account is based.

It will be well to begin with a word of warning which is given by Père Poulain.[1] Père Poulain warns his readers not to confuse the mystical state termed spiritual marriage with those sensible marriage ceremonies enacted in ecstatic vision between the soul and Jesus Christ of which we read in the lives of the saints. These ceremonies, consisting usually in the gift of a ring by Jesus, sometimes precede and sometimes accompany the conclusion of the true spiritual marriage. Sometimes they occur when that marriage has been already accomplished, on the occasion of an increase of the mystical union.

Such a symbolic ceremony was that recorded in the Life of St Catherine of Siena, wherein she received a wedding ring from the Infant Jesus ; such, also, a similar vision of Gemma Galgani. Another modern instance is the double ceremony in which Sister Gertrude Mary was wedded first to the Word, then a few weeks later to the Holy Spirit. Here, however, there was no gift of a ring. It is clear that Sister Gertrude could not have entered the state of spiritual marriage on both occasions. The latter ceremony therefore was probably on the occasion of an increase in the

[1] *Les Graces d'Oraison*, xiv. 22.

marriage union already effected. Many, on the other hand, enter this final state of mystic union without any such phenomenal accompaniment. Moreover, a far greater number of souls reach mystical marriage than the minute handful who have received a nuptial vision.[1] Indeed St John of the Cross himself never experienced any such vision.

It is indeed evident that, whatever be their significance and degree of objectivity, such sensible or imaginary phenomena are but symbols of a spiritual reality, which reality is, as we have seen, by no means identical wherever there is identity of external symbolism. Nuptial symbolism is, moreover, of more frequent occurrence in the case of feminine than of masculine mystics, and is at least in part conditioned by the natural character of the recipient soul. Souls inclined to represent their spiritual experience by sensible images are more likely subjects of such visions than others of a less imaginative type. For although these visions are by no means wholly subjective, they postulate, like similar phenomena, the co-operation of a certain subjective disposition in their recipient. The true mystical marriage is a purely spiritual union effected in the very centre of the soul, a region far removed from sense-derived images.

We must also keep in mind that, since the term marriage is itself a symbol derived from the world of sense, it can be applied to various degrees of the soul's union with God. Fr. Terrien, S.J., devotes to this matter the fifth chapter of the fifth book of his theology of sanctifying grace, *La Grace et la Gloire*. He there points out that the nuptial symbol is justly applicable and is, in fact, applied to (1) the union of the Church as a whole with Christ ; (2) the union with Christ of every soul in the state of grace ; (3) the special union of virgins with Christ and in particular of nuns ; (4) the spiritual marriage of the mystics. To these we may add the sacramental union of the communicant with the Sacred Humanity, to which, as Fr. Terrien points out in a later chapter, the nuptial symbolism has also been applied. Fr. Terrien enumerates the characters which justify the use of this symbol to describe the union with Christ of every soul in a state of grace. We should observe that these characters are common *in different degrees and modes* to all the unions enumerated above. They are (1) mutual love—that is, union of wills ; (2) fidelity, an indissolubility either

---

[1] Dr Imbert, according to Père Poulain (*loc. cit.*), enumerates seventy-seven instances of these bridal visions.

relative or absolute ; and (3) fruitfulness—that is the production of supernatural works, indeed of a supernatural life. It is therefore plain that the mere use of nuptial terminology and images is insufficient to determine the nature of the spiritual union thus described.

After these two preliminary warnings there is another question that must be solved before we enter on our inquiry into the nature of mystical marriage—namely, the question who in this marriage is the bridegroom of the soul. Hitherto we have spoken of union between the soul and God. Fr. Terrien, as we saw, speaks of the union between the soul and Christ. Indeed St Paul constantly speaks of the grace-union as a union with Christ, a participation of Christ's life, an incorporation into Christ's body, a life in Christ.* It is, however, evident that in mystical marriage the bridegroom is not the Sacred Humanity, the man Christ Jesus. It may be that the union is ushered in by a symbolical marriage ceremony with Jesus, but the union itself is not directly referable to Him as man. For the Sacred Humanity is as we know present only in heaven and in the Most Blessed Sacrament. Therefore it is not present in the soul of the mystic.[1] Indeed it is impossible that His body could be present in the soul, and His soul is never where His body is not, for they are inseparable. The mystics do, however, often speak of the spiritual marriage as contracted with the Second Person of the Trinity, the Divine Word. In the *Spiritual Canticle* the Bridegroom is regarded as the Word—that is, Christ in His Godhead—and to this state St John applies the texts of St Paul : " I live, now not I but *Christ* liveth in me " and " He that cleaveth to the Lord " (Jesus Christ) " is one spirit." [2] Other passages, however, speak of union with the Holy Ghost [3] or with the Blessed Trinity. Sister Gertrude Mary speaks of a special union with the Word, and also of a special union with the Holy Ghost. Mother Cecilia speaks more generally of God. We may surely draw the conclusion that the Bridegroom is the Trinity—the one God in three Persons. It is a maxim of theology that the Persons of the Trinity have everything in common save the relations which constitute their personal

---

[1] The singular opinion of Cardinal Cienfuegos that the human Soul of Jesus is habitually present in the soul of the communicant is surely as untenable as it is universally rejected.

[2] *E.g., Living Flame*, st. 1.

[3] *Spiritual Canticle*, st. 22.

distinction, and that therefore every Divine operation whose term or end is a creature—that is, a term external to the Godhead—is common to the three Persons. But the union of the soul with God through grace is a Divine work whose term is the created soul, hence this work in all its degrees and modes must be common to the three Persons of the Trinity.[1] It is therefore the Triune God Who is the Bridegroom in the mystical marriage. If St John and others seem to refer that union especially to the Second Person, the reason is twofold. In the first place, the Sacred Humanity that is one person with the Word is the cause and in a large degree the means whereby that union has been attained by the soul; and, moreover, the closer our union with God, the closer are we united, though in a different and less intimate fashion, with the Humanity that is in hypostatical union with God. Indeed it is in virtue and in measure of our incorporation into the mystical body of the Word Incarnate and Glorified that we are united with God in the union of grace and mystical experience, so that the measure of our supernatural union with God is the measure of our union with Christ and our incorporation into His Body. The other reason for this appropriation is that the Word in virtue of His procession from the Divine self-understanding is the manifestation and representation of God (" the express image of His Person "). In this transforming union the mystic possesses a special consciousness of God which may be regarded as His manifestation and representation in the soul, though indeed it is a consciousness of the Godhead possessed in common by the three Persons. Therefore, regarded under this aspect, the union is appropriated to the Word, as it is to the Holy Ghost under its aspect of will-union. Consequently when St John is regarding mystical marriage in its aspect of intuition he refers it to the Word; when, however, he has chiefly in view the will-union he refers it to the Holy Ghost. That the Blessed Trinity is the true Bridegroom of this nuptial union is indeed stated explicitly in *The Living Flame*. " We should not regard it as incredible . . . that the promise of the Son of God should be accomplished in this life in a faithful soul—namely, that if any man should love Him, the

[1] Petavius, however, postulated a special union with the Holy Spirit. The contrary is the opinion most generally received by theologians. Nevertheless the language of Scripture does seem in favour of the Petavian doctrine. Perhaps the real difference is unimportant. When the Holy Ghost inhabits the soul the Blessed Trinity inhabits it—whether or no the inhabitation be in its mode effected through the Third Person as such.

U

Most Holy Trinity would enter into that soul, and would dwell within it, by a divine illumination of the understanding in the wisdom of the Son, a delectation of the will in the Holy Ghost, and a powerful and mighty absorption of the soul itself in the abyss of the Father's sweetness " (*Living Flame*, st. 1). If possible, even clearer is the following passage :—" The soul explains that the Three Persons of the Most Holy Trinity, the Father, Son and Holy Ghost, are they who accomplish in the soul this Divine work of union.   Therefore the hand, the wound and the touch are in substance one and the same thing, and these names are only employed to express effects peculiar to each.   The wound is the Holy Ghost, the hand is the Father, and the touch is the Son.   Thus the soul magnifies the Father, the Son and the Holy Ghost, by extolling these three great graces and gifts which they accomplish in it, in that they have changed its death into life, by transforming it into Themselves."   He proceeds to explain that the wound is love—the will-union ; the touch is a taste of the Divine Wisdom, the intuition of the consciousness, and the hand is the transformation of the central substance or ego out of its natural selfhood to be henceforward a recipient and participator of the infinite Godhead.   He then concludes : " Although the Three Persons are here referred to severally on account of the special properties of these three effects, the soul addresses itself to the Unity, saying *Thou* hast changed it into life, for the Three Divine Persons co-operate, and so the entire operation is attributed to Each and to All " (*Living Flame*, st. 2).

For further explanation of this appropriation I refer the reader to Fr. Terrien's work on grace,[1] or indeed to any theological text-book.   Suffice it here to realise that whatever the language of St John or other mystics may at times suggest, the mystical marriage is quite simply a state of extraordinary union between the soul and God—the one Godhead in three Persons.

When the mystics such as St John and Mother Cecilia treat of spiritual marriage, they describe it chiefly by means of similes or by the use of expressions susceptible of very various inter-pretations.   It is only by comparison of one simile with another, and of one expression with another, that a certain more or less definite notion arises in the mind.   This notion is not indeed an apprehension of what the mystical marriage is, as a conscious state of spiritual experience, but an external indication of the

[1] Book V., chap. i.

relationship between the soul and God which effects and conditions that experience. I will try to state what the notion is which has risen in my mind after careful study of the descriptions given by St John and by Mother Cecilia. From that standpoint I will proceed to examine the language of St John and Mother Cecilia by which that notion was originally suggested to me. My notion is this. The mystical marriage or transforming union is a state of habitual possession by God of the centre of the soul—that is, the root of the will and cognition, especially the root of the will —together with an habitual consciousness of the presence of God in the centre of the soul, and of his possession of that centre.[1]

When this habitual union is realised in act, that act is a Divine influx into or motion of the central functions of the soul, volition, cognition and their concomitant affection from the centre of which He is in habitual possession. The effect of that influx and motion is that, while the transforming union is thus in act, the activities of the soul subject to this influx and motion are receptacles of the Divine activity, which is God Himself, so that the soul partakes in this activity. Its volition is then the Divine volition received by its volition, its cognition is similarly the Divine self-knowledge received in its cognition, though this participation is of necessity veiled so long as this bodily life continues. As the transforming union increases, as it does increase indefinitely till death, it comes ever more frequently and more powerfully into act. Previously to the transforming union the Divine operation upon the activities of the soul was external to them. Now God acts in and through them. For henceforward these activities are, when the union is in act, participations or receptions of the Divine operation. Previously to the mystical marriage there was no habitual possession of the centre [2] by God and therefore no habitual consciousness of that possession—that is to say, no habitual consciousness of His possessing Presence in

---

[1] According to Père Poulain, an habitual consciousness of the Divine Presence may precede the Transforming union. He instances St Teresa (*Les Graces d'Oraison*, p. 22). If this be the case, this habitual consciousness would be, however, a consciousness of God's presence to the centre, not of His intrinsic possession of the centre as the new principle of the soul's life, in the manner described in the text. St John, however, seems to teach that an habitual sense of God's presence is confined to mystical marriage (*sup*. 39).

[2] There was, of course, an " habitual presence " in the centre. Owing, however, to the limiting selfhood that presence was not a possession, as now when that resistant limit has been removed.

the very ground of the psychical life. Now, however, this consciousness is habitually present. If in the prayer of quiet the presence of the Beloved in the dark chamber was felt, if in ecstasy His hand was grasped, in mystical marriage He is enfolded in a close and continuous embrace. I also figure the transforming union by the following image. The centre of the soul is filled with God like a reservoir full of water, for its capacity has been emptied of selfhood by the antecedent purgation. When the transforming union is in act the flood-gates of this reservoir are opened and the Divine water pours out and fills the channels, the activities or functions of the soul. The sole reason why the union is not always in act is a certain dependence of the soul on the body and occupation by the bodily activities which survives the destruction of the internal barrier of selfhood effected in the night of spirit. To this habitual possession and its transient acts Mother Cecilia refers when she says : " The faculties are already divinised in habit, and in act they are often divinised " (*Trans.*, st. 6). The faculties are habitually divinised by God's felt possession of their root, actually when their entire activity is the reception of His. When the more external activities supervene, the Divine possession is only felt at the root of consciousness and will, always, however, ready to fill both functions of the centre now thus consciously God-possessed. This difference between the continuous union and its transient though increasingly frequent acts is laid down by St John. "Though the soul," he says, " be always in the high estate of marriage ever since God has placed it there, nevertheless actual union in all its powers is not continuous, though the substantial union is. In this substantial union, however, the powers of the soul are very frequently in union and drink of this cellar, the understanding by knowledge, the will by love and so forth. We are not, therefore, to suppose that the soul, when it says that it went out, has ceased from the substantial union " (*i.e.* the conscious union in the substance of the soul or central ego), " but only from the union of its faculties, which is not and cannot be continuous in this life " (*Spiritual Canticle*, st. 26). This distinction, however, between the habitual state and its acts is not so clear in every passage in his writings. It is very often difficult to tell whether a description applies to the habitual state or to its actualisation. Indeed both are often treated together as constituting the complete union. Even when the union is not in act, in principle the life or activity of the soul is Divinely possessed and Divinely moved, and is thus a reception and participation of the Divine life or activity that is of the Divine Being. Moreover, as the acts of union grow more frequent, the Divine possession of the soul becomes more complete, though in principle effected since the first entrance of the soul into the transforming union. Because the life of the soul now proceeds from God operating in and through its life, it is a participation of the Divine life thus lived within it.*

St John and Mother Cecilia speak of this union as a transformation of the soul " *en Dios.*" The preposition *en* may mean in or into. In my opinion it is by the latter that it should here be rendered. The soul is transformed into God because its life is a participation of His, because its natural and therefore essentially limited activity has been destroyed (save for certain sensible functions which must endure so long as life lasts) and has been replaced by a reception of His unlimited activity. Everything that I have said is scant by comparison with the strong expressions used by our authors to describe the identification of the soul's interior life with God present and operative in the soul. The spiritual marriage, writes St John, " *is a complete transformation into the Beloved : whereby they surrender each to the other the entire possession of themselves* together with a certain consummation of the union of love " (*Spiritual Canticle*, st. 22).

The soul's consciousness of the Divine possession of its centre and of the Divine life proceeding thence to be its own life is thus expressed by St John. The soul " usually feels that it embraces " the Bridegroom " so closely that it is in truth an embrace by means whereof the soul lives the life of God. . . . And now that the soul lives a life so happy and so glorious as this life of God, what a sweet life it must be—a life wherein God sees nothing displeasing, and where the soul finds nothing irksome, but rather tastes and feels the glory and delight of God in the very substance of itself now transformed into Him " (*Spiritual Canticle*, st. 22). " We may say in truth," he writes in another passage, " that such a soul is clothed in God, and bathed in the Divinity, and that not as it were on the surface but in the interior spirit, being clad in the Divine delights in the abundance of the spiritual waters of life. . . . This fulness will be of the very being of the soul " (*Spiritual Canticle*, st. 25). " As a draught diffuses itself through all the members and veins of the body, so this communication of God diffuses itself substantially in the whole soul, or rather, the

soul is transformed into God. In this transformation the soul
drinks of God in its substance and in its spiritual faculties "
(*Spiritual Canticle*, st. 26). St John is here evidently speaking
of the habitual union and its acts as one complete union.

Elsewhere he writes : " In that soul wherein abides no desire,
neither images, nor forms nor affection for any created object,
the Beloved dwells most secretly, and the purer the soul and the
greater its estrangement from everything but God, the closer and
more intimate is His embrace. This dwelling is secret, because
neither the devil nor the human intelligence can attain to this
place and embrace, so as to have knowledge of its nature. *But in
this state of perfection the Divine presence is not a secret to the soul
itself, for that soul enjoys a perpetual sense of this intimate embrace.*
. . . The Beloved is usually as it were asleep in this embrace
of the bride, in the substance of the soul, and the soul has usually
a strong sense and enjoyment of His presence " (*Living Flame*,
st. 4).

Moreover, this habitual consciousness of the Divine presence
in the centre is in this passage expressly distinguished from
the acts of the Divine union which St John calls " awakenings "
of God in the soul.   He then proceeds : " The soul, however, is not
always conscious of these awakenings, for when the Beloved effects
them, it seems to the soul that He is awaking in her bosom, where
before He was, as it were, asleep, so that although the soul felt
and enjoyed His presence, He seemed to be asleep. When,
however, either of the two parties is asleep, the mutual communication of knowledge and love ceases, until both have
awakened " (*Living Flame*, st. 4). This passage also explains
the acts of union, the awakenings, as Divine motions in the understanding and will proceeding from God, felt as inhabiting and
possessing the centre—that is, the root and ground of these cognitive
and conative functions. Moreover, St John proceeds to point
out that this habitual sense of the central Presence is the dis-
tinguishing characteristic of this supreme state of union, whereas
in earlier stages souls " do not ordinarily feel the Presence of God,
but only when He effects certain sweet awakenings, which,
however, are not of the same kind with those already described "
(the acts of the transforming union), " neither indeed are com-
parable with them " (*Living Flame*, st. 4).[1] To this continuous
sense of the Divine possession of the centre may be referred the

---

[1] See, however, p. 315, note.

words of Mother Cecilia : " Now that the soul's battle is over "
(*i.e.* its purgation is complete), " its centre is glorified by the
continuous touches of God's substance. . . . Even if the soul suffer
severe pains in its lower part, these pains are destroyed by the
substance of God within it " (*Trans.*, st. 3). The soul has thus
finally reached an abiding condition of transformation wherein
" its substance is bathed in the living water of God " (*Trans.*, st. 2).
" Now the soul beholds the Holy One of Israel present in its
centre" (*Trans.*, st. 4).

" The soul," says Mother Cecilia, " now sees that its centre is
living in the life of God. The impetuous force that proceeds
from this Divine life (in whose immensity the soul is grounded
with a Divine tranquillity in this life wherein it lives and is transformed) occasions it a glorious satisfaction in the presence and
fruition of its Beloved, to which it can give no other name, save
this of its desired end, for it is the most infinite good that could
be desired " (*Trans.*, st. 8). " The soul, or rather its better and
more substantial part—namely, its essence " (the centre)—" is
filled with and transformed into this Divine substance and force,
that has consumed and changed it into Himself " (*Trans.*, st. 11).
" The most powerful and infinite Deity bathes the centre of the
soul which He now keeps in Himself " (st. 16). " The soul beholds
its centre united and satisfied with the very substance of God "
(*Union*).

This conscious possession of the centre by God is the cause of a
permanent peace in this state which excludes the spiritual sufferings hitherto experienced. St John indeed in *The Living Flame*
says distinctly that " the soul is now incapable of suffering "
(st. 1). On the other hand, in the thirty-ninth stanza of the
Spiritual Canticle he tells us that in this life the soul " still
suffers, in some measure both pain and harm." There is no reconciliation of these contradictory statements in the writings of
St John. For this we must turn to Mother Cecilia. There we
find several passages which inform us that suffering is now confined to the lower part of the soul, and is unable to disturb the
peace of the centre in its continuous enjoyment of God's presence,
so that the central ego is now free from suffering, although the
lower and more exterior functions of the soul still suffer. " Even
if the soul suffer severe pains in the lower part, those pains are
destroyed by the substance of God within it " (*Trans.*, st. 3).
" It is the lower part of the soul that suffers. The centre is always

calm in this state " (st. 6). " The soul is fixed in God as in its true centre, wherein it is lost and absorbed, and therefore that peace admits no disturbance. When trouble or suffering occurs in the lower part, this central peace absorbs that pain into itself with such sweetness and strength that it passes away like a shadow " (st. 8). " In the exterior and lower parts the soul does not cease to suffer pain. The central substance, however . . . does not feel pain. . . . If the soul feels any pain, it is . . . in the inferior part alone, and it is very speedily consumed by the superior part " (st. 10). This co-existence of peace and joy in the centre with suffering in the lower functions is exemplified in the last illness of St Catherine of Genoa. With her the external torment seems to have been the normal occasion of an increased central joy (Baron von Hügel, *Mystical Element*, vol. i., p. 199). Moreover, these sufferings of the lower functions or faculties are now no longer purgatorial, but entirely expiatory of the sins of others, as were those of Our Immaculate Lady. Indeed this expiatory suffering has at times been permitted by special dispensation of God to attain the central ego and to over-cloud its peace and its consciousness of the Divine presence. Although this is not hinted either by St John or Mother Cecilia, it is evident both from the compassion of Our Lady and from the lives of certain victims of expiation who had indubitably been raised to the state of mystical marriage. An instance of this is the death-bed dereliction of Gemma Galgani.[1] This exception, however, is far from disproving the general truth of Mother Cecilia's teaching of the peace and freedom from pain enjoyed by the central ego in virtue of its continuous fruition of the Divine presence.

The efflux of this Divine presence and operation in the centre into the central functions of the soul, which constitutes the act of the transforming union, is clearly stated by St John. " As a draught," he says, " diffuses itself through all the members and veins of the body, so this communication of God diffuses itself substantially into the whole soul. . . . In this transformation the soul drinks of God in its substance and in its spiritual faculties. In the understanding it drinks wisdom and knowledge, in the will the sweetest love, in the memory refreshment and delight in the recollection and sense of its glory " (*Cant.*, st. 26). This Divine efflux is, if possible, even more clearly expressed by Mother Cecilia.

---

[1] *Life*, pp. 344-348.

" The soul," she tells us, " that now lives in this Divine life feels in a very special manner that a stream of life is proceeding from its centre. It sees that this stream of life springs from the substance of God (Who is the life of the centre) and flows down into the faculties and lower part, which enjoy a ray of that hidden life that is within itself " (*Trans.*, st. 4). " The flood of glory received from God in the centre spreads and extends itself to the lowest part " (st. 15). " When God penetrates the essence of the soul there issues from His very Being eternal and infinite a ray of light, or surge of water (though it is really neither of these, but the very Being of God), which transfuses the soul. . . . The soul has a sweet sense that this ray is piercing through it with a gentle movement, issuing, it would seem, from its very centre, which is grounded in God. . . . From time to time God makes this motion like a surge of water flowing forth from a reservoir, a ray proceeding from the sun or the sweet perfume that is smelt when a vial of fragrant liquid is stirred. The mighty God, Who dwells in the centre of the soul, effects this movement, and from the centre it spreads to the extremities. This most powerful and infinite Deity bathes the centre of the soul, which He now keeps in Himself, and issuing from thence He bathes the entire soul and body. . . . The entire Being is bathed by the Being of God ; while this Divine ray of the Deity endures, it fills the entire soul and body " (st. 16). " That which God communicates to the essence of the soul overflows to its higher part and proceeds from thence to the lower part and to the body " (*Union*).

Thus when the act of this union attains its utmost fulness and power the entire soul, even in its lower functions, is filled and impelled by the Divine influx. At other times, however, during the act of this union the Divine influx fills the higher functions of the soul alone and leaves the lower body-informing functions in their natural operation. When this is the case the soul has the experience of a double life, almost of a double personality.[1] Its higher life or activity, now God-informed and God-impelled, seems to be cut off from its lower life. " The higher and lower portions of the soul," says St John, " seem to it . . . to be so far apart that it recognises two parts in itself, each so distinct from the other that neither seems to have anything in common with the other, being

---

[1] This is not to be confused with the rare pathological condition of double personality when there exist two apparently distinct egos or selves in one person with no conscious link between them.

in appearance so far removed and apart. And in reality this is, in a certain manner, true, for in its present operation, which is wholly spiritual, it has no commerce with the sensual part" (*Dark Night*, ii. 23). This experience is mentioned by Blessed Angela of Foligno, who says: "I saw in me two parts, as if a division had been made in me, and on one side I saw love and all good that was from God and not from me, and on the other I saw myself dry and that from myself there was no good thing" (*Visions and Instructions*, chap. xxv., p. 81).[1]

At the opening of *The Living Flame* St John returns to his favourite simile of fuel and fire, which he has already used to illustrate the action of the second night, to illustrate now the distinction between the habitual transforming union and its acts, which acts increase indefinitely, both in frequency and in intensity. "The flame of love," he writes, " is the spirit of the Bridegroom, that is the Holy Ghost, Whom the soul now feels within itself, not only as a fire that holds it consumed and transformed in sweet love, but as a fire which, beyond this, burns within it and darts forth a flame. . . . Whenever that flame shoots forth it bathes the soul in glory, and refreshes it with the temper of Divine life. . . . The difference between the transformation in love and the flame of love *is that between habit and act*, and is like the difference between burning wood and the flame it emits, for the flame is an effect of the fire that is present in the wood. We can therefore say of the soul in this state of transformation of love that this transformation is its ordinary habit, and that it is like wood which is continuously in the fire, and that its acts are the flame, begotten of the fire of love, which darts forth with a vehemence proportionate to the intensity of the fire of union" (*Living Flame*, st. 1). This divine activity outflowing from the centre through the psychical functions is, as we have seen, received by these functions in such wise that their activities are rendered divine, because they are now receptions or participations of the Divine activity infused into them. This doctrine of the deification of the

---

[1] See also *Spiritual Journal* of Lucie Christine, ed. Poulain, Eng. trs., p. 47. This experience was, however, undoubtedly given before the transforming union. The same phenomenon was produced in this and in like instances by a similar but not identical cause—namely, the transient seizure of the central powers by God as it were *ab extra*, as distinguished from His internal efflux from the continuously possessed centre that occurs in the act of the transforming union.

higher and more interior activities of the soul [1] by their reception of the Divine activity is distinctly affirmed in many passages by St John of the Cross and Mother Cecilia.

In the third stanza of *The Living Flame* St John says that the virtues and attributes of the soul are those of God Himself, only in a shadow, because the soul's comprehension of God is imperfect. At the very opening of this book we read that " In this state the soul cannot make acts, but the Holy Ghost effects them all and moves the soul to them. Hence all the acts of the soul are Divine, because the soul is moved and operated by God " (*Flame*, st. 1). And elsewhere he says, speaking of the intuitional element of the act of union, " the soul is renewed and *moved* by God to behold this supernatural sight " (*Flame*, st. 4). Of the divinisation or deification of the understanding—that is, of the intuition—Mother Cecilia speaks thus : " When the understanding and natural reason have passed away . . . the things of God are understood supernaturally above all understanding and above all reason " (*Union*). " The Beloved infuses into the soul *certain rays of the Divine Being* which make the soul resplendent with their life, sanctity and beauty. In this . . . mutual vision, wherein the two lovers are contemplating each other, the soul sees the beauty of the Beloved. *Its understanding does not form this vision* to which the soul cannot attain, though it receives as much light and knowledge as its capacity suffers. It is raised to a supernatural condition that it *may be made Divine and may understand after a Divine manner* " (*Transformation*, st. 11). And again : " The understanding . . . now understands *divinely*, since the former *human* mode of understanding has passed away " (*Transformation*, st. 6). These passages, however, fail to explain clearly in what this new divine understanding and love consist. A clearer explanation is to be found in the passages that will now be cited. In the second stanza of *The Living Flame* is to be found a passage already quoted in which St John tells us that the soul has mortified—that is, has put to death—its entire nature and that as the result of this its operations and affections have been rendered divine. St John proceeds to explain and emphasise this deification. " The understanding," he says, " that previously to this union understood naturally by the force and vigour of its

---

[1] The lower activities cannot of their nature be thus divinised, being corporeal in their dependence and reference. Their participation in the Divine Union is therefore but a sensible sweetness.

natural light through the bodily senses, is now moved and *informed* by another and a far higher principle, God's supernatural light wherein the senses have no part. The understanding has now therefore been rendered divine, since in virtue of this union the understanding of the soul and that of God are all one. The will also which formerly loved after a mean and dead fashion with its natural affection is now changed into a life of divine love, because it now loves after a sublime fashion *with a divine affection*, moved by the force and power of the Holy Ghost in Whom it lives now a life of love, since by virtue of this union the soul's will and the will of the Spirit are one sole will. . . . The natural desire that once possessed only capacity and strength to taste the sweetness of the creature that works death is now changed into a Divine taste and sweetness, moved and satisfied henceforward by another principle . . . because it is united with God, and it is therefore now solely the desire of God. In fine, all the motions and operations and inclinations which sprung formerly from the principle and force of the soul's natural life are now in this union changed into divine motions dead to their own operation and inclination and alive in God. For the soul . . . is now wholly moved by the Spirit of God. Hence . . . the understanding of such a soul is the understanding of God, its will the will of God, its memory the eternal memory of God, and its delight the delight of God. Moreover, the substance of such a soul, although it is not the substance of God, since it cannot be substantially converted into Him, nevertheless since it is thus united with Him and absorbed into Him, is God by participation of God." In this passage a distinction is drawn between the substance of the soul, which is not and cannot be changed into God, and its functions or activities, which are changed into His operations. If that change had been understood by St John in some unreal or restricted sense, this distinction would lose its point, for as this very passage affirms, there is a sense in which the substance may be said to be God—namely, by union and absorption. The meaning of this absorption will be discussed later. The truth to be realised at present is that although the substance may be truly said to become God, that is only in a restricted and non-literal sense, whereas in contradistinction to the substance the deification of the activities or functions is affirmed without qualification. The essence of this deification is, that whereas the activities proceeded formerly from a natural principle, they are now actuated and informed by God.

But an activity that proceeds from God as its principle is a Divine activity or operation. Therefore these activities or operations of the soul are Divine activities received in the soul. This is confirmed by the words of Mother Cecilia's *Treatise on the Union of the Soul with God.* " By this death in God," she writes, " wherein the soul dies to all its knowledge, consciousness, understanding and love, God becomes the life of the soul. He is now wisdom in the soul making her supernaturally wise, consciousness whereby the soul is conscious of itself in Him, not in its own self-consciousness. . . . He is love also in the soul wherewith it loves. These souls therefore love God . . . with the very love of Him Whom they love which He infuses into them." " Blessed," she exclaims, " is the soul that understands God with His own understanding, because He grants it His own understanding wherewith to understand Him. Blessed is the soul that loves God with His own love, because He grants it His own love wherewith to love Him." Again, in the thirty-eighth stanza of the *Spiritual Canticle*, St John says that in heaven " The understanding of the soul will be the understanding of God and its will the will of God," and " its love will be His love," for the soul will then love God " with the will and strength of God Himself, being made one with the very strength of love wherewith itself is loved of God." He proceeds to add that " in the perfect transformation . . . of the state of spiritual marriage . . . *the soul loves in a certain way through the Holy Ghost* "—that is, the principle from which her acts of love proceed is the Holy Ghost. In the following stanza he says that the soul in heaven will " breathe in God the same aspiration of love which the Father breathes with the Son, and the Son with the Father, which is the Holy Ghost Himself, Who is breathed into the soul in the Father and the Son in that transformation so as to unite it to Himself." He adds that even on earth the soul " united with God and transformed into Him breathes in God to God that very divine aspiration which God breathes in Himself to the soul when it is transformed into Him. . . . The blessed in the life to come and the perfect in this thus experience it." In other words, the deification of the activities of the soul in spiritual marriage is identical in principle with the deification of the activities of the souls blessed in heaven, since the former is the beginning of the latter. " Nor," proceeds St John, " is it to be thought impossible that the soul should be capable of so great a thing as that it should breathe in God, as God in it, in the way of participation. For, granted that

God has bestowed upon it so great favour as to unite it to the most Holy Trinity . . . is it something incredible that it should exercise the operation of its understanding, its knowledge and its love, or, to speak more accurately, *should have it all done* in the Holy Trinity together with It, as the Holy Trinity Itself ?   This takes place by *communication and participation*, God Himself effecting it in the soul, for this is to be transformed in the Three Persons in power, wisdom and love." The soul, Mother Cecilia tells us, knows God " by a Divine experience " and "participation of His Divine Being." " It is a certain participation of His Divine Substance " (I have termed it of His activity. In God both are one and the same thing), " of that same substance which in heaven is beheld openly " (*Trans.*, st. 12).

Antonius of the Holy Ghost, a later mystical theologian of this same Carmelite school, tells us that "the soul does not so much act as *receive*, though certainly it gives its consent. It does not so much behold and love as *find in itself* that very intuition most glorious, and love most ardent of God " (*Directorium Mysticum*, Tract 4, Disp. 1, sec. 2). Elsewhere he says that the transformation of the soul into God is effected "through an expulsion of its own nature in a perfect (full) participation of the Divine Nature by an extraordinary gift of sanctifying grace and in a participation of the Divine Understanding by a sublime light of contemplation and of the Divine Will by most fervent love " (Tract 4, Disp. 4, sec. 4).

This "receptionist" explanation of the union of mystical marriage and a fortiori of the beatific vision has surely been sufficiently established by the explicit affirmations of St John and of Mother Cecilia. It may, however, appear to some of my readers so pantheistic that they will at once reject it as unorthodox. Indeed Fr. Terrien in his treatment of the beatific vision (*La Grace et la Gloire*, Bk. IX., chap. iii.) rejects as pantheistic in tendency the doctrine that in the beatific vision God's own vision of Himself is participated by the saints (p. 167). But in his explanation of the nature of sanctifying grace in the first volume he insists that grace is a " permanent and very intimate participation of the Divine nature," as St Peter tells us, " by grace we are made *divinæ naturæ consortes* [partakers of the Divine nature] " (Bk. II., chap ii). This participation is then explained by Fr. Terrien as a participation in the operations proper to God alone, as their first principle, and of which therefore no creature can be the first principle. The Divine Operation wherein we thus participate is, he tells us, here expounding the common teaching of the fathers, schoolmen and theologians, the Divine self-knowledge or self-vision—a vision which of ourselves we cannot, being creatures, possess. This participated vision to which we have access through grace alone is further declared to be " a radiation that takes place within ourselves from that which is highest, most intimate, most deep and most naturally incommunicable in the Divine Substance." I fail to see any real distinction between this teaching and the participation-vision which he condemns elsewhere.[1] Moreover, if the Divine self-vision is thus communicated to the soul and received in its consciousness, His self-love must similarly be communicated to the soul and received in the will, for between God's self-vision and self-love there is no real distinction. Again, since the Divine Substance is one with the Divine self-vision and self-love, that substance itself must be communicated to and received in the soul. Surely receptionism is thus deducible from the principle laid down by its seeming opponent.

Nor is the receptionist explanation of mystical marriage confined to the Spanish school of mysticism. It is, on the contrary, to be found in mystical writers of all places and periods. From the vast mass of possible testimony I can only quote a few representative statements of very diverse provenance, which will, however, amply prove the universality of receptionism. The participation and reception of the Godhead by the soul is affirmed very clearly of the intuitional element of the union in a locution spoken by Our Lord to the Ven Battista Vernazza, quoted by Baron von Hügel (*Mystical Element*, vol. i., pp. 356-357). " I generate My Son, having an infinite cognition of Myself ; similarly I generate thee, *by infusing into thee that same cognition*. But (this) My cognition is without measure ; and thine shall be according to that measure which I shall by My goodness be impelled to give thee, in such wise that of this cognition and of thine intellect there shall be

---

[1] Fr. Terrien may have meant to condemn *only* the identification of the participated vision with the *lumen gloriæ* (an identification, however, expressly taught by Antonius a Spiritu Sanctu : *Directorium Mysticum*, Tract 3, Dist. 4, sec. 5). He identifies, however, this " radiation " with created grace and so speaks of an "*écoulément crée de cette nature incréée*"—" a created emanation of the Uncreated Nature." This expression seems a contradiction in terms. Surely created grace is not the " participation of the Divine Nature," but merely the ground and principle of that participation inhering in the nature of the participator.

effected one identical thing; so that I shall place My Word, My Concept, which I possess within Myself in thee, according to that capacity for it which I shall deign to give thee; and so that, again, thy spirit shall be a son within My Son, or rather one only son with Him. Thus shall I have Generated thee." Though this statement is directly concerned only with the intuition, it is obvious that the principle it affirms is applicable to the entire union.

From the Netherlands Ruysbroeck teaches the same doctrine. "All the powers of the soul," he says, "must give way, and they must suffer and patiently endure that piercing Truth and Goodness *which is God's self*" (*Book of Supreme Truth*, chap. viii., trs. Wynschenk Dom). "Their bare understanding is drenched through by the eternal Brightness, even as the air is drenched through by the sunshine. And the bare uplifted will is transformed and drenched through by abysmal love, even as iron is by fire" (*Supreme Truth*, chap. xi). "He feels God within himself . . . as the quickening health of his being and all his works" (*Supreme Truth*, chap. vi). "All our powers fail us and we fall from ourselves into our wide-opened contemplation and become all One and one All in the loving embrace of the Threefold Unity. Whenever we feel this union" (the transforming union in act) "we are one being, and one life and one blessedness with God" (*The Sparkling Stone*, chap. xii). "In the transformation within the Unity all spirits fail in their own activity, and feel nothing else but a burning up of themselves in the simple Unity of God. . . . In this transcendent state the spirit feels in itself the eternal fire of love . . . and it feels itself one with this fire of love. . . . If it observes itself, it finds a distinction and an otherness between itself and God; but *where it is burnt up*" (in the Divine influx constitutive of the act of this supreme union) "it is undifferentiated and without distinction, and therefore it feels nothing but unity : for the flame of the love of God consumes and devours all that it can enfold in itself. . . . Through this intimate feeling of union" the soul "feels itself to be melting into the Unity : and, through dying to all things, into the life of God. And then it feels itself to be one life with God" (*Sparkling Stone*, chap. iii). "All those men who are raised up above their created being into a God-seeing life are one with this Divine Brightness, and they are that Brightness itself, and they see . . . by means of this Divine light" (*Adornment of the Spiritual Marriage*, Bk. III., chap iii).

" Every creaturely work . . . must here cease, for here God
works alone in the high nobility of the spirit . . . the spirit itself
becomes that Breadth which it grasps. And God is grasped and
beheld through God " (*Spiritual Marriage*, Bk. III., chap. ii).
" The spirit receives the Brightness which is God Himself, above
. . . every creaturely activity. The loving contemplative . . .
finds himself, and feels himself, to be that same Light by which
he sees " (*Spiritual Marriage*, Bk. III., chap. i).

The entire union must therefore consist essentially in this
reception of the unlimited activity, life and being (all are one) of
God, by and in the activities, life and substance of the soul. " The
detached man," says Suso (*Autobiography*, trs. Knox, p. 220),
" must consider the presence of the all-penetrating Divine essence
in Him and that *He is one of its vessels*." Here we have at least
the underlying principle of receptionism. And again : " In this
merging of itself in God the spirit passes away, and yet not wholly,
for it receives indeed some attributes of the Godhead " (p. 245).
" When the spirit has passed out of itself . . . there shines forth
out of the Unity a simple light, and this light streams out from the
three Persons into the purity of the spirit. When this light falls
upon the spirit, it sinks down out of itself, and all that belongs to
self ; the activity of all its powers comes to an end " (*i.e.* their
activity is now reception of the Divine influx), " and it is divested
of its operations and its self-existence " (p. 247). " This man"
(the highest mystic) "*finds his created spirit seized upon by the
super-essential Spirit* and drawn into that which it never could
have attained to in its own strength. This entry of the spirit into
God strips it of all images, forms and multiplicity, and it becomes
merged with the three Persons in the abyss of their indwelling
simplicity " (p. 252).

Similar is the language of St Catherine of Genoa. " When,"
she said, " the soul is transformed, then of herself she neither
works nor speaks nor wills nor feels nor hears nor understands,
neither has she of herself the feeling of outward and inward, where
she may move. In all things it is God Who rules and guides her
without the mediation of any creature " (*Vita*, chap. xviii., quoted
by Miss Evelyn Underhill, *Mysticism*, p. 528, who believes it to
be authentic). Certainly authentic are other even more striking
sayings of this Saint. " MY ME," she said, " is God, nor do I
recognise any other Me except my God Himself. God is my Being,
My Me, my Strength, my Beatitude, my Delight. My being is

x

God . . . by a true transformation of my Being." How could receptionism be affirmed more strongly than by sayings such as these ? Turning from the fourteenth century of Suso and Ruysbroeck and St Catherine's fifteenth century to our own days, we find the same receptionism in the saying of Sister Elizabeth of the Trinity, a Pauline mystic of great worth. " I love God with His own love ; it is a double current between Him Who is and her who is not " (*Life*, Eng. trs., p. 83). If the operations of the will are thus receptions of God's love, the other operations of the soul must similarly be receptions of the Divine action. " In heaven," she says again, and this must hold good in an inferior degree of the mystical marriage, " each soul lives no longer its own life, but the life of God. The soul ' reflects ' God's whole Being and is a fathomless abyss into which He can flow and outpour Himself, a crystal through which He can shine and view His own perfections and splendour " (*Life*, p. 96). " I am Elizabeth of the Trinity—that is to say, Elizabeth disappearing, submerged in the Three."

The same receptionism is clearly taught by another modern mystic, Sister Gertrude Mary. " At the end of my prayer," she writes, " I participated by a mysterious communion in the power of the Father, the wisdom of the Son, the goodness and charity of the Holy Ghost. . . . God the Father said to me : ' Participate in the power of the Father. . . . Participate in the wisdom of the Son. . . . Participate in the goodness and the charity of the Holy Ghost ' " (extracts from her *Diary*, pp. 141-142). Even clearer is the language of her greater contemporary, Lucie Christine. " In such happy moments," she writes of the act of this transforming union,[1] " it is no longer I who am there ; it is He. I see myself no longer, I only see Jesus. I am not destroyed, but His life takes possession of me, dominates and absorbs me. . . . I adore Him, but the Divine Action penetrates and transforms my adoration ; *the Divine Being thinks, lives and loves in me*. I live no longer except through Him " (*Spiritual Journal*, Eng. trs., p. 237). " The soul is so one with God in the mystery of union that if, in that passive state, she formulates distinct interior acts, she feels that God penetrates her prayer itself, her prayer is one with Him, *she speaks God* " (p. 259). " It was given my soul to know the effect that this grace operates,

---

[1] Or perhaps of its anticipation in the transient because habitless act of the Betrothal.

which is a veritable passing of the soul in God, the abstraction of her own life to give place to the Divine life " (p. 271). " There is no more Thee nor me, the soul now no longer knows how to distinguish herself from Him Whom she loves ; nothing remains but God alone " (p. 264). " Not only does " God " allow Himself to be seen, He must likewise give Himself to the soul as the eye which sees and the spirit which hears. The soul then feels all her own proper operations suspended and useless and her life itself flows into God where she knows herself no longer, seeing only Him, living through the Father, knowing through the Word, loving through the Holy Ghost " (pp. 305-306).

Such is the witness of mystics chosen, as it were, at random. It is a witness that could be multiplied indefinitely. But, indeed, we need go no further than the prince of Christian mystics, St Paul himself, to find this receptionist teaching. Does not the Apostle declare in the words I have quoted as a text for this chapter, " I live, now not I, but Christ liveth in me " ? In other words, the interior life of St Paul's soul is simply a reception of the Divine life, which is the life of Christ. Elsewhere he tells the Colossians that in Christ "dwelleth all the fulness of the Godhead corporeally. And," he continues, " you are filled in Him "—filled, evidently, with a participation of the fulness of the Godhead that is one Person with Christ.* St Paul, it is true, addresses all Christians in grace and therefore says little or nothing of the especial reception of God in mystical marriage. This union is, however, but the completion of more imperfect receptions granted to all in a state of grace. Therefore the principle of receptionism is truly Pauline, and Sister Elizabeth evidently found the doctrine in his epistles. This interpretation of the Pauline and therefore of Catholic teaching is approved by the emphatic language of Wilhelm and Scannell in their *Manual of Catholic Theology*, and their teaching is but a reproduction of that of the great modern theologian of grace, the German Scheeben. In this *Manual* we read that " in the beatific vision creatures are united to God as intimately as if they were one with Him ; God, as the *principle*, the subject matter and the final object of all their spiritual life, replenishes, *penetrates* and *pervades them* " (p. 494). The beatific vision is, however, as a supernatural union with God, anticipated, though in lesser degree, by the act of the transforming union. Therefore to this act of union may be applied the receptionism so plainly taught in the above-quoted passage.

Moreover, if receptionism be untrue—that is, if the supernatural union between the soul and God through grace and its
fulfilment glory be less than I have understood it to be—the strong
statements of the mystics must be, as indeed Père Poulain actually
terms them (*Les Graces d'Oraison*, chap. xxii), *exaggerations*. But,
as we have seen, it is a commonplace of the mystics that the reality
of their experience immeasurably exceeds any possible verbal
or conceptual interpretation. If, however, their interpretation is
an exaggeration of the true nature of the experience, the exact
contrary is the case. Hence the union experienced must be immeasurably closer, higher and more real than their explanation of
it. Therefore their " receptionist " statement of that union cannot
exceed, but must fall short of, the reality. Receptionism is the
highest conceivable interpretation short of a pantheistic identification of the soul and God which would destroy the Divine
transcendence and would deprive the entire mystical process of
its significance and worth, since that process would end in the
annihilation of its subject. Therefore the receptionist interpretation is the least inadequate explanation of the inconceivable
reality of the supreme union between the soul and God, or, more
truly, the only adequate interpretation, because it is itself so inadequately comprehensible.

Scheeben cites from Goudin a most important passage in
which he insists that the promise of Scripture that we shall be
made partakers of the Divine Nature is to be understood in the
strictest sense. " The words," he says, " wherein God declares
His gifts to us are not to be understood as hyperbolical language "
(exaggerations), " expressing more than the reality of which they
speak. On the contrary, we must firmly believe that the reality
is in excess of its verbal expression. If, however, grace were not
a proper and physical participation of the Divine Nature, but
merely a moral participation, the words quoted above, in which
the worth of grace is declared to be such that it constitutes its
possessors partakers of the Divine Nature and sons of God, would
obviously be an exaggeration and true only when understood not
in their proper sense, but only in an improper and less real sense.
Hence grace is not merely a moral participation of the Divine
Nature, but a participation in the strict sense of the term
and therefore a physical participation " (*Dogmatik*, French
trs., vol. iii., p. 476, translated by myself). Thus not only the
language of the mystics but the very words of Scripture itself

are a misleading exaggeration, unless receptionism be true. Receptionism, therefore, far from being a pantheistic exaggeration, is the unanimous teaching of the mystics, the " orthodoxy " of mystical theology ; it is also the doctrine of dogmatic theology from the New Testament to the best modern text-books. In this reception of the Divine Being and Activity in and through the being and activity of the soul, and in this reception alone, is and will be fulfilled that participation of the Divine Nature to which the Christian is called and has been supernaturally exalted.

We have seen from the above teaching of theologians that sanctifying grace even in its lowest and most ordinary degree involves a true participation and reception by the soul of the life of God and therefore of His self-knowledge and self-love, and that every act done in and from grace (here actual grace is meant) is a certain reception of the Divine Self-knowledge and Will (see Scheeben, *Dogmatik*, French translation, vol. iii., pp. 528-531). This reception is not, however, manifest as it is in mystical union and more perfectly in the transforming union. It is also far more partial and, so to say, external. It is a fundamental apprehension of the Divine Act by the central ego, not, as in this supreme union, an entire possession of the latter by the former. The principle of the soul's activity is not, as in this union, God-received by the soul, but the soul in supernatural union with God. Nevertheless the life of Grace is essentially a reception of the Divine life and activity by and in the soul, a reception which increases in degree and in completeness of permeation, and therefore in consciousness, until it is made perfect in the beatific vision wherein the life of the soul is wholly a reception of God's Self-vision and Self-love and in these of His Being, as He eternally is and acts in the ineffable fecundity of the Blessed Trinity. "The elevation," Scheeben tells us, " of the created image of God " (the soul) "to a deiform likeness is fundamentally a copy and consequently a multiplication, extension and manifestation, indeed in a certain sense, a repetition of the eternal generation " (of the Son, the Word). It reveals externally the infinite fecundity of this generation in itself and the magnificence of its product. Moreover, when considered formally as a communication of the Divine Nature by love, it is a reflection, multiplication, extension and manifestation of the eternal procession of the Holy Ghost. The unfolding of the deiform life " (the life of grace) " in the creature by the knowledge and the love of God as He is in Himself presents a reflection of the eternal productions of the Word and of the Holy Spirit, a reflection wherein the divine productions are formally recognised and honoured as such" (translation from the French translation of Scheeben, *Dogmatik*, vol. iii., sec. 1000, p. 745).

This reflection and extension of the Blessed Trinity in the grace-union with God, and His special Self-communication and indwelling in the soul constituted by that union, so secret and so potential in its lower degrees, is supremely realised and manifested[1] in the act of the mystical marriage, as it has been explained above. For we have seen the act of this union to consist in the reception of the Divine Self-knowledge in the cognition of the soul, of the Divine Self-love in the volition of the soul, both receptions proceeding from the Divine possession of the central substance. The generation of the Son from the Father as the hypostatic expression of His Self-knowledge is reflected and extended or continued in the reception of the Divine Self-knowledge by the soul, thus fully constituted the Adoptive Son of God. The procession of the Spirit from the Father and the Son as their mutual love, the Divine Self-love, since the ground of that mutual love is the common Deity of both, is reflected and extended or continued in the reception of the Divine Self-love by the soul, thus fully constituted the temple of the indwelling Spirit. Moreover, in the soul's reception of the Divine Self-knowledge the Word is given to the soul and the soul is specially united to the Word. In like manner in the soul's reception of the Divine Self-love the Holy Spirit is given to the soul and the soul is specially united with the Holy Spirit. Thus is the transforming union a manifestation and extension of the inner fecundity of the Godhead, the Divine life in which are grounded the processions constitutive of the Blessed Trinity, and thus is the soul in that union an external and created reflection and continuation of the Blessed Trinity.

As the purgation of the soul from its natural selfhood is substantially one and the same in the night of spirit and in Purgatory, so also is this participation and reception of the Divine life by the functions of the soul whereby the activities of the soul become the activity of God received in them identical in substance and principle in the mystical marriage and in the beatific vision. If the night of spirit is the anticipation and revelation of Purgatory, so is the transforming union the foretaste, revelation and be-

---

[1] That is, supremely in this mortal life. The unveiled vision of heaven is a still higher and more complete realisation and manifestation.

ginning of Heaven. The transforming love which is God's love received in the soul through its participation of the Divine Self-love is the beginning of the beatific love, and the veiled but intense and potent consciousness of God received by the soul through its participation of the Divine self-consciousness is the dawn of the beatific vision.

We must not, however, imagine that the activity of the soul is substantially destroyed by being thus rendered a reception and participation of the Divine Activity. Even in heaven "the will of the soul will not be destroyed" (*Canticle*, st. 38). Neither in mystical marriage nor in heaven will the acquired habits of knowledge be lost by their subsumption by the higher wisdom " of the Divine Knowledge " (*Canticle*, st. 26).

In the fifteenth stanza of the *Transformation of the Soul in God* Mother Cecilia tells us that the natural operations, far from being destroyed, are perfected when thus occupied and filled by the operation of God. In the third stanza of *The Living Flame* St John, speaking of the illumination of the soul by the splendours of Divine knowledge, describes the co-operation of the soul in this illumination with the Divine influx of which it is the receptacle by the simile of inflamed air. "This illumination," he says, " of splendours wherein the soul shines forth together with the heat of love is not like that caused by material lamps which illuminate with their flames the surrounding objects . . . for the soul is within these splendours. . . . Nay, further, it is . . . transformed into and made these splendours . . . so that it is like the air inside a flame, enkindled and transformed into the flame. For the flame is simply inflamed air, and the motions and splendours caused by that flame belong neither to the air alone nor to the fire alone . . . but to the air and fire together, and the fire makes the air which it holds inflamed within itself accomplish these effects. After this fashion we are to understand that the soul with its powers is illuminated within the Divine splendours.

"The motions of this Divine flame are the work not of the soul alone, that has been transformed into the flames of the Holy Ghost, nor of the Holy Ghost alone, but of both together, for the Holy Ghost moves the soul as the fire moves the inflamed air."

The interior spiritual functions or faculties are indeed, as we saw, but aspects of the central ego. Since that ego is not destroyed by this union with God, neither can they be destroyed by it. We should say rather that when the transforming union is in act the operations of the soul proceed from God as their active principle and from the soul's own function or activity as a passive principle receiving the Divine action.   Hence, as St John tells us, the good works of the soul " proceed from God and the soul together," [1] from God as the primary agent or first principle, from the soul as the recipient which though passive in relation to the Divine operation received, nevertheless is active in that very reception.   Moreover, so long as this life endures and the vision of God is veiled, this reception is free and therefore meritorious.[2]   Pantheism positing the Divine action denies the created human reception of that action.   Catholicism in its completeness of positive teaching affirms the co-existence and co-operation of both.   Such co-existence and co-operation exist indeed in every act that proceeds from Divine grace.   In the earlier stages of union, however, the work of grace was but to set in motion the active principle of the soul to work after its own natural and limited fashion.   In the transforming union, and a fortiori in heaven, the Divine influx has become itself the first principle of the action which is effected in the soul in a Divine and unlimited fashion, and the activity of the soul is now but the reception of that Divine operation.   In the ordinary activities that proceed from grace we may say that God causes the soul to act.   In this perfect union God rather acts in the soul, whose action is now simply the reception of His.   This change of proportion between the action of God and that of the soul has been gradually effected by the destruction of the limits formerly opposed to the Divine action by the natural operations of the soul arising out of its own created and therefore limited selfhood, which was then their first principle.   Nothing hinders now the complete possession of the psychical functions by the operation of God, which is effected in, through and with these functions whenever the transforming union is in act.

Thus in this transforming union the activity of the soul is made perfect in its entire reception of the activity of God, and in this union are fulfilled the words of St Augustine : " When I shall with my whole self cleave to Thee . . . my life shall wholly live, as wholly full of Thee " (*Confessions*, x. 39, trs. Pusey).

The degrees of grace and hence of reception found in the acts

---

[1] *Canticle*, st. 30.

[2] Ruysbroeck indeed seems to teach the contrary (*Sparkling Stone*, chap. ix). If he is right, his assertion can only be understood partially of the actual love of God divinely received in the act of this union.

of the soul, though normally passing imperceptibly one into another, may be roughly distinguished as the six following :—

1. Morally good or indifferent acts elicited in a state of grace by purely natural motives. These receive some influx of grace and merit from the radical union of the will with God in charity, which charity commands and virtually motives the substance at least of these acts. The act, however, is itself essentially natural, albeit united radically with the supernatural grace-union of the soul with God, as being the act of a soul thus united (see Terrien, *La Grace et la Gloire*, vol. ii., pp. 26-55, Bk. VII., chaps. iii. and iv).

2. Acts accomplished with an actual co-operation and influx of grace, but principled by the natural selfhood in union with God.

3. Acts accomplished in virtue of special illuminations and motions of grace. These are explained at length by Father Baker (*Holy Wisdom*, second section of first treatise). In these acts the direct motive is a special operation and reception of God, Whose share in the act is thus larger than in the precedent degree. Natural selfhood, however, is still the predominant active principle of the act, not, as in mystic union, a predominantly passive and recipient principle.

4. Mystical unions lower than the transforming union. In these the Divine operation and its reception are evident in the union itself, and are more complete and interior, possessing and permeating the very substance of the act or union.

5. The acts of the transforming union. Here the Divine operation proceeds from a continuous and conscious permeation and possession of the centre by God, and is thus far more complete and interior even than in the last degree.

6. The beatific vision-union. In this the soul has naught of its own. Its entire life is the reception of the divine life. Hence all its knowledge and will are receptions of the divine self-knowledge and self-will, without any limit of natural extra-godly life or operation remaining.[1] This interpretation of the act of spiritual marriage or transforming union, as essentially consisting in a

---

[1] To prevent any possible misunderstanding I beg the reader to bear in mind that this increasing operation of God in and through the operation of the soul, until that operation becomes wholly a reception and participation of the divine operation, is in all its degrees effected not by any change in the essentially immutable Godhead, but by the action of created grace. This created grace establishes a new relationship of the soul to God, whereby it thus receives and participates in His Being and operation. In the final degree this work is effected by the completion and crown of grace—namely, the Light of Glory.

reception of the Divine activity—that is, of the Godhead Itself—in the functions or activities of the soul, is confirmed by an instructive analogy. For thus understood the mystical marriage reveals to us the spiritual significance of a type principle which runs through the higher orders of natural being, the principle of sex. It is undeniable that unhealthy Gnostic speculations have been rife in this province. Nevertheless we cannot suppose a principle so potent and so far-reaching to lack a profound spiritual meaning. The principle of sex begins first with plants and is thenceforward continuously present until it reaches humanity. In human nature sex differentiation transcends its physiological basis and enters the domain of psychology.[1] The difference between man and woman is far deeper and wider than the corporeal distinction. The contrary assertion of Plato in the *Republic* was an error, an error which has been unhappily resuscitated by the more extreme feminists of our own day. Men and women are naturally complementary in soul, as well as in body. Even where physical union has been altogether transcended, as in the case of priests and nuns, indeed in the religious sphere as such, the masculine and feminine elements of human nature continue this mutual co-operation and supplement of their distinctive characters. Nearly all the great movements in ecclesiastical history have been the joint work of men and women. Every great order save the Jesuit has had its feminine counterpart. (If, indeed, there are no Jesuitesses in name, they exist in fact, in the nuns of the Sacred Heart.) St John Chrysostom is assisted by the saintly deaconess Olympias, St Benedict has a fellow-worker in St Scholastica, St Francis finds sympathy, understanding and support in St Clare, St John of the Cross carries out the Carmelite Reform in conjunction with St Teresa, and St Francis of Sales is for ever joined in his work and in our remembrance with St Jean de Chantal. Even in the supreme work of our Redemption through the Incarnation and death of Christ, the second Adam, a woman co-operates most intimately, Mary the second Eve. Now whether we regard sex on its lower and transitory physical plane, or on its higher and enduring spiritual plane, we find that it represents the distinction and complement of donation and reception.[2] It is essentially,

---

[1] This has, of course, begun in the case of the higher animals, but in them the physical differentiation enormously outweighs in importance the psychological.

[2] Modern physiology in opposition to the mediæval belief (see Dante, *Purg.*, 25) teaches, it is true, the equal co-operation of the female element in the formation

therefore, a type and expression of these two fundamental aspects of reality, action or donation and passivity or reception. It may perhaps be asked how there can be a co-operation of the sexes if woman is the receptive and man the active element. But we must remember that reception is itself an activity, modifying by its own conditions that which it receives, a passive-activity, if I may so term it. A further answer is surely to be found in the nature of woman's contribution. That contribution is essentially the faithful conservation of the ideas and energy received in the first place from the man. In the stress and fatigue of practical life the man is apt to lose the first clearness of his perception, the first strength of his impulse. He finds these again stored in the woman. St Francis, for example, in his times of despondency and apparent failure found in St Clare the fresh and full ideal and life which he had originally imparted to her. The female sex is thus the treasure-house wherein is stored and guarded the spiritual riches gathered by masculine activity. In this work of faithful conservation, represented by Mary when " she kept all her son's words in her heart," is manifest the essential character of womanhood as reception, for perfect reception implies conservation.[1] The union and mutual co-operation of the two sexes on all its planes and in all its forms is thus symbolic of the union between the soul and God. For we have seen that in this union the soul is the recipient of the Divine Being, which is pure energy—the *actus purus*—and that the higher, closer and more intense the union the more completely is the soul the receptacle of that Divine activity. The union between Christ and the Church is symbolised as a marriage. for the same reason, since the Church is the receptacle of the activity and self-donation of Christ, her life a full and continuous reception of His life. St Anselm raises the question why we should not as well represent the relationship between the first and second Persons of the Trinity by the relation of Mother and Daughter as by that of Father and Son. The answer is, I think, that a feminine relationship would be contrary to the nature of

of the embryo. This, however, does not affect the fact that in generation itself the male element is donation-action—the female reception and *qua* reception passivity, although, to use an oxymoron, an active-passivity.

[1] We must, however, bear in mind that in the souls of many men there is an element of distinctively feminine character and in the souls of many women a distinctively masculine element. These psychological sex gradations will be most of all apparent in the sphere of spiritual life and work, and will modify the broad distinction insisted upon in the text.

God as pure activity. The creature differs from the creator essentially in its potentiality and consequent need to receive from without in order to self-actualisation, whereas the Creator is in Himself the entire and eternal Actualisation of His Godhead. The soul is only then fully actualised to the utmost of its capacity, when it is wholly recipient of the Divine activity, as we have seen it to be in this mystical marriage. The use of the term mystical marriage is thus explained and justified by this interpretation, and by this interpretation alone. The fact of this mystical marriage and its fulness, the beatific union, thus discovers the inner significance of the type principle of sex, and conversely the existence of this principle in its enormous depth and scope is a powerful witness to the truth and reality of the supernatural union of which it is the analogue and symbol.

Further light will be thrown on this Divine Action in and through the central functions of the soul by the consideration of certain passages in which St John and Mother Cecilia attempt to give an indication of its character, as experienced respectively in either function, as experienced in the understanding or spiritual consciousness, and as experienced in the will. Of these two the Divine Action in and through the will, the will-union, is the most fundamental aspect of the transforming union. I shall therefore speak first of this reception of the Divine Love in the will. In the thirty-eighth stanza of the *Spiritual Canticle* St John points out that in heaven " as the understanding of the soul will be the understanding of God and its will the will of God, so its love will also be His love. Though in heaven the will of the soul is not destroyed, it is so intimately united with the power of the will of God that it loves Him as strongly and as perfectly as it is loved of Him, both wills being united in one sole will and one sole love of God. Thus the soul loves God with the will and strength of God Himself, being made one with that very strength of love wherewith itself is loved of God. This strength is in the Holy Ghost, in Whom the soul is there transformed." St John proceeds to say that in this state of mystical marriage the soul loves in a certain way through the Holy Ghost, Who is the giver of its love. Therefore the love of the soul in mystical marriage is the beginning of the infused Self-love of God that will be its love in heaven, and its love now is thus an infusion into the will of God's own self-love. " These souls," writes Mother Cecilia, " love God no longer with their natural love alone, but also with the very love of Him Whom they love, which He infuses into them. Hence it is that they no longer love Him solely or chiefly with their own acts. They receive and support God's own love in themselves " (*Union*). " I saw," says Blessed Angela, "that it was not I that loved . . . but that the love was from God alone " (*Visions and Instructions*, ch. xxv., p. 81). In this infusion of God's own love into the soul the transforming union is especially grounded. For it is as the root or apex of the will that the centre is consciously possessed by God in the habitual union, and thus the will is the function through which especially the central ego grasps and attains the unlimited Being and Goodness that is God. Hence the act of this union is primarily an act of the will in love, the Divine self-love received in the will. " The act of this union," St John tells us, " consists more in the inflamed fire of love than in aught else " (*Living Flame*, st. 2). The reception in the will of God's own love is thus the predominant aspect and constituent of the act of the transforming union. This infused fire of Divine love, so painful in the night of spirit, is now a joy inexpressibly deep because it is satisfied by the veiled fruition of its infinite object. St John speaks of this fire of love as a sweet wound. " Inasmuch," he says, " as this Divine fire now holds the soul transformed into itself, not only does that soul feel a wound, but is made one entire wound of ardent fire. It is a strange and noteworthy fact that although this fire of God is so ardent and powerful that it could burn up a thousand worlds with greater ease than our earthly fire a wisp of flax, it does not consume and destroy the soul wherein it burns after this fashion, nor even causes that soul the least affliction. On the contrary, it deifies and delights that soul in proportion to the strength of the love, glowing and burning sweetly within it " (*Living Flame*, st. 2). There is now no longer any limiting attachment to any particular created good for the sake of its own limited self, and therefore no limit to bar the free and full reception of the unlimited love—that is, the unlimited God. There is no conflict and therefore no pain. Mother Cecilia echoes this teaching. " This light," she says, " is a Divine fire that consumes without burning and tormenting like created fire. Little by little the soul melts away and is consumed in this Divine fire, receiving ever more completely the qualities and properties of Him Who makes this communication to it. He is in His very substance light and fire of love most potent, most strong and most beautiful " (*Transformation*, st. 1). Elsewhere she describes

this same infusion of love under the image of air. The stanza
proceeds to tell us that God's " Divine Spirit stirs a breeze of love
and unites the soul with its Beloved," the Triune God. " The
love of the Father and Son is an eternal love that is essentially God.
Hence the true God that communicates Himself to the soul and
breathes in it unites it with Himself and with the Father and the
Son in this sovereign delight. The soul is conscious of this
breathing of the Holy Ghost. . . . The Holy Ghost effects this
stirring in order to manifest Himself and to make His presence
felt in this Divine delight. . . . The soul in whom the Holy
Trinity dwells . . . receives unceasingly these Divine breathings "
(*Transformation*, st. 9). In the third stanza of *The Living Flame*
St John describes how from the supernatural knowledge of the
Divine attributes, now communicated to the soul, there arises a
fire of love. Each attribute infuses into the will a special love
and all together unite into one immense fire of soul that absorbs
the entire soul. It is surely to this conflagration of love that we
may apply a passage in the second stanza of this same work where
St John tells us that " the entire universe appears to the soul a sea
of love, wherein it is drowned, neither can it discover any term
or end where this love ceases."

Indeed the will or conative activity is now one boundless love
of the unlimited goodness. Hitherto love has been limited by the
limited goods and by the limited notions of the Divine Goodness
which alone are cognisable by the natural understanding. Now
the will partakes in the unlimited self-love of the Unlimited.
" Nothing," says Mother Cecilia, " brings the soul so nigh to God,
nothing guides it more surely to Him, than love, by which it is
united with Him. . . . From the beginning love was emitting
sparks of itself whereby to enkindle the soul. It was love that
burnt up and consumed all the obstacles that kept back the soul
on this journey, and it is love that is leading it blindly in this Divine
darkness that is the light of God. This is the work proper to love.
This blind power guides the soul better and teaches it more,
because it leads the soul to a larger possession of God in the union
with Him than all the lights and revelations together. . . . Love
. . . gives the soul more of God than any other means and finally
unites it immediately with Him after a different and more special
manner of union than it previously possessed " (*Trans.*, st. 11).
Yes, truly, love is the beginning, the middle and the end of the
way to God. It is a blind power, as Mother Cecilia terms it,

because it ever transcends the limits of clear vision and involves an element of faith in its apprehension of that which it cannot comprehend. This is true even of human love. Two persons do not fall in love because they know each other's worth. Their love is a faith in a worth not distinctly seen. Knowledge arises later, for knowledge of souls is born of love, not love of knowledge.[1] The pragmatists would extend this to all knowledge. Though we cannot grant this, it is at least true that the lover is always a pragmatist. In human love, indeed, the faith of love may be, and alas! too often is, an illusion, a credulity. The particular object does not possess the worth that love believed to be there. But the instinct of love is not deceived. There is an unlimited worth behind and beyond the limited created values which, if taken as absolute, are illusory. In and beyond the unworthy human beloved is the one Beloved of all creatures, Whose presence is dimly felt in the earthly love. In the love of God, the unlimited, the faith of love cannot be misplaced and deceived. In this mystical marriage, when the soul's love has become a reception and participation of the substantial love Himself, it finds its full satisfaction, and this fruition of love fills the soul. " My only occupation is love," sings the soul in St John's *Canticle*. " It is quite clear," he says, " that the soul which has attained the spiritual betrothal " (this must be understood here of the mystical marriage) " knows nothing else but the love of the Bridegroom and the delights thereof, because it has arrived at perfection, the form and substance of which is love. . . . The more a soul loves, the more perfect it is in its love, and hence it follows that the soul which is already perfect is, if we may say so, all love ; all its actions are love, all its energies and strength are occupied in love " (*Canticle*, st. 27). So he proceeds, repeating again and again through the entire passage the dear name of love, like a composer who recurs continually to one *motif*. You would think the passage a description of the first days of two lovers, when the hours are filled with nothing but the expression of their love, when all they see, hear and do is significant only of that love which gives all things done or felt a new meaning and worth hitherto unknown, and when for them the entire universe moves around a new centre, the supreme, nay, the sole, reality, their love. This auroral glory, doomed as it is to fade all too quickly, is but a dim reflection and a faint

[1] Love is indeed preceded by an obscure intuition or instinct. That, however, is not clear knowledge.

indication of the Divine rapture of love that fills the soul in this
state of spiritual marriage.   Here there is no illusion, no decay, no
end.   It is the beginning and first-fruits of an eternal love, this
boundless love that fills the soul to overflowing.   Love working
through faith has drawn the soul onward and outward beyond the
limits of self and creatures into the unlimited love that is indeed
the one Absolute Reality, underlying and transcending all things,
the cause, the meaning and the worth of all positive being.   To
this progress of the soul in blind love to the Divine Union we may
apply the wonderful lines of Shelley that describe the journey of
Asia and Panthea to the secret cave of Demogorgon under the
image of a boat guided seaward by sweet music.   By the music we
may understand love, by the boat the soul, and by the ocean God.

> My soul is an enchanted boat
> Which like a sleeping swan doth float
> Upon the silver waves of thy sweet singing.
>
> It seems to float ever, for ever,
> Upon that many-winding river,
> Between mountains, woods, abysses,
> A Paradise of wildernesses ;
> Till like one in slumber bound
> Borne to the ocean I float down, around
> Into a sea profound of ever-spreading sound,
> And we sail on, away afar,
> Without a course, without a star,
> But by the instinct of sweet music driven ;
> Where never mortal pinnace glided.
> The boat of my desire is guided.
> *Realms where the air we breathe is love,*
> Which in the winds and on the waves doth move,
> Harmonising this earth with what we feel above.
>
> *Prometheus Unbound,* Act ii., sc. 5.

" Realms where the air we breathe is love " : the transforming
union is this new world, the Kingdom of God now come in the
fulness of power.   All is now love, for all is known to reflect love
and to subserve love, to be love's gift and love's ordering, even
that which opposes love most.   In this love all things are made
one and known to be one, for all the barriers of created limitations,
by which they excluded each the other, are destroyed in the
Absolute Unity of the unlimited love.   All things are thus seen
to be harmonised and unified in the unity of love, whence they proceed and whither they tend, the ground of their being the law of

their becoming and their final end. Life itself is now known to be love, life uncreated, love absolute, created life the offspring, the image and the minister of that love, at which it aims in all its forms and degrees, save only the sinful will, and even that serves perforce.

Now at last the soul understands that love is the explanation of that experience which is often so painful and so incomprehensible. Like Dame Julian, it knows that " love was His meaning," and that there neither is nor can be any other. Faith still remains, for the soul cannot yet see how this is so, how evil can be so wholly subject to love that it does not overthrow or disturb its absolute rule. But it apprehends, with an intuition deeper and more certain than any natural knowledge, that so it is and so it must be. For love the soul has lost all things and itself, and in losing them has lost only the limits that barred it from the infinite love that is All without limit. In this boundless love the soul has found itself and all things, life immune from age and death, worth supreme, indefectible, unlimited, reality perfect and entire, God Himself. It has found *Love*, and " *Love is enough.*"

From this glimpse of the perfect will-union of love we must now return to consider the conscious or cognitive aspect of the act of union, its intuition. This intuition is a supernatural knowledge far surpassing any and every kind of natural knowledge. " When the understanding," says Mother Cecilia, " and natural reason have passed away . . . the things of God are understood supernaturally, above all understanding and all reason " (*Union*). In the twenty-sixth stanza of the *Spiritual Canticle* St John speaks of the divine knowledge now possessed by the soul. He dwells, however, rather on its negative than upon its positive character. He insists on its absolute transcendence of natural earthly knowledge, which is " in its eyes the lowest ignorance," so that " the divinely wise and the worldly wise are fools in the estimation of each other; for the latter cannot understand the wisdom and science of God, nor the former those of the world." He points out how this divine wisdom completely detaches its possessor from the knowledge of earthly things and even from the understanding of evil. This latter effect is to be explained by the fact that evil *qua* evil is sheer negation and limit, and the soul now partakes of the wholly positive and unlimited self-knowledge of God. In this positive knowledge the nonentity of evil, as being but a negation and defect of being, is made known by its disappearance in this

Y

intuition from the field of perception.   So in Dame Julian's vision of the Divine Immanence in creatures " sin was not showed," because it " is no deed "—that is to say, is purely negative (*Revelations*, chap. xi).   In the third stanza of *The Living Flame* St John describes at length how the soul enjoys a special knowledge of those aspects of God that are termed His attributes, and of all these as one simple Being.   " If we would understand what are these lamps to which the soul here refers, and how they burn within her and emit light and heat, we must remember that God in His one simple Being is all the virtues and grandeurs of His attributes. . . . Since He is all these things in His simple Being, and since He is united with the soul, whenever He deems it good to grant the soul this knowledge, the soul sees distinctly in Him all these virtues and grandeurs, to wit omnipotence, wisdom, goodness, mercy and the like.   Moreover, since each one of these is the very Being of God in one person, either the Father, the Son or the Holy Ghost, and since each of these attributes is thus God Himself, and God is infinite light and infinite fire divine . . . each one of these His attributes . . . and virtues gives forth the light and heat of God Himself.   Inasmuch as the soul in one single act of this union receives the knowledge of these attributes, God is to that soul many lamps together, each one of which emits a distinct light of wisdom and a distinct heat " (of love).   " The soul possesses a distinct knowledge of each, whereby it is inflamed with love."   It is hard to explain more clearly a knowledge which to us who possess it not is and must be a sealed book.   I understand by it that in this act of infused knowledge the soul perceives that all those spiritual ideas or type principles which are in various degrees and modes manifested in the world of creatures, and becoming, of sensation and sense-derived conceptions, which is the object of our natural experience, are present in absolute and unlimited fulness of being in God, and that each is one with the other in His Unity. The entire value that is the positive being of creatures consists in their participation in these Divine attributes.   The truths discovered by science are participations of God's absolute wisdom, the beauty of landscapes, of beautiful faces, pictures and poems, a participation of His absolute Beauty.   Now the soul having been freed from the essential limits of these created participations apprehends in the mystical intuition the presence of these absolute ideas that were mirrored so imperfectly in creatures.   The soul has achieved such a vision as that spoken of by Plato in the

Symposium, wherein the soul, having ascended the ladder of things beautiful, rising continuously from more limited to less limited beauties, suddenly beholds Beauty Absolute. "He who has learned to see the beautiful in due order and succession when he comes toward the end will suddenly perceive a nature of wondrous beauty . . . a nature which in the first place is everlasting, not growing and decaying, or waxing and waning . . . not fair in one point of view and foul in another . . . but beauty absolute, separate, simple and everlasting, which, without diminution and without increase or any change, is imparted to the ever-growing and perishing beauties of all other things" (*Symposium,* 211, trs. Jowett). Such is the veiled vision of the transforming union. Here, however, all the ideas are apprehended together as aspects of the One Absolute Being Who is them all. Mother Cecilia speaks of this same intuition in the first stanza of *The Transformation of the Soul.* "Even to the understanding," she says, "there are granted certain openings through which are discovered to it some rays of the Divine and resplendent countenance of the Divine Persons and Substance. . . . Although in this life this Divine Lord cannot be seen as He is in Himself, as the blessed behold Him in Heaven, He discovers Himself to the soul in a most secret Divine vision, so that those who experience it are able to affirm with great certainty and truth that they see God in this Divine fashion. . . . Not only do these souls behold and gather an infinity of goods and riches that proceed from God Himself ; they go further and *enjoy a Divine consciousness and knowledge of His Being.* If you were shown the riches of one whom you held in great esteem, when all the force of your love was directed to that person himself, the riches would not satisfy you, for you must needs enjoy his personal presence. In like manner all the riches communicated to the soul that are not the touch and Divine consciousness of God's substance cannot wholly satisfy the soul that must needs receive them in the very essence and substance of Him whom it loves. Great is the difference between those whose thirst is satisfied with a few tiny pools, though even these are the gift of God . . . and those whose thirst is unquenchable save by the fruition of Himself, in Whom they drink in its source and fount the vein of delicious living water. In this wise do certain souls enjoy and delight in that unfathomable sea which is the boundless expanse of the glorious waters of the Being of God. This is the Divine Sight whereon they feed their gaze, a sight that must of

necessity be revealed to the soul whose entire life is in God.   Even
the twilight that consists in a great satisfaction divinely given is
insufficient.   Such a soul must finally behold and ever gaze upon
the life wherein it rejoices. . . . It is a sight that wholly bathes
the soul in glory. That glory makes it beautiful, that beauty makes
it pure, that purity makes it brilliant, that brilliance clothes
it in Divine rays and splendours.   This vision enlightens the soul
in its light, makes it true in its truth, one entire love in its love,
holy in its holiness and full of grace in its Divine grace. . . . This
vision, moreover, fills the soul with blessings innumerable. . . .
Such is this vision, whereon the eyes of the soul are fixed so firmly,
that in this vision it beholds all things, and as it regards them
in Him and by Him, it sees them, as it were, bathed and penetrated by Him their lord, so that when that soul regards them as
they are in themselves, they appear like accidents without a
substance " (*Transformation*, st. 1).

The world of creatures apart from God is now phantasmal and
unreal—a world of shadows—for the real being of creatures is perceived to be in God—their participation of Him.   In themselves
they seem " but accidents without a substance."   The sensible
world, once so solid, so inevitable, so powerful, so attractive and
so claimful that it all but hid from sight the world of spirit and
God Himself, is now disclosed in its true character—in its nothingness, in its illusion, in its unreality—" such stuff as dreams are
made on." [1]   Over against this phantom universe God stands
revealed as the One Reality, and the creatures are seen to be real,
only so far as they partake of His Reality.   Thus is fulfilled that
conversion from appearance to reality, from the exterior to the
interior, from the sensible to the spiritual, and from creatures to
their uncreated Source and Ground, which is the substance of the
mystical way and the entrance of the soul into eternal life.

Mother Cecilia stresses the fact that it is the *substance* of God
Himself that is the object of this intuition—though, we must
always bear in mind, veiled.   After the act of union has passed,
she says, the soul sees " that it has seen God with no human
sight . . . a most supernatural vision of God Himself in His
Divine Being " (*Union*).   It is an intuition of God as the sole
Reality by comparison with Whom all creatures are mere illusion
and nothingness, and of that One Reality as the unification of all
the type ideas its aspects, and as the ground and true substance

[1] This unreality is of course *comparative* (see Chapters I. and VI. *ad fin.*).

of all creatures, since God is eminently their positive being. The nature of this apprehension is unintelligible to us, the fact of it is indubitable for those who accept the testimony of the mystics. Elsewhere Mother Cecilia says that these souls " understand everything with a certain immensity " (st. 6). By this is meant that the soul sees one unlimited Being underlying and partially manifest in each created particular, so that every creature is now an entrance, wide or narrow, into the Divine Infinity. For the soul now contemplates creatures from God's point of view, in virtue of its reception of the Divine knowledge. " Since the soul is placed in the consciousness of God, it is conscious of things as God is conscious of them " (*Living Flame*, st. 1). It is a knowledge of all things in their Divine source, not, however, distinctly understood as in heaven, but apprehended in an obscure but most vivid and certain intuition as proceeding from, present in and unified by their Divine origin and ground. " The blessed soul that is so fortunate as to attain this wound knows all, tastes all and doth all it will " (*Living Flame*, st. 2). This knowledge of all things in God is stated more fully and explicitly by St John in the fourth stanza of *The Living Flame*, where he envisages the Divine consciousness infused into the soul as a Divine motion within it. " This awakening," he says, " is a movement of the Word in the substance of the soul, a movement of such greatness, lordship and glory and of a sweetness so intimate that it appears to the soul as though all the balsams, aromatic spices and flowers throughout the world were handled and shaken, being turned over to give forth their sweetness, and that all the kingdoms and lordships of the world, and all the powers and virtues of heaven were moved. Neither is this all. All creatures—that is, the virtues, substances, perfections and graces of all things created—shine forth and make the same motion, all together and in one, inasmuch as all things, as St John saith, are life in Him, and in Him they live and are and move, as the Apostle also tells us. Hence when this mighty Emperor moves in the soul . . . all things appear to move with Him, just as in the earth's motion all the natural objects thereon move, as if they had been nothing. . . . Here, however, they not only appear to move, but they all discover the beauties of their being, power, loveliness and graces, *and the root of their duration and life*. The soul perceives how all creatures, whether above or here below, possess their life and strength and duration in God. . . . And although it is true that the soul perceives that these things

are distinct from God, inasmuch as their being is created, and sees
them in Him with their strength, root and vigour, this soul perceives so clearly that God is in His Being all these with infinite
eminency that it knows them better in His Being than in themselves " (*Living Flame*, st. 4). " Since God is ever, as the soul
now sees Him, moving, ruling and bestowing being, power, graces
and gifts in all His creatures, possessing them all in Himself, in
virtue, presence and substance, the soul sees what God is in Himself and what He is in His creatures in one sole vision."

This knowledge of creatures in God, as grounded in His Being
and participators of His Being, is termed by St John their " morning knowledge," in contrast to our natural knowledge of them as
they are in themselves apart from their Divine Source and Ground,
a knowledge that is but " evening knowledge." [1] This morning
knowledge of creatures in God embraces both the created universe
as a whole and individual persons and things, in so far as they are
possessed of positive being.   From this source proceeded the sympathy between the saints and dumb animals, their love and their
fellowship with plant life and even with yet humbler forms of
being.   For the saints saw God in all things, and all things in God.
Their harmony and fellowship with creatures in God was the concomitant, indeed the result, of their union with God, the source
and ground of all creatures, and of their consequent knowledge of
creatures in Him.

This intuition or veiled knowledge of God as the source and
ground of all things created and the unity of the type-ideas, His
attributes, together with the intuition of all creatures as contained
eminently in Him, is often accompanied by a certain intellectual
understanding—more or less continuous—of the mystery of the
Blessed Trinity, an intellectual vision, as it is termed, of that
mystery.   By this vision is meant, I believe, an infused conviction
that the Godhead is and must of Its Nature be possessed by three
Persons, is therefore essentially self-communicating, a threefold
subsistence of one infinite Reality.   This vision is spoken of by
St Teresa and other mystics as a concomitant of the transforming
union.   It is, however, mentioned neither by St John nor by
Mother Cecilia.   It cannot therefore constitute an essential part
of this union.   It is external to it, an additional grace.   Its chief
value for the philosopher of mysticism is its witness to the fact

---

[1] This is derived ultimately from St Augustine's commentary on the first
chapter of Genesis.

that mystical experiences are not always of a nature common to all creeds, but that there are certain experiences, not merely exterior and sensible phenomena that are so largely subjective in their conditions, but interior, purely spiritual and attaching to the very highest states of union, which are distinctively Christian and can only be enjoyed by a Christian mystic.[1] To the mystical undenominationalist the intellectual vision of the Trinity must be sheer illusion. It stands, however, on as high a level of validity as the mystical union, which it so frequently accompanies, for it is equally spiritual, equally independent of the senses and equally self-evident to its recipient. It is therefore illogical to accept the latter as objectively valid and to reject the former.

This discussion, however, of the positive consciousness of the soul in the act of the transforming union, which is the intuitional aspect of that act, must not render us oblivious of the indistinct and veiled character of this intuition of God. God Himself is beheld immediately, but not as He is in Himself. Even the intuition of the Divine attributes is an intuition of the type-ideas as existent in Him, not an open sight of the Divine Nature as It is in Itself. In this life there is ever a veil over the face of God. " God does not show Himself with the clearness with which He is seen in heaven, but is veiled " (*Transformation*, st. 11). " The communication made under a veil in this life . . . although of the same Divine Being Whom we shall enjoy hereafter . . . is very different from the least degree of the glory of eternity, for in this life the Divine communication, however great, is always covered and under a veil " (st. 12). Though the soul's " intuition knowledge and vision is of the very Substance of God. It is always veiled " (st. 1).

" God," says St John, " removes from before the soul some of the many veils and curtains that are outstretched before it. . . . He then shines through and there appears dimly through the veils (for all the veils are not removed) an outline of that countenance so full of graces " (*Living Flame*, st. 4).

Though mystical marriage is the dawn of that midday where God feeds His saints with the beatific vision of Himself, it is still

---

[1] These Christian experiences are granted to Christians alone, because God will have dogmatic truth made known only through human preaching and faith yielded to that external authority. " Faith cometh by hearing. . . . How shall they hear without a preacher ? "

" the night of faith in the church militant." [1]   Gideon's pitchers,
still unbroken, conceal the lamps within.[2]   There is indeed a
sense in which even the heavenly midday is a night, the night of
the Divine infinity which no created intellect can ever fathom
even in the fullest reception of the Divine Self-knowledge.   There
are always depths in God to which even the beatific vision cannot
pierce.   St John, therefore, terms that vision in the *Canticle* the
serene night.   Nevertheless it is not night as on earth.   It is on
earth that the veil hangs to the end before the Holy of Holies
and hides the Divine Presence within.   After death that veil is
no more.

Nor only is there in the state of mystical marriage this veil of
faith.   It is true that in the act of this supreme union the soul, as
we saw, apprehends God as the source and eminent possessor of
all created Being, and the Unity of those spiritual idea-types that
we call His attributes.   This knowledge, however, passes into a
deeper consciousness, a consciousness which we may term negative, a simple consciousness of the infinite transcendence of the
Godhead present in the soul, as infinitely exceeding the highest
knowledge of Him that the soul can possess.   This consciousness of
the Divine infinity, of a reality wholly incomprehensible, is so fundamental in the act of this union that the conscious aspect of that
act appears from this standpoint a knowledge of infinite ignorance,
a darkness.   This darkness arising from the Divine Transcendence
which accompanies the highest intuition of the transforming
union has been expressed with great clarity, force and beauty by
Sister Gertrude Mary.   " I entered," she says, " into contemplation of the Infinite Being and His greatness. . . . The further my
interior gaze penetrated, the deeper it plunged into unfathomable
depths.   I still gazed, and God appeared ever greater to me.
These immeasurable grandeurs unfolded themselves unceasingly
to my eyes, and I always seemed only at the starting-point.   I
could only perceive in the darkness one tiny point of the greatness
. . . of the Infinite Being.   I say in the darkness, for God hides
Himself as if behind a thick veil.   I see Him and yet not clearly.
I feel His Presence and yet in no sensible manner. . . . Oh, what
beauty will burst upon our eyes when this veil is removed "
(extracts from *Diary*, pp. 178-179).

Similar is the language of Blessed Angela of Foligno.   " There
was a time," she says, " when my soul was exalted to behold God

[1] *Ascent*, Book II., chap. iii.   [2] *Ibid.*, chap. xi.

with so much clearness that never before had I beheld Him so distinctly. . . . Afterwards did I see Him darkly, and this darkness was the greatest blessing that could be imagined, and no thought could conceive aught that would equal this. Here, likewise, do I see all Good. . . . The soul delighteth unspeakably therein, yet it beholdeth naught that can be related by the tongue or imagined in the heart. It seeth nothing, yet seeth all things, because it beholdeth this Good darkly—and the more darkly and secretly the Good is seen the more certain is it and excellent above all things. Wherefore is all other good which can be seen or imagined less than this, because all the rest is darkness, *and even when the soul seeth the divine power, wisdom and will of God*" (the intuition of God in and through His attributes described in *The Living Flame of Love*) "*it is all less than this most certain Good.* Because this is the whole and those other things are but part of the whole." [1] This darkness, which is the supreme intuition of the Transcendent Deity, is often mentioned by Mother Cecilia, who refers to it several times in her *Treatise*. The Divine "communication," she tells us, "is termed darkness. He who enters farthest into this darkness enters farthest into the light of God, the light that shineth in the darkness of the creature's limited capacity and that darkness understands it not" (*Transformation*, st. 1). "The more deeply the soul enters into this union" (the mystical union with God), "the more is it darkened by the greater light that it receives from its transformation into God. However hard I might try, it would be impossible to explain how the soul is now blinded by this Divine light" (*Transformation*, st. 10). Elsewhere Mother Cecilia dwells at greater length on this negative consciousness attendant on the act of union, which act she describes as a flight of the centre into God. "I have now," she says, "to speak of the greatest communication of all. . . . This communication is effected in the immensity of the soul's very centre. The soul takes flight into the immensity of God, a flight so divine into Him that the senses and faculties, indeed all the lower part, completely miss it. In solitude is the soul raised to God in this flight, knowing with certainty that it has entered farther into Him, with Whom it is now united. . . . In Him it abides wholly lost, and in Him transcends all the limits of reason, and of all that is natural and sensible. The soul flies to God in a Divine slumber, completely dead to all things. This is a most Divine and in-

[1] *Visions and Instructions*, chap. xxvi.

expressible experience. It is the highest summit of pure contemplation, for it wholly destroys all the operations of the soul
and renders it not merely entranced, but dead to all its natural
activities and operations." "Nevertheless," continues Mother
Cecilia, "when this highest contemplation has passed away,
wherein the soul is so completely blind, it is left with increased
capacity and strength to attend to any matter whatsoever "—that
is, of course, when the union is not in act. . . . " However, during
the time that this flight and deepest entry into God endures,
the soul sees nothing, but enjoys in darkness Him Who is present
with it, not knowing nor understanding how " (*Transformation*,
st. 4). Elsewhere Mother Cecilia says: "While this Divine
silence, wrought in the heaven of the spirit, endures, the understanding is wholly lost in the excess of its object. . . . The soul's
greatest fruition of God, therefore, is when the understanding
is blind, in darkness, and suspended in God, Who, since He
transcends all understanding, leaves the intelligence blind and in
darkness. . . . The mighty force effected by God in the soul . . .
suspends the faculties " (*Transformation*, st. 6). "The understanding . . . is not admitted to the substance of this Divine
work, which is wrought in the essence of the soul. The inferior
parts of the soul, therefore, remain lost, blinded and dazzled by
this infinite good. Thus to remain is the best work which the
understanding does or could do. Further, it cannot attain, so
great is the force that overthrows and absorbs it. Although it
understands divinely that which God wills it to understand . . .
it does not attain that which is greatest and best of God's self-
communication, for this is granted solely to the essence (*i.e.* the
centre) of the soul." By this is meant that the act of union is
grounded in the Divine possession of the centre which is beyond
all understanding. "This substantial communication is the
principal work of God in the higher part of the soul, to which the
lower faculty cannot attain, but must be content with that which
its capacity can reach, the perception that there is being given to
the essence of the soul a good that is beyond understanding.
Since the understanding sees that it cannot help, but must rather
hinder, it suffers itself to fail and be lost, yielding to the forces
that attack it. Indeed it could not do otherwise at the presence of
this infinite greatness and light that overpower it. In this Divine
darkness the understanding is illuminated more divinely than it
could have been by any possible intuition or conception that fell

short of this infinite excellency " (*Transformation*, st. 12). "The motion of the very Being of God is so strong and sweet that it overpowers the entire soul" (*Transformation*, st. 16). This blinding of the cognition or spiritual consciousness is thus twofold. Though the understanding is filled by the divine self-knowledge communicated to it, it cannot fathom the central source of the Divine efflux. Moreover, its natural perception is destroyed by that effluent flood.

When the transforming union is in act all the functions of the soul are thus filled to overflowing with God, for His Divine Operation that is His Very Self is received in them all. Hence they fail in themselves and become the channels of this Divine activity that infinitely exceeds their capacity. The functions of the soul are overwhelmed by the communication of an energy which is infinite, being God Himself. The understanding is raised into the incomprehensible Godhead, the will is inflamed by Him, with His own self-love. Thus the act of union in its twofold aspect is an imbibition of God by the entire soul. This imbibition, however, may also be regarded as an absorption of the soul into the unlimited Godhead. Our authorities dwell on this aspect of absorption or fusion of the soul into the Divine Being. It is surely needless to insist once again that this absorption or fusion is not that imagined by pantheism and Buddhism, an absorption which destroys the created being of the soul and the functions that are essential properties or aspects of that being. Such an absorption would leave nothing to be absorbed. Unless, indeed, we postulated growth in the Divine Being, a grotesque conception incompatible with the Divine infinity, eternity and immutability demanded by religious experience and taught by the revealed faith of the Church —that is to say, incompatible with the nature of Absolute Reality[1] —such an annihilation would stultify the entire spiritual process. What value or significance could there be in the creation of the soul and in its spiritual growth if, at the end, that soul must pass into sheer nothingness, leaving the Godhead unchanged and unaffected ? Neither is it possible to regard the absorbed soul as continuing to exist, but without self-consciousness. Such an existence would be no better than annihilation. A soul perpetu-

---

[1] If God thus grows, at what degree of His Being did the growth begin ? Mr Wells seems to answer at nonentity from which the garnered experience of humanity has gradually built up its God. The best criticism of such a conception of deity is to try to think it out.

ally unconscious would be a spiritual nonentity, entirely without worth. True absorption into God or fusion with Him must therefore be the conscious reception of God by the entire soul, a conscious participation of His Divine Life, a conscious union with His Godhead, a consciousness of His self-consciousness. It will thus be a God-consciousness, in which the soul is conscious also of itself and of other creatures; not directly, indeed, but as known in the Divine self-knowledge.[1]   Moreover, our study of the transforming union in habit and act has shown it to consist in an absorption into God through the reception and imbibition of the Godhead by the substance and functions of a created spirit, conscious of this imbibition.   There is therefore no danger of pantheistic misinterpretation of the passages that I must now quote, which insist on the reality and fulness of this inconceivable absorption in God, the absorption of a self that has lost its limited selfhood by participation in the unlimited Godhead.

" The soul," says St John, " is now detached not only from all outward things, but even from itself.   It is, as it were, undone, assumed by and dissolved in love—that is, it passes out of itself into the Beloved " (*Canticle*, st. 26).   " God . . . in the omnipotence of His unfathomable love absorbs the soul into Himself with greater violence and efficacy than a torrent of fire a single drop of the morning dew which resolves itself into air " (*Canticle*, st. 30).   " The soul is absorbed into the Divine life " (*Living Flame*, st. 2).   The absorption of the soul into God, or fusion of the soul and God, is imaged by the union of a small light with a light enormously greater.   " As in the consummation of carnal marriage there are two in one flesh, so also when the spiritual marriage is consummated between God and the soul there are two natures in one spirit and love. . . .   So when the light of a star or of a candle is joined and united to that of the sun, that which gives light is not the star nor the candle, but the sun, which contains the other lights diffused within itself " (*Canticle*, st. 22). " In this state God and the soul are united as a window is with the the sun's ray, or coal with the fire, or the light of the stars with that of the sun " (*Canticle*, st. 26).   " We may say that the light of God and the light of the soul are all one, since the natural light of the soul is united to the supernatural light of God, and

---

[1] I speak here of this absorption as it is when finally complete in the beatific vision.   Need I add that self-knowledge in God is better and truer than self-knowledge in self ?

now the supernatural light alone is shining. It is as when
the light created by God (on the first day of creation) was
united with the light of the sun, so that now the sunlight alone
shines, although the former has not ceased to exist" (*Living
Flame*, st. 3). "God and the soul," says Mother Cecilia, "are
now united as one water with another, or one light with another,
so that they do not admit of division. Or rather their unity is
greater than that of these examples, for God in the most pure
subtlety wherewith He unites Himself with the soul, bestows
upon it His own qualities, so that it is made light in the light,
water in the water" (*Transformation*, st. 13).

"The union is far closer than that of one fire with another or
one water with another, for they are corporeal things, and God and
the soul spiritual substances" (*Union*). Material objects can never
interpenetrate so intimately as spirits interpenetrate. Another
reason why the union exceeds even that of two waters or lights
is that the created being is nonentity by comparison with the uncreated Being into which it is absorbed. It follows that in this
union only one member possesses true and full Being, the other
member being simply the reception of that fulness of Being by a
comparative nothingness. This, indeed, seems to be Mother Cecilia's
meaning when she says : "Since Our Most High God is Who He
is, it is not strange that union with Him changes and transforms
the soul with such force of love into the Being of the Beloved, and
that this transformation into so strong and so Divine a Being takes
it out of itself and its natural activity to supernatural and Divine
activities. . . . When united with God the soul is immense, in
Him it is life, in Him sanctification and perfection. The soul
attains to be God in God, because it is united with God Himself,
and in this permanent union comes to possess certain qualities
wherein it closely resembles Him. In this union that which is
nothing is God, that which is death is life, that which by sin is
corruption is sanctification" (*Union*). In other words, the soul's
reception of God dwarfs into comparative non-existence its created
being that receives Him. It is for this reason that mystics confer
upon a soul in this union, as does Mother Cecilia in the passage
above quoted, the name of God. Because its entire being and
activity is a reception of God, it is God, deified by participation
of God. Language could not express more concisely or more
eloquently the completeness of its absorption into the Godhead.

Mother Cecilia emphasises this deification in the following

passage :—" This Divine force is so powerful that it undoes and consumes the soul as the sea a drop of water. . . . God as a most strong and powerful lover takes such possession of the soul that is united with Himself that it is changed into Him by this Divine transformation. . . . God is a Divine and eternal Being . . . mighty, strong and infinite, and He is very life. If, then, this eternal and Divine life reveals Himself more fully to the soul, and the soul participates in Him with greater force, it is no wonder that He Who is so strong should undo the soul to remake it more like to Himself, to make light that which was dark, to purify that which was impure ; until finally He receives and changes it wholly into Himself. The soul, indeed, does not lose its own nature, for either party in this union remains in its own being. But the union is so Divine in the subtlety wherewith the one party penetrates and saturates the other that the creature is changed into the Creator, although still remaining a creature and He the Creator. By its reception into God the soul is deified and possesses the properties and qualities of the Creator, Whose force is so infinite that He hides it until He has strengthened the soul to its endurance. . . . We must not understand that the soul loses its natural being to be made part of the nature of God, for this is an impossibility. . . . When, therefore, the soul is said to lose its being, that being is meant that was previously in the soul oppressed by human things and attached thereto, that being which through them was made a being of sins. . . . As a result of this Divine transformation the soul remains changed and converted into God in this union. . . . Everything in the soul is entirely subject and yielding to the immensity of God Who . . . has taken possession of everything and by the force of His Spirit spiritualises the soul and keeps it in Himself. . . . Since the soul is thus in God, it often feels that its interior substance is like a glass window penetrated by the rays of the sun " [1] (*Transformation*, st. 16).

If possible, even bolder is her language in another passage. " It even seems," she says, " as though in a certain fashion His Majesty wills to place the soul on an equality with Himself and to raise it to Himself in order to make it God together with Himself. Indeed it may be truly said that this participation of God by the soul is now so great that not only is it like God, but God and the Son of the Most High. . . . It is now God's will to raise the soul after this exalted fashion to this participation of Himself and to be

[1] *Cf.* St John.

the life that is given it for its support, which life is His very Being. He wills the soul so to abide in Himself that the creature no longer has any consciousness of itself, but resolved in itself into nothing, lives in the life of its God and faints and dies in Him. All that was its own has now been destroyed. The Divine essence is now its own, for into the Divine essence its own essence has been transformed, and therein it abides, consumed and converted into Divine fire, in the fire of God that consumed it, peaceful in the peace of God, wise in His wisdom. . . . The force that has consumed such souls in its substance is so infinite and eternal, so active and potent, that though they handle everything, nothing enters into them, save as accidents lacking substance. . . . So powerful is the effect of the perpetual and abiding union that the continuity of the substantial touches " (the frequent acts of union, together with the habitual consciousness of God present and possessing the centre) "makes the soul one substance with the substance of God. . . . The entire natural being of the soul is lost or rather is glorified into a Divine being. Its substance is undone and changed into God, because that substance is now deified and transmuted into Him. It is true that on every soul is stamped the image of God, and He keeps all souls in His essence, conferring upon them life and being. The being of the transformed soul, however, is now undone and changed in a very special manner, being changed and transformed into the Essence of God " (*Union*). I cannot comment on these marvellous words ; they must speak for themselves to every reader as he is capable of their reception. Only let no one cry blasphemy that she makes the soul thus to become God. " Christ became Man," said St Athanasius, " that we might become God." This is not a solitary utterance. Through the fathers and schools from Clement of Alexandria to St Thomas, with especial emphasis in the Latin Augustine and the Greek Cyril, is repeated this bold language of the deification of the Christian soul by its grace-union with God and participation of His Deity.[1] As recipients of the infinite Divine Being, "partakers of the Divine nature " through sanctifying grace, we are already gods in potency. If the language of deification is no longer so freely applied to the ordinary Christian in a state of grace as it was by many of the Fathers, it is because a long and bitter experience has made us realise how extremely potential is the deification of the

---

[1] See Scheeben, *La Dogmatique*, vol. iii., and Fr. Terrien, *La Grace et la Gloire*, Book I., chap. iv.

average Christian.[1] Nevertheless, wherever sanctifying grace is present, that potency or germ of deification exists. In this transforming union the potency is passing into act, for the barriers of natural selfhood have been destroyed. "The soul has now no door" of limited volition or consciousness "shut against God's Divine Being."[2] "It is the highest mystery and bliss of rational creatures that although they are so little, indeed nothing, in respect of God, He raises them into Himself. . . . The more this nothing annihilates itself the more is it enabled to extend its capacity in the immensity of God, because it is in this nothingness, undetained by any limited thing. . . . When the soul is strengthened by the Divine infinity it can no longer be contained within the limits of its own natural strength and capacity and of its own nothingness, but abandons itself wholly to the greatness of its God" (*Transformation*, st. 16). "The soul journeys . . . to God in immensity without any limited road or way in her interior essence. . . . The soul is no longer attached to any creature whatsoever, for it has now transcended all the limitations of reason, of creatures, of all finite conceptions of God. God has set its feet in a large room, in a Divine heaven, that is higher than heaven itself, because it is the Creator of heaven. Herein the soul extends, dilates and travels in the freedom of infinity, not needing any road, for in the boundless expanse it has gone forth from all roads that now lie behind it, for its travels thereon are ended. A stage in the journey has been reached when the Divine immensity lies open before the soul, and the further it travels therein the more it realises its infinity." "God shows Himself to the soul in His immensity in an immense and unbounded place that is in Himself and without any limited way, for His way now is in the sea and His path in the mighty waters and His footsteps are not known" (*Trans.*, sts. 12, 11). Such is the end of the Divine philosophy of the unlimited that I have endeavoured to expound throughout this book, absorption in the Unlimited because all limits have been destroyed. Mother Cecilia expresses this by a simile to which she recurs with especial fondness, the simile of a man immersed and drowned in the ocean. In one passage she regards this ocean as the centre of the soul, capable of receiving the infinite life of God because created after His image and grounded in " His very life

---

[1] Similar to this has been the restriction in the use of the term "saint" applied by the Apostolic and subapostolic writers to all Christians indiscriminately.

[2] *Union.*

and essence " (*Transformation*, st. 1). Elsewhere that ocean is the infinite Godhead. The soul " is now drowned in the deep ocean of the Deity, wherein it finds no limit or measure or particular path or way, but one simple Goodness " (object and satisfaction of the will that seeks and finds an unlimited good) " immense and eternal " (*Transformation*, st. 12). " The way of the soul lies amidst . . . the deep sea of the Divinity " (*Transformation*, st. 12). It is, however, towards the end of *The Treatise of the Union* that Mother Cecilia elaborates the simile. She is explaining how, even when the transforming union has been attained, the soul can be immersed ever more deeply in the Divine immensity. " When once the soul has received this continuous union . . . its task . . . is to join itself more closely to Him to Whom it is joined already, to receive in greater power the Divine Substance received already, to surrender itself to Him with a fuller self-abandonment, to penetrate deeper into Him, to live more intimately in His life. . . . The substantial touches no longer cause any sense of novelty, because the soul always has present to itself the Substance of God. But it understands without understanding that it enters deeper into Him. That soul is like a person drowned in the sea. When he enters the sea first, before he is drowned, he is conscious of his own natural life and of the water contending against it, until little by little he is wholly drowned." This drowning is accomplished when the soul enters into the transforming union. " Let us imagine that after his drowning he were able to retain some interior and supernatural consciousness, as is now the case with the soul, for the more completely the soul is dead the intenser is its life, and the more it is drowned the more is it satisfied. This man would thus feel or understand that after death he was dying more completely, and after drowning was being drowned more completely, and that the more completely he was drowned the deeper did he sink down into the profound depths of the sea. . . . Suppose also that this sea were so deep that it had no bottom, and that as the drowned man sank down into the depths he discovered ever greater beauties and treasures (for indeed in our God such treasures are contained, seeing that He alone can attain to the infinite comprehension of His own infinite Being), this would present some faint likeness of that which now passes in the soul " (*Union*). I should like this illustration to fill the imagination of all who may read my book. It sums up the entire doctrine of mystical theology. To pass beyond all the limits of

z

our created life and its activity and to sink deeper and deeper,
ever deeper, into the boundless ocean of the Divine infinity, the
entire soul filled with that unlimited Life or Being that is the
Absolute and the All, this is the end for which God has created
and regenerated the soul of man, with its quenchless craving for
an unlimited good that is for an unlimited life.   This fruition of
the Unlimited has begun for a few—unhappily a very few—in
mystical marriage and is consummated for all the saved in the
beatific vision of heaven.   For mystical marriage is the entrance
into eternity and the foretaste of heaven.   For those who have
reached it, death is but a deeper plunge into the same boundless
ocean in which they are immersed already.   Unless it be for
expiation that death is but a transport of love of extraordinary
force and sweetness that breaks the thin web of earthly life which
still veils the open vision of God (see *Living Flame*, st. 1).   The
transforming union and the beatific vision are one and the same
possession and contemplation of the infinite Godhead, differing
solely in manner and degree.   This fruition of the Unlimited and
therefore absolutely real Being of God, already begun on earth in
spiritual marriage, complete hereafter in the beatific vision of
heaven, this and nothing less will satisfy our souls.[1]   For this
fruition of the Unlimited is perfect knowledge, perfect love and
perfect happiness.   Every ambition of youth, every yearning of
age, every motion of desire, every joy real or imagined, *in all they
possessed of positive being*, are now found without illusion and without limit in God.   Every vision of physical beauty, every melody
of earthly music, sunset light after rain, scarlet poppies ablaze
in the corn-fields, the furnace of an August moon rising behind
dark fir-trees, the still ecstasy of a summer garden at night, the
ever-changing sea, dawn enthroned on the hills, the perfect forms
of the Parthenon frieze, the lucent and joyful colours of Angelico,
an organ thundering through the lofty vaults of a Gothic minster,
violins thrilling with love and yearning with desire, the magic of
a plain-chant Jubilus, the music of Wagner, soul-searching and
soul-burning, his mighty storms of passion, his softer notes of
tender, mournful longing, his raptures of triumphant possession,
the love-lit eyes of some dear human countenance, the tones of
a voice, precious alike for the singer's sake and the song, all these

---

[1] This statement requires modification as regards those souls who are in a
state of mere nature—*e.g.* the unbaptized infants.   Here I leave such out of
account.

are possessed here in the perfect fulfilment of that Divine reality of which they were but shadows and sacraments. They will indeed be found also hereafter in material beauties worthy to be abiding sacraments of the spirit of which they will be wholly translucent. Even these, however, will be of little worth by comparison with the present spiritual fulfilment. Spiritual beauty— the beauty of noble deeds, lofty thoughts, inspiring visions and loving hearts—is now drunk immediately from its unlimited source. It is the same with truth. Vast hypotheses of science, inexpressible intuitions of an art, wherein truth and beauty are wed, revealed dogmas of faith—all are found in the Truth that is absolute and all-sufficing. Life is also herein, that life which is an impulse in the veins when the morning is fair, the air keen and the years few, that life which is the foe of dullness, monotony and convention, that life for which we long and to which we cling, even when we can least understand or justify our longing and clinging, ours now in inexhaustible fulness. No more negation, no more self-denial, no more asceticism.[1] These were but the means, albeit the sole means, by which the limits of independent selfhood and limited desires could be destroyed. They have no place in the end which is wholly positive : unlimited life, unlimited knowledge, unlimited love. The Resurrection stage has also begun, in part, even here on earth. The confident naturalism of the early Greeks,* and of ourselves, too, during a few favoured moments when we feel that this earthly life is good and beautiful, and nature the all-sufficient key-bearer and dispenser of Reality, but destroyed long since by bitter experience, returns once more fulfilled and transcended by this new life of supernature triumphant and complete. This infinitude of delights is, moreover, one, an absolute unity which is perfect harmony and therefore perfect peace. But this peace is also a boundless energy of love infinitely intense and passionate in its purity from all the limits that make earthly love so scant, so unsatisfying, often so gross and so vile. The soul loves by participating in that love Divine that made the perfectly self-satisfied God assume our humanity to buy our love by suffering and death. Each Person of the Blessed Trinity is the necessary uncreated and intrinsic receptacle of the unlimited Godhead and term of the unlimited Divine activity. In the transforming union

---

[1] This is, of course, strictly and fully true only of the perfect fruition of heaven. On earth there is always (1) a body that weighs down and wars against the soul and (2) the suffering of expiation.

in part, wholly in heaven, the soul is, if we may use the expression, a contingent, created and extrinsic receptacle of the Godhead and term of His activity.   But whereas the intrinsic Divine receptacle and term comprehends and exhausts the Divine fulness received, the created receptacle and term falls infinitely short of comprehension and exhaustion.   Though one with the Unlimited, recipient and partaker of the Unlimited, its own being is finite because created.   It is, as it were, lost and absorbed in the Unlimited that exceeds it infinitely.   Therefore eternity cannot exhaust its vision or satiate its love.   There can never be the weariness of satiety because there can never be an end.   The ancient Beauty is ever as new as its first vision.   The entire life and history of mankind, alike individual and social, is a yearning and a striving, unconscious or conscious, ill or well directed towards the boundless ocean of the Unlimited.   Thither leads the path of sanctifying grace.   The mystical way has taken the soul beyond the shore of that ocean and down into its depths.   Souls unspeakably blest, immersed in this Divine Ocean, unbounded activity is yours that is also undisturbed peace, insatiate desire that is infinite satisfaction, inexhaustible knowledge that retains for ever the awestruck wonder which arises from the realisation of limitless realms of being that are and must ever be unknown.   The Unlimited alone can fill the human soul, and that Infinity may be ours, for it is God, and God offers us Himself.

APPENDIX TO CHAPTER XII

THE RELATIONSHIP BETWEEN THE TRANSFORMING
UNION AND THE BEATIFIC VISION

I HAVE already discussed at length and, as I hope, have sufficiently proved the substantial identity between the passive night of spirit and purgatory. Is there also an identity of substance between the transforming union and the beatific vision of heaven ? It is surely evident that a complete identity between any mystical union on earth, however exalted (apart from the doubtful possibility of an extraordinary miracle), and the open vision of heaven is precluded alike by the conditions of man's life of probation in this world and by the teaching of Scripture (" No man hath seen God at any time "). On the other hand, there must be some community and therefore some identity between all supernatural receptions of the Godhead by the soul, whether in this life or in the next. Our question is therefore whether the identity is sufficient to be justly termed a substantial identity. I have not been able to find any full discussion of this question.[1] An answer may,

---

[1] Antonius a Spiritu Sanctu (*Directorium Mysticum*) treats the question incidentally in a number of scattered passages. He is, however, vague and even self-contradictory. In Tract 4, Disp. 4, sec. 13, he says that apart from the extraordinary case of a transient admission to the Beatific Vision God is not seen *per essentiam*. Since, however, God and His Essence are indistinguishable, and the soul in the highest mystical experience does see God, it must in some sense see His essence. In some passages Antonius denies that the experimental knowledge of God in the mystical union is an intuition. In other passages, however, he speaks of the soul as having a " simple intuition of the truth," and that " mystical theology is truly termed *intuitio*." Again, he sometimes says that God is seen in the highest mystical union " by a species that perfectly represents Him " (Tract 4, Disp. 4, sec. 4). But elsewhere I find "perhaps it can be better said that this light . . . communicated to the understanding is a *certain participation* of the light of glory and so disposes the understanding that God is *immediately* united with it " (in other passages he denies that it is the light of glory or an *immediate* perception of God) " after the fashion [*in ratione*] of an intelligible species " (and therefore He is not seen only by a created species, as affirmed above), " so that God is indeed seen in Himself, though not clearly and perfectly as in glory " (Tract 4, Disp. 1, sec. 8). It may be said that this latter passage refers to a lower union than that referred to in the former quotation which is concerned with mystical marriage—but surely if the intuition in its lower form

however, be found by a consideration of the nature of mystical experience. Mystical experience comprises, as we have seen, two fundamental constituents, a conational or will-union and a cognitional union or intuition. As regards the former there is surely no substantial difference between the transforming union and the beatific love of the saints in heaven. Both are the Self-love of God received in the will, and the latter differs from the former only in degree. An identity of principle exists also in the cognitional element or aspect of union ; for the intuition of the transforming union and the beatific vision are alike receptions of the Divine Self-knowledge. There is, however, a most important divergence, a divergence not of degree only but of kind. The intuition of the transforming union, although an immediate per-ception of the Godhead, is not a clear vision, as will be the beatific vision. God is immediately apprehended by a supernatural con-tact and grasp of His Godhead, but there is no comprehension of His Nature. On the contrary, the highest intuition is the most negative, the fullest perception of an incomprehensible infinitude. It is true that even in the beatific vision the unlimited Godhead will never be fully comprehended. But there will be such a measure of comprehension as will amount to a clear, unveiled vision of the Divine Nature. On earth, on the contrary, the supreme intuition is a dark though intensely certain and vivid apprehension of the Divine Presence.[1] If, therefore, we mean by substantial identity an identity of principle, there is a substantial identity between the transforming union and the beatific vision.[2] If, however, we mean an identity which admits only of differences that leave unaffected the essence of the experiences under com-parison, this identity, though fully present in the case of the night of spirit and purgatory, is not thus present in the case of the trans-

is immediate without created species, and by a participation of the *lumen gloriæ*, *a fortiori* is this true of a higher form.   At the opening of his book Antonius gives both views without deciding between them.   As will be seen from the text, my own opinion is that expressed by Antonius in the last quotation.   It is con-firmed indirectly by Antonius when he calls faith the participation of the light of glory (Tract 3, Disp. 1, sec. 5), as the light of glory is itself a participation of the Divine Understanding (Tract 3, Disp. 4, sec. 5).

[1] It is impossible in treating of a matter so far beyond the province of normal experience to employ words with any pretence of scientific accuracy and dis-tinction.   Language can only indicate.

[2] There is indeed an identity of principle between every operation of sanctifying grace and the union enjoyed in heaven.   The least operation of sanctifying grace possesses in common with the beatific vision the character of a supernatural reception of the Divine Being and Operation.

forming union and the beatific vision. For in the cognitive element there is a difference between the two unions which suffices to establish a difference of kind, the difference, namely, between veiled intuition and unveiled vision, between apprehension of God's Presence and comprehension real, though partial, of His Nature.   It remains, however, true that there is sufficient identity between mystical marriage and the beatific vision to justify us in regarding the former as the beginning, foretaste or dawn of the latter.

CHAPTER XIII

ON THE MYSTICAL INTERPRETATION OF SCRIPTURE

Every light that comes from Holy Scripture comes and came from this supernatural light. Ignorant and proud men of science were blind, notwithstanding this light, because their pride and the cloud of self-love had covered up and put out the light. Wherefore they understood the Holy Scripture rather literally than with understanding and taste only the letter of it . . . they get not to the marrow of it, because they have deprived themselves of the light, with which is found and expounded the Scripture ; and they are annoyed and murmur, because they find much in it that appears to them gross and idiotic. And, nevertheless, they appear to be much illuminated in their knowledge of Scripture, as if they had studied it for long ; and this is not remarkable, because they have, of course, the natural light from whence proceeds science. But because they have lost the supernatural light infused by grace, they neither see nor know My Goodness, nor the grace of My Servants.

> St Catherine of Sienna,
> *Dialogue*, trs. Algar Thorold. Abridged
> Edition, pp. 184, 185.

God's revelation to man does not consist of a number of isolated facts about Himself, but is a revelation of the means whereby fallen man may be reunited with Himself, the revelation of the economy of grace. This economy centres in God-Incarnate Our Saviour Jesus Christ and in His mystical body, the Catholic Church wherein His Divine Work of restoration is continued and applied. The Judæo-Christian revelation is wholly and solely concerned with this dispensation of grace uniting man to God. If it also teaches us a doctrine concerning God in Himself, the mystery of the Blessed Trinity, this is because that doctrine is implied in the economy of redemption wherein the Second Person is Incarnate and the Third Person [1] indwells the Church and the individual soul for their sanctification. The Bible, however, was

---

[1] By appropriation say the majority of theologians.

inspired and given to the Church as a [1] source and instrument of this revelation. Hence that alone which concerns the union of man with God by grace and its economy is the subject matter of Scripture. When, however, we read the Bible we find a very great deal which is apparently external or unessential to this economy of grace. Throughout the Hebrew portion of the Book of Esther, for instance, there is no mention whatsoever of God. What is the bearing on our salvation of the temporal deliverances of the Jewish people ? Do the life and acts of Jewish heroes, such as Samson, Gideon, Jephthah, or even of Moses, of Abraham or of Jacob, make any difference to the Catholic to-day ? What concern have we with the ceremonial prescriptions of the Levitical law long since abolished ? If, indeed, nearly all the Old Testament were suddenly lost to us, Catholics would still possess the entire Christian revelation [2] in the New Testament and tradition. It is, therefore, evident that the surface meaning of much of the Old Testament, which is temporary, local and carnal, cannot be the *primary* meaning of the Holy Ghost. That we must seek in an inner sense, in a mystical or allegorical interpretation. The existence of this sense is amply vouched for by the authority of Scripture itself. The Gospel interprets typically the story of the brazen serpent and of Jonah in the whale's belly. St Paul plainly tells us in Galatians that the story of Isaac and Ishmael was an allegory— that is to say, that its primary meaning and intent is allegorical (Gal. iv). In 1 Corinthians he presents an allegorical interpretation of certain incidents of the Exodus. The rock, he says, whereof the Israelites drank in the wilderness was Christ. A large element of type or allegory is contained in the use made in the Epistle to the Hebrews of the strange figure of Melchisedec. When we turn to the uninspired Fathers by whose unanimous consent the Catholic must interpret Scripture, we find that this allegorical interpretation is in the highest favour with them. It is especially marked in the Alexandrine school, and also, lest any suspect the method, for the theological errors of Origen, in that great father whose teaching has moulded Latin theology ever since, St Augustine. The only school which looked with more or less disfavour on the allegorical interpretation was the school of Antioch, which accordingly soon lapsed into the rationalising heresy of Nestorianism. Indeed the only member of this school

[1] Not, however, as Protestants maintain, the only source and instrument.
[2] As interpreted and developed by the infallible definitions of the Church.

who entirely rejected the allegorical interpretation, Theodore of Mopsuestia, was one of the leading supporters of this heresy. He represents the culmination of an anti-allegorical tendency visible even in St John Chrysostom.[1] The mediæval writers are saturated with this mystical interpretation. There is no need to give instances. Every mediæval theologian, dogmatic or mystical, is an instance. If in our days this mystical interpretation is less in favour, it is because, by an easily intelligible reaction from Protestant bibliolatry, the Scriptures themselves are less studied than they were of old. The argument from authority is amply supported by the argument from reason. This argument is derived from that mystical philosophy which I have endeavoured to explain in my previous chapters. The principles on which the validity of the mystical interpretation of Scripture is founded may, however, be resumed briefly here.[2] The human understanding is in this life conditioned by the information of the bodily senses. The human intelligence cannot apprehend God as He is. The highest knowledge of God in this life is that which is termed negative, the apprehension, that is to say, of God as wholly transcendent of all the concepts and categories of our understanding. It is not even true that He exists in the same sense that creatures possess existence. We know that God is, not what He is. We do, however, know that all that is in the creature is in God eminently after an infinitely higher fashion, so that this infinite difference is not thereby destroyed. God, therefore, has revealed and communicated Himself to us by means of creatures, who cannot, indeed, adequately represent Him, but who reveal as much of our relationship to Him, actual and possible, as can be made known, who serve as channels of His grace and who point beyond themselves to Him. Nor are these creatures pure spirits, because pure spirits are too distant in nature from man, who is composite of soul and body, to be knowable by him directly.[3] It is through the human and the material that God reveals Himself to men and unites Himself with men. The economy of grace is essentially sacramental. In this sacramental economy, however, there are various levels. There is the lowest level in which the material

---

[1] See Newman, *Development of Christian Doctrine*. For this more detailed information I am indebted to Fr. Joseph Rickaby, S.J.

[2] For a fuller discussion see Chapter IV.

[3] Except in an extraordinary supernatural way, and then only with an obscure and veiled knowledge.

object is solely a type or symbol of the spiritual reality. Such were the Jewish sacraments. Such are the non-sacramental rites and ceremonies of the Church to-day. Then we have the level in which the material symbol is the channel of a special grace given through it—such are the Christian sacraments which effect what they signify. Above that is the level at which the material sign is in a particularly intimate relation to God. Such is the Blessed Sacrament of the Altar wherein the species [1] of bread and wine veil the Real Presence of God Incarnate. Above all is the Incarnation itself at once the basis and the crown of the entire sacramental economy. In the Incarnation the infinitely transcendent and therefore unknowable God made a particular created Soul and Body one Person with Himself—so that Jesus Christ is both God and Man, the infinite Creator, and a created Nature, spiritual and corporeal, though in virtue of the hypostatic union no creature. It is clear that at these various levels the relation between the outward appearance and the inward reality is infinitely diverse. That which is merely symbolic must be transcended and in a sense set aside in order to reach the spiritual reality. The Humanity that is one Person with God can never be transcended. Mother Cecilia tells us in her *Treatise on the Transformation of the Soul in God* that the sacred Humanity and the mysteries of Our Lord's earthly life should be understood in a progressively more spiritual fashion— that is to say, that the contemplative must realise ever more fully the infinite Deity of Our Lord underlying His human life and actions. This Sacred Humanity, this Life and these Actions cannot, however, be set aside and forgotten, because they are essentially and eternally by personal union the life and actions of God Himself. Therefore the primary meaning of the Gospel Narrative is the plain historical meaning. Though there is also an allegorical interpretation of the episodes of Our Lord's life, this is secondary in value. Any neglect or depreciation of the literal sense of the Gospel in the interests of an allegorical meaning hidden beneath it would be profoundly un-Catholic. The same holds good of the other writings of the New Testament (apart from the Apocalypse, which is essentially a book of types and images). The Epistles teach the dispensation of grace, its channels, the sacraments, its social organisation, the Church, its law, charity. These are, indeed, types and sacraments of heavenly things, but are also

---

[1] The species are not, of course, material in the sense of being material substances, but as being the accidents of material substances.

in themselves the most solid and profound realities of our religious life on earth.   Here, therefore, the allegorical sense is wholly subordinate.   The Old Covenant, on the other hand, is essentially a sacramentum, of which the New Covenant is the *res*.   " The law," it is written in Hebrews, " having a shadow of the good things to come, not the very substance of the things."   But the Old Testament is the written account of the dispensation of the Old Covenant.   Therefore it also is essentially a shadow of good things to come—namely, Christ, His grace and His Church. " The whole kingdom of the Hebrew nation," wrote St Augustine, " was one great prophet, because the prophet of one Great One. Wherefore in those among them, who were taught within by the Wisdom of God, we must, not in what they said only, but also in what they did, search for prophecy of the Christ Who was to come, and His Church ; but in the rest of that nation, collectively in those things which were done in them or to them by God." . . . " God so accounted of these men [the saints of the Jewish law], and at that time made them such heralds of His Son, that not only in what they said, but in what they did, or what happened to them, Christ is sought, Christ is found " (quotations from St Aug. Opera by Dr Pusey in note to St Aug. *Confessions*, iii. 14).   The very strangeness of many of the stories told in the Old Testament, the inadequate ethical level displayed in many incidents recorded, are signs to point us to the hidden meaning.   Are we, for instance, scandalised by Jacob's deception of his father ?   " Si diligenter et fideliter attendatur," comments St Austin, "non est mendacium, sed mysterium " (" If it be considered diligently and faithfully, it is no lie, but a mystery ").   No one had been more offended by the superficial difficulties of the Old Testament than St Augustine himself, until St Ambrose's preaching at Milan taught him to look below the surface of the letter to find the interior spirit.   It is undeniable that the literal meaning and truth of the Old Testament is to-day clouded by the difficulties raised even by a moderate historical criticism.   To what degree the Old Testament is historical truth of the letter can only be decided, if at all, by the consensus of competent scholars.   Without anxiety we may abandon to them a question devoid of religious significance. The mystical interpretation is the primary sense intended by the Holy Spirit.   If we receive and study that sense according to the teaching and practice of the great Catholic theologians of the past, we can leave the minor matter of the letter to the solution of future scholarship. Whatever be the final verdict, if a final verdict be attainable, on the literal sense of the Old Testament writers, the sense of the Divine Author, the mystical or typical sense, remains unaffected. And it is this sense which possesses religious value for us. It is certain from authority and reason alike, that every event, whether or no it be historical, is certainly an allegory, that the Old Testament history is a series of inexhaustibly significant types of Christ and His mysteries. Christ and His mysteries are thus the substance of the Old Testament. Never has this principle been stated more clearly than it is by St John of the Cross in the nineteenth chapter of the second book of *The Ascent of Mount Carmel.* He is speaking primarily of the prophecies, especially of the prophetic visions, but his words are applicable to the whole of the Old Testament. "It is clear," he says, "that the prophecies do not always mean what we understand by them, and that the issues do not correspond with our expectation. The reason is that God is infinite and most profound,[1] and therefore His prophecies, locutions and revelations involve other conceptions, other meanings, widely different from those according to which we measure our own perceptions; and they are the more true and the more certain the less they seem so to our understanding." St John proceeds to give examples of prophecies never fulfilled in their literal meaning. He then continues : "This is one of the many ways in which souls deceive themselves in the matter of revelations and Divine locutions. They understand them in the letter and according to the husk. . . . The chief purpose of God in sending visions is to express and communicate the spirit which is hidden within them and which is very hard to be understood. This is much more abundant than the letter, more extraordinary, and surpasses the limits thereof. . . . The letter killeth," saith the Apostle, "but the spirit quickeneth. We must therefore reject the letter and abide in the obscurity of faith, which is the spirit, incomprehensible by sense. . . . The Jewish nation understood not the prophecies, for it followed after the milk of the rind and the breasts of sense. For God spoke to them the doctrine of His own mouth and not of theirs, and that in another tongue than theirs. . . . It was not possible for these not to be deceived because they relied on the literal, grammatical sense." St John then refers to the prophecies which seemed to foretell a temporal

[1] Trs. David Lewis slightly altered.

rule of the Messias, and after pointing out that their literal meaning was never fulfilled, he continues : " The Jews, *blinded by the letter of the prophecy*, and not understanding the true spiritual meaning it involved, put Our Lord God to death." Finally St John points out that the spiritual fulfilment absorbs the literal, as the greater the less, containing it, so to speak, eminently, even as God contains created worth eminently in Himself. Since this is so, we should not be disturbed by any difficulties raised in regard to the literal sense of the Old Testament, which, however true, is at best a mere husk and rind, a killing letter, but should cleave to the inexhaustible spiritual reality veiled and figured by the letter which is God Himself, and His dispensation of grace to man, in Christ and in His body the Church. As the Jewish ceremonies are not only dead, but deadly, to us who have reached their substance, so also the literal sense of the Old Testament, if regarded as the sole or even as the primary sense, is deadly, taking away the true sense and profit of Scripture to our souls. That such was the constant instruction of St Ambrose to his flock we learn from St Augustine's *Confessions*, where he says : " With joy I heard Ambrose in his sermons to the people oftentimes most diligently recommend this text for a rule, The letter killeth, but the spirit giveth life ; whilst he drew aside the mystic veil, laying open spiritually what, according to the letter, seemed to teach something unsound " (*Confessions*, vi. 6, trs. by Pusey).

But, it may be objected, this mystical interpretation is purely arbitrary, a figment of the interpreter's own brain foisted into Scripture. Moreover, the allegorical interpretation is infinitely diverse, and the interpretation of one commentator is at variance with the interpretation of another. No doubt, like all true principles, allegorical interpretation has often been misapplied or pushed too far, so as to become mere phantasy. We must, however, recollect that the spiritual sense is not finite like the literal, but extends to the infinity of God Himself and contains the inexhaustible significance of His mysteries. Therefore the mystical significance of one prophecy or type comprises a rich variety of applications and senses, none of which, nor indeed all together, can exhaust that significance. In a degree this is true even of profane art, which in proportion to its greatness is sacramental of spiritual realities. A great picture or poem has a different message to different spectators or readers and suggests meanings far beyond the conscious intention of the painter or poet. Yet these are contained implicitly in the work of art—not arbitrarily foisted into it. It is the more superficial and more material art whose message is confined to the limited and external understanding of its author.[1] If, then, the mystical sense of Scripture were tied down to one distinct concept, it would be but an outer husk or letter. Indeed the difference between the incidents of the Old and New Testaments is but this, that in the latter case its depth of spiritual meaning, its true significance, belongs to the incident itself, in the former to the reality of grace signified and foretold by the incident. For example, the feeding of the Israelites with manna is not in itself of inexhaustible significance, but only in its reference to the Blessed Sacrament, whereas the institution of that Sacrament by Our Lord is itself a fact whose meaning is inexhaustible.

Nevertheless there is an underlying unity in all right mystical interpretation. However the detailed application may vary, the spiritual sense of Scripture is harmonious and unified. Wherever we take up the Bible the underlying teaching is the same. The more the critics point out divergencies of outlook, of ethical depth and the like in the letter, the more strongly does this inner unity come into view. Suppose it to be shown—I do not for a moment say that this has been proved—that the sacred writers were not conscious of this fundamental unity, that would only serve to prove the action of one Inspiring Spirit, the true Author of all. Moreover, no book of Scripture, above all, no book of the Old Testament, must be taken apart from the entire canon. The meaning of the Holy Ghost in that book is determined by its place and function in the full cycle of the completed canon eternally present in the mind of the Divine Author of Scripture. Taken by itself, the teaching of a particular book must often be inadequate, that half truth which, if left unsupplemented, would amount to an error, though true as far as it goes. We must therefore interpret the incomplete and more superficial teaching of an earlier book by the deeper, fuller and more complete doctrine of a later. This also is mystical interpretation. The sole adequate way in which this unity of principle could be shown would be the detailed interpretation of Scripture passages. This I must leave to the further study of any reader who cares to undertake it. The unity to be sought and found throughout the Bible is the revelation of the

[1] Is there any need for me to say that all the meaning of Scripture is eternally present to the true author of Scripture, God Himself ?

economy and operation of grace.   It is the doctrine of the working of grace restoring fallen man and reuniting him to God,
through the Incarnation, through the extension of the Incarnation,
the Church and her sacramental system, and through the application of the Incarnation and its fruits, by means of Church and
sacraments, to the individual soul.   So long as the letter is inter-
pretated in reference to this economy of grace, the interpretation
is valid and fruitful, and the most superficially diverse passages
and texts will yield one harmonious substance of spiritual truth.
From Genesis to the Apocalypse one self-consistent doctrine will be
revealed to the reader who uses this key.   I can but mention one
or two instances here as illustrative of my meaning.   The Babylon
of Nabuchodonosor is identical in its spiritual significance and in
its relation to the Church of God with the Babylon of the Apocalypse—namely, the Rome of Nero—and both with the Babylon
of to-day, repaganised Western Europe, whose view of Catholic
Christianity is so ignorant and so hostile.   Tyre is one in spiritual
meaning—that is to say, in its relation to the economy of grace
—with the great mercantile states of later days, such as Carthage,
Venice and modern England.   When Jeremias speaks in the
third chapter of his prophecy of the revolted ten tribes who have
cut themselves off from the spiritual commonwealth of Judah,
having forsaken the centre of spiritual unity, the priesthood and
temple at Jerusalem, is he not speaking also of the Christian bodies
which have forsaken the centre of spiritual unity in Christendom,
the Pope and Church of Rome ?   " Return, O ye revolting
children, saith the Lord, for I am your husband : and I will
take you, one of a city, and two of a kindred, and will bring you
into Sion."   Is not this fulfilled in our day in the individual conversions to the Catholic church ?   It is no arbitrary twisting of
the sense to interpret Jerusalem by the Church, the Aaronic by
the Christian priesthood, the idolatrous empires of Hebrew times,
as the pagan, whether or no nominally Christian, empires of later
days, if, as is the case, the spiritual values of these things, their
significance for the dispensation of grace [1] are identical throughout.
The unity and harmony of the mystical interpretation is thus the
guarantee of its truth.

---

[1] It is true that the Aaronic priesthood did not minister as the Christian grace-
conferring sacraments.   They exercised, however, the same function in the typical
economy of the Old Testament sacraments as the Christian hierarchy in the
fulfilled economy of the Christian sacraments.

For the entire Judæo-Christian history is simply the history of the economy of grace in the world, the supernatural order at work in and largely against the natural.[1] " Two loves," says St Augustine, " built two cities. The love of God built Jerusalem, the love of the world Babylon." Thus for St Augustine these loves, supernatural charity and self-love or concupiscence, are the two great foes. Natural love of our neighbour has never yet built a great world order, for it is only rendered possible by a confusion of mind that will not trace issues to the end. Now these two opposing orders, the former the work of grace, freeing man from the bondage of the finite and raising him to union with God, and the latter the work of fallen nature aided by the evil spirits, bringing man into bondage to his own selfish desires and superficial life and thus keeping him apart from God, are seen at war throughout Scripture from Genesis to the Apocalypse. Indeed, long ere man was made and fell, the strife began in heaven when the great intelligences, now known as the evil angels, rejected supernatural charity. We see the two opposing forces in the history of Cain and Abel, in the contrast between the descendants of Cain, the inventors of the arts of civilisation and the first city builders, and the descendants of Seth, in the enmity between the Canaanites, Egyptians, Philistines, Syrians, Assyrians, Babylonians and Greeks on the one hand, and the chosen people of Israel on the other, in the combined hostility of Pharisees and Sadducees, of Herod and of Pontius Pilate to the Divine Head of the supernatural order, Christ Our Lord, and finally in the endless struggles, either open or secret, between the world and its rulers and the Church and her ruler the Pope.* The essential contest is always the same ; the sole change is the progressive realisation on both sides of the true issue at stake. But, indeed, I have said enough, I think, to indicate sufficiently the consistency, the harmony and therefore the unity of Scripture, when all is understood, either as a type of grace and the supernatural order of grace, or as an actual revelation or embodiment of that grace and order. The ancients distinguished three species of mystical interpretation, the allegorical, the moral and the anagogical. Dante speaks of them in his letter to Can Grande and interprets in these three ways the first verse of Psalm cxiii. The allegorical sense

---

[1] Not that the natural is in itself opposed to the supernatural. It is the adhesion to mere nature in opposition to the Divine call to transcend it which causes the conflict.

2 A

refers to Christ, the moral to the soul in her life here and now, the anagogical to the soul's lot hereafter. It seems to me that a clearer division would be into the following three senses: (1) the reference to Christ ; (2) the reference to His body, the Church; (3) the reference to the individual soul, either in her state on earth or after death, as best fitted the text to be expounded. In so far as the Church and the soul are conformed to Christ, the principles manifested in His life are applicable to them. That this is the case in regard to the Church has been most clearly and most beautifully expounded by the late Mgr. Benson in his series of sermons entitled " Christ and the Church." The individual soul also can only reach Christ's glory by following in His steps, if not here on earth, hereafter in purgatory. Moreover, the Church is, in a sense, the soul writ large, as Plato pointed out in the *Republic* in regard to the state. Therefore, just as Plato found justice in the state first, then in the soul, so we may find the principles and operation of grace in the Church first, then in the individual soul. The spouse of the Canticles is alike the faithful soul, especially the supremely and perfectly faithful and grace-filled soul of Our Immaculate Lady, and also the Church. There are, moreover, innumerable side lines of reference, harmoniously converging into one of these central lines of interpretation. For instance, a text may refer equally well to the soul's deliverance from sin to grace, from this life to the next, or from purgatory to heaven. All these forms of mystical interpretation, however, refer to one and the same sacrament or fulfilment of the dispensation of grace. May this brief chapter serve to call attention to this interpretation of Scripture, to point out a path of exegesis, whereon the fathers of old ever walked, but which of late we have so sadly neglected. For the neglect of this interpretation has been and is a source of evil and scandal, both religious and ethical. For example, the Father of Jesus Christ is represented as the author of such hideous savagery as the massacre of the Amalecites. Further, such deeds have been employed as a Divine sanction of religious persecution. Pope Pius V. abused the Amalecite massacre as a sanction for the massacre of Huguenots, the English Puritans as a sanction for the massacre of Irish Catholics. Moreover, we have ourselves witnessed the employment of the Old Testament to hallow the cruelty and hatred of war. The ancient mystical interpretation, the favourite interpretation of the Church since the Apostles, cuts the ground from under such abuses. This should not be its least recommendation.

CHAPTER XIV

THE WITNESS OF NATURE MYSTICISM TO THE TEACHING OF CATHOLIC MYSTICISM STUDIED IN THE MYSTICISM OF RICHARD JEFFERIES

The Queen of the south shall rise in judgment with this generation and shall condemn it, because she came from the ends of the earth to hear the wisdom of Solomon. St Matthew xii. 42.

Consider the lilies of the field, how they grow : they labour not, neither do they spin. But I say to you that not even Solomon in all his glory was arrayed as one of these. St Matthew vi. 28, 29.

The Living God . . . left not Himself without testimony, doing good from heaven, giving rains and fruitful seasons, filling our hearts with food and gladness. Acts xiv. 16.

God . . . hath made of one, all mankind . . . that they should seek God, if haply they may feel after Him or find Him, although He be not far from every one of us, for in Him we live and move and are. Acts xviii. 26-28.

If ever a period or civilisation has forgotten God, has been without God in the world, it has been Western European civilisation of the nineteenth (must we add the twentieth) century. Misinterpreted science and unregulated industrialism together accomplished in great measure the impious boast of a certain French statesman and extinguished the lights of heaven from the spiritual firmament of countless souls. Paganism has returned once more. Nevertheless, as in the pre-Christian paganism, God gave some knowledge of Himself to favoured souls, who lacked the light of revelation ; so also has He similarly favoured certain modern pagans who, although they may have possessed an external knowledge of Christianity, never understood its true meaning. As we have seen, the end of the Christian revelation and sacraments is the union of the soul with God, a union whose highest stage here on earth is the union-intuition of the mystic. In divers fashions and in various degrees God grants the immediate knowledge and union of mystical experience to many souls whom obstacles external or internal beyond their power to remove have debarred from the acceptance of revelation. Such were Plotinus and the great Sufis. Among these in our own days was Richard Jefferies, the great nature mystic of the nineteenth century. He was not, however, merely a nature mystic—that is, one who enjoyed that peculiar sense of the immanence of God in nature which has been possessed in greater or lesser degree by all poets and artists. By special grace he was raised to a higher level, to an intuition of God as apart from and infinitely transcendent of the creation which He has made. This great mystic, this prophet and priest of the Unknown God, built to His worship an altar whose stones were intuitions of the Divine presence, its hangings the richly embroidered and brilliantly coloured tapestries of nature's loom and tincture, its ornaments, the plate and jewels of a prose that is pure poetry. Thereon he offered a fragrant incense of that adoring prayer which is the aspiration of the soul to the infinite God, Who alone can satisfy its need, alone fill its emptiness. But the nineteenth century turned a deaf ear to his message, leaving him to die in penury, while it wasted its praise and treasure on those who exploited the new power of machinery that a minority might enjoy increased comfort and wealth, now declared the sole realities. Catholics, on the other hand, because they possess the revelation so long denied altogether, never completely granted to Jefferies, have often eyes only for his errors and his denials—and fail to perceive how much truth he learnt and taught. To point out the reality, depth and value of the truth thus learnt and taught by Jefferies will be the object of this chapter. The truth contained in the message of Richard Jefferies will prove to be an external confirmation of the teaching of Catholic mysticism as we have studied it in St John of the Cross and Mother Cecilia. As such his teaching possesses a special interest for us, a special claim on our attention. Jefferies, however, has another if quite secondary title to our study and affection, his incomparable insight into nature, not merely an external knowledge of natural objects—though he is indeed an observer of unrivalled diligence and accuracy—but a sympathetic understanding of the inner life of nature and of the spiritual values therein expressed. The greatest book written by Jefferies is his spiritual autobiography, *The Story of My Heart.* In this alone does he reveal the inmost aspirations, the deepest intuitions of his God-thirsty soul. In his other works his mysticism is an undercurrent which rarely comes to the surface. They are for the most part sketches of nature, of the life of the country-side and its denizens, whether plants, animals or human beings. This intimate knowledge of nature was the starting-point of his mysticism. Therefore the student of Richard Jefferies should begin with these nature sketches. I do not think it would profit any, save the ardent naturalist, to wade through all his writings, at any rate not continuously. The capacity of the soul to receive ideas and images is, after all, limited, and even more limited is its capacity to receive emotions and æsthetic impressions. When, however, the mind grows too weary to be any longer capable of entering into the emotions and impressions received by Jefferies from the scenes and happenings which he describes with such wealth of detail, these descriptions become, what a certain clergyman complained that his writings were, a mere cataloguing of the minutiæ of nature. Happily his work largely consists of short, independent sketches. Each sketch is a vivid presentation of some phase of the life of nature, or of man in his closest contact with nature. Typical books are two collections of reprinted articles entitled *The Life of the Fields* and *The Open Air*. *The Open Air* begins with some of his finest writing, a sketch entitled " The Pageant of Summer." This is a description of a summer's day in the fields, not amidst scenery of peculiar grandeur or extraordinary beauty, but such as would be afforded by any walk through our English country-side. Green rushes, hedgerow weeds, an oak, humble bees, the blue butterflies peculiarly dear to Jefferies, and our most common birds, these are the elements out of which he weaves for us the gorgeous pageant of summer. Never has any man spoken better of Nature ; never has she found a more loving or more faithful interpreter. The imagination of Jefferies, which is of the type termed by Ruskin penetrative, lays bare her secrets. He plunges us deep into her life. The reader feels that life in its strength, its fulness, its mystery, flooding the world like a mighty ocean. Listen to the magic words in which Jefferies reveals this to all who have ears to hear him : " As the wind wandering over the sea takes from each wave an invisible portion, and brings to those on shore the ethereal essence of ocean, so the air, lingering among the woods and hedges —green waves and billows—becomes full of fine atoms of summer. Swept from notched hawthorn leaves, broad-tipped oak leaves, narrow ash sprays and oval willows, from vast elm cliffs and sharp-taloned brambles ; under-brushed from the waving grasses and stiffening corn, the dust of the sunshine was borne along and breathed.   Steeped in flower and pollen to the music of bees and birds, the stream of the atmosphere became a living thing.   It was life to breathe it, for the air itself was life.   The strength of the earth went up through the leaves into the wind.   Fed thus on the food of the Immortals, the heart opened to the width and depth of the summer, to the broad horizon afar, down to the minutest creature in the grass, up to the highest swallow.   Winter shows us Matter in its dead form, like the Primary rocks, like granite and basalt, clear but cold and frozen crystal.   Summer shows us Matter changing into life, sap rising from the earth through a million tubes, the alchemic power of light entering the solid oak ; and see ! it bursts forth in countless leaves, living things leap in the grass, living things drift upon the air, living things are coming forth to breathe in every hawthorn bush.''   In this passage has been struck one of Jefferies' key-notes, his intuition and union with the life of nature.   This intuition was the first stage of his mysticism, as yet wholly natural, the mysticism of the artist and poet. It is the contemplation of nature by the natural man, whose sense of communion with her life has not yet been dimmed or destroyed by the interposition of an artificial culture.   The poetry of Homer is thus steeped in this sympathetic intuition of nature.   His nature similes are cameos glowing with the colour of the object described, whose essence is revealed by some epithet which brings it before the reader in its living reality.   Jefferies has returned to this primitive communion with the life of nature by breaking through the barrier of a conventional civilisation, which in the world of Homer did not yet exist.   The very style of Jefferies has taken this Homeric colouring, almost the Homeric rhythm.   In the midst of the nineteenth century Jefferies has recaptured the unsophisticated freshness of the world's youth.   He has rejected the world, and his reward is at least that sought by a kindred soul, the poet Wordsworth, when he exclaimed :

> " Great God !   I'd rather be
> A pagan suckled in a creed outworn,
> So might I standing on this pleasant lea
> Have sight of Proteus rising from the sea
> Or hear old Triton blow his wreathed horn.''

That mankind will not seek this vision is to Jefferies bitterness of soul.   The plea, foreknown to pass unheeded, that men will withdraw awhile from the sordid effort of getting and spending to enter into the life of Nature, to drink of her wine and to receive of her treasure is the burden of his exquisite idyll, " Saint Guido." It is this communion with the life of nature that made Jefferies long so intensely for bodily vigour, with its resultant capacity to enter more deeply into that life, to live with its fulness, to energise more intensely, in harmony with the mighty energies of the universe. It is this longing, and no Epicurean desire for animal pleasure, that inspires the outburst of vehement desire for physical strength in the passage that follows p. 120 in *The Story of My Heart*. It is this longing that is expressed in the same book in the second petition of " The Lyra Prayer," " to make a discovery or perfect a method by which the fleshly body might enjoy more pleasure, longer life and suffer less pain." This desire is, of course, wholly natural and pagan, for the life desired is the limited life of physical nature, but it is really *natural*, not like much modern paganism, unnatural, and the natural, not the unnatural, is the basis of the supernatural. Nor is this union-intuition of the life of nature of necessity destroyed by the supernatural. Is it not the inspiration of that beautiful Easter Sequence by Adam of St Victor, which begins, " Mundi renovatio," and of its kindred Processional " Salve festa dies " ?

Noble, then, is the lower level of Jefferies' intuition, but it is only the lower level. In *The Story of My Heart* we have a transcendent mysticism also. This is chiefly to be found in the opening chapters and in the last pages. The middle of the book is chiefly occupied either by the purely natural and lower level intuition or by bad philosophising, which often denies the very truths which intuition had affirmed.

The level of Jefferies' mysticism to which we first rise from the purely natural level hitherto described is that in which the phenomena and forces of nature are felt as sacramental of a higher soul life, of spiritual realities which they symbolise and express. Matter is now felt to be the expression and embodiment of spirit. Beautiful forms and colours, indeed all natural objects, convey in terms of matter spiritual ideas, of which ideas these forms are the natural sacraments. Contemplation of natural beauties and forces, so as to receive into the soul the spirit at once revealed and hidden therein, may be termed a reception of these natural sacraments. To speak thus is in no way to disparage the infinitely higher supernatural sacraments [1] which are the

---

[1] Surely it is unnecessary for me as a Catholic to point out that I do not apply the term sacrament here or elsewhere in its strict theological sense to anything save the seven rites so termed by the Church.

crown of the entire sacramental economy whereby God reveals Himself to the embodied soul of man. This sacramental reception is Jefferies' contemplation of nature on this level of his mysticism. "I spoke to the sea," he writes. "I desired to have its strength, its mystery and glory. Then I addressed the sun, desiring the soul equivalent of his light and brilliance, his endurance and unwearied race."[1] "My soul prays that I may gather a flower from them, that I may have in myself the secret and meaning of the earth, the golden sun, the light, the foam-flecked sea."[2] "Drinking the lucid water . . . I absorbed the beauty and purity of it. I drank the thought of the element ; I desired soul-nature pure and limpid."[3] And again : "Everywhere the same deep desire for the soul nature ; to have from all green things and from the sunlight the inner meaning which was not known to them."[4] Yet again, as he contemplates the vast cycle of æons through which natural forces have worked, he says : "With all that time and power I prayed, that I might have in my soul the intellectual part of it, the idea, the thought."[5] And in yet another place he exclaims : "Let divine beauty "—he is referring to the beauty of the human body—" bring to me divine soul."[6] "I was not more than eighteen," he tells us, "when an inner and esoteric meaning began to come to me from all the visible universe, and indefinable aspirations filled me. . . . There was a deeper meaning everywhere. The sun burned with it, the broad front of morning beamed with it ; a deep feeling entered me while gazing at the sky in the azure noon and in the star-lit evening."[7] Elsewhere he says : "I was aware of the grass blades, the flowers, the leaves on hawthorn and tree : I seemed to live more largely through them, as if each were a pore through which I drank. . . . I was plunged deep in existence, and with all that existence I prayed."[8] Thus does Jefferies reverently receive the sacraments of nature and rise thereby to a higher plane. This reception is essentially an intuition of God as present in creation, yet other than the creation wherein His Presence is apprehended. Intuition of the Divine immanence is essentially constitutive of nature mysticism, as opposed to the higher and purely supernatural mysticism. Nevertheless, even in nature mysticism at this higher level there is surely present a supernatural element,

[1] *Story of My Heart*, pp. 4, 5. Ed. 1907. [2] *Ibid.*, p. 11. [3] *Ibid.*, p. 21.
[4] *Ibid.*, p. 13. [5] *Ibid.*, p. 19. [6] *Ibid.*, p. 25.
[7] *Ibid.*; p. 199. [8] *Ibid.*, pp. 14, 15.

a co-operation of Divine grace. For this sense of the sacramental character of the material universe is a perception of the truth, that all things are made and sustained by God, of Whom they are a true though infinitely inadequate revelation, that His Being is in them and works through them, and that all that they are is in Him eminently so that their positive being is a participation of His. We have, however, already seen that the intuition of this truth constitutes an essential part of the intuition of the super-natural mystics, even of those whose teaching is most severely transcendental, and that it is emphasised by St John of the Cross and Mother Cecilia.

It is true that the immanental intuition in which these super-natural mystics beheld this truth was not the same as that of the nature mystic. It was a consequence and concomitant of their direct intuition of the transcendent Deity, whereas the latter was given on a far lower level and by a far inferior mode as an indirect intuition of the hidden immanence of God in creatures. There-fore, whereas the former intuition is essentially supernatural, the basis of the latter is natural. Nevertheless the truth common to both intuitions argues for the working of grace in the production even of the lower and more natural intuition. Moreover, as we have seen, the lower intuition when it has attained this sacra-mental plane is of God as distinct from the creation in which He is immanent. This also points to the working of grace. There-fore, though I cannot prove a supernatural element and co-operation in the nature mysticism of Jefferies, even at his second and mediate level of intuition, there is good reason to posit that supernatural element and co-operation. I therefore claim with confidence the presence of such a supernatural element and operation in this second and sacramental level of Jefferies' mysticism, which is pre-eminently his nature mysticism.

We saw above that Jefferies' sense of the life of nature gave birth to a prayer for a fuller natural life, for a deeper and wider share in this natural life and energy. His deeper intuition of a spiritual reality in and behind the life of nature gives birth to a deeper prayer, no longer wholly natural. On p. 30 of *The Story of My Heart* Jefferies expressly distinguishes this higher prayer " the far deeper emotion in which the soul was alone con-cerned " from the lower " Lyra " prayer for a fuller and more powerful life in the natural order. This deeper prayer was, he tells us, essentially inexpressible. " I felt," he says, " an emotion of the soul beyond all definition ; prayer is a puny thing to it and the word is a rude sign to the feeling." [1]   Again : " One of the greatest difficulties I have encountered is the lack of words to express ideas. By the word soul, or psyche, I mean that inner consciousness which aspires. By prayer I do not mean a request for anything preferred to a Deity. I mean intense soul-emotion, intense aspiration." [2] This prayer of Jefferies possesses two essential properties of mystical prayer : (1) it transcends intellectual formulation ; (2) it proceeds from the radical ego, which is also the root of the will, is thus the aspiration of the centre of the soul, of the synderesis. [3]   We should also note how miserably inadequate was the so-called Christianity learnt by Jefferies in his youth, in which prayer is conceived as essentially a begging for particular favours, usually of a temporal nature. This prayer of Jefferies is not for any particular object, another essential character of mystical prayer or contemplation. He says, indeed, in so many words that it was not for an object. [4]   On the same page, however, he also says : " What I laboured for was soul-life, more soul-nature, to be exalted, to be full of soul-learning." His desire was an unlimited desire for spiritual reality, for an infinite and ineffable soul-life, a life or being insusceptible of definition. This ineffable and unlimited soul-life or spiritual reality is, as we saw, often conceived as the spirit immanent in nature. In varying degrees, however, it is realised as transcendent of nature. The realisation of this transcendence constitutes the third and highest level of Jefferies' mysticism, a level which is most decisively and entirely supernatural. Indeed its obvious supernaturalism is a further argument for the existence of supernatural co-operation on the mediate level of nature mysticism from which it sprang. " From all the ages," so writes Jefferies, " my soul desired to take that soul life which had flowed through them." [5]   " I prayed that . . . my soul might be more than the cosmos of life." [6]   " That I might have the deepest of soul-life, the deepest of all, deeper far than all this greatness of the visible universe and even of the invisible ; that I might have a fulness of soul till now unknown and utterly beyond my own conception." [7]

---

[1] *Story of My Heart*, p. 5.   [2] *Ibid.*, p. 202.
[3] This latter character I conclude from Jefferies' account of his prayer. There is, of course, no explicit statement to this effect.
[4] *Story of My Heart*, p. 8.
[6] *Ibid.*, p. 16.   [5] *Ibid.*, p. 14.
                                                                [7] *Ibid.*, p. 17.

This sense of a soul-life transcendent of physical nature is expressed still more plainly in another passage. " Now, this moment give me all the thought, all the idea, expressed in the cosmos around me " (immanental and sacramental level). " Give me *still more*, for the interminable universe, past and present, is but earth ; give me the unknown soul, *wholly apart from it*, the soul of which I know only that when I touch the ground, when the sunlight touches my hand, *it is not there* " [1] (transcendental level). He perceives also that his own soul is nearer akin to this unknowable soul-life than is physical nature. " The mystery," he says, " and the possibilities are not in the roots of the grass, nor is the depth of things in the sea ; they are in my existence, in my soul." [2] Who can doubt the transcendent and supernatural character of this utterance ? Do not all the mystics from St Augustine downwards cry out that God dwells hidden in the centre of the soul, and that there and there alone can He be sought and found ? Indeed the language of Jefferies in the two passages last quoted echoes that famous passage of the *Confessions*, which begins : " I asked the earth and it answered me, ' I am not He ' " (St Aug., *Confessions*, x. 9). At first, indeed, this sense of the transcendent spirit-being seems solely, or at least normally, to have been given through the instrumentality of natural beauties. This was not, however, invariably the case, for Jefferies tells us that this same thought rose in his mind in the deepest darkness of the night.[3] As time progressed the need of nature images became less. " It " (the prayer) " is now less solely associated with the sun and sea, hills, woods or beauteous human shape. It is always within. It requires no waking, no renewal ; it is always with me. I am it ; the fact of my existence expresses it." [4] This increasing transcendence of images is, as we have seen, characteristic of that progressive purgation from the limits of the finite, which is the negative way of mysticism, as it is taught, for instance, in *The Ascent of Mount Carmel*. This complete transcendence of creatures finally attained by Jefferies in his irrepressible aspiration, which is supreme prayer towards the all-transcendent Reality apprehended by mystical intuition beyond thought and expression, is most powerfully affirmed in the concluding passage of his book. " The great sun," he there writes, " burning in the sky, the sea, the firm earth, all the stars

---

[1] *Story of My Heart*, p. 20.   [2] *Ibid.*, p. 35.
[3] *Ibid.*, p. 17.   [4] *Ibid.*, pp. 27, 28.

of night are feeble—all, all the cosmos is feeble : it is not strong enough to utter my prayer-desire. My soul cannot reach to its full desire of prayer. *I need no earth, or sea, or sun to think my thought.* If my thought part, the psyche, were entirely separated from the body and from the earth, I should of myself desire the same. In itself my soul desires, my existence, my soul-existence is in itself my prayer, and so long as it exists, so long will I pray that I may have the fullest soul-life." [1] This ascent from intuition of the Divine immanence in nature to intuition of the Divine transcendence, indeed the entire process from the first purely natural level onwards, is closely paralleled by a Catholic mystic contemporary with Jefferies. In her *Spiritual Journal* [2] Lucie Christine gives a detailed and very beautiful account of her rise from the purely natural intuition of the life of nature (Jefferies' first level) through the "mixed" intuition of God immanent in nature yet other than and thus transcendent of nature to the third purely supernatural intuition of His transcendence. "Everything beautiful," she writes, "fascinated and fired my soul with enthusiasm. The first glimpse of the sea from the cliffs drew tears from my eyes. I often remained whole hours contemplating its immensity without being able to express what I felt." Here is the first, purely immanental and natural intuition. "I sought Thee, my God, in all things beautiful, and in all things I found Thee. I asked Thee of the sea. . . . Thou wert reposing in its depths. . . . I met Thee in the impenetrable gloom of forests, I saw Thee pass in the lightning flash. . . . I have felt Thee in the hidden travail of nature. I sought Thee at the hands of all creatures, and they all replied, 'Behold, He is here.'" This is the immanental-transcendent intuition of the second level—in which, as Lucie distinctly tells us, the supernatural is present. "Soon I felt something strange. . . . Everything I had admired . . . still appeared to me equally beautiful ; nevertheless I could no longer enjoy it as before. As the stars fade away in the light of the sun, so everything grew pale in the glance of God upon my soul ; I gazed on sea and land and saw only God." [3] Here is the third and wholly transcendental level, a level completely supernatural, the level of which Jefferies speaks in the passage last quoted. The very language of Lucie in this passage closely re-

[1] *Story of My Heart,* pp. 206, 207.   [2] English translation, pp. 131-134.
[3] This passage has been already quoted in Chapter V. but is so apposite to this explanation of Jefferies' mysticism that I venture to cite it again here.

calls that of Jefferies, in particular her account of the mediate intuition which is the higher intuition of the nature mystic. Lucie Christine thus confirms and explains in the light of her full Catholic faith the intuition of Jefferies on all its levels.

The Unlimited soul-life, this Reality beyond image and concept transcendent of nature wherein It is immanent, which is the object of Jefferies' highest prayer and intuition, is, of course, known to the Christian mystic as God. Jefferies refuses to term it God. On the contrary, he says : " I realise the existence of an inexpressible entity infinitely higher than Deity"[1]; and elsewhere: "I prayed that I might touch to the unutterable existence infinitely higher than Deity." [2] " I know that there is something infinitely higher than Deity." [3] Jefferies' denial of God is, however, wholly verbal, at least when he is expressing his mystical experience. A Being identical with the Divine Being experienced by Christian mystics is that Divine Being, is God. The reason for Jefferies' verbal denial is that he understands by God the anthropomorphic and therefore limited deity of his childhood's creed. How anthropomorphic and limited his notion of the Christian God was is seen in the words on p. 106 : " Go higher than *a* god ; to the Entity unknown." No one who understood Christian theism could speak thus of *a* god, as if there might be many gods. Jefferies was obviously ignorant of the true Catholic Theism. Had he known it he would have recognised the Being in whose communion and intuition his inner life consisted. He enjoyed an intuition of God, as infinite and therefore unknowable by any human concept. He falsely imagined the Christian god to be finite and comprehensible by such concepts. Hence his very intuition of God made him reject the false notion which he had formed of the Godhead as the object of Christian belief. Fidelity to the true theism really taught by the Church, to the negative knowledge of Dionysius and the schools, a theism which he had learned by his mystical intuition, compelled him to deny the existence of the idol which he had mistaken for the God of Christian theism. His agnosticism is therefore the agnosticism of St John of the Cross, not that of Herbert Spencer, and his verbal atheism proves his attainment of the true theism.

Jefferies' ignorance of his own theism is indeed a warning to us who believe never to allow our intellectual or spiritual life to outgrow our understanding of the Catholic Faith. If this should

---

[1] *Story of My Heart*, p. 57. [2] *Ibid.*, p. 6. [3] *Ibid.*, p. 206.

happen, we must amend the defect by a deeper study of our creed. Otherwise we shall either stunt our spiritual growth by confining it within the religious ideas that we have outgrown, or we shall lose our faith entirely.   One of these two evils is the inevitable result of a false identification of the Catholic Faith with a superficial, often a childish, understanding of it.   We learn also from Jefferies that the line of demarcation between atheism and theism has often been wrongly drawn.   The real test is not verbal profession. Everyone who makes the limited his end alike of will, of thought and of intuition and has thus said in his heart, "There is no God," is an atheist, no matter how theistic or even Christian his external profession.   Everyone who apprehends, whether by will, by thought or by intuition, the unlimited and therefore spiritual Being existent in and beyond the limited is in very truth a theist, no matter how inadequate or perverted his intellectual formulation of that apprehension, nay, even if such formulation be entirely lacking.[1]   If we do not apply this test we shall be led to absurd results.   We shall be obliged, for instance, to label the deeply religious Buddha an atheist, the irreligious and rationalist Voltaire atheist.*   We must therefore apply the test not of verbal profession, but of the limited or unlimited nature of aim and apprehension.   Nietzsche is in the depths of his soul a theist, for his message ends with *ewigkeit*, eternity, the unlimited.   On the other hand, Mr Snooks, of Ealing, who attends eleven o'clock service on Sunday for the sake of respectability, but whose entire soul *in all its functions* is confined by limits, is a veritable atheist.   Jefferies is therefore a theist, however loudly he may affirm and imagine the contrary.[2]   Indeed his account of the Object of his mystical intuition is even verbally identical with the mystical theology of the Areopagite whose doctrine has met with such entire acceptance and veneration by the Church.   For his verbal atheism passes over into that transcendent and therefore negative statement of theism which is found in Dionysius.   Jefferies' teaching of "the unutterable existence infinitely higher than deity—the inexpressible entity infinitely higher than deity—something better than a god—something higher than a god—something

[1] Pantheism *of the higher type* is a *perverted* formulation of theism as understood here in a wide and untechnical sense.

[2] Obviously I do not maintain that Nietzsche was a theist in the technical sense—for that would mean that his discursive reason accepted theism, which, of course, was not the case.

infinitely higher than deity," is but an echo of the Dionysian doctrine of "the Super-Deity Which is above all superessentially" —the "Triad Supernal, both *super*-God and super-good—He Who is super-source, beyond even the so-called Deity and Goodness, seeing He is beyond source of Divinity and source of Goodness— He Who neither is Deity." Clearly Jefferies and Dionysius teach one and the same theology, expressed in a terminology almost identical. Only, unhappily, Jefferies, unlike the Areopagite, did not know that the Christian God is this super-divine Deity in Whom both alike believed.

In the third chapter Jefferies reaffirms his doctrine of an Entity that " is in addition to the existence of the soul, in addition to immortality and beyond the idea of the deity." " I think there is something more than existence." [1] He proceeds, however, to inform us that this intuition of an unknowable Being beyond all we can think or imagine is his own discovery, a Fourth Spiritual Idea gained for man ! " There is," he continues, " an immense ocean over which the mind can sail "—this super-Deity "upon which the vessel of thought has not yet been launched. I hope to launch it." How astonished he would have been to read this newly discovered truth, this fourth idea, in Dionysius or in St Thomas, this doctrine that God is above existence, as creatures possess and understand it. In this very book Jefferies utters a wish that all the writings of mediæval philosophy might be destroyed as unreal figments coming between man and reality. Had he only read those writings, he would have found them centred around the very doctrine fondly imagined to have been now dis- covered for the first time by himself. So orthodox, indeed, is the teaching of Jefferies that we can obtain from his book the essential principles of Christian monotheism as taught or presupposed by the Christian mystics. Only the doctrine of the Trinity is absent which rests on revelation alone, and is only manifested to those mystics who have first learned it from the Church. The Divine Infinity, incomprehensibility, immanence and transcendence, all these we have seen taught by Jefferies. It is also clear from the above quotations that he conceived of the unknowable Being as essentially nearer to spirit than to matter ; it is "the thought that lies therein . . . the spirit that I feel so close." [2] It is a " Soul-Entity." [3] Jefferies teaches us in effect that the Ultimate Reality, though in Itself unknowable, is known by its works and

---

[1] *Story of My Heart*, p. 54.   [2] *Ibid.*, p. 43.   [3] *Ibid.*, p. 54.

is more adequately, though still infinitely inadequately, represented by personal spirit than by impersonal matter, is therefore
supra-personal, not infra-personal.   We have seen that Jefferies
also taught that it is through the soul that we are in closest
relationship with this Ultimate supra-personal (and therefore
personal) Being.   Jefferies feels that his own soul is capable of so
intimate a union with this Divine Being that it *seems* at times to
be identical with that Being or life.   The infinite soul-life which
he seeks, though given from without, is to be in a true sense his
own soul-life.   This is, of course, to affirm the possibility of the
transforming union of the soul with God, of the deification of the
soul.   The third chapter is devoted to a description of Jefferies'
experience of eternity and immortality as more real and more
ultimate than time and mortality, just as spirit is more real, more
ultimate than matter.   Jefferies feels himself rapt out of time into
the Now of eternity.   " This Now is eternity. . . . We are . . .
in eternity." [1]   " I cannot understand time.   It is eternity now.
I am in the midst of it. . . .   Now is eternity ; now is the immortal
life.   Here this moment. . . . I exist in it. . . . To the soul
there is no past and no future ; all is, and will be ever, in now." [2]
" I dwell this moment in the eternal Now that has ever been and
will be." [3]   There is perhaps in this passage a certain confusion
between the eternal now of God and the soul-time of the finite
spirit which transcends clock-time (see von Hügel).   But the
experience of eternity is there.   Jefferies' intuition is the temporary
entrance of the mystic into the everlasting Now of eternal life, no
mere experience of a Bergsonian duree and becoming.   It is rather
Suso's experience of " a breaking forth of the sweetness of eternal
life felt as present in the stillness of unvarying contemplation." [4]
A consequence of this experience of eternal life is a conviction of
personal immortality, that the soul which thus enters into eternity
cannot die with the time-subject body.   It is true that Jefferies
also says that the eternal life apprehended transcends immortality
and emphasises its unknowability.   Here, however, Jefferies has
again in view the popular notion of a future life which is but the
unending continuation of our time-life on earth, and this concept
he rightly rejects, as all mystics have rejected it.

In this same chapter Jefferies points out that miracles,

---

[1] *Story of My Heart*, p. 45.   [2] *Ibid.*, p. 43.   [3] *Ibid.*, p. 49.
[4] *Life*, trs. Knox, p. 10.   See also Lucie Christine, *Spiritual Journal*, Eng.
trs., pp. 52 and 64.

interventions of the ultimate spiritual reality and of superhuman spirits in the phenomena and order of nature, are not only possible but in a sense perfectly natural.[1] " I see no reason at all why they should not take place this day." He even witnesses to the existence of superhuman finite spirits. " The air," he says, " the sunlight, the night, all that surrounds me seems crowded with inexpressible powers, with the influence of souls, or existences." [2] Miracles and angels laughed out of court by modern enlightenment, as Jefferies laughs out of court the mediæval treatises on these matters, are here affirmed as facts of spiritual experience by the mystic who of all others is most eager to be free from all traditional teaching, to be alone with reality, without the mediation of church, creed or philosophy. I cannot conceive any more convincing vindication of the fundamental principles of Catholic theology and mysticism. The intuition of Jefferies, the verbal atheist, indeed the real sceptic of non-mystical moments, is a powerful apologia for the truth of Catholic theism and mystical theology.

Jefferies bears witness not only to the Object but also to the Method of mystical theology, as we find it in the Christian mystics. It is true that he sets out from the Divine Immanence in nature, which for the Christian mystics is a secondary intuition consequent on achieved union with God. But Jefferies, as we saw, has also attained to God transcendent, and has done so by the only possible way, the negative way—the way that rejects the limitations of finite beings in order to attain to the Infinite Being. Like them, Jefferies had to purify the will from limited attachments, the consciousness from limited forms. To the former purgation many passages bear witness. In the preface he says : " The surroundings, the clothes, the dwelling, the social status, the circumstances are to me utterly indifferent. . . . The pageantry of power, the still more foolish pageantry of wealth, the senseless precedence of place, I fail words to express my utter contempt for such pleasures or such ambitions." Jefferies also practised the purgation of the consciousness from limited forms. In chapter six he relates the preliminary stage of this purgation, his refusal to allow himself to be imprisoned by the " endless and nameless circumstances of everyday existence, which by degrees build a wall about the mind so that it travels in a constantly

---

[1] *Story of My Heart*, pp. 48, 49.
[2] P. 49. See also top of same page.

narrowing circle." To effect this he used to take solitary walks, for he too had learned the truth of God's promise to the soul : " I will lead her into solitude, and there will I speak to her heart." But he went further, and as he rose from God-immanent to God-transcendent he learned to exclude even the well-beloved forms of nature. " Sometimes," he says, " I have concentrated myself, and driven away by continued will all sense of outward appearances, looking straight with the full power of my mind inwards on myself." [1] He proceeds to tell us how he found within himself an ego not wholly comprehensible, through which he was brought into contact with an unknown life, that was really, though he could not so name it, the Being of God. " I find ' I ' am there, an ' I ' I do not wholly understand or know [the normally subliminal centre]. . . . Recognising it, I feel on the margin of a life unknown, very near, almost touching it " (the intuition of God's especial presence in the unlimited centre).[2] We thus find the fundamental principles of St John's active night or purgation stated and practised by Jefferies. The passive purgation has also a certain counterpart. Not only did he detach himself from sensible forms during his highest contemplation, but, as we saw above, these forms tended to fall away from him of themselves. Indeed the entire mystical portion of Jefferies' book is the active achievement and the passive gift of that escape from the limits of the finite into the infinite which is the essence of the mystical way. Moreover, God sent him the great purifier that invariably accompanies, indeed conditions, high mystical insight—namely, suffering and external failure. Lacking recognition, in crippling poverty, compelled to long periods of uncongenial drudgery, he was also, during his later years, the victim of an internal ailment that caused him the most acute suffering. Indeed *The Story of My Heart* was largely written amidst intense physical agony.

It is true that his purgation did not possess the intensity or the completeness of the purgation of the great Christian mystics. Neither did his mystical experience possess the height, the perfection or the personal love of their experience. It lacked the personal love of the Christian mystic for His Incarnate Lord, it lacked the sense of sin and of the need of redemption, was, in a word, open to St Augustine's criticism of Neoplatonism. It also lacked the height of Christian mysticism. Jefferies never reached the supreme degrees of union. For that very reason it lacked its

[1] *Story of My Heart,* p. 49.   [2] *Ibid,* p. 50.

completeness. The centre of Jefferies' soul found God in intermittent intuition and union—but his whole soul was not subjected to the centre and its experience. Lower levels of experience remained side by side with the higher, only half distinguished from them. Such was that naturalistic Homeric level frequent with him to the end. Although his will was fundamentally united with the will of God through his love of the Unknown Deity, in union with Whom he found his highest good, he was by no means wholly resigned to the Divine disposition of his life. Moreover, despite his efforts to achieve entire independence of all previous speculation, his intellect was still enslaved by the false tenets of the dominant philosophy of the nineteenth century, a pseudo-scientific materialism. His discursive reason often denies the affirmations of his mystical intuition. He refuses to credit the actual occurrence of miracles, although he has seen their possibility and likelihood. Still worse, he is ready to believe that after all death is the extinction of the ego and its resolution into the material elements! He is therefore eager to realise human happiness in this world, and is apt to translate his mystical aspiration after the life of God into the lower key of a desire for the enjoyment by posterity of a full, powerful and happy life on earth. His realisation that man's nature requires the completion and expression of a perfect soul by and through a perfect body, the principle which underlies the Catholic doctrine of the Resurrection, is distorted by his this-worldly perspective into the craving for a beautiful and active body in this life. Thus his intellect is at strife with his mystical intuition. The normal Jefferies is not at one with Jefferies the mystic. It may seem strange that God should have permitted these intellectual errors to co-exist with mystical union and intuition. We must remember, however, that many opponents of religion attempt to explain away the witness of mysticism by denying its independence.[1] Its intuition is, they say, but the reflex of a creed previously accepted. Richard Jefferies gives the lie direct to this assertion. So far as any creed dominated him, and that was only in part, it was dogmatic materialism. The creed of his childhood—an imperfect Christianity childishly understood— he rejected with contempt. But the work of the spirit of God in his soul overcame the philosophy of his extra-mystical intelligence, and compelled him to bear witness to the Light in an age of darkness, to affirm an experimental knowledge of God and eternal life

---

[1] *E.g.* Prof. Höffding, *Philosophy of Religion* (pp. 102 *seqq.*).

which his lower reasoning denied. His witness even extended to the affirmation of the theism taught by Christian mystics, of the soul, of eternity, of angels and of miracles, although this witness was so strangely unconscious. That is for us his supreme value— the *testimonium animæ naturaliter Christianæ*—given with a clearness and intensity of conviction never exceeded by any other non-Christian mystic. Nor was he left to the end in his intellectual ignorance. As he lay on his bed of sickness, nigh to death, Christian faith was infused into him. This faith was indeed very imperfect, being limted by an ultra-Protestant individualism which rejected all church membership. Nevertheless it was the knowledge of God, clear and certain now to the discursive reason, as well as to the intuition of the centre, and thus accepted by the whole man. It was, moreover, the knowledge of Jesus. For all the truth and beauty of non-Christian mysticism, the Christian reader may well feel what St Bernard felt when he said : "*Si scribas, non sapit mihi nisi legero ibi Jesum.*~ *Si disputes, aut conferas, non sapit mihi nisi sonuerit ibi Jesus*" ("Naught that is written hath savour to me, but I may read therein Jesus. No disputation, no conference hath savour to me, except I may hear therein Jesus") (serm. in Cant. 15). To all such it must be a joy to know that when Jefferies came to die that Divine name uttered in fervent prayer was among the last words to pass his lips. Having used so well the light and gift of his mystical knowledge of God, he was given the one great gift yet lacking, the knowledge of God Incarnate, into Whose membership he had indeed been baptized, but Whom he had never truly known. His faith [1] as a Gentile was far beyond that of the majority in the Christian Israel. Therefore, like the centurion of old, he found Christ, and in Christ the healing of his lower nature, the servant of the already united centre, and his translation from the obscure knowledge of God on earth, for him in his intellectual infidelity, doubly obscure, to the clear vision of Heaven, wherein he drinks at its source that fulness of unlimited soul-life for which he thirsted so deeply. "*Euge serve bone et fidelis quia in pauca fuisti fidelis supra multa es constitutus, intrasti in gaudium Domini tui*" ("Well done, thou good and faithful servant, because thou hast been faithful in a few things thou art set over many, thou hast entered into the joy of Thy Lord").

---

[1] I mean the *faith* of his mystical intuition.

CHAPTER XV

ST JOHN THE POET

All is done, every haunting form is gone. . . . Far, far away, like a steely light upon the horizon, a watery plain, a line of trembling waves, the sea. The river runs down to it. The sea seems to run up to the river. She fires him. He desires her. He must lose himself in her.

JEAN CHRISTOPHE,
English trs., vol. i., p. 90.

ART must ever remain the most adequate expression of spiritual intuition and experience. The quasi-scientific treatment in *The Ascent of Mount Carmel* and *The Dark Night* broke down of necessity, and passed over into the poetry of the *Spiritual Canticle* and *The Living Flame of Love.* Yet even the two former treatises were comments on a poem, and the poem contained far more than the comment could ever express. St John has left us some twenty-three poems inclusive of the three whose commentary is his prose works. They are of very unequal value; there is but one positively bad and the best is of supreme worth. Like all poetry, the poetry of St John is truly accessible to those alone who can read it in the original.

Most of the poems are based directly or indirectly on nuptial imagery, on the mutual love of Bride and Bridegroom. This imagery was fundamental for St John, different in this from Mother Cecilia, who, like St Catherine of Genoa (see Baron von Hügel, *Mystical Element*), prefers a more impersonal imagery. A lengthy presentation of the Incarnational economy which occupies a consecutive series of nine poems, called Romances, is based on the nuptial union between the Word and the elect, His bride. His longest poem is a paraphrase of the Canticle of Canticles, and the finest of all his poems, *The Dark Night*, describes the meeting and embrace of the lover and the beloved. Other leading ideas are transcendence of clear knowledge, dissatisfaction with creatures and longing for death. The fundamental principles of St

389

John's mystical teaching are summed up, often with great force, concision and clarity. The fifth poem,[1] entitled *An Ecstasy of Contemplation*, is perhaps the best example of this. It is simply St John's doctrine of transcendence and the nature of mystical intuition expressed in beautiful verse. There is little imagery and none that is not explained in the poem itself. In other poems, such as that of *The Dark Night*, all is unexplained imagery. These latter are poems in a far higher sense than the former, since art, of which poetry is a species, consists essentially in the embodiment of spiritual intuition in material images.* Sometimes St John falls into the besetting sin of allegorical literature, the formation of a grotesque image in the interest of the allegory. An instance of this is to be found in the twelfth stanza of the *Spiritual Canticle*. This reads :

> O crystal well !
> Oh, that on thy silvered surface
> Thou wouldst mirror forth at once
> Those eyes desired
> That are outlined in my heart.

To the careless reader this stanza would suggest a well of clear and still water bathed in sunlight, whose surface shone like a sheet of bright silver, and in that silver-bright sheet the appearance of the face of the Beloved, as faces are reflected in clear water and in a shining surface of silver. Such an image would be altogether beautiful and consistent. When, however, the prose explanation is read, it is realised that the surface is not called silver or silvery, but silver-plated. The well is the substance of the faith and the silver-plated surface the definitions and dogmas beneath which that substance is hidden—like gold plated over with silver. But it is evident that the two images of a clear well and of metal plating do not cohere and that their union is grotesque. The image is sacrificed to the allegory. Again, in the ninth poem the principal image is that of a fountain, the Divine Being. But the three Persons of the Blessed Trinity are said to dwell in one living water. Surely the image of the joint habitation of one place by three persons does not consist with the image of a fountain. Worse is the concluding stanza, where St John says that—

> The living fountain for which I long
> I see in this Bread of Life.

---

[1] I number the poems in accordance with the Edicion Critica.

The image of a fountain springing from a piece of bread is surely grotesque in the extreme. In a poem based on the imagery of a fountain of water the inconsistent imagery of bread should have been avoided.

Moreover, from the purely æsthetic point of view, it is a pity that the impassioned melodies of the *Canticle* should end on a note of discordant flatness:

> None saw it,
> Neither did Aminadab appear.
> The siege was intermitted
> And the cavalry dismounted
> At the sight of the waters.

The artistic error is all the worse because the preceding verse is most beautiful and would have formed a worthy ending. Moreover, the original ends with a far more beautiful image: "Flee, my beloved, and be like the roe and the young hart on the mountains of spices." Here also the allegorical interest has overpowered the artistic. We must remember, however, that even Dante did not avoid this trap in the allegory which concludes the *Purgatorio*, for we find Prudence figuring in the mystic procession with three eyes, although a three-eyed maiden would be a monster. Sometimes the poetry is injured by excess of fidelity to a paraphrased original. Thus in the twentieth poem a mystical paraphrase of the exilic psalm, *Super Flumina Babylonis*, St John has felt himself obliged to introduce that final verse of fierce wrath against Babylon: "Blessed shall he be that taketh thy children and dasheth them against the stones." In order to retain this verse he has to end his poem with the following stanza:—

> He will me, thy weeping captive,
> With thy little children take,
> And to Christ the *Rock* will bring them.
> I have left thee for His sake.

The feebleness and formlessness of this verse are in striking contrast with the energy of the original ending. Moreover, the verse is suggestive of the final conversion of all worldlings, a doctrine far indeed from the mind of St John. How much better art it would have been to omit a verse which did not harmonise with the interpretation of the psalm adopted in this poem.

These instances of disharmony between form and matter,

between expression and idea, are, after all, rare. In general the poetry is no unworthy embodiment of the doctrine it conveys.

I am not competent to discuss the literary form of the poems since I am unacquainted with Spanish literature. It seems to me clear, graceful and musical. St John was a careful student of artistic form and used the best models. *The Living Flame* is, he tells us, composed in the manner of Boscan. A favourite device is the repetition, exact or almost exact, of the same line at the end of each verse. This line is the key-line of the poem in which the main thought is expressed. It occurs in six poems. The respective key-lines of these poems are " *muero porque no muero* " (" I die because I am not dead "); "*toda sciencia transcendiendo* " ("all knowledge transcending "); " *que le di a la caza alcance* " (" that brought the prey within my grasp "); " *un no se que, que se halla per ventura* " (" a something, I know not what, that has happily been found "); " *aunque es de noche* " (" though it be night "); and " *el pecho del amor muy lastimado* " (" his breast cruelly torn by love ").

The series of Romances which set forth the economy of the Incarnation, as a theological exposition in metre, challenges comparison with Aquinas' *Lauda Sion*. The comparison does not result to the advantage of the Romances. They lack that fire of ecstatic jubilation which inflames the dogmatic statements of the eucharistic sequence, the same fire that burns in the rhapsody which opens Father Faber's *Treatise on the Blessed Sacrament*. Their very metre is monotonous, especially when prolonged through the entire series of poems. But, indeed, even the *Lauda Sion* could not have been thus prolonged. Its flame would have been stifled under the mass of fuel. Nevertheless these Romances possess some beauty, although of a very placid, uninspired type.

Then we have a number of poems of varied merit, expressive of particular aspects of the mystical way—diverse emotions of the soul's love. Among these are the twenty-second poem, *Si de mi Baja Suerte* (the longing for a consuming love that will penetrate the Divine Heart), and the preceding poem, *Del Aqua de la Vida* (the thirst of the soul for the full fruition of heaven). Interpolated in this is a long passage of more than doubtful authenticity—a description of heaven in the style of Bernard of Cluny's *Hora Novissima* and St Peter Damian's *Ad Perennis Vitæ Fontem*. It is quite well done, but its dwelling on material images, such as pearls, is somewhat unjohannine. We remember the passage in

The Ascent of Mount Carmel where St John says that a mountain of gold or pearls contains, after all, no more than the single pieces of gold and the single pearls of which we have actual experience. Akin to these are the seventh poem, of detachment from creatures, and the sixth of the attainment of God. Neither is specially noteworthy. The fourth poem of longing for death, with its refrain, " I die because I am not dead," is a noble expression of this feeling. We may note in particular the image of the fish out of water, found, of course, elsewhere, as representative of the mystic in this life. Very beautiful is the poem that describes the satisfaction of the soul in its experience of the unknowable Godhead in mystical intuition, " something, I know not what, that happily is found." Best of this group is the *Ecstasy of Contemplation*. I do not know that its poetical achievement is better than that of the others. Its power lies in its clear expression of the mystical knowledge that is nevertheless ignorance. This entire group of poems, like the Romances, falls short in being a direct exposition of spiritual truth rather than its expression through material imagery. It is only half poetry, therefore far less poetical, than much of the prose-writing. In the ninth poem, the poem on the fountain that flows by night, we have more imagery and therefore truer art, and more suggestion of an infinity beyond the letter. In the more or less disembodied poetry hitherto discussed there is a false suggestion that the poem, since it directly expresses the spiritual meaning, is adequate to that meaning. In the embodied poetry we know that we are dealing with symbols and sacraments of the unlimited and inexpressible. Only in this fountain poem the embodiment is not complete and the underlying meaning breaks through disconcertingly. In the tenth poem, on the other hand, the embodiment is entire. Nevertheless this poem is the most unsuccessful of all, because that embodiment is hopelessly inadequate. Not that the embodiment is ugly ; it is, on the contrary, quite pretty. But it is only pretty, and prettiness is ugly in religious poetry. The poem allegorises the love of Christ for the human soul by the figure of a shepherd mourning for his shepherdess who has slighted and forgotten him. The effect is a pastoral, resembling closely a Watteau group, or those Chelsea figures that adorn the cupboards and mantelpieces of collectors of old china. But the artificial loves of Chelsea shepherds and shepherdesses can never image the love of Christ for the soul. It is strange indeed that the stern mystic of Carmel could ever have written this poem. The

Edicion Critica unhesitatingly accepts its authenticity, so I suppose we can but remember that Homer nods at times. Certainly if St John wrote these verses there is no reason to deny his authorship of *The Thorns of the Spirit*, where a solid substance of mystical doctrine is tricked out with similar prettiness of playful endearment. Here the first word strikes the wrong note —*Un pastorcico*—a little shepherd ! Only in the final verse we are surprised by the sudden emergence of a deeper tone when the Crucifixion is spoken of—and we are jarred by the contrast, as by the sight of a crucifix in an elegant drawing-room.

There remain now for discussion but three poems of undoubted authenticity, but these three exceed in value all the others together. They are the three whose comment constitutes the four great prose works of St John. All three are embodied and they are poetry and art in the fullest and most complete sense. *The Living Flame* suffers, I think, by comparison with its commentary, which is even more poetical than the poem itself. When compared with the purple passages so frequent in this prose poem, the verses, beautiful though they are in themselves, must appear somewhat meagre. The *Canticle* is far finer poetry, though we must, of course, make a large deduction from its merit as largely due to the beauty of its inspired original. Nevertheless it is not slavish imitation, no Tate and Brady paraphrase. It is, on the contrary, full of original touches of exquisite beauty. Mr Lewis has given us two versions—one in prose, the other in verse. Personally I vastly prefer the former—it is so much simpler and more faithful to the original. Of all its forty verses the two that have impressed themselves most deeply on my imagination are the following :—

> My Beloved is the mountains,
> The solitary wooded valleys,
> The strange islands,
> The roaring torrents,
> The whisper of the amorous gales,
> The tranquil night
> At the approaches of the dawn,
> The silent music,
> The murmuring solitude,
> The supper which revives and enkindles love.

Do not say that the murmuring solitude is unreal, a perverted symbolism. If you think that you can never have been alone in

the depths of a pine wood on a summer day. There is perfect
solitude, undisturbed stillness, and yet the air is as full of murmurous sound as it is of heat and light. So is it with the mystic when
alone with God. His detachment and his peace are perfect, and
yet he is plunged into an infinite activity. For the silent music,
think of Shelley's line : "Music, when soft voices die, vibrates in
the memory." The silence that follows noble music is the suprem-
est music, just as the negative intuition that follows the positive
teaching of dogma is the truest and most positive knowledge of
God. The rest of these two stanzas possesses this exquisite
delicacy of suggestion at an almost equal level. In all this, too,
St John is most himself ; there is nothing in it that is borrowed
from the Song of Songs. But indeed this is among St John's
finest poetic effects, the infinite suggestion of silence and its
equivalent, the peace of soft and subtle sound. Nor could any
poet express better a similar suggestion, the mystical significance of night and of that first spring of dawn when the night
is most felt. Nietzsche approaches him in his midnight conclusion to *Zarathustra*, but he had to introduce the loud sound of a
clock. This thought of night has led me to St John's masterpiece
—his one poem that is absolutely perfect, without flaw, the poem
of *The Dark Night*. I cannot refrain from transcribing it at length,
and with it the Spanish original, that even those who cannot
understand the Spanish may not miss its music—an indispensable
part of the effect :

CANCIONES

1. EN una noche oscura
   Con ansias en amores inflamada,
   Oh dichosa ventura !
   Salí sin ser notada,
   Estando ya mi casa sosegada.

2. A oscuras, y segura
   Por la secreta escala disfrazada,
   Oh dichosa ventura !
   A oscuras, en celada,
   Estando ya mi casa sosegada.

3. En la Noche dichosa
   En secreto, que nadie me veiá,
   Ni yo miraba cosa,
   Sin otra luz, ni guiá,
   Sino la que en el corazón ardiá.

4. Aquesta me guiaba
   Más cierto que la luz de medio diá,
   A donde me esperaba,
   Quien yo bien me sabia,
   En parte, donde nadie pareciá.

5. Oh Noche, que guiaste,
   Oh Noche amable más que el alborada ;
   Oh Noche, que juntaste
   Amado con amada,
   Amada en el Amado transformada !

6. En mi pecho florido,
   Que entero para el solo se guardaba,
   Allí quedó dormido,
   Y yo le regalaba,
   Y el ventalle de cedros aire daba.

7. El aire de el almena,
   Cuando ya sus cabellos esparciá,
   Con su mano serena
   En mi cuello heriá,
   Y todos mis sentidos suspendiá.

8. Quedéme, y olvidéme,
   El rostro recliné sobre el Amado,
   Cesó todo, y dejéme,
   Dejando mi cuidado
   Entre las azucenas olvidado.

STANZAS

1

IN a dark night,
With anxious love inflamed,
O happy lot !
Forth unobserved I went,
My house being now at rest.

2

In darkness and in safety,
By the secret ladder, disguised,
O happy lot !
In darkness and concealment,
My house being now at rest.

3

In that happy night,
In secret, seen of none,
Seeing naught myself,
Without other light or guide
Save that which in my heart was burning.

4

That light guided me
More surely than the noonday sun
To the place where He was waiting for me
Whom I knew well,
And where none appeared.

5

O guiding night ;
O night more lovely than the dawn ;
O night that hast united
The lover with His beloved,
And changed her into her love.

6

On my flowery bosom,
Kept whole for Him alone,
There he reposed and slept ;
And I caressed Him, and the waving
Of the cedars fanned Him.

7

As His hair floated in the breeze
That blew from the turret,
He struck me on the neck
With his gentle hand,
And all sensation left me.

8

I continued in oblivion lost,
My head was resting on my love ;
Lost to all things and myself,
And, amid the lilies forgotten,
Threw all my cares away.

This poem beggars all comment. How shall I dare to appraise a beauty that is so inexpressible ? All I can say seems profanation. The mystical experience that is its subject matter has woven for itself a garment of the most subtle and exquisite loveliness. The external image is a complete picture, and is as adequate as any symbol that artistic intuition could devise. Not once does the spiritual significance mar the consistent harmony of the picture that embodies it. Not once by the introduction of a discordant figure does the external imagery fail to suggest the spiritual reality behind it. The reader may perhaps object to the striking of the Bride in verse seven. But the mention of the *gentle* hand tells us that the blow is not a brutal and painful stunning, but a supreme touch of powerful love that suspends the senses of the Bride in a rapture of bliss—the climax of the embrace. Nor does the transformation of the Beloved into the lover really pass beyond the symbol. As part of the symbol it is the close union of human love in which two hearts may be said to become one. The picture is consistent throughout, perfect and flawless. And what a picture it is! It is a warm summer night of the south fragrant with the rich scent of the cedar-wood and the lilies. The vast boughs of the cedars sway through the gloom as the breeze moves gently among them. Beneath all is blackness save for the white gleam of the lilies. Through the trees looms the turret of some fantastic Oriental building—reminiscent of the Alhambra or the Alcazar of Seville. (Surely the very word "almena" is of Moorish origin.) But this is but the external setting, an atmosphere plenteously charged with suggestion of passionate love in which the meeting and embrace of the lovers is placed. There is the Bride, who has escaped the would-be hindrance of her household by the secret ladder and in disguise, while all are asleep. There is He who awaits in the darkness, the lover undescribed, because He is indescribable, Himself. The transformation follows, the embrace and the sleep of the Divine Lover. It is impossible to say these things in other words. Only the words of the saint are able to unite so intimately the earthly type and the spiritual antitype, to fuse so completely intensest passion with perfect purity.[1] For the power and the life of the poem are a white heat of spiritual passion. That heat moulds the imagery and burns through it. Every detail is aglow with it, even the turret, the cedars and the lilies. In every supreme work of art the feeling of the artist thus moulds and penetrates the material embodiment, as life moulds and penetrates every limb of the human body. I have designedly termed this spiritual passion white heat in contradistinction to the red heat of earthly and physical passion. The former heat is so much more intense than the latter. To realise this we have but to compare the masterpieces of earthly passion with this poem. Their fire, more expansive and more brilliant, pales before the concentrated intensity of this spiritual flame. So far as my acquaintance with art and

[1] Be it remembered that the purity of this supernatural passion has been a purity obtained and only obtainable by a total mortification and relentless crucifixion of the flesh and its desires.

literature extends, I know of nothing nearer to this Dark Night than the passage in praise of night in the second act of Wagner's *Tristan und Isolde*.* The fire there does indeed burn almost as fiercely as in this poem. But it does so precisely because it transcends the sensuous love, that forms its immediate fuel. It tends to pass over into the spiritual passion of an infinite love. It cannot, however, free itself from the idolatry of its finite object, from the bondage of its sensuous conditions. Hence it ends in tragedy, a tragedy not really due to the external circumstances, but inherent in its very nature. In the poem before us the passion flames forth unchecked by any limitation because it is perfectly pure—and purity is essentially freedom from limits. But perhaps some among my readers, I hope but a few, may be shocked at the notion that there is any passion in religion. For good people differ from saints and sinners alike in this, that they are afraid of passion, and therefore afraid of life. They charge to the account of passion and life, for passion is but life in its intensest vigour, the limits that distort and sully it in fallen sense-bound humanity. Hence they take refuge from both in a cold and uninspired moralism and in an artificially closed circle of thought and practice. The result is that the stream of life leaves them behind in their backwaters as it sweeps onwards, a turbid, muddy, often destructive, but always mighty, force. I do not blame this attitude of the good. It is often their only safeguard. They lack the capacity to purify and spiritualise passion, and therefore must avoid it entirely. Only let not such expect to help and save those who will and must live with the fulness of life, who must love passionately.

Unlike these good people, the saints have not fled from passion. They have transformed it and raised it to a higher level where it is freed from the limitations of sense. Some have done this from the outset, and have never, or little, felt the appeal of earthly and sense-bound loves. Others, like St Augustine, have learnt by experience the emptiness and unreality of the limited, and so have come to find rest in an infinite love that is the intense passion of pure spirit.[1] If the saints have withdrawn from life, it has been to find a fuller life from which the limits of that lower life would

---

[1] I know there are philosophers who, like Abbot Vonier, would limit emotion and passion to the sense-conditioned activities of the soul. I regard this as a profound error—an error which logically involves the substitution, as the ideal, of the apathy of the stoic sage, for the love of the Sacred Heart.

have debarred them. If they have withdrawn from love, it has been to find a mightier love, from which the limits of that lower love would have debarred them. But they have never shunned life and love in themselves. Never have they shunned passion that is the fulness of both. And after all it is self-evident that the spiritual passion of this Dark Night exceeds the passion of earthly love, as the fire of the sun the fire of a candle. It is indeed true that even earthly passion, when deepest and most intense, tends to transcend its physical and limited occasion and ground. The passion of Wagner's Tristan is not to be confused with that of a Fyodor Karamazoff.[1] The common element of sense is in the higher passion merely a limit which is the source of idolatry, discord, illusion and tragedy. The final message of Ibsen—the symbolic drama—*When We Dead Awaken*—is that life is love passionate and intense—and that only in such love is reality touched—the rest is deception, bondage and spiritual death. Moreover, such love draws upwards ever upwards to the mountain peaks—that also Ibsen knew. But he cannot in his unbelief escape the limits of the sensible and the finite. The snowy sun-lit pinnacle remains an unattainable aspiration. The pagan artist cannot enter or lead us into the promised land that his dying eyes beheld from his Pisgah summit. Only with the mystic is passion, love or life, call it which you will, free to attain its unlimited satisfaction, the sole satisfaction possible. I seem perhaps to have wandered far from the poem before us—I have in reality declared its essence. It *is* this passion that is pure love, this love that is pure passion, this purity that is passionate love, this pure passion and love that is fulness of life. The restraint of the verses is not the externally imposed restraint which was but the means of destroying limits. It is the unity of entire concentration. The passion reaches its height in the cry of the fifth stanza, "O noche, che guiaste," a stanza whose very language recalls that of the night passage in *Tristan*. Thenceforward the fulfilled passion passes into the peace of perfect satisfaction—when its energy is no longer desire but possession.

A somewhat similar transition from desire to satisfaction is also found in our Wagner passage. There, however, it soon passes on the intrusion of the lower earthly element of human love, the limit of its limited object. It is indeed finally restored.[2] But

---

[1] The sensualist in Dostoievsky's novel, *The Brothers Karamazoff*.
[2] In Isolde's death ecstasy.

this restoration is the effect of a transcendance of limits unwarranted by the sense-conditioned and therefore tragic passion
of Tristan and Isolde and arising out of the poet's intuition of the
Infinite, the supreme intuition of his art, bearing unconscious
witness to the truth of mystical experience. In this poem of
St John the peace of satisfied love is not as with Wagner a vision
of what should or might be, but a present reality. Once attained,
it endures for ever, an eternal sleep of oblivion in respect of the
limited death-in-life of creatures, an eternal awakening in the
unlimited fulness of the life of God. This fulness of passionate
love that is infinite satisfaction is peace and slumber from the
unfulfilled desire which renders earthly passion so destructive and
spiritual passion a purgatorial anguish. The raging torrent has
flowed out into the calm depths of the ocean. It was but the
narrowness of its bed that made the water so rough. Now that
its force has been set free it is perceived no longer. Even so
does the passion that beats throughout this poem pass into the
perfect peace of that mystic marriage and sleep among the lilies,
the peace of perfect attainment, of entire fruition. In this
marriage are fulfilled all knowledge and all art, all striving, all
desire, all love and all life. This marriage union is the limitless
Being of God eternally filling the eternal emptiness of the soul.
It is harmony without discord, freedom without bond, reality
without illusion, satisfaction without striving, love without
longing, yes without no, and life without death.

EPILOGUE

In the Unlimited all things are ours, ours in potency even now, for even now the Unlimited Godhead is ours by grace. Therefore in all things and through all things He may be found and praised by the Christian soul. To Thee, then, O God, do we turn and would gather together all to offer in praise to Thee.

Through the vast expanse of space, the bounds whereof no human eye or mind can reach, the image of Thine infinity—praise be to Thee, O Lord.

Through the countless suns of fire that burn therein, giving light and warmth to hidden worlds, the homes of other children of Thine to us unknown, other sheep not of our fold, praise be to Thee, O Lord.[1]

Through the long preparation of man, and the earth his dwelling through æons of evolution and creation, the image of Thy Patience, praise be to Thee, O Lord.

Through the sapphire dome of the sky, and through its tapestries of cloud, snow-white or dyed with purple and flame, the image of Thy Heavenly dwelling-place, even Thy Godhead inaccessibly exalted, praise be to Thee, O Lord.

Through the sun enthroned therein, giver of light and of heat, of strength and of joy, whose rising is our hope, whose setting is our consolation, the image of Thine Incarnate love, praise be to Thee, O Lord.

Through the moon whose light is mystery and tender grace, image of Thy Mother, and through the stars far-burning in the abyss of night and space, that lift our thoughts to Thee, emblems of Thy saints, praise be to Thee, O Lord.

Through the earth, our school, and our hostel on the way to Thee, the footstool of Thy feet, clad in the overflowings of Thy Beauty, praise be to Thee, O Lord.

Through the dark awe of the storm, the image of Thy wrath

---

[1] For the orthodoxy and probability of belief in rational beings other than men and angels see a series of articles by Bishop John Vaughan in *The Catholic Review* of 1914.

against sin, and through the darker peace of night, the mirror of Thine incomprehensibility, praise be to Thee, O Lord.

Through the soft refreshment of the rain and the dew, images of Thy grace, praise be to Thee, O Lord.

Through the sea also do we give Thee glory. Its ever-changing surface reflecting the passing hues of the sky above, to-day unruffled calm, crystal-clear, to-morrow raging billows, the foam-crested steeds of the tempest, images the soul of man. But its vast expanse and unfathomed depth image Thine Infinity. Delight is it and wonder, but pain also and terror and death, to those that voyage thereon, refreshment to those that bathe, but merciless death to those that drown. Herein does it present the unsolved riddle of life, whose understanding is hidden with Thee. Through this mighty ocean glorious and free, its enthralling beauty and relentless rage, whose robe is of light ' and shade many tinted, subtly woven, and whose canopy is the firmament, praise be to Thee, O Lord.

Through the mountains ancient and solemn, robed in royal vesture of forest and snow, storm-mantled and star-crowned, the image of Thy Majesty, the source of the flowing streams that gladden the earth and make fertile its vineyards and corn-fields, even as Thou art the source of the living water of the Spirit, praise be to Thee, O Lord.

Through the still lakes hid in the folds of the hills, types of contemplative souls hidden in Thine Almightiness, praise be to Thee, O Lord.

Through the rivers also, swift and strong, do we give Thee glory. Their source is the clear spring gushing forth from the mountain cave overhung with dark trees. Their course is fringed with poplar and willow and decked with reeds and loosestrife and water-lilies. But their end is the wide sea that absorbs them into itself. Thus do they set forth the soul whose source is Thine Almighty power, whose way is Thy loving care—that is, her protection, refreshment and beauty—and whose end is Thine Immensity.

Through the meadows starred with cowslips and daisies and girt with trailing hedgerows sweet with violets, an image of the Peace that Thou alone dost bestow, praise be to Thee, O Lord.

Through the forests where the light is green and the silence is peace and awe together, the image of Thy hiddenness, praise be to Thee, O Lord.

Through the olive-yards where the dark-eyed peasants of the south gather the grey berries, the source of oil, through the vine-yards where the purple must is trodden, through the corn-fields whose swaying ears are heavy with the people's bread, types of Thy Sacraments, praise be to Thee, O Lord.

Through the hope of spring, the full life of summer, the wistful satiety of autumn and the asceticism of winter, praise be to Thee, O Lord.

Through the mighty forces of inorganic nature, whereby matter is disposed for the use of life, and Thy Power is shown forth, praise be to Thee, O Lord.

Through the life and growth of plants, through the feelings and instincts of animals and through the living forces that are manifest therein, ever striving to attain a fuller, a more unlimited life, a closer resemblance to Thee, praise be to Thee, O Lord.

Through the universal motion of Thy creation wherein every creature in its own scope seeks a fuller participation of Thy Being, praise be to Thee, O Lord.

Through the singing of the birds, the music of the wind in the trees, the scent of the grass and leaves after rain, praise be to Thee, O Lord.

Through the comfort and help we have of animals, our dumb fellow-servants, praise be to Thee, O Lord.

Through the beauties of earth, whether in sky, in sea, in meadow, in woodland, or in the face of man or woman, hints of Thy beauty, praise be to Thee, O Lord.

Through the human body—its strength, its comeliness—the tabernacle of Thy Spirit, praise be to Thee, O Lord.

Through our bodily life, the foundation and condition of entrance into Thy Divine life eternal, praise be to Thee, O Lord.

Through the human understanding powerful to discover the wonders of Thy handiwork, praise be to Thee, O Lord.

Through the human heart able to love the good and the beautiful, to pity the weak and the sinful and to follow and to receive the higher love of Thyself that Thou dost give, praise be to Thee, O Lord.

Through all the simple tasks and delights of daily life, praise be to Thee, O Lord.

Through all-consoling friendships, tender sympathies and natural pieties, praise be to Thee, O Lord.

Through the love of parent and child, brother and sister,

husband and wife, broken reflections of Thy One Infinite love, praise be to Thee, O Lord.

Through the disappointments, bereavements and sufferings, whereby we learn that there is no satisfaction or repose of heart in the transitory and the limited, but only in the eternal and the Unlimited, even Thyself, praise be to Thee, O Lord.

Through the course of human history, wherein the rise and fall of empires, the conflict of peoples and the development of arts and of ideas, of institutions and of moralities are overruled by Thy Providence to the accomplishment of Thy Will and the manifestation of Thy Truth, praise be to Thee, O Lord.

Through the inventions whereby man has bent the strong forces of nature to his stronger will—a triumph of spirit over matter—praise be to Thee, O Lord.

Through the hypotheses and laws of science do we give Thee glory. They are forms wherein are revealed Thine operation and law in the universe, and the unity of its manifold phenomena, the reflection of Thy Oneness. In them is beheld Thy Wisdom—reaching strongly from end to end and disposing all things sweetly in the beauty and the harmony of energies and lives ordered and tempered by Thy Providence. Thus is understanding of the work, worship of the Worker, even Thyself, O eternal Wisdom. Through the knowledge of science, praise be to Thee, O Lord.

Through the intuitions of art, expressed through the yielding matter, their instrument and vehicle, do we give Thee glory. Therein the Unlimited Reality of Spirit—Thyself, O God—is shown forth to those who have sight to behold it, whether it be in the sculpture of frieze and statue, in the architecture of temple and cathedral, in the drawing and colour of pictures, in lyric and drama, or in prose rhythmic and gracious. Thus in art the invisible is seen, the inaudible is heard, the intangible is touched and the unknowable is known. Through the sacraments of art, praise be to Thee, O Lord.

Through all there is of truth in any philosophy or human creed, however limited and distorted by undue denial of other truths, praise be to Thee, O Lord.

Through all that there is of beauty in any form or example of art, however limited, by scantiness of perception and inadequacy of expression, praise be to Thee, O Lord.

Through the errors and deficiencies of knowledge and science, and through the insoluble antinomies of philosophy do we give

Thee glory. They teach us that the reality of our experience grounded in Thine Infinite Being is incomprehensible by the narrow and shallow thoughts of human reason. Thus do they invite us to pass beyond these limits into the immensity of loving faith. Through our ignorance, praise be to Thee, O Lord.

Through the ugliness that mars all created beauties, so that our hearts are inflamed with longing for Thy absolute beauty, praise be to Thee, O Lord.

Through the natural knowledge of Thyself, immanent in the heart and conscience of man, through that craving for the infinite that is the source and ground of natural religion, and through the religious experience wherein Thou dost reveal Thy presence as the Unknown God, whose altars are the imperfect creeds of the world that man has shaped, praise be to Thee, O Lord.

Through the supernatural revelation of Thy truth given first to the Jews in part and in shadow, completed through the Gospel of Christ Thy Son, and developed in His Body, Thy Catholic Church, in whose fulness is gathered all the truth of human philosophies and creeds, praise be to Thee, O Lord.

Through the dispensation of Thy grace, whereby man is raised from the natural to the supernatural, from time to eternity, from the limited to the Infinite, and from himself to Thee, whereby he is deified a god by participation of Thyself, praise be to Thee, O Lord.

Through the Incarnation of Thy Word to be our fellow-man, that as a fellow-man we might know and love Thee, praise be to Thee, O Lord.

Through His bitter Passion, wherein He redeemed us from the limits of sin that barred us from Thyself and revealed Thee as love, praise be to Thee, O Lord.

Through His Resurrection, Ascension and Glory, wherein are shown forth the first-fruits of the future glory of.Thy People, praise be to Thee, O Lord.

Through the descent and indwelling of the Spirit in our souls, the source and wellspring of our new life of grace, praise be to Thee, O Lord.

Through the Catholic Church, the guardian of Thy truth and the steward of Thy grace, praise be to Thee, O Lord.

Through the seven Sacraments of Thy Church, channels of sanctifying grace, extensions of the Incarnation and the crown of the sacramental dispensation of nature and art, wherein matter is the symbol and vehicle of spirit, praise be to Thee, O Lord.

Through the Most Blessed Sacrament of the Altar, Thy tabernacle among men, wherein Thou dost dwell with us in Thine Incarnate Word, Who in this Sacrament is the daily offering of our praise, the daily sacrifice for our sins, and the daily food of our weakness, praise be to Thee, O Lord.

Through the saints that, through Thy grace, have destroyed the limits of sin, nature and selfhood and even on earth have attained the unlimited fruition of Thine infinite Being, praise be to Thee, O Lord.

Through the vision of prophets transcending the limits of time and space, through the preaching of Apostles destroying the limits of pagan ignorance and Jewish legalism, through the heroism of martyrs overthrowing the limits of earthly power, force and ambition, through the mortification of monks and hermits escaping the limits of worldly prosperity, comfort, moderation and respectability, that satisfaction with a bounded and careful goodness which is the death of Thy love, through the supernatural wisdom of the fathers and doctors scorning the limits of human prudence and earthly science, through the purity of virgins overpassing the narrow limits of earthly love in the freedom and spiritual passion of a supernatural love of Thee, praise be to Thee, O Lord.

Through the holy souls that have enjoyed in any measure the mystic union that is a participation of Thine Infinity, praise be to Thee, O Lord.

Through the teaching and practice of mystical theology that declares and offers this escape from the unsatisfying limits of creatures into the all-satisfying, unlimited Fulness of absolute goodness, beauty and truth, praise be to Thee, O Lord.

Through the countless hosts of angels, those pure spirits free from the limits of the body who penetrate with their loving contemplation the depths of Thy Being that remains notwithstanding infinitely unfathomable, praise be to Thee, O Lord.

Through Thine immaculate Mother, free from her first conception from the limits imposed by sin and ever enjoying a union with Thee and a participation of Thy Godhead beyond the measure of any creature save herself alone, praise be to Thee, O Lord.

Through the most Sacred Humanity of Thy Son, one Person with Thyself, in Whom Thine Infinite Godhead is mirrored, and Thine unknowable Deity is revealed, wherein Thou, O God, art Thyself a man, praise be to Thee, O Lord.

In Thine Immanence in all Thy creatures as the source of their being and life we render Thee adoration and glory.   By this Thine immanent presence and guidance Thou dost change many creatures into new forms less narrowly limited because possessed of further degrees of being, and thereby nearer to Thee, enjoying a larger measure of Thy Being and representing Thee more fully.   Through Thy hidden operation in Thy creatures, praise be to Thee, O Lord.

Through the special relationship in which the souls of the just are placed towards Thyself so that Thou dost dwell within them after a peculiar and most intimate fashion, praise be to Thee, O Lord.

In Thine Infinite Transcendence of creatures, so that Thou art incomprehensible by any save Thyself, and art hidden in the darkness of Thine Infinity, praise be to Thee, O Lord.

In Thy Most Simple Unity wherein Thou dost embrace and make one an infinite multiplicity and variety, praise be to Thee, O Lord.

In Thy Peace untroubled by change, wherein Thou dost give rest to our souls, praise be to Thee, O Lord.

In Thine Energy boundless and eternal, wherein Thou dost move all things, and dost act through the souls united with Thyself, praise be to Thee, O Lord.

In Thine Omnipotence, whereby Thou canst do all that intrinsically is possible, praise be to Thee, O Lord.

In Thy Love for man, whereby Thou hast sent Thy Son to die for our sins, hast given Him for our food, and Thyself for our reward, and wherein Thou dost seek our souls with unwearied patience, dost lead them towards Thyself with Thy secret wisdom and dost unite them to Thyself in a union, inconceivably intimate, praise be to Thee, O Lord.

In Thy Beauty whereof all beauties are shadows, in Thy Truth whereof all truths are fragments and indications, in Thy Goodness the ground and measure of all values, praise be to Thee, O Lord.

In Thy Trinity of Persons, in the Oneness of Thy Deity, wherein each Person possesses and is possessed by the fulness of Thy Godhead, praise be to Thee, O Lord.

In Thy Fulness of Being without limits, whereby Thou alone art and we are not, praise be to Thee, O Lord.

In Thy Reality beyond all being, thought and value, wherein Thou art Nothing and All things, praise be to Thee, O Lord.

In all things Thou art, and Thou art beyond all things, and all things are in Thee, and all things apart from Thee are not.   Only

EPILOGUE

Thou art in their nothingness, for they are limited, and their limit is lack of being, but Thou art unlimited, fulness of Being, and Thou dost will to be ours for ever, that in Thee we may live Thy life without limits in Thine infinity. We thank Thee, O Lord, and we worship Thee, and we give Thee glory. Praise and silence be to Thee, O Lord.

NOTES

Note for p. 28 (1).—Mr H. G. Wells, also an exponent of a "pluralist" divinity, is apparently being forced by his religious experience to the affirmation of an ultimate and universal God. (See *The Undying Fire*, esp. chap. vi.)

Note for p. 28 (2).—Personal because the suprapersonal is more, not less, than personal, as we know personality.

Note for p. 31.—By comparison adequately. We could attain a perfectly adequate knowledge of anything only by comprehension of the ultimate Reality, in which all things are grounded. Since this latter knowledge is impossible, so also is the former.

Note for p. 41.—Nevertheless there is an arresting unity of mechanical disposition throughout the plane of inorganic matter. The solar system repeats itself everywhere, from the constitution of the electron to the stellar "universe."

Note for p. 49.—Mr Bertrand Russell tells us that "the Aristotelian doctrines of the schoolmen come nearer in spirit" (than the Kantian metaphysic) "to the doctrines which modern mathematics inspire" (*Mysticism and Logic*, p. 96).

Note for p. 53.—The relationship between two scientific laws mutually interdependent affords a suggestion of this Simple Unity of mutually inclusive aspects. But no activity proceeding from a created principle can understand this Unity.

Note for p. 60.—Herbert Spencer's *Unknowable* does, however, contain eminently all conceivable perfections. In so far as he maintained this, his "agnosticism" was that of the mystics. (See *First Principles*, i. 5, quoted by Mr Greenwood, *The Faith of an Agnostic*.) Indeed it seems to me that the agnostic tends to agree with the mystic in the Dionysian doctrine of transcendence while rejecting his belief in communion with the Absolute.

Note for p. 62.—*Lit.*, "Which we ourselves can attain." The general sense requires us to understand this of all attainment, intellectual as well as actual.

Note for p 81.—We are aided to apprehend this one-sided relationship between creatures and God by the reflection that the relationship between creatures on diverse planes of being is not strictly and in all respects mutual. For example, a pet animal whose happiness, nay, whose very existence, depends on the will of a master who would perhaps be scarcely affected by its death is surely more related to him than he to it. So also with a tool and its maker. Its existence as a tool depends on him. The toolmaker, able to make a multitude of tools, depends very little on that particular tool.

Note for p. 147.—Because I speak of the "eternal suffering" of hell, I do not accept the traditional view of a physical fire torment. This view has never been defined by the Church and lacks the consensus of the fathers. Indeed I do not believe in any pain extrinsic to the necessary consequences of the soul's eternal self-exclusion from supernatural union with God. On the entire subject of eternal punishment I accept in substance the view expounded by Baron von Hügel (*The Mystical Element of Religion*, vol. ii., pp. 218-230).

Note for p. 156.—To prevent any possible misunderstanding that might arise from a hasty reading, I would point out to any who do not accept the teaching of Jesus and His Church as to the existence of a personal devil, that his non-existence would not affect in the very least anything that I say in this section.

Note for p. 173.—By orthodox mystics I mean men who were both mystics and orthodox. Many Quietists—*e.g.* Madame Guyon—were genuine mystics.

Note for p. 180.—It is but fair to point out that this most unfortunate passage is representative only of the weakest aspect of Miss Underhill's mysticism. It is the result of her unintentionally pantheistic identification of God's immanent activity in creatures with "Becoming." This identification, already made in her magnificent psychological study of mysticism, her *Introduction to Mysticism*, has unhappily worked itself out in her later books in a practical deification of creatures and in a defective apprehension of degrees of value and reality.

Note for p. 192.—Blake's doctrine of free love, so strange in a man whose life was of stainless purity, arose from his apprehension that perfect love excludes any exclusive property in its possession. Unhappily, he imagined that this perfection could be realised under the essentially limited and therefore imperfect conditions of human sex love in this mortal life, though this love normally involves its lower and animal element—an element which is necessarily an exclusion and an appropriation.

Note for p. 204.—It must be admitted that many of these visions of St Teresa long preceded her attainment of the Resurrection stage of the mystic way, and though they *may* be anticipations of that stage, they may, on the other hand, be of purely natural origin.

Note for p. 231.—I need hardly remind my readers that this *a priori* condemnation of anti-Catholic private revelations is hypothetical upon acceptance of the Catholic revelation—and is no part of the *philosophy* of mysticism.

Note for p. 233.—Recently the Rev. Joseph Petrovits has shewn that the authenticity of this promise is open to grave doubt.

Note for p. 304.—It should, however, be remarked that in his central formula "in Christ" St Paul refers not to the personal but to the mystical Christ—namely, Christ's entire mystical body, members and head together. Of this body, of which Christ is the head, the Holy Ghost is the indwelling and informing soul. Hence for St Paul the formula "in Christ" is practically equivalent to its concomitant formula, "in the spirit."

Note for p. 309.—Madame Guyon appears to have disregarded this important distinction between the habit and the act of mystical marriage and to have treated the state as one continuous act. Hence she maintained the immediate divine actuation of every psychosis of souls in this state. Thus arose a claim to the divine inspiration and infallibility of all her acts and writings. This was, I believe, her fundamental error (see the study of Madame Guyon in Delacroix, *Etudes*).

Note for p. 323.—The immediate sense of this latter text is indeed that Christians, as members of Christ's body, attain the complete and full spiritual life in and through union with their Head. But this life, as the former text shews, is the Divine life of God, incarnate in Jesus Christ.

Note for p. 355.—This "confident naturalism" is, however, always breaking down and dissolving into utter pessimism. A grey atmosphere of profitless labour and sorrow without hope overhangs the world of Homer, for all the simple delight in life and nature experienced in moments of strength and success. We may also remark Herodotus' story of Cleobis and Biton.

Note for p. 369.—It is indeed true that Popes have often struggled against secular powers for the sake of temporal dominion. But the majority of conflicts between the Papacy and governments have been waged on behalf of the spiritual aims of the Church.

Note for p. 382.—Though Voltaire's attitude of scoffing hostility to religion merits severe condemnation, in fairness we must not forget his services to the cause of morality and humanity, his noble opposition to political oppression, judicial cruelty and war.

Note for p. 390.—The spiritual intuition embodied by art may be of any immaterial reality—not necessarily a religious or moral intuition. When the object of the intuition is moral evil—that is, some spiritual idea or force as unduly limited by evil will, or, it may be, of evil spirits—its embodiment is an art perverse and morally evil, such as the drawings of Aubrey Beardsley.

Note for p. 399.—Since this was written I have read Fr. Martindale's comparison between Wagner's *Tristan* and *The Dark Night*. His treatment is, however, on different lines to my own.